Sorcerer Hunt

Book 2

by Satoru Akahori & Ray Omishi

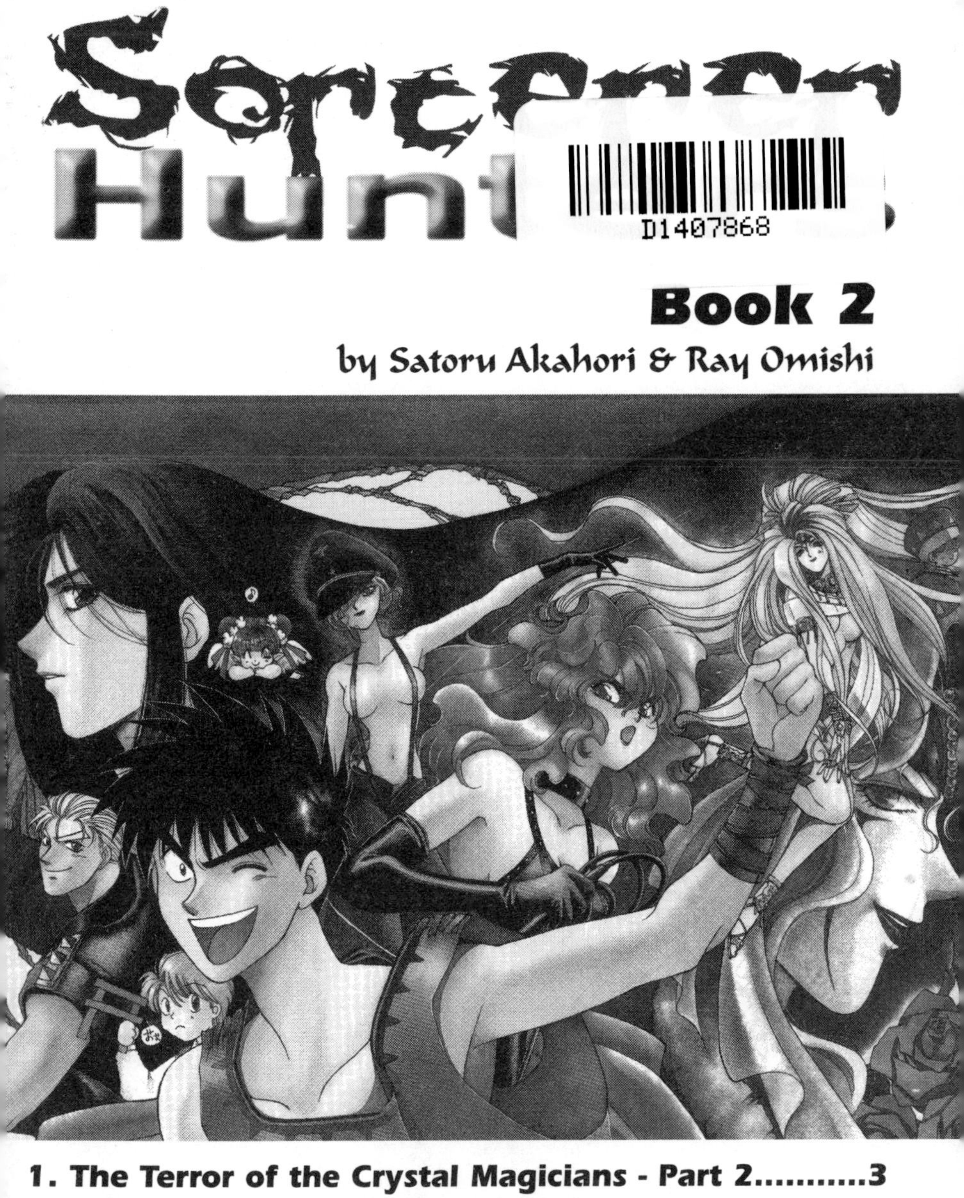

TOKYOPOP PRESS Presents
Sorcerer Hunters 2 by Satoru Akahori & Ray Omishi
Mixx Manga Premium Edition is an imprint of Mixx Entertainment, Inc.
ISBN: 1-892213-54-0
First Printing July 2000

10   9   8   7   6   5   4   3   2   1

Story originally appeared in TOKYOPOP Magazine issues 3-6 through 4-1 in its entirety.

Translator - Anita Sengupta. Retouch Artist - Wilbert Lacuna. Graphic Assistant - Steve Kindernay.
Graphic Designer - Akemi Imafuku. Associate Editor - Jake Forbes. Editor - Mary Coco.
Production Manager - Fred Lui. Director of Publishing - Henry Kornman.

Email: info@mixxonline.com
Come visit us at www.TOKYOPOP.com.

MIXX ENTERTAINMENT, INC.
LOS ANGELES - TOKYO

The Terror of the Crystal Magicians - Part 2

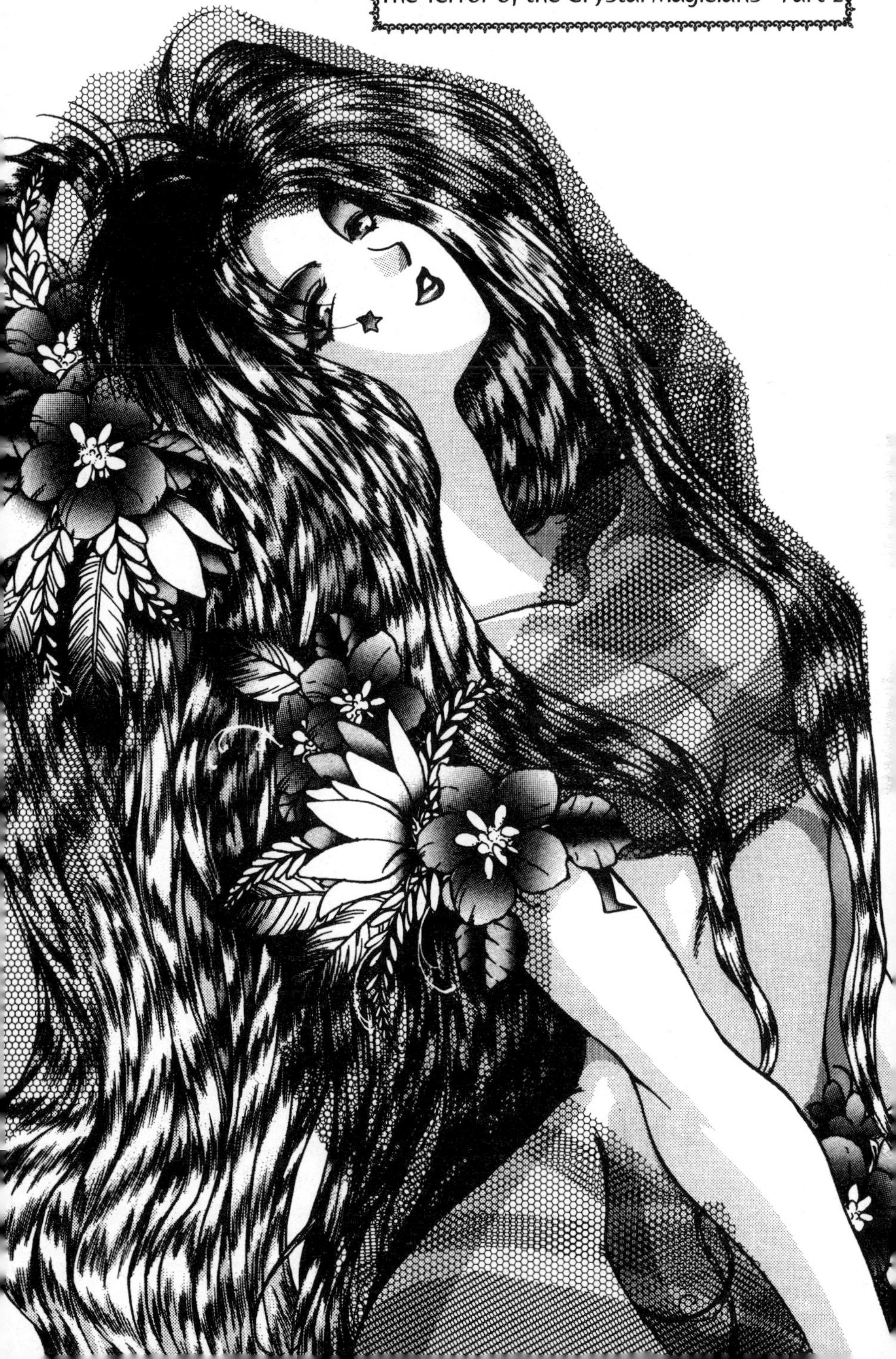

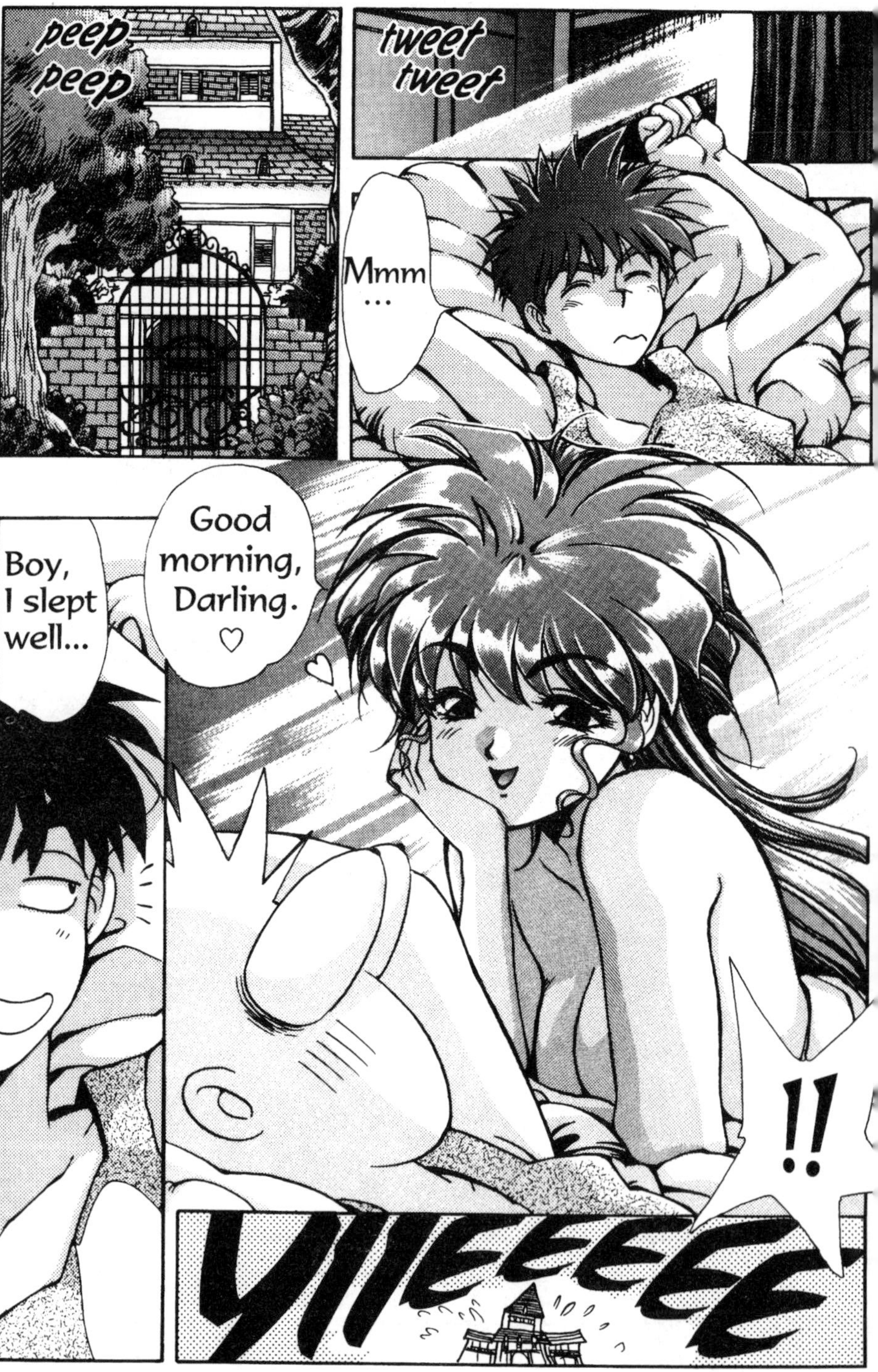
peep peep
tweet tweet
Mmm ...
Boy, I slept well...
Good morning, Darling. ♡
!!
YIIEEEEEE

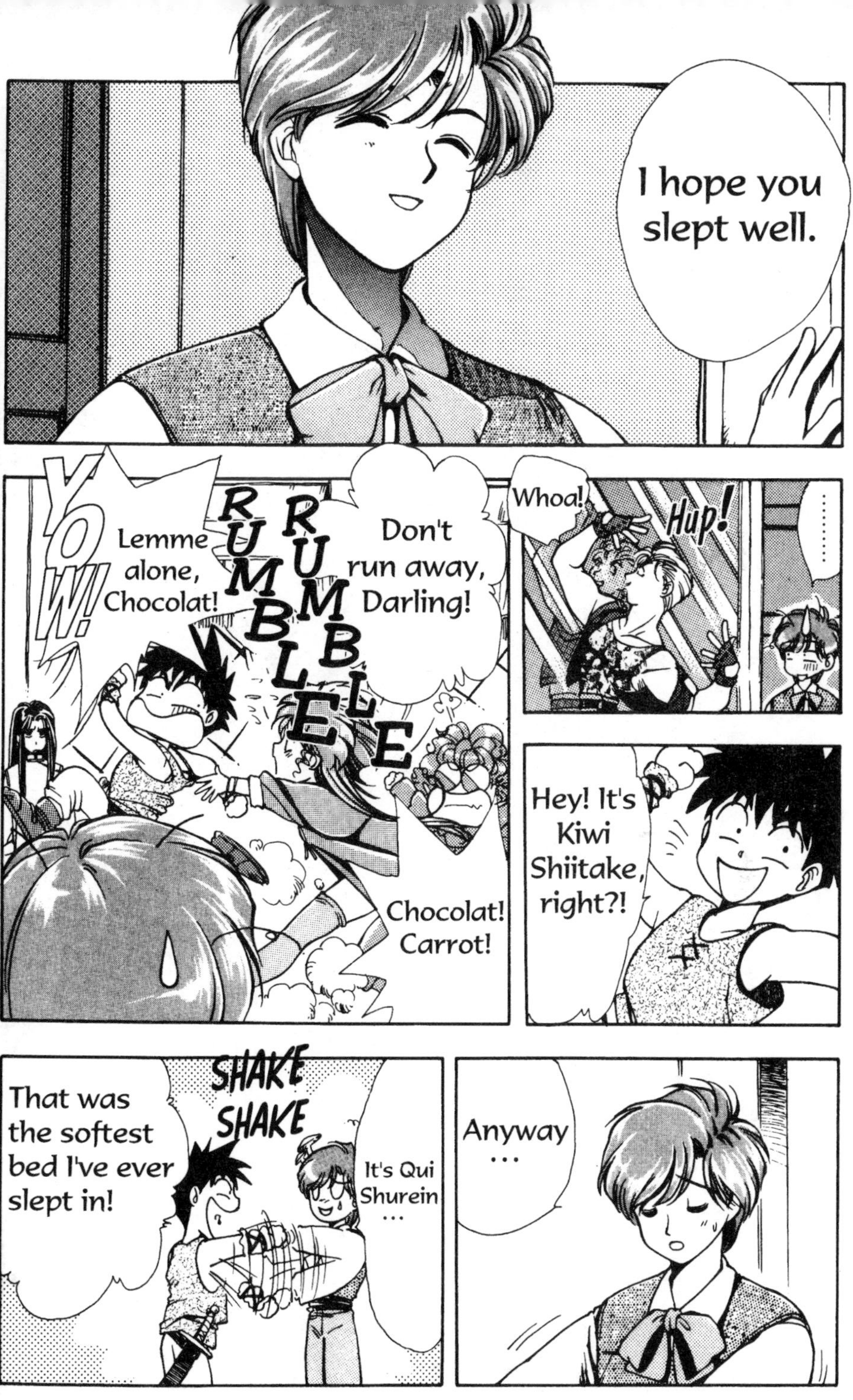
I hope you slept well.
YOW!
Lemme alone, Chocolat!
RUMBLE RUMBLE
Don't run away, Darling!
Chocolat! Carrot!
Whoa!
Hup!
......
Hey! It's Kiwi Shiitake, right?!
That was the softest bed I've ever slept in!
SHAKE SHAKE
It's Qui Shurein ...
Anyway ...

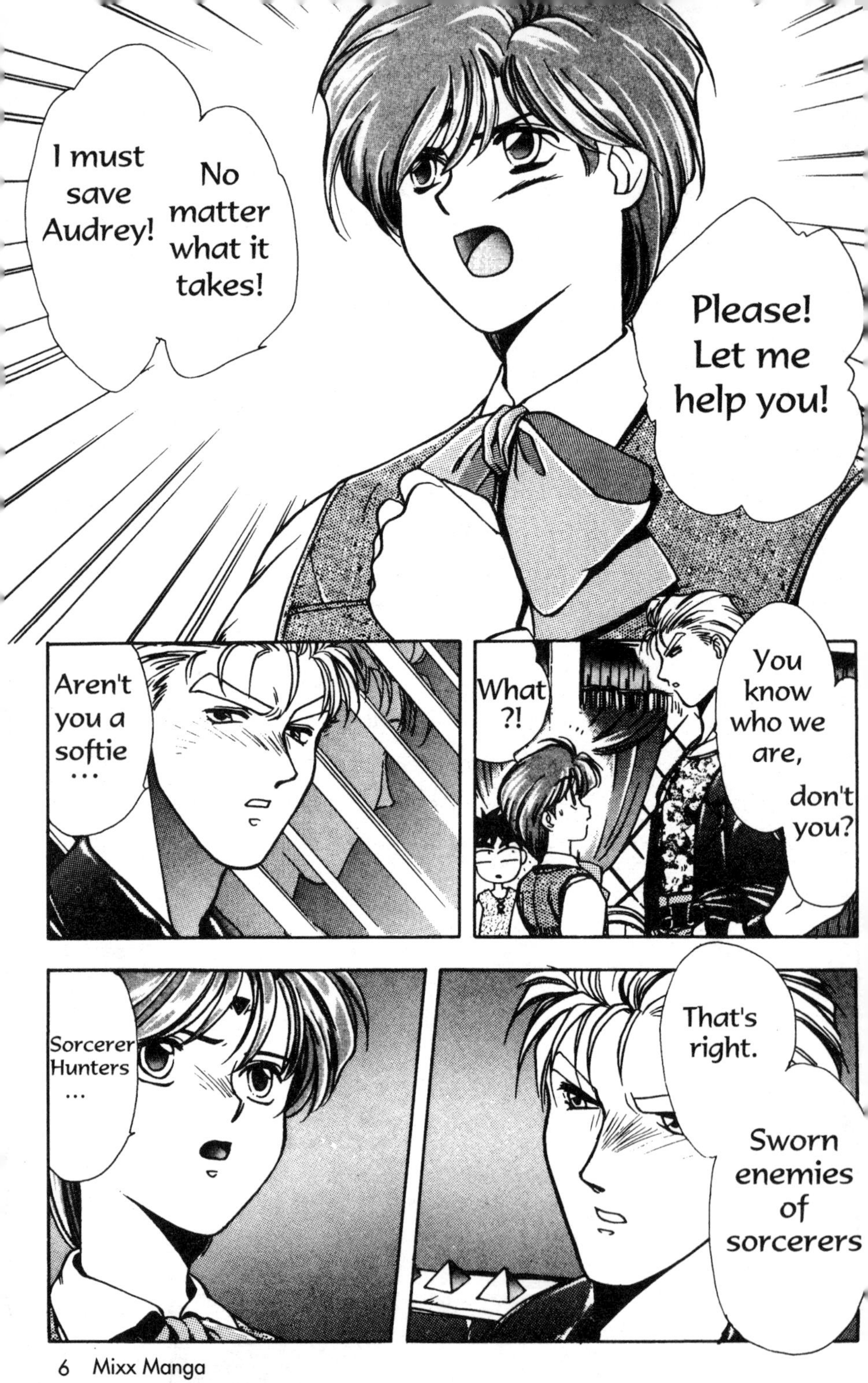
I must save Audrey!
No matter what it takes!
Please! Let me help you!
Aren't you a softie ...
What?!
You know who we are, don't you?
Sorcerer Hunters ...
That's right.
Sworn enemies of sorcerers

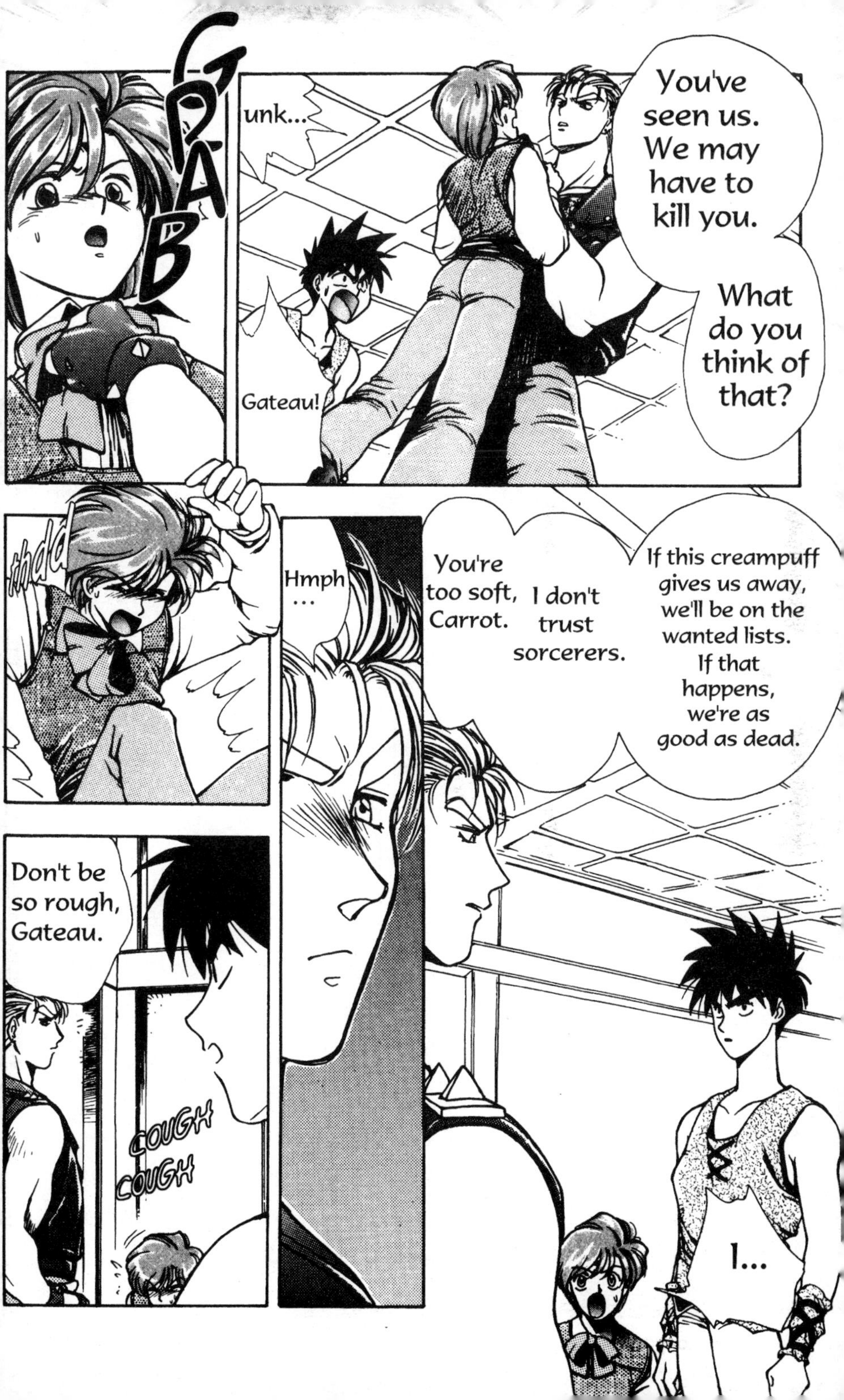
GRABB
unk...
Gateau!
You've seen us. We may have to kill you.
What do you think of that?
Don't be so rough, Gateau.
COUGH COUGH
Hmph...
You're too soft, Carrot.
I don't trust sorcerers.
If this creampuff gives us away, we'll be on the wanted lists. If that happens, we're as good as dead.
I...

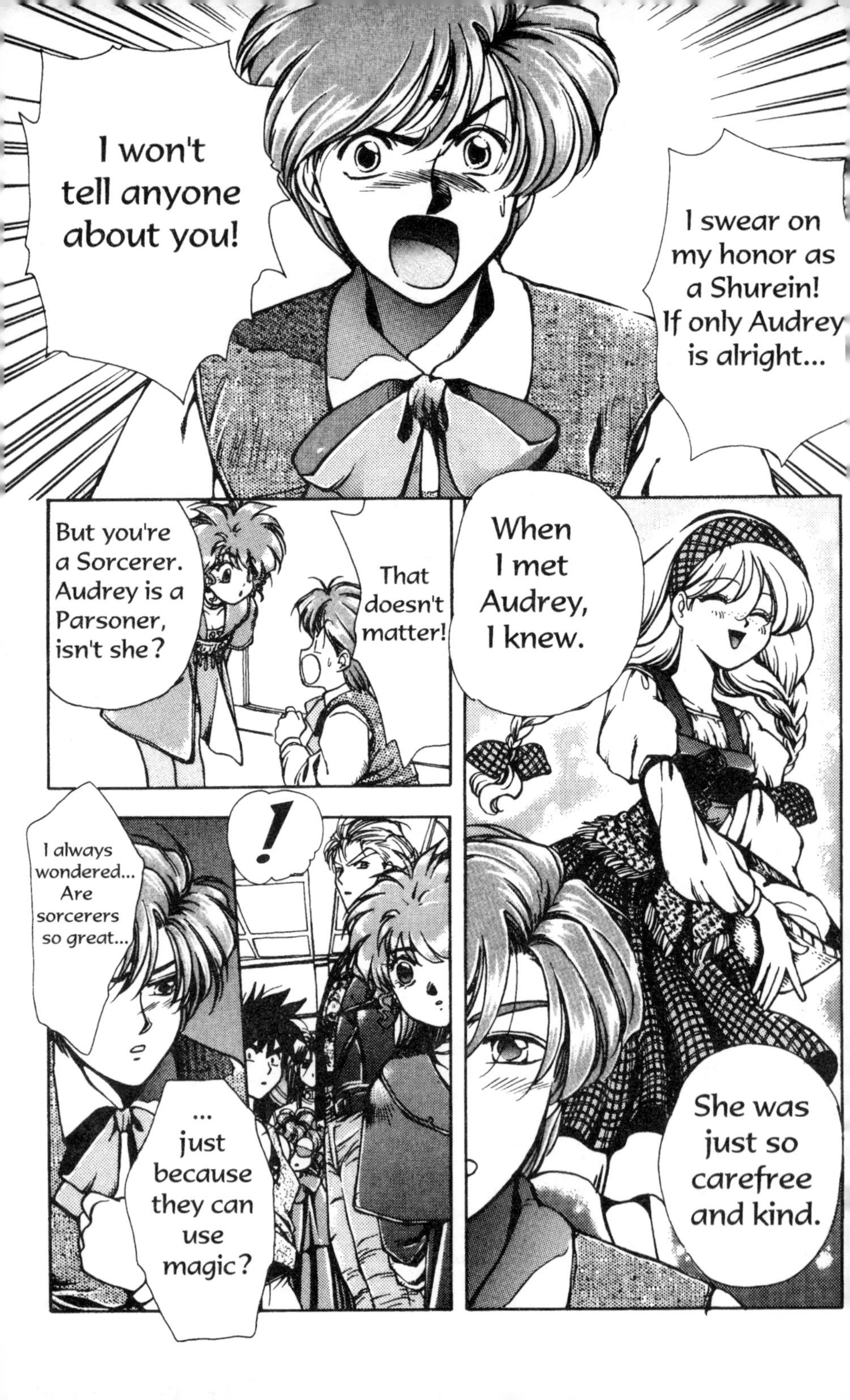

I won't tell anyone about you!
I swear on my honor as a Shurein! If only Audrey is alright...
But you're a Sorcerer. Audrey is a Parsoner, isn't she?
That doesn't matter!
When I met Audrey, I knew.
She was just so carefree and kind.
I always wondered... Are sorcerers so great...
!
... just because they can use magic?

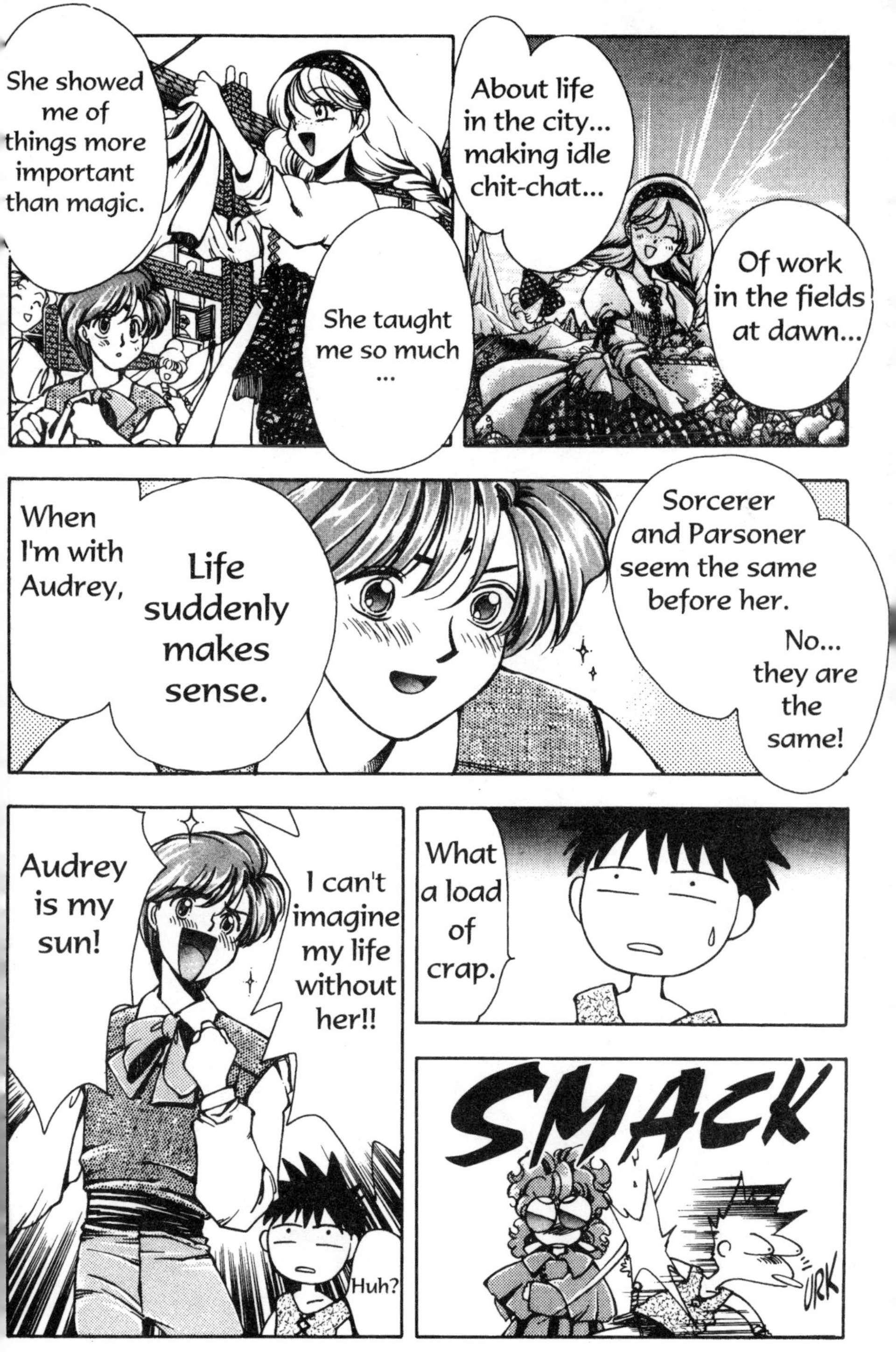
She showed me of things more important than magic.
She taught me so much ...
About life in the city... making idle chit-chat...
Of work in the fields at dawn...
When I'm with Audrey,
Life suddenly makes sense.
Sorcerer and Parsoner seem the same before her.
No... they are the same!
Audrey is my sun!
I can't imagine my life without her!!
Huh?
What a load of crap.
SMACK
URK

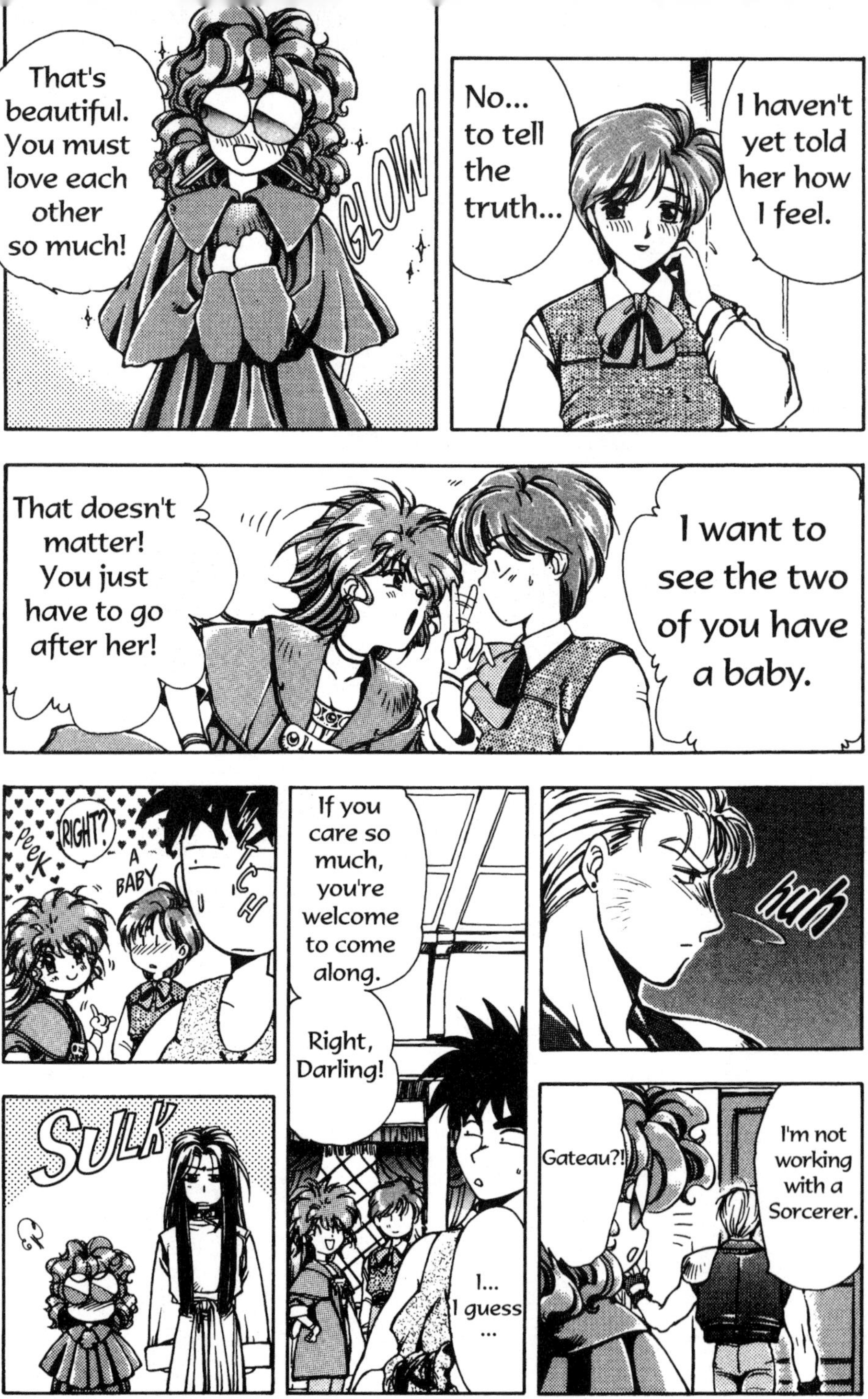
That's beautiful. You must love each other so much!
GLOW
No... to tell the truth...
I haven't yet told her how I feel.
That doesn't matter! You just have to go after her!
I want to see the two of you have a baby.
PEEK
RIGHT?
A BABY
TWITCH
SULK
If you care so much, you're welcome to come along.
Right, Darling!
I... I guess...
huh
Gateau?!
I'm not working with a Sorcerer.

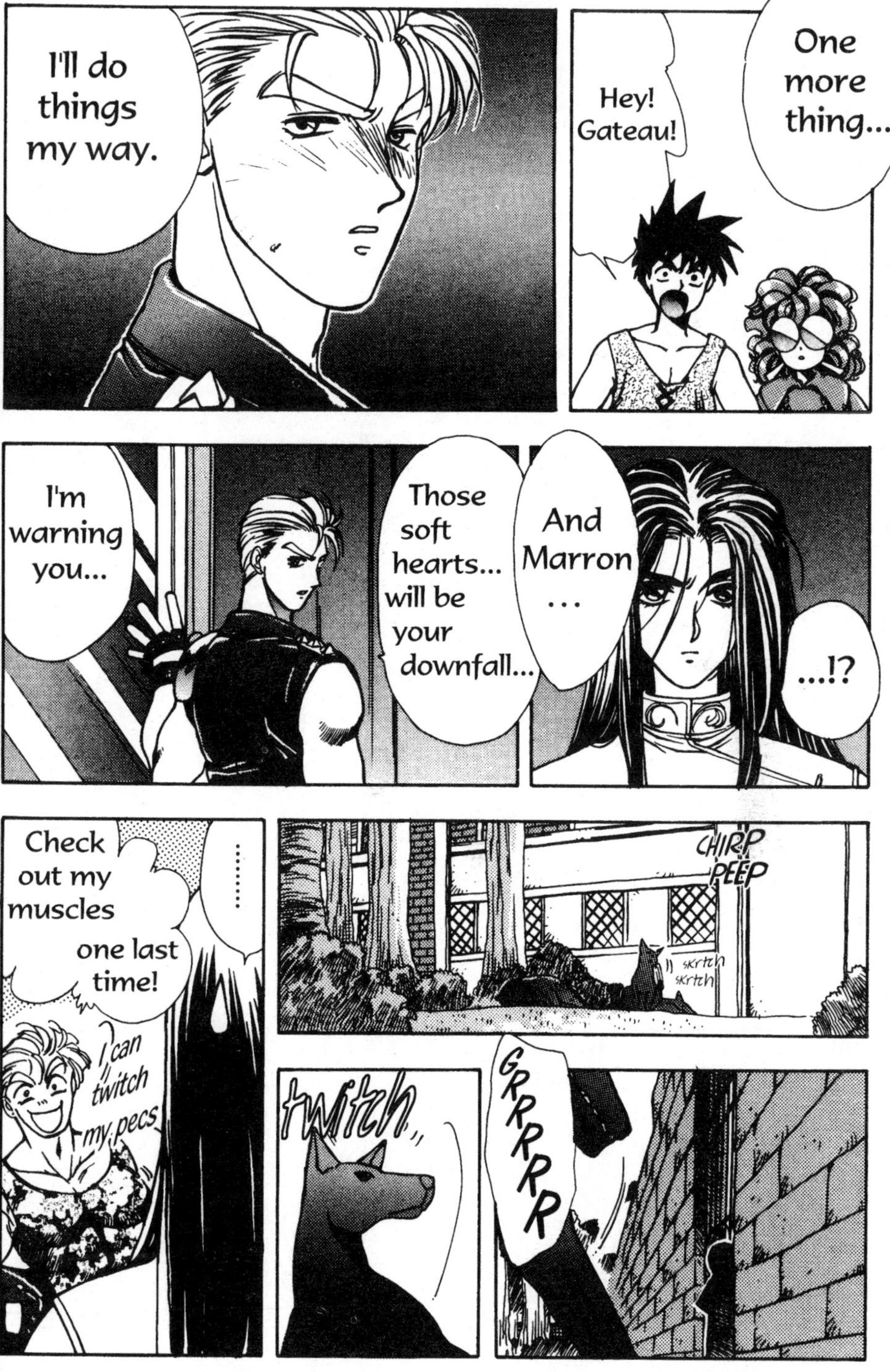
I'll do things my way.
Hey! Gateau!
One more thing...
I'm warning you...
Those soft hearts... will be your downfall...
And Marron ...
...!?
Check out my muscles one last time!
....
I can twitch my pecs
CHIRP
PEEP
skrtch skrtch
twitch
GRRRRR

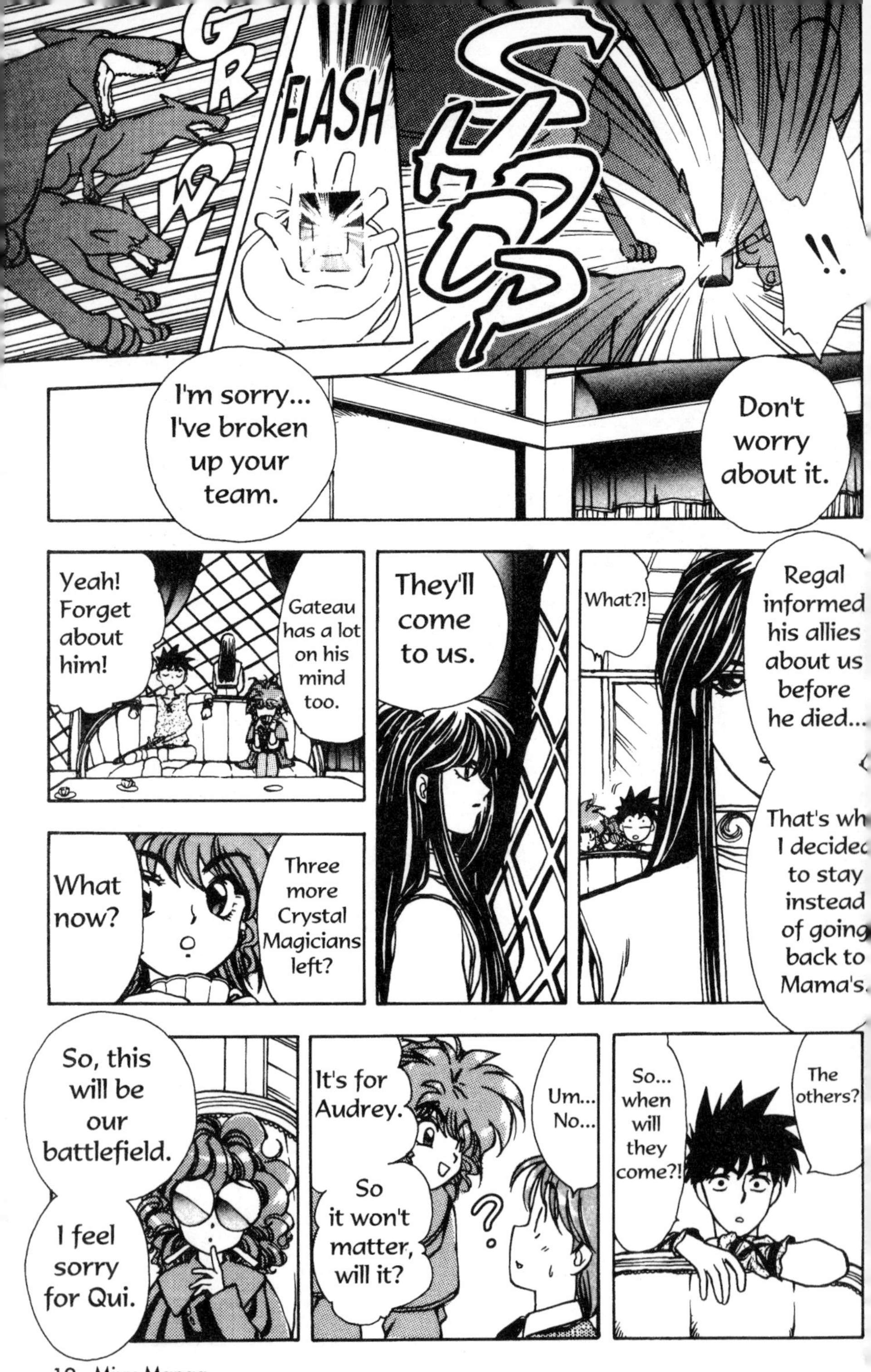
GROWL
FLASH
!!
I'm sorry... I've broken up your team.
Don't worry about it.
Yeah! Forget about him!
Gateau has a lot on his mind too.
What now?
Three more Crystal Magicians left?
They'll come to us.
What?!
Regal informed his allies about us before he died...
That's wh I decided to stay instead of going back to Mama's.
So, this will be our battlefield.
I feel sorry for Qui.
It's for Audrey.
Um... No...
So it won't matter, will it?
So... when will they come?!
The others?

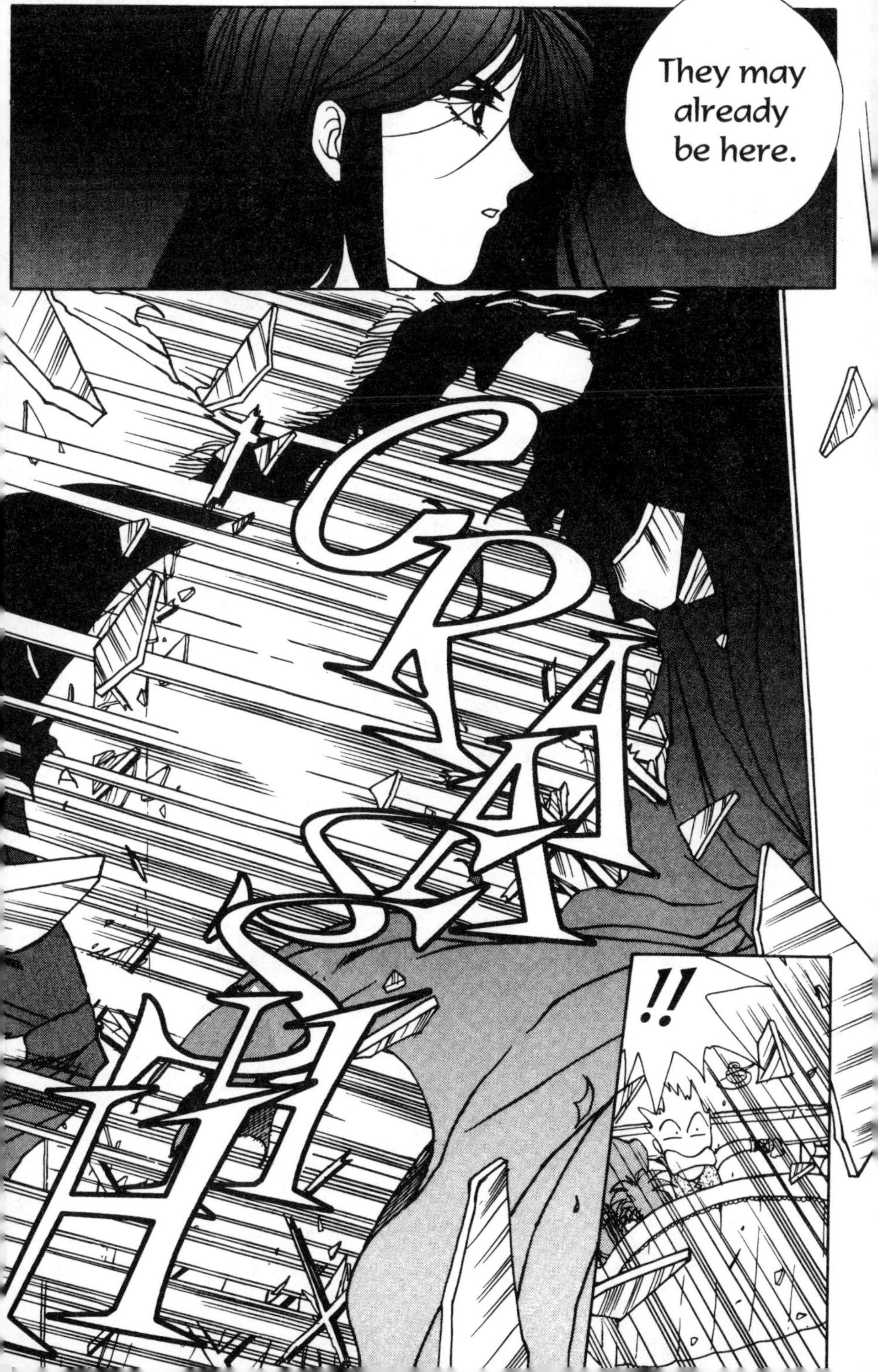
They may already be here.
CRAASH
!!

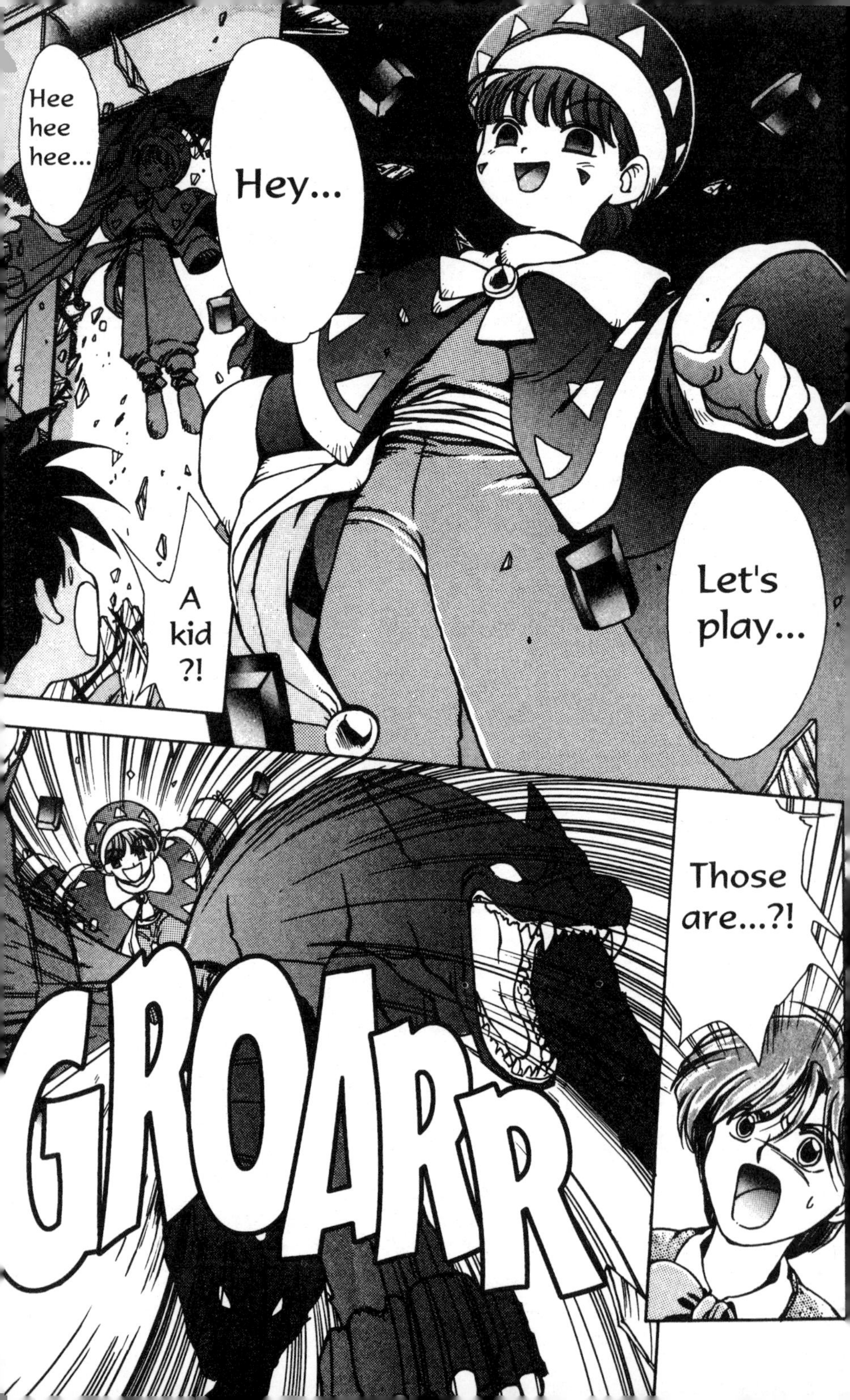
Hee hee hee...
Hey...
A kid ?!
Let's play...
GROARR
Those are...?!

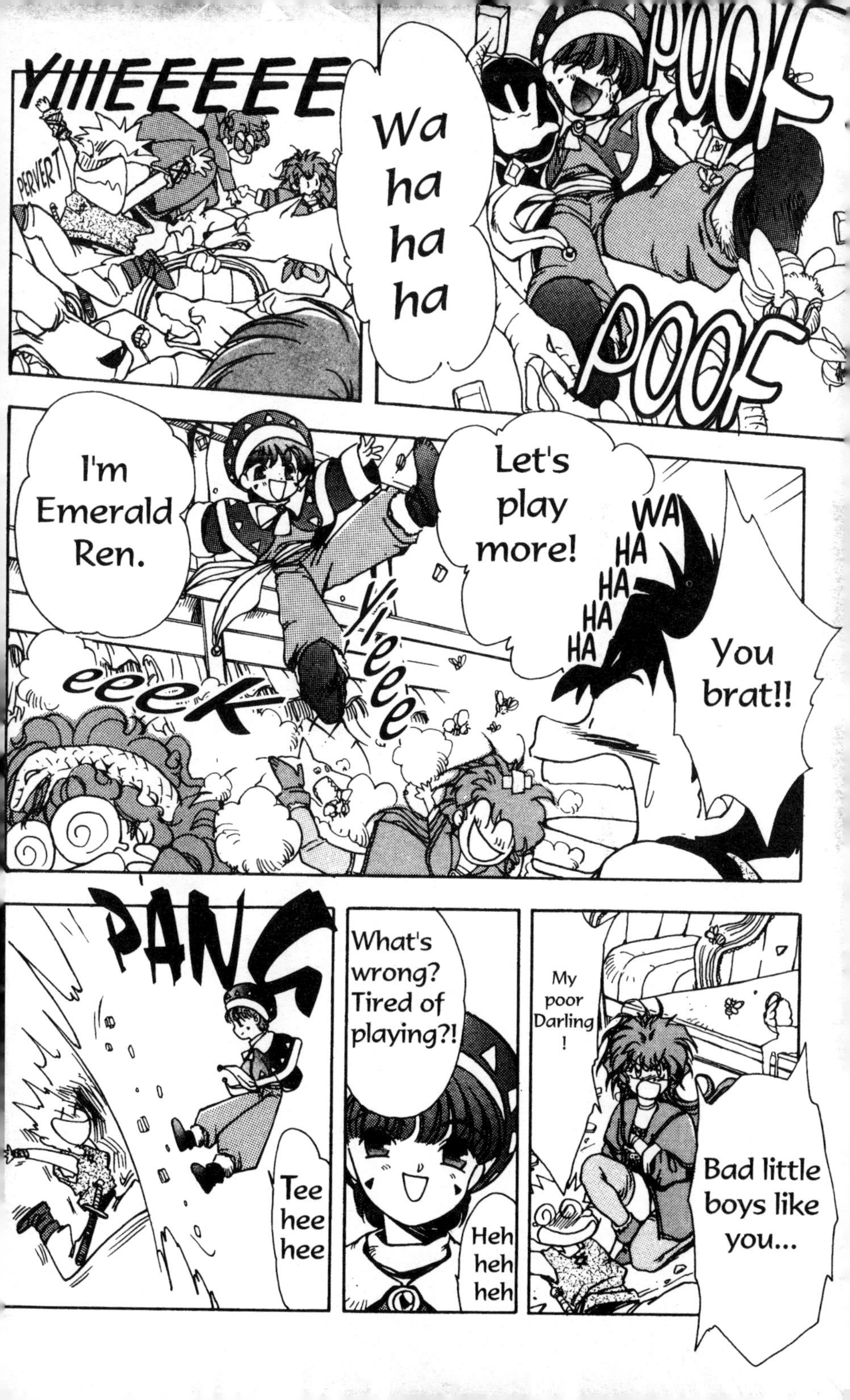
YIIIEEEEEE
PERVERT
POOF
Wa ha ha ha
POOF
I'm Emerald Ren.
Let's play more!
YIeeee
eeek
WA HA HA HA HA HA
You brat!!
PAN
Tee hee hee
What's wrong? Tired of playing?!
Heh heh heh
My poor Darling !
Bad little boys like you...

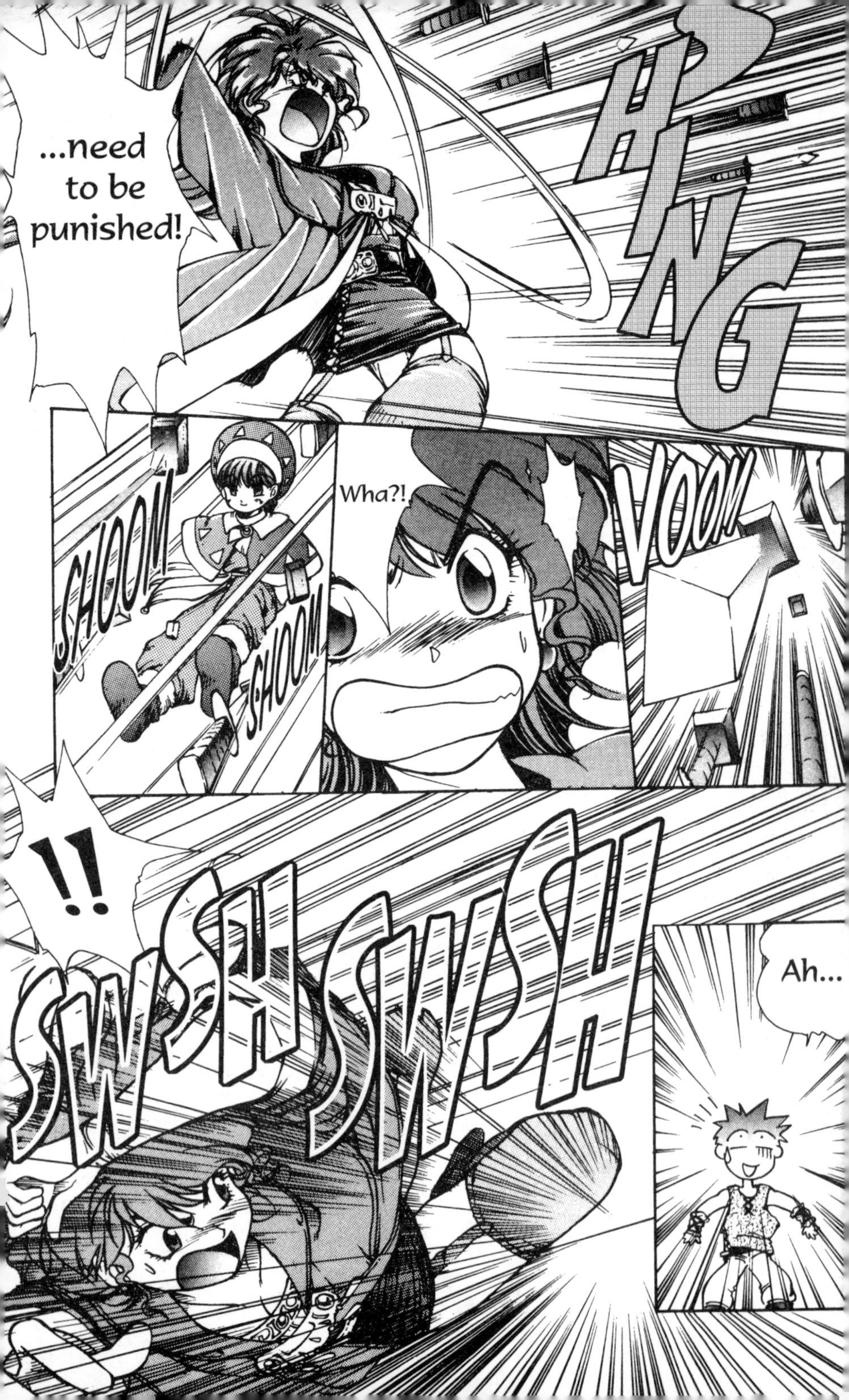
...need to be punished!
SHOOM
SHOOM
Wha?!
VOOM
!!
SWISH
SWISH
Ah...

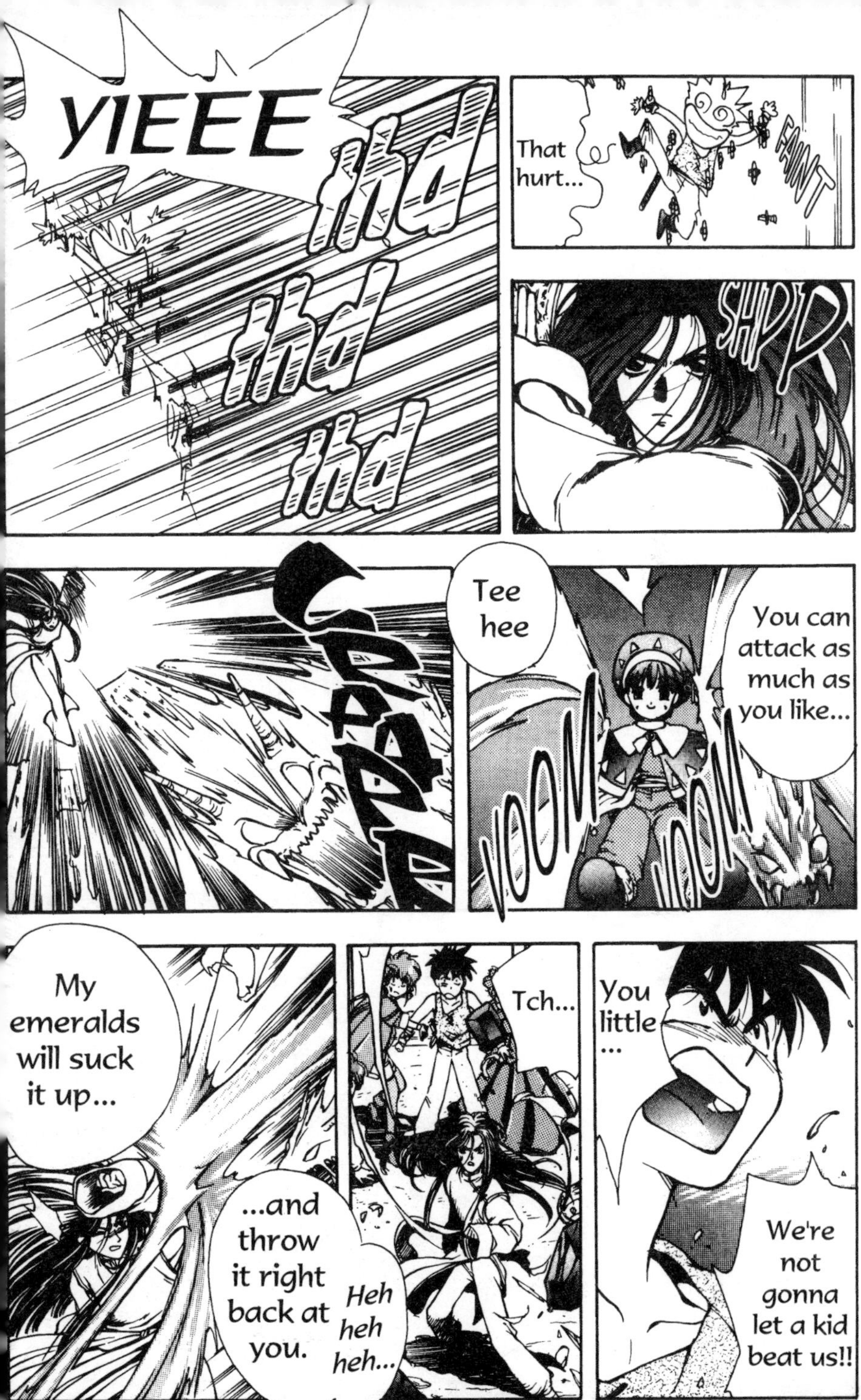
YIEEE
thd
thd
thd
That hurt...
FAINT
Tee hee
You can attack as much as you like...
VOOM
VOOM
My emeralds will suck it up...
...and throw it right back at you.
Tch...
Heh heh heh...
You little ...
We're not gonna let a kid beat us!!

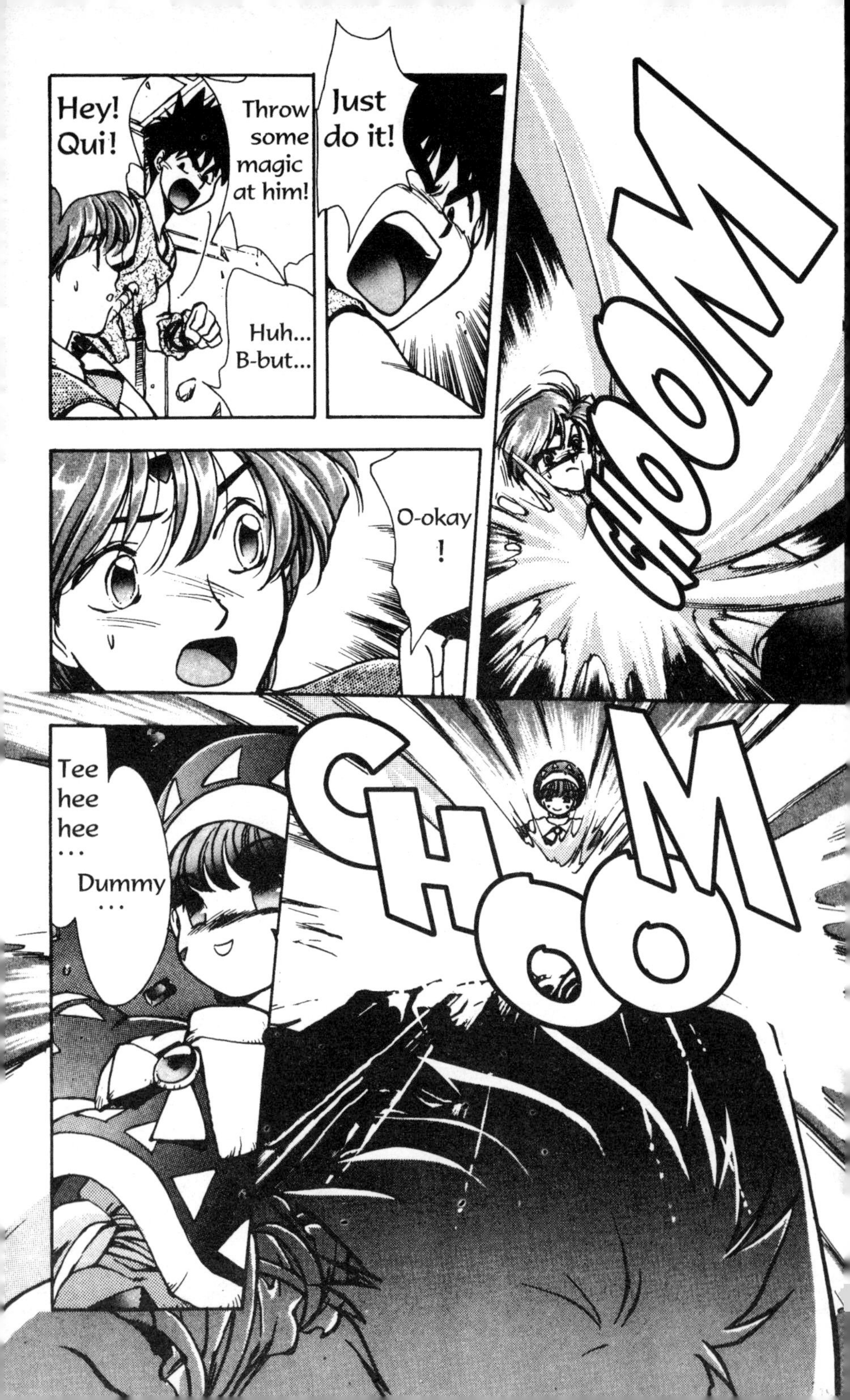
Hey! Qui!
Throw some magic at him!
Huh... B-but...
Just do it!
O-okay!
CHOOM
Tee hee hee...
Dummy...
CHOOM

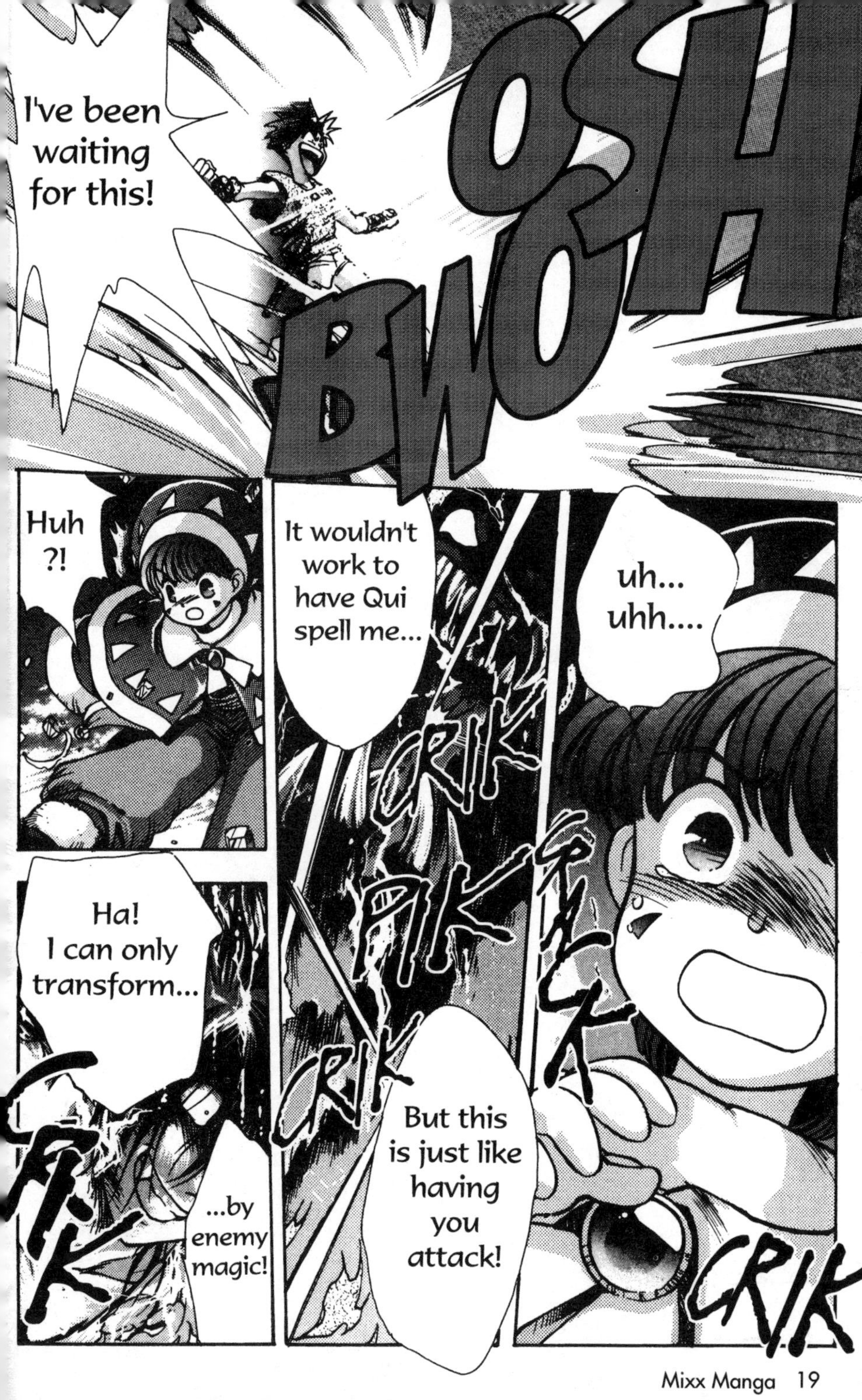
I've been waiting for this!
BWOOSH
Huh ?!
It wouldn't work to have Qui spell me...
CRIK
PIK
CRIK
uh... uhh....
Ha! I can only transform...
...by enemy magic!
But this is just like having you attack!
CRIK

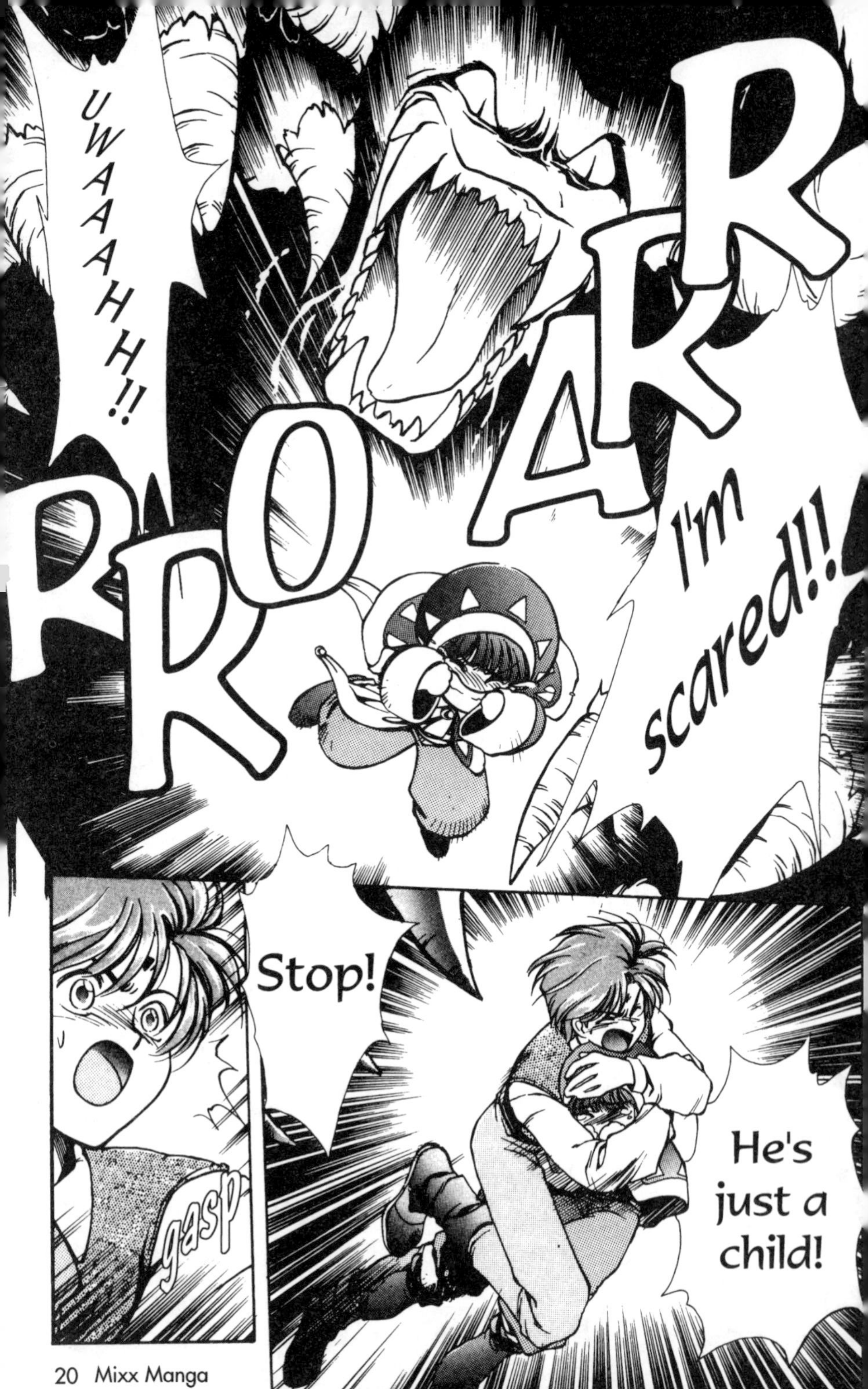
UWAAAAHH!!
ROOAARR
I'm scared!!
Stop!
gasp
He's just a child!

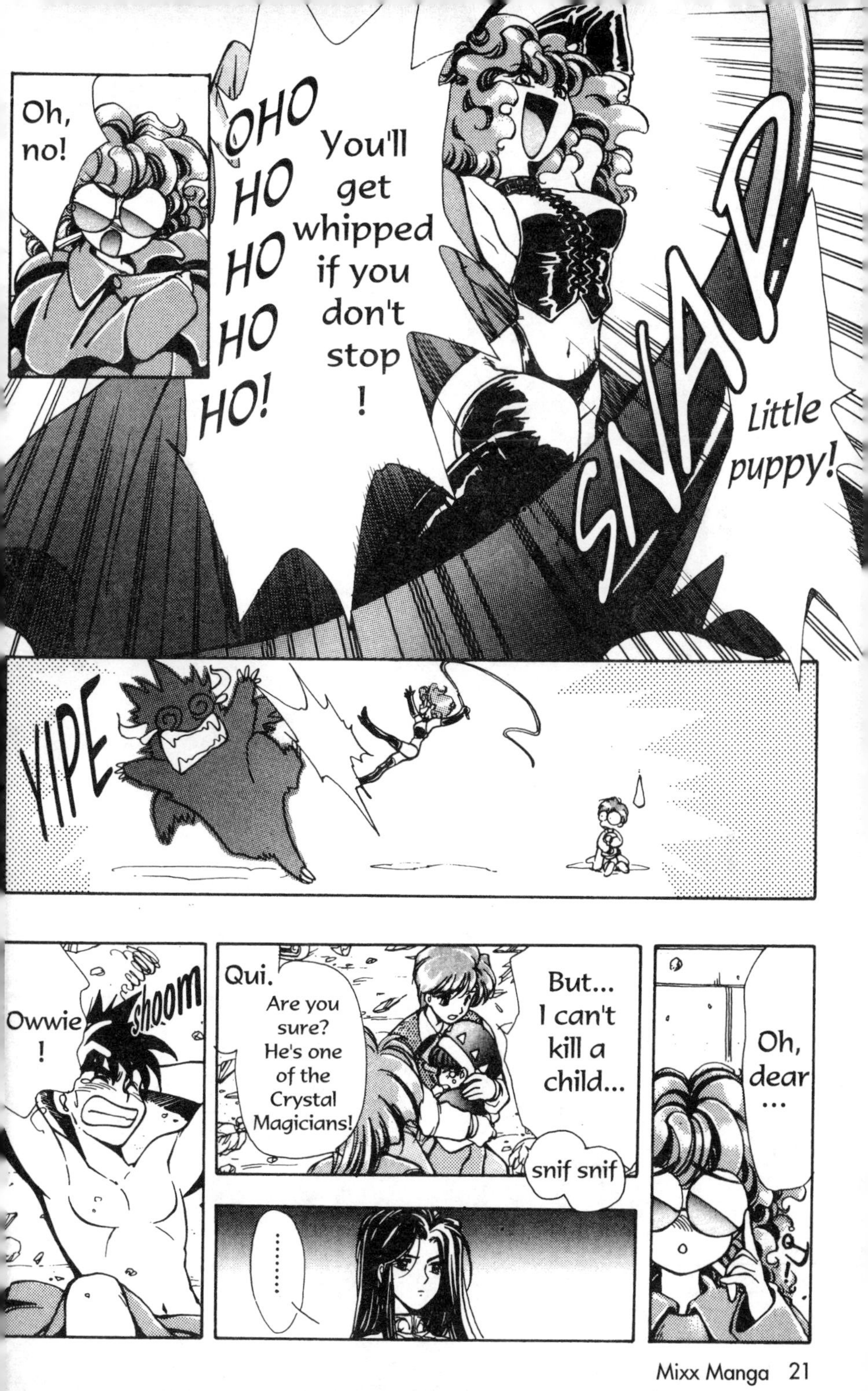
Oh, no!
OHO HO HO HO HO!
You'll get whipped if you don't stop!
SNAP
Little puppy!
YIPE
Owwie!
shoom
Qui.
Are you sure? He's one of the Crystal Magicians!
But... I can't kill a child...
snif snif
......
Oh, dear...

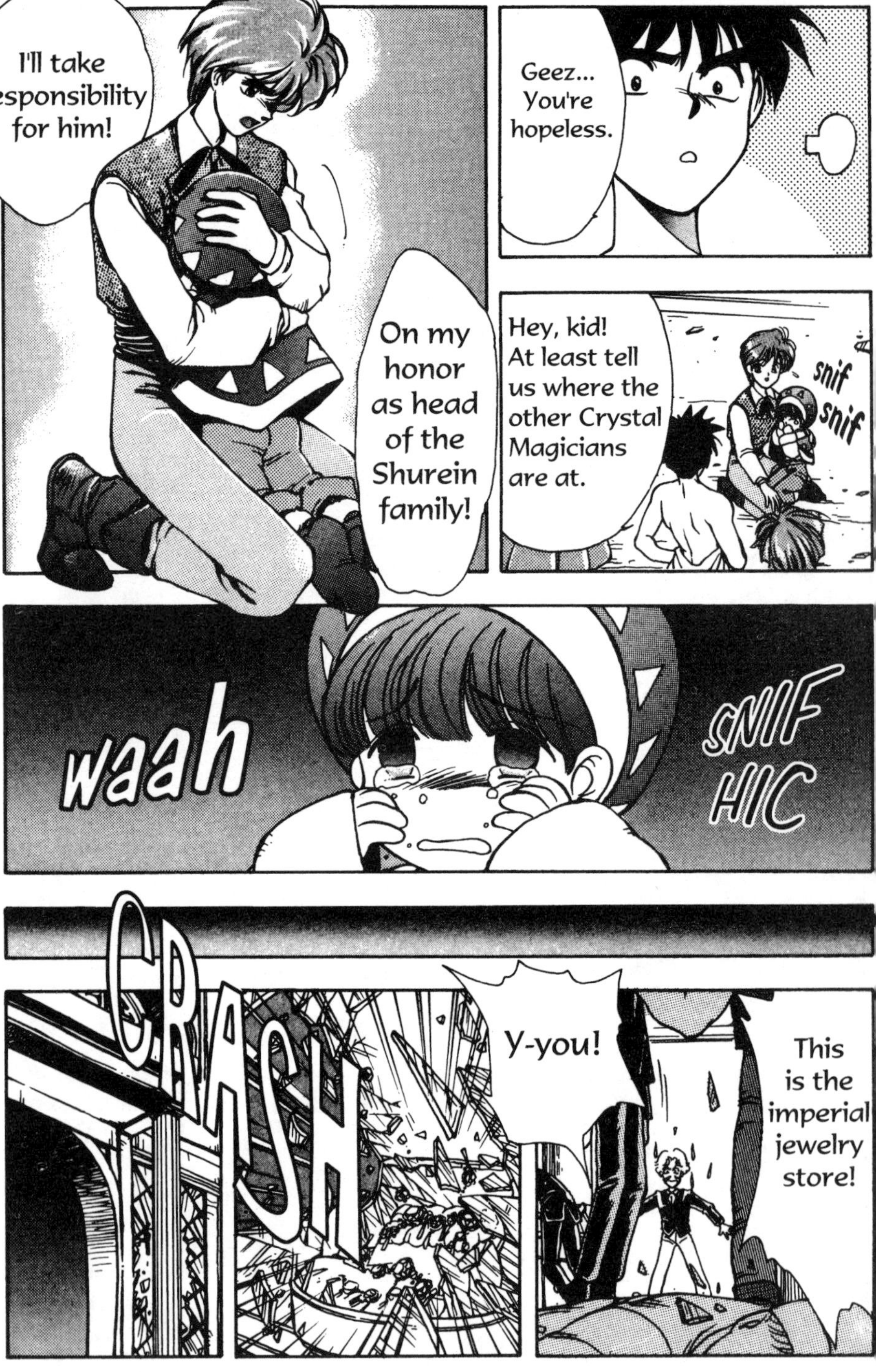
I'll take responsibility for him!
On my honor as head of the Shurein family!
Geez... You're hopeless.
Hey, kid! At least tell us where the other Crystal Magicians are at.
snif snif
waah
SNIF HIC
CRASH
Y-you!
This is the imperial jewelry store!

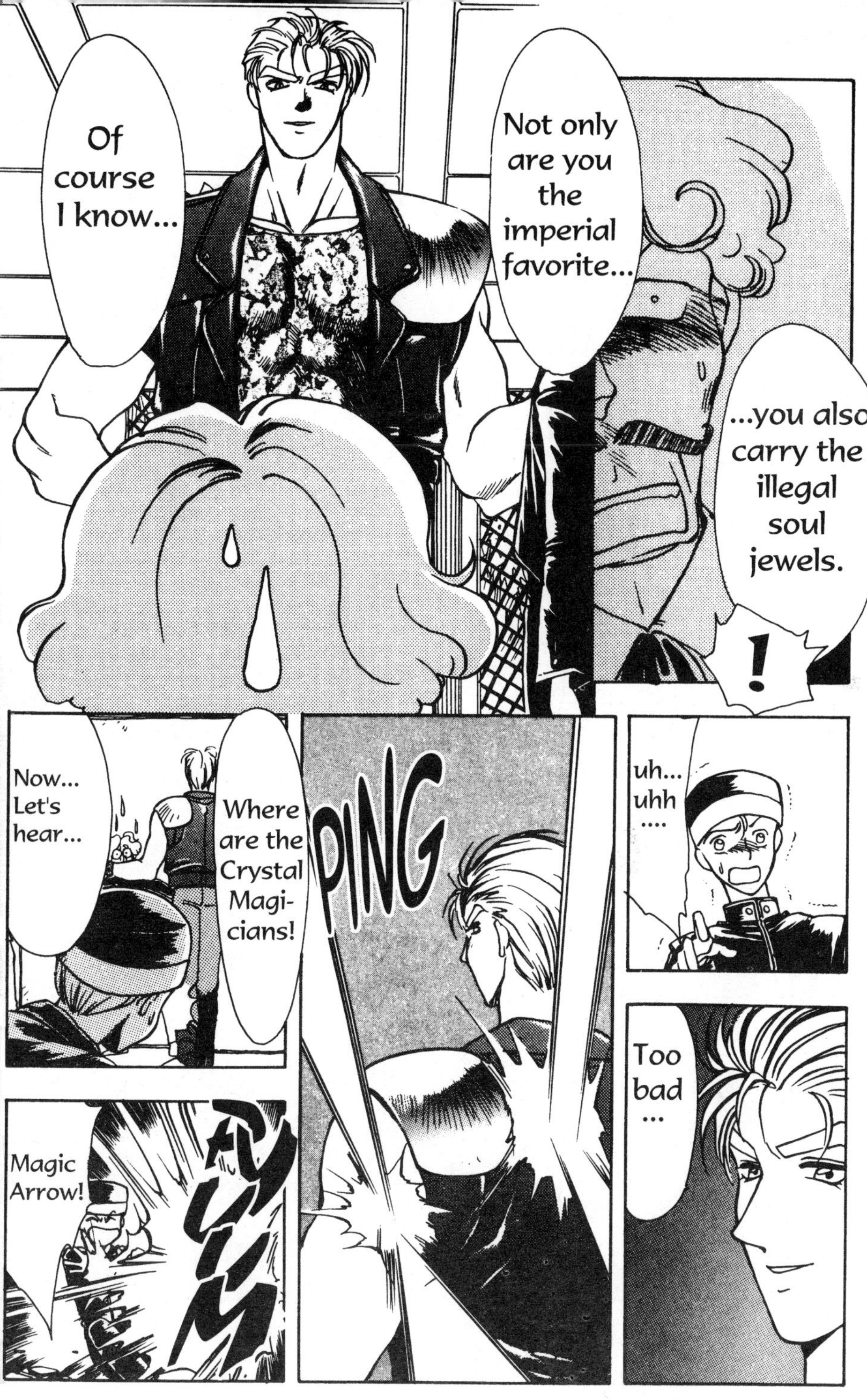
Of course I know...
Not only are you the imperial favorite...
...you also carry the illegal soul jewels.
!
Now... Let's hear...
Where are the Crystal Magi-cians!
PING
uh... uhh ....
Magic Arrow!
Too bad ...

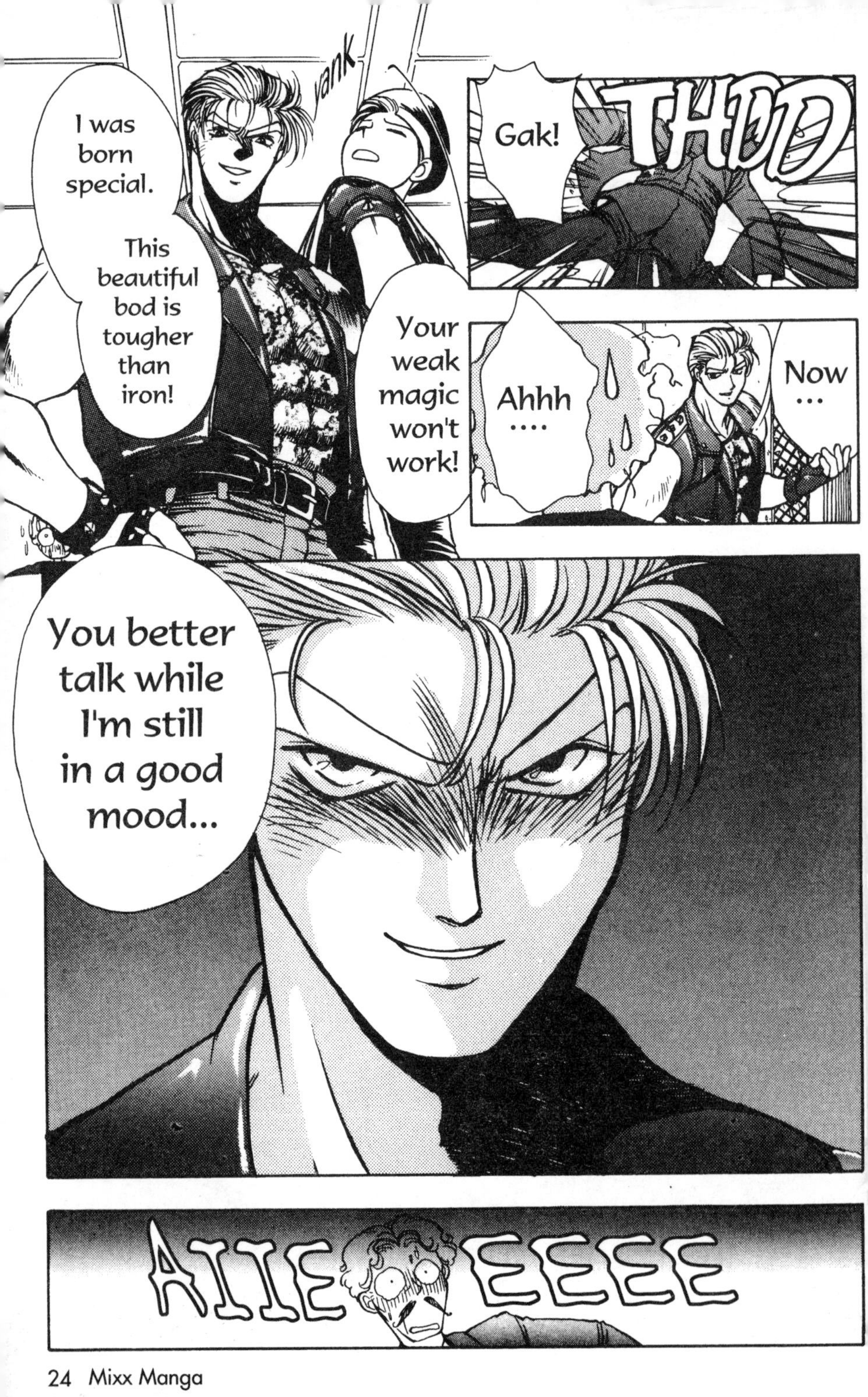
I was born special.
This beautiful bod is tougher than iron!
yank
Your weak magic won't work!
Gak!
THUD
Ahhh ....
Now ...
You better talk while I'm still in a good mood...
AIIEEEEE

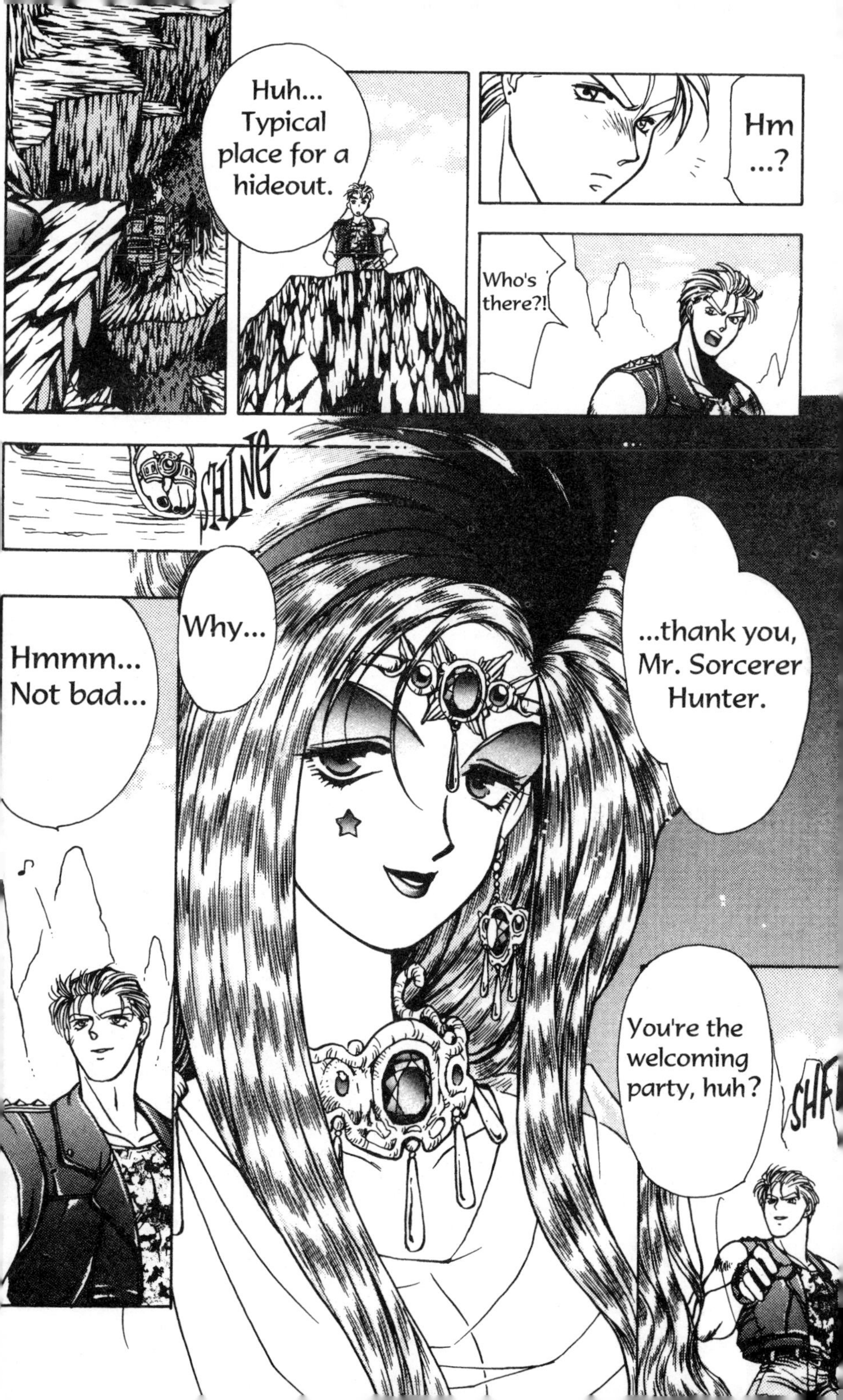
Huh... Typical place for a hideout.
Hm ...?
Who's there?!
SHING
Hmmm... Not bad...
Why...
...thank you, Mr. Sorcerer Hunter.
You're the welcoming party, huh?

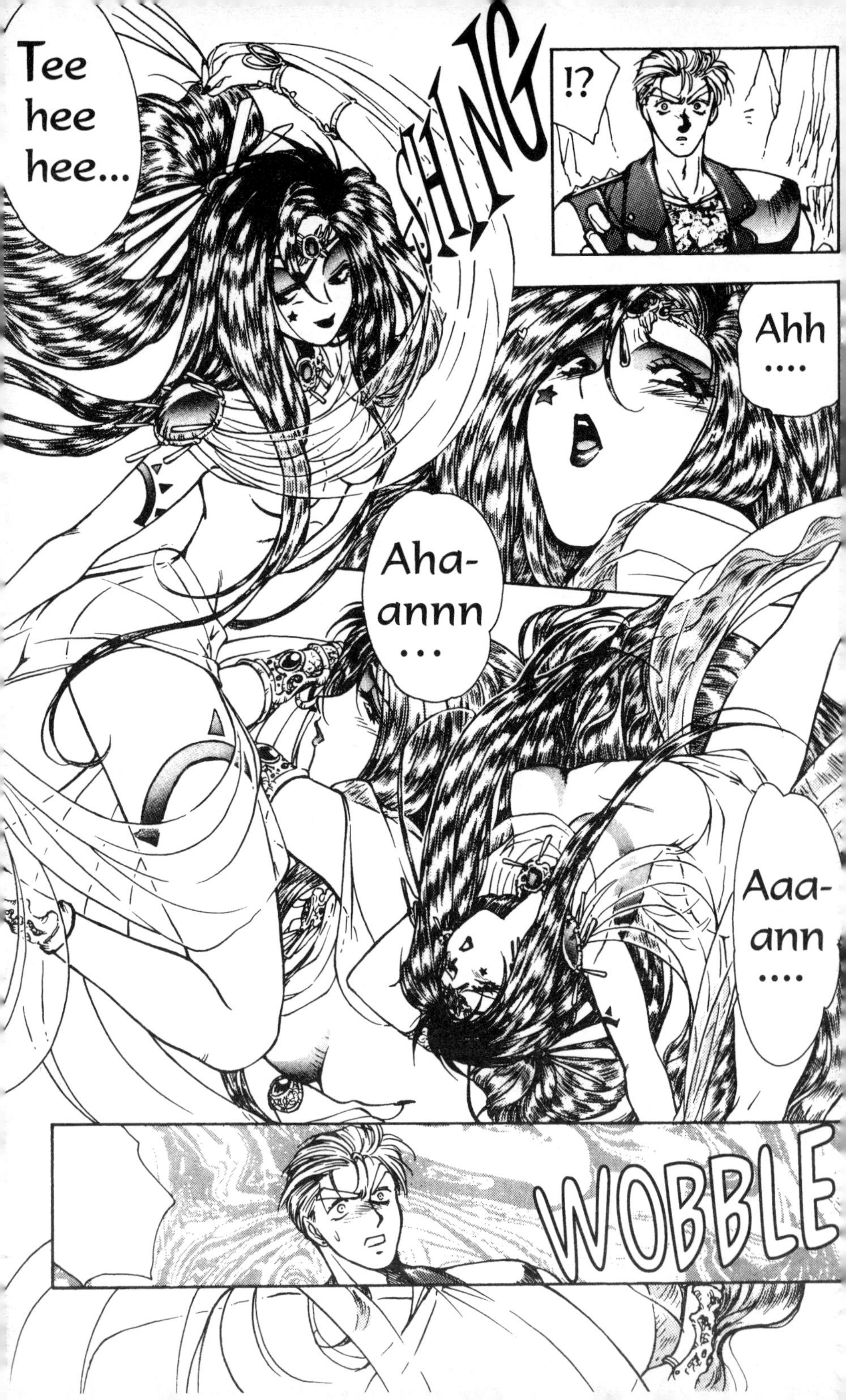
Tee hee hee...
SHING
!?
Ahh ....
Aha-annn ...
Aaa-ann ....
WOBBLE

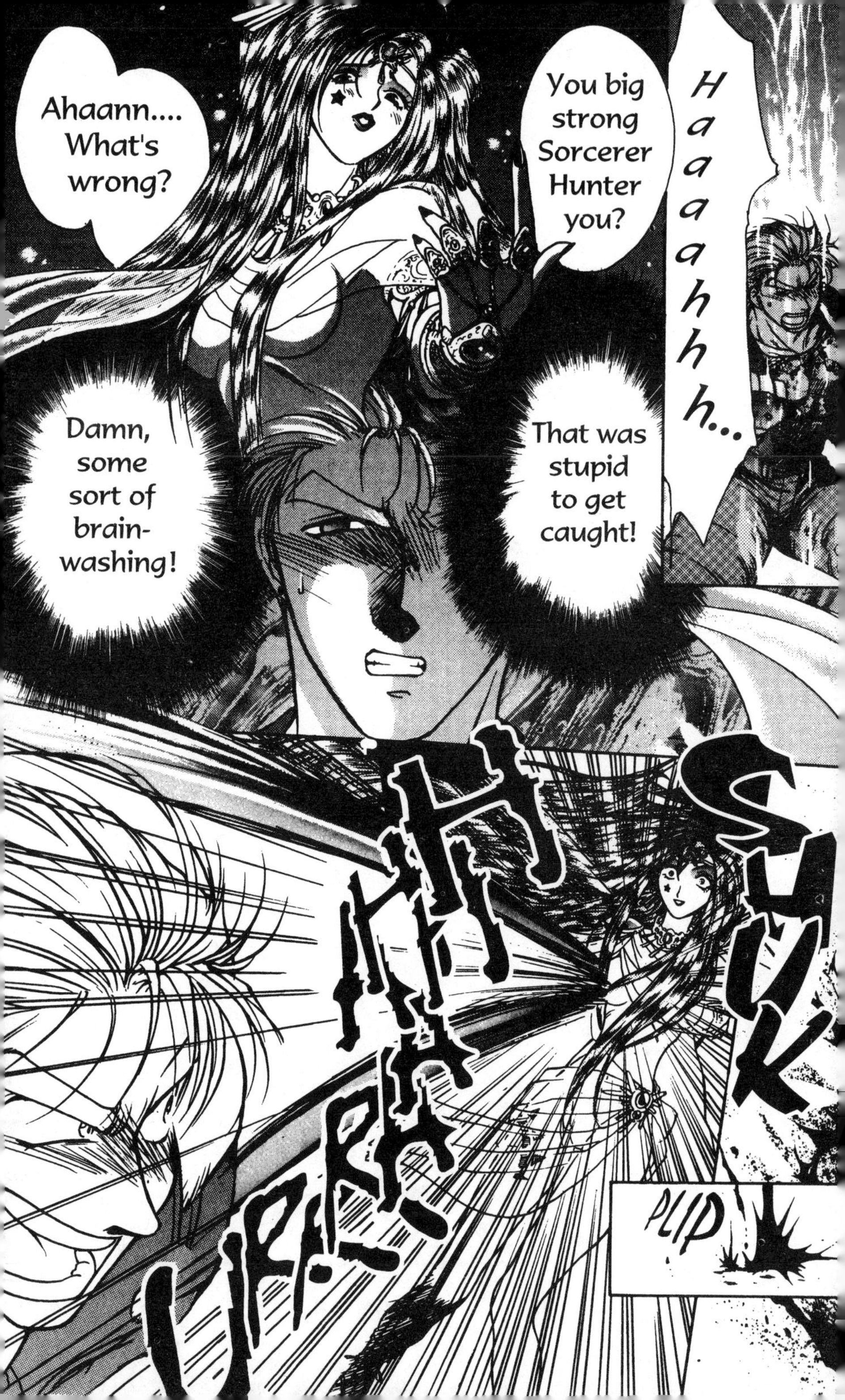
Ahaann.... What's wrong?
You big strong Sorcerer Hunter you?
Haaaaahhh...
Damn, some sort of brain-washing!
That was stupid to get caught!
VRRK
SHK
PLIP

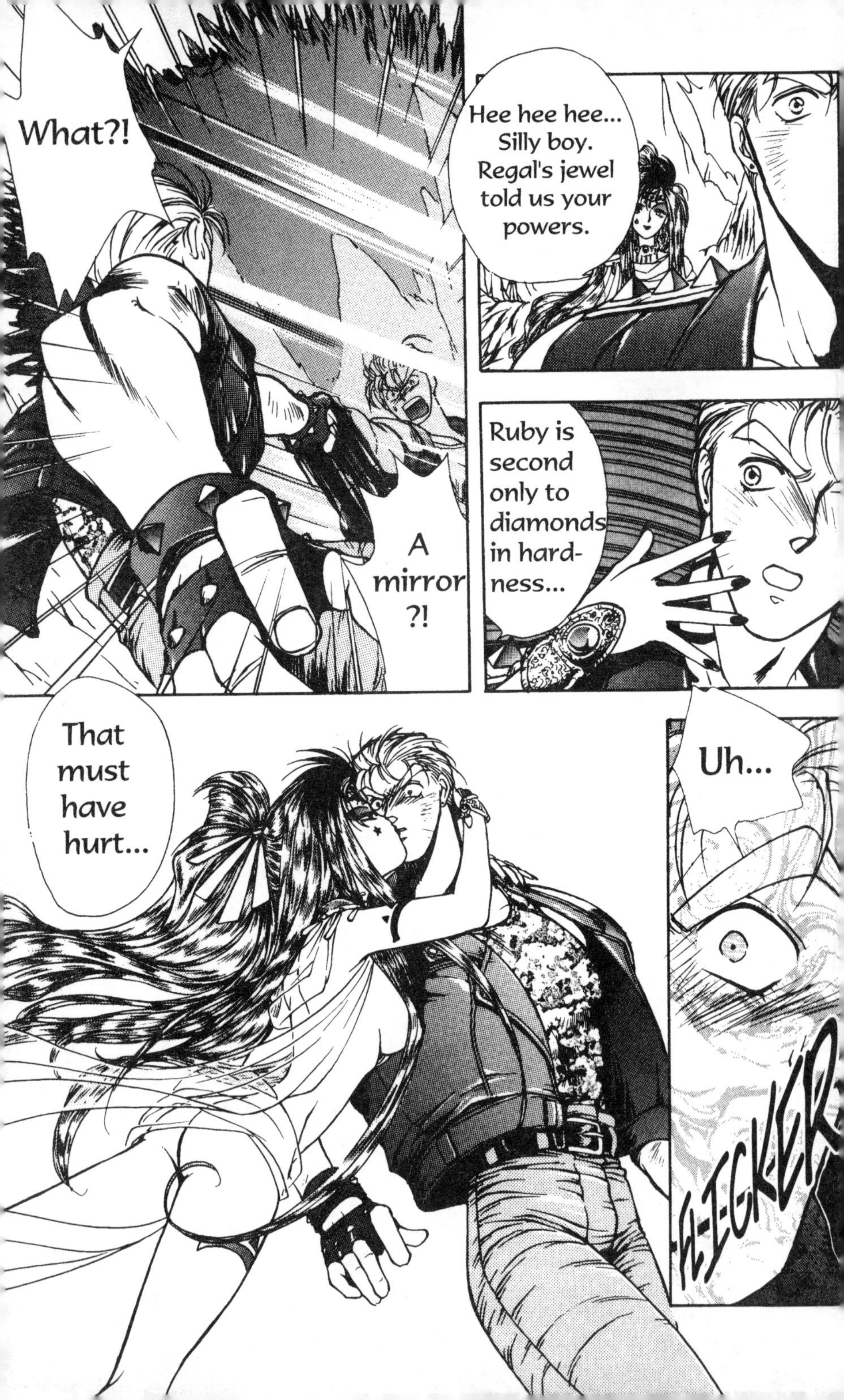
What?!
A mirror ?!
Hee hee hee... Silly boy. Regal's jewel told us your powers.
Ruby is second only to diamonds in hard-ness...
That must have hurt...
Uh...
F-L-I-C-K-E-R

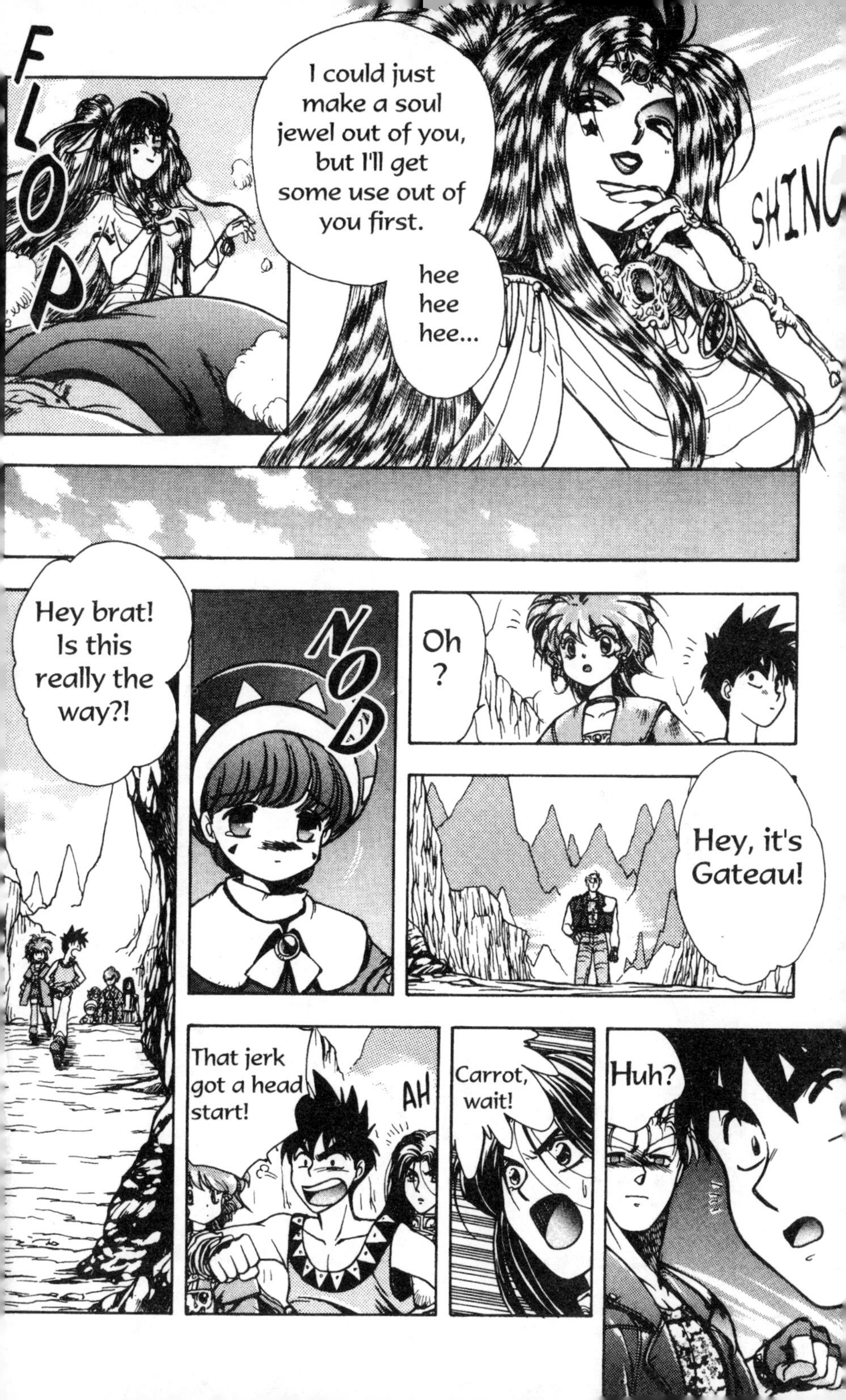
FLOP
I could just make a soul jewel out of you, but I'll get some use out of you first.
hee hee hee...
SHING
Hey brat! Is this really the way?!
NOD
Oh ?
Hey, it's Gateau!
That jerk got a head start!
AH
Carrot, wait!
Huh?

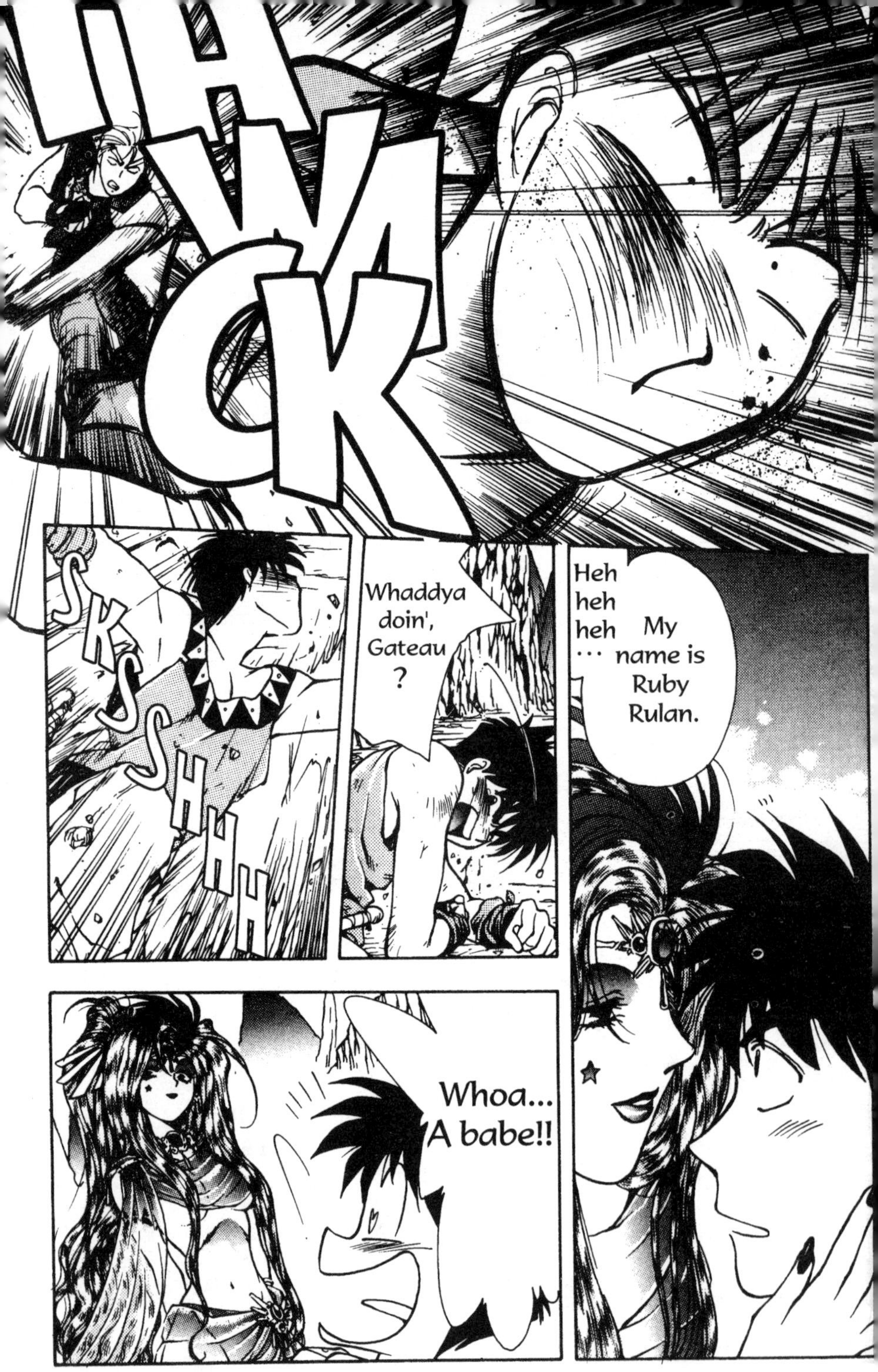
WHACK
SKSSHHH
Whaddya doin', Gateau?
Heh heh heh... My name is Ruby Rulan.
Whoa... A babe!!

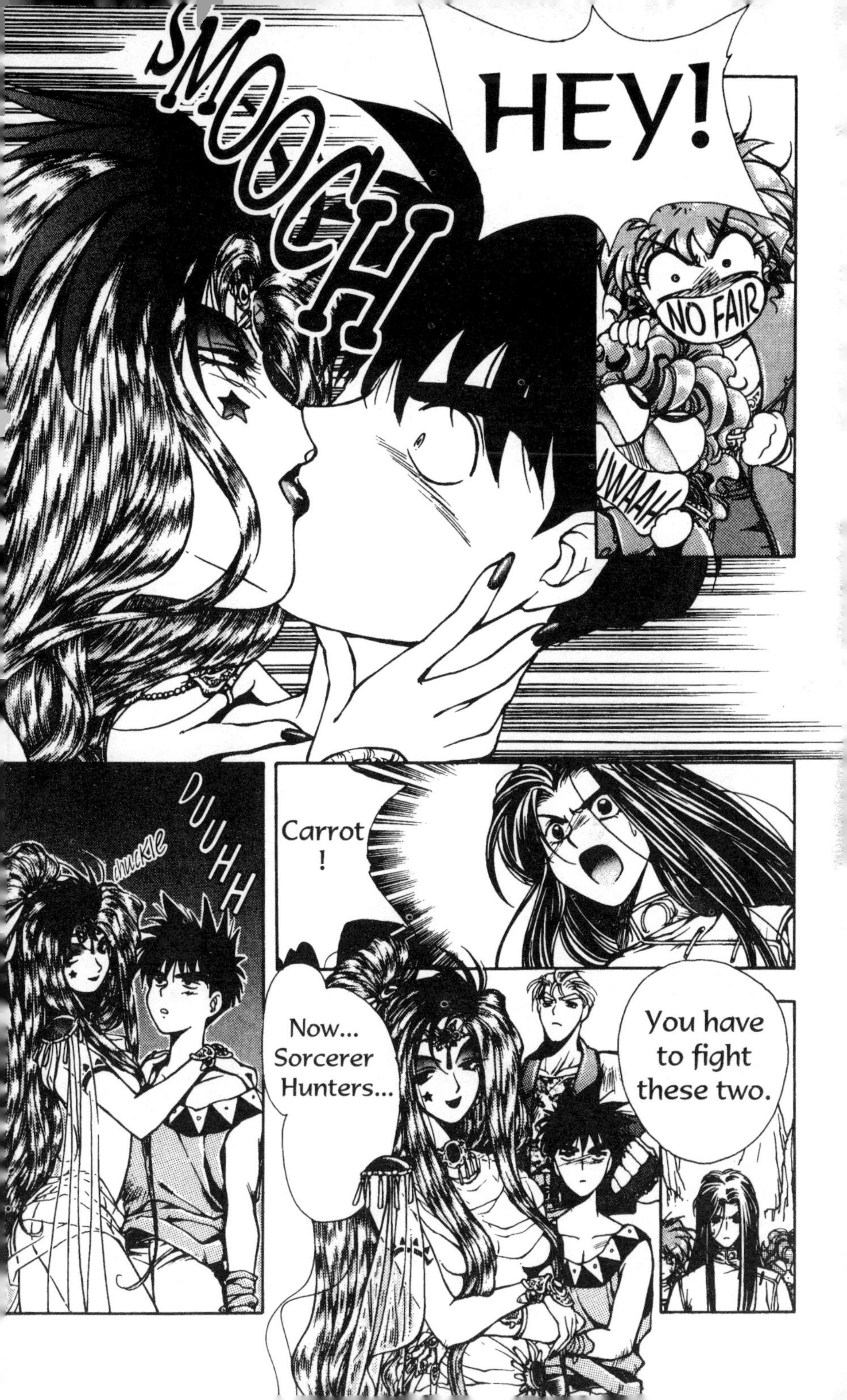
SMOOCH
HEY!
NO FAIR
WAAAH
chuckle
DUUHH
Carrot!
Now... Sorcerer Hunters...
You have to fight these two.

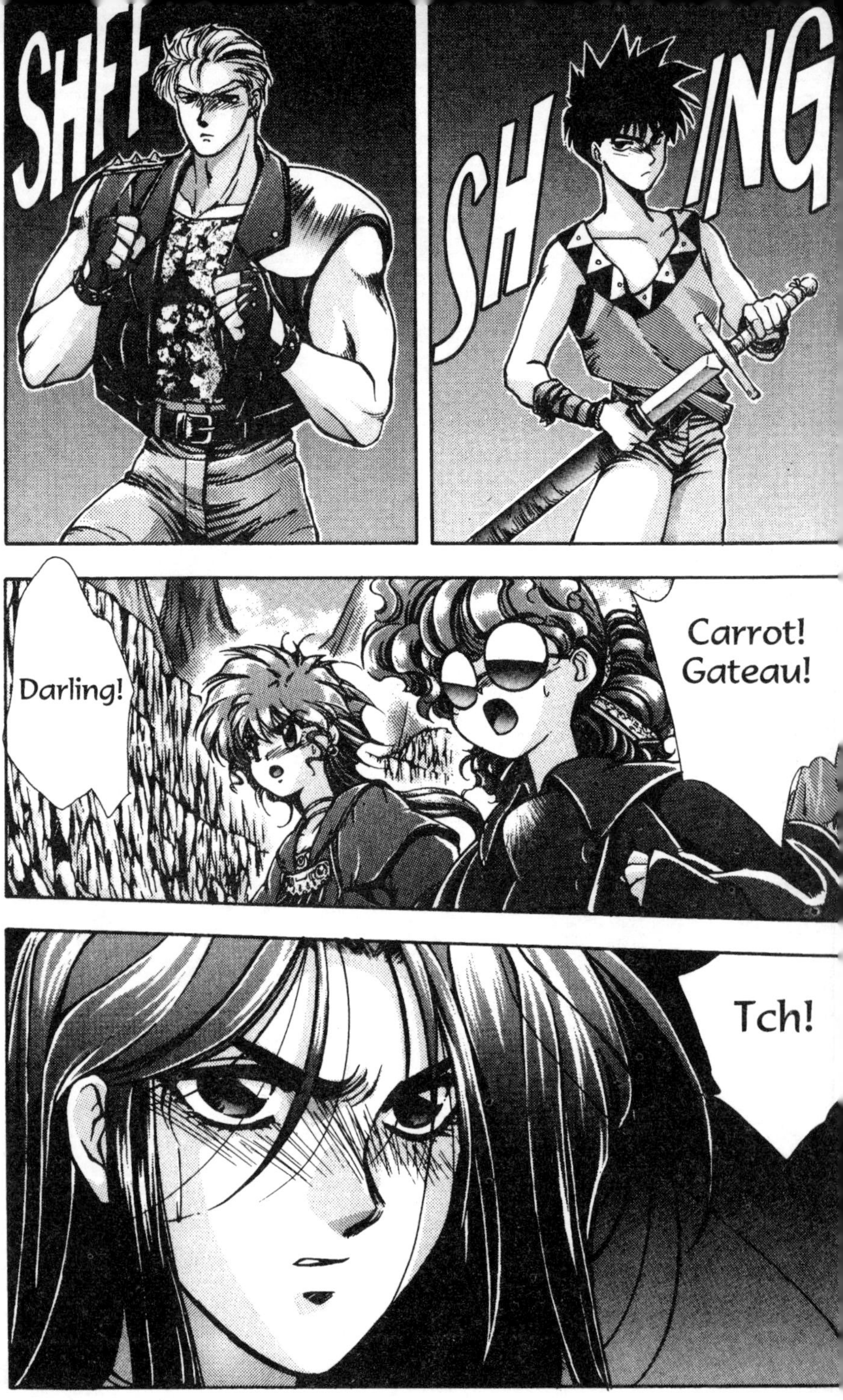
SHFF
SH ING
Darling!
Carrot!
Gateau!
Tch!

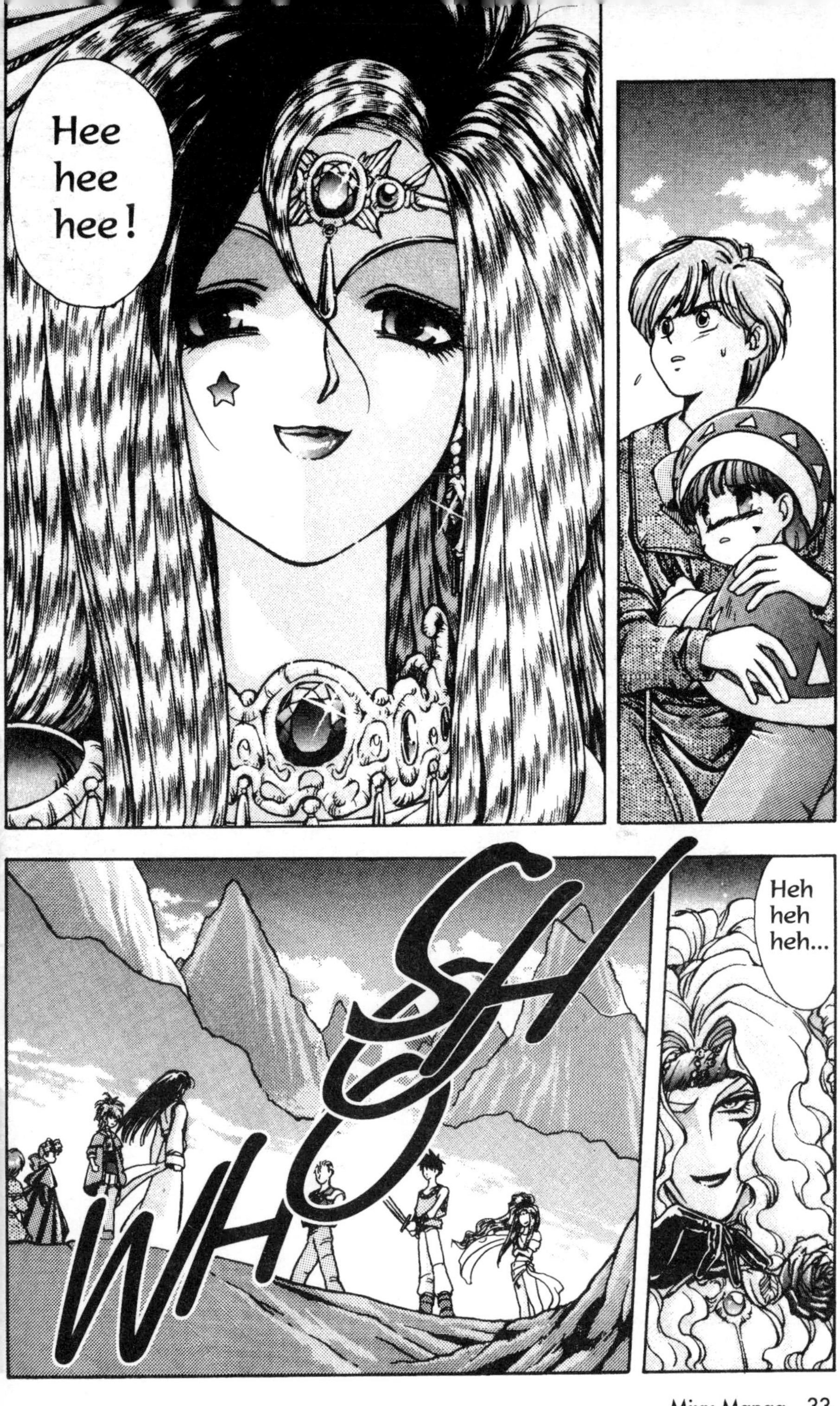
Hee hee hee!
WHOOSH
Heh heh heh...

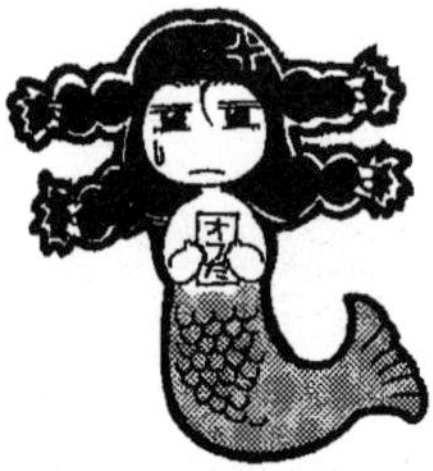
オフだ

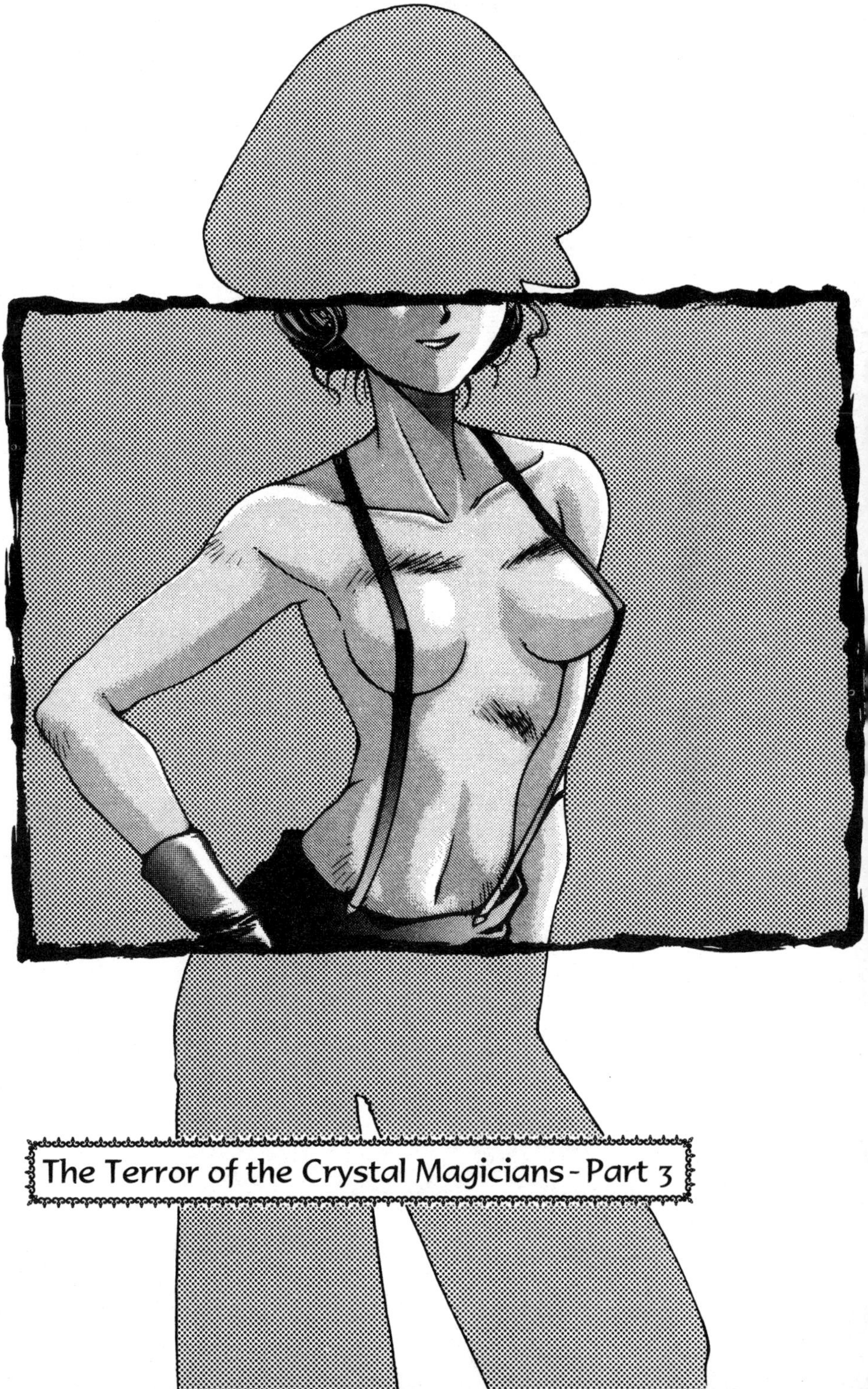
The Terror of the Crystal Magicians - Part 3

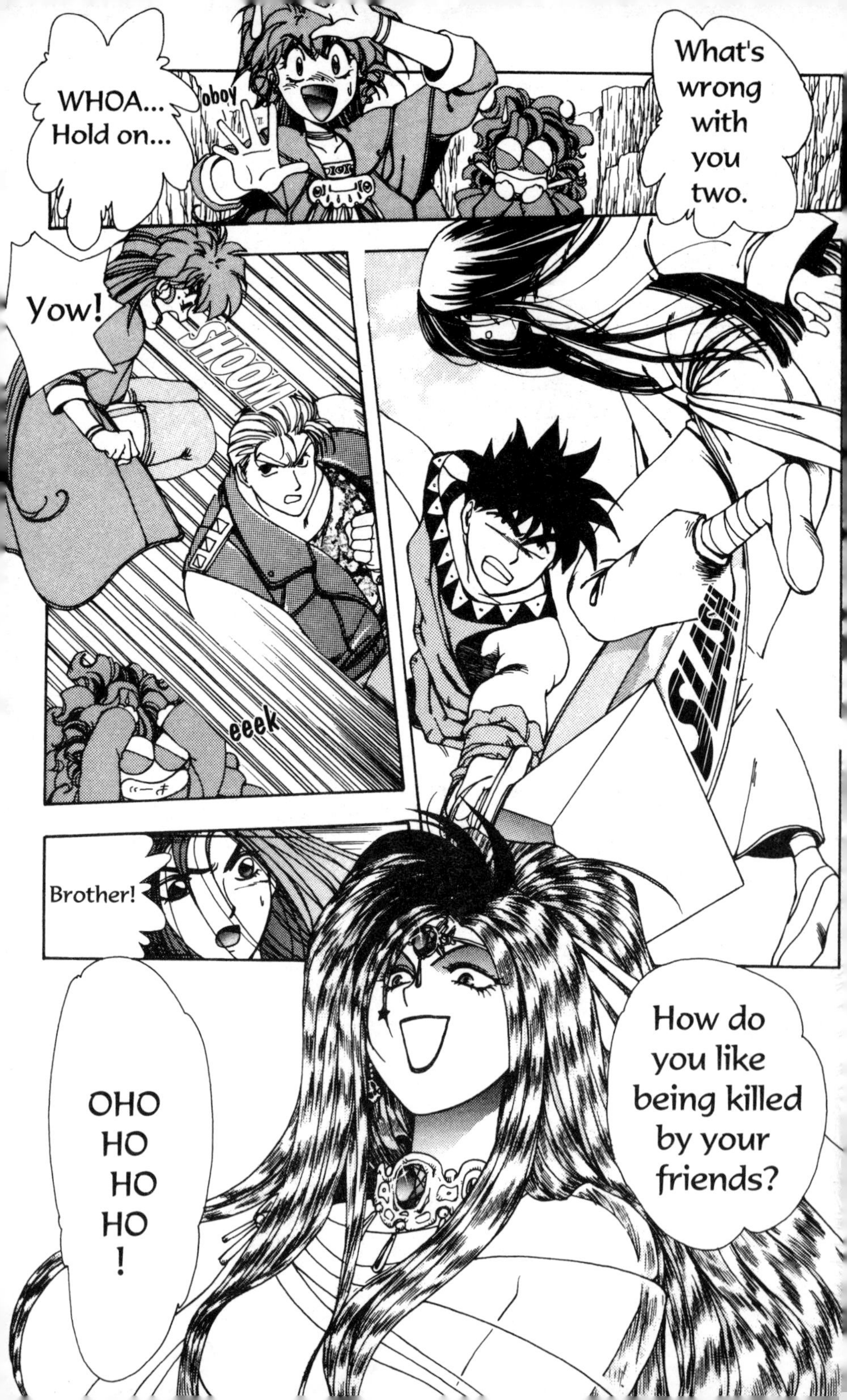
WHOA... Hold on...
oboy
What's wrong with you two.
Yow!
SHOOM
eeek
SLASH
Brother!
OHO HO HO HO !
How do you like being killed by your friends?

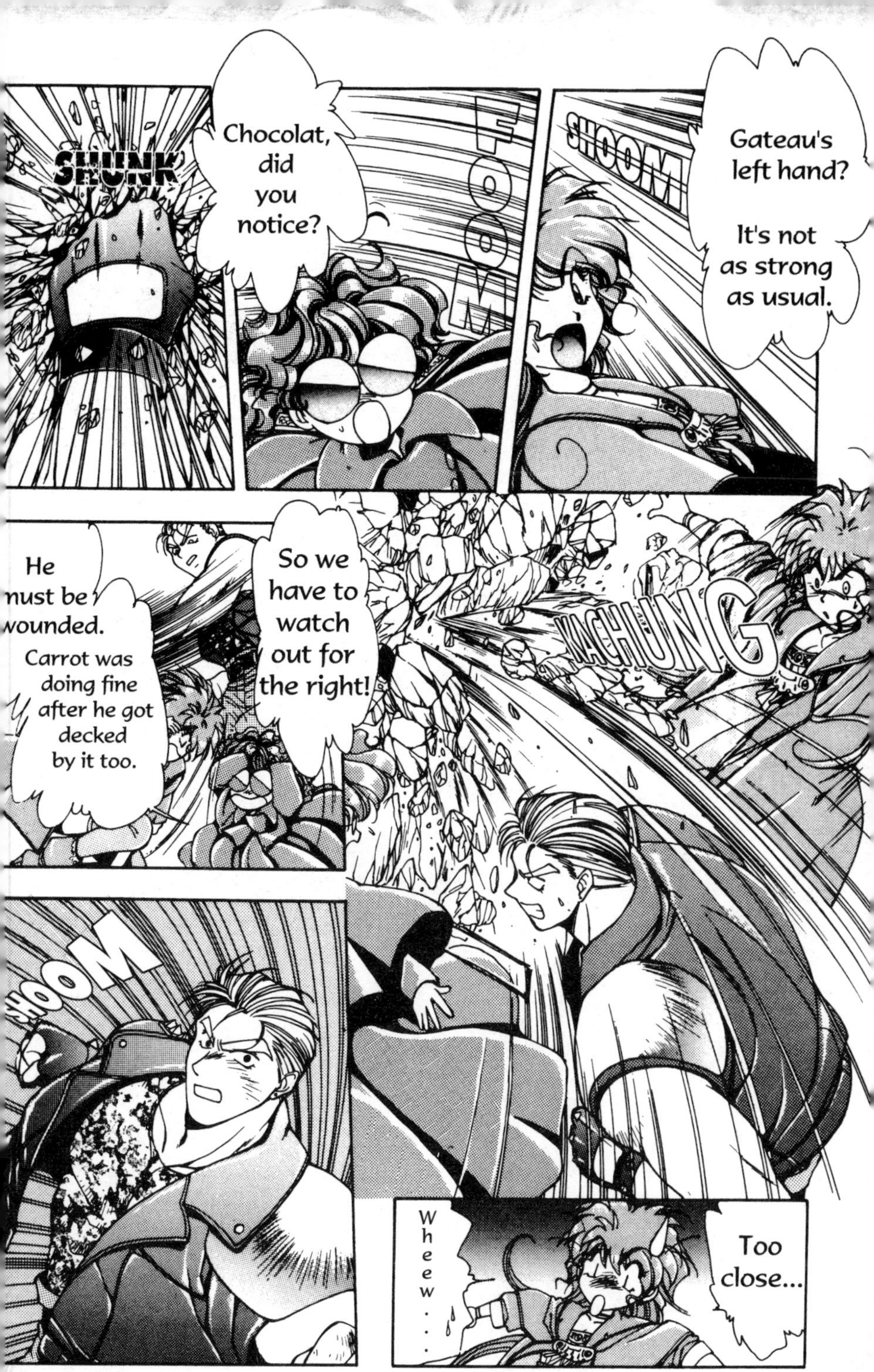
SHUNK
Chocolat, did you notice?
FOOM
SHOOM
Gateau's left hand?
It's not as strong as usual.
He must be wounded.
Carrot was doing fine after he got decked by it too.
So we have to watch out for the right!
VACHUNG
SHOOM
Wheew...
Too close...

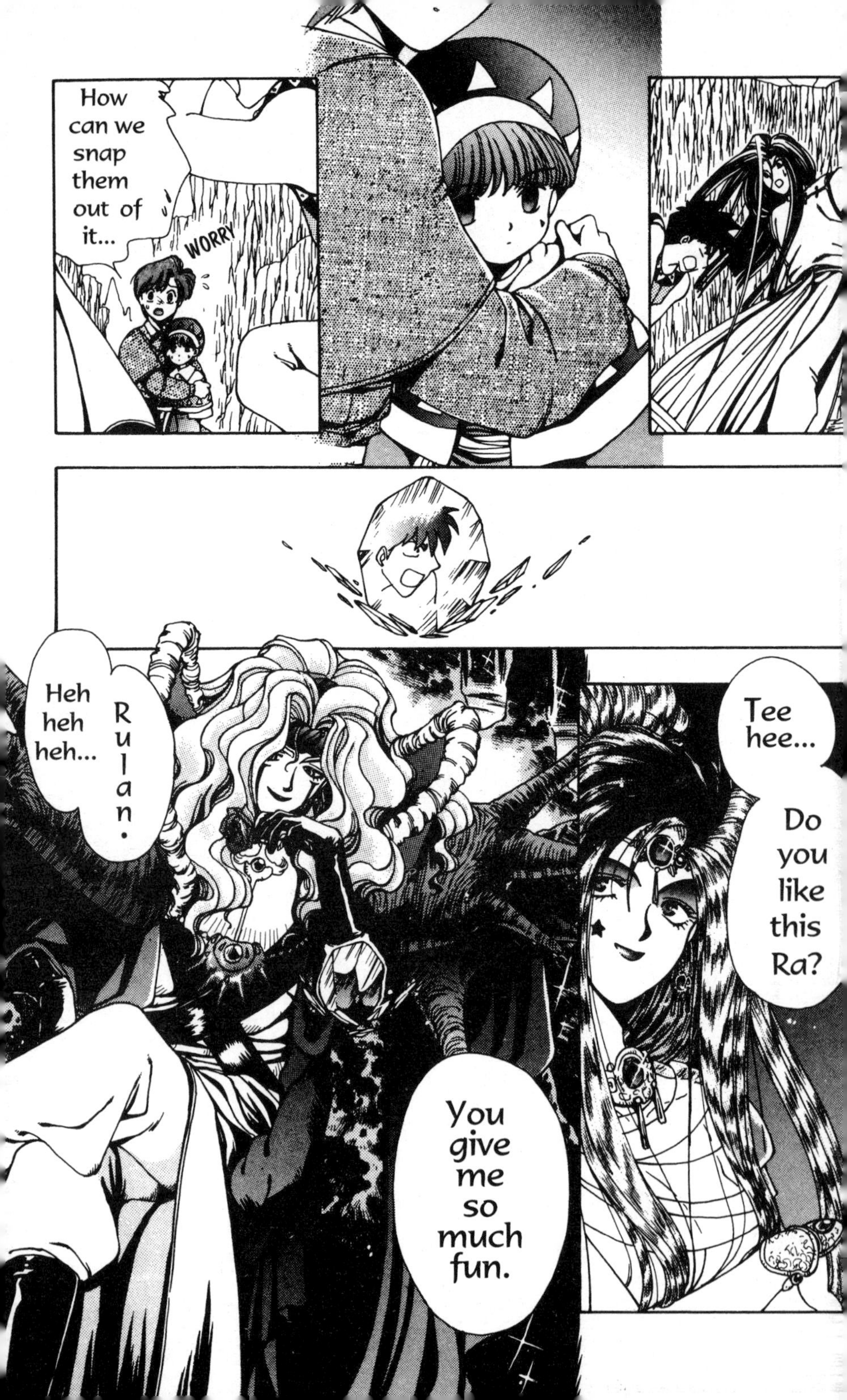
How can we snap them out of it...
WORRY
Heh heh heh...
Rulan.
Tee hee...
Do you like this Ra?
You give me so much fun.

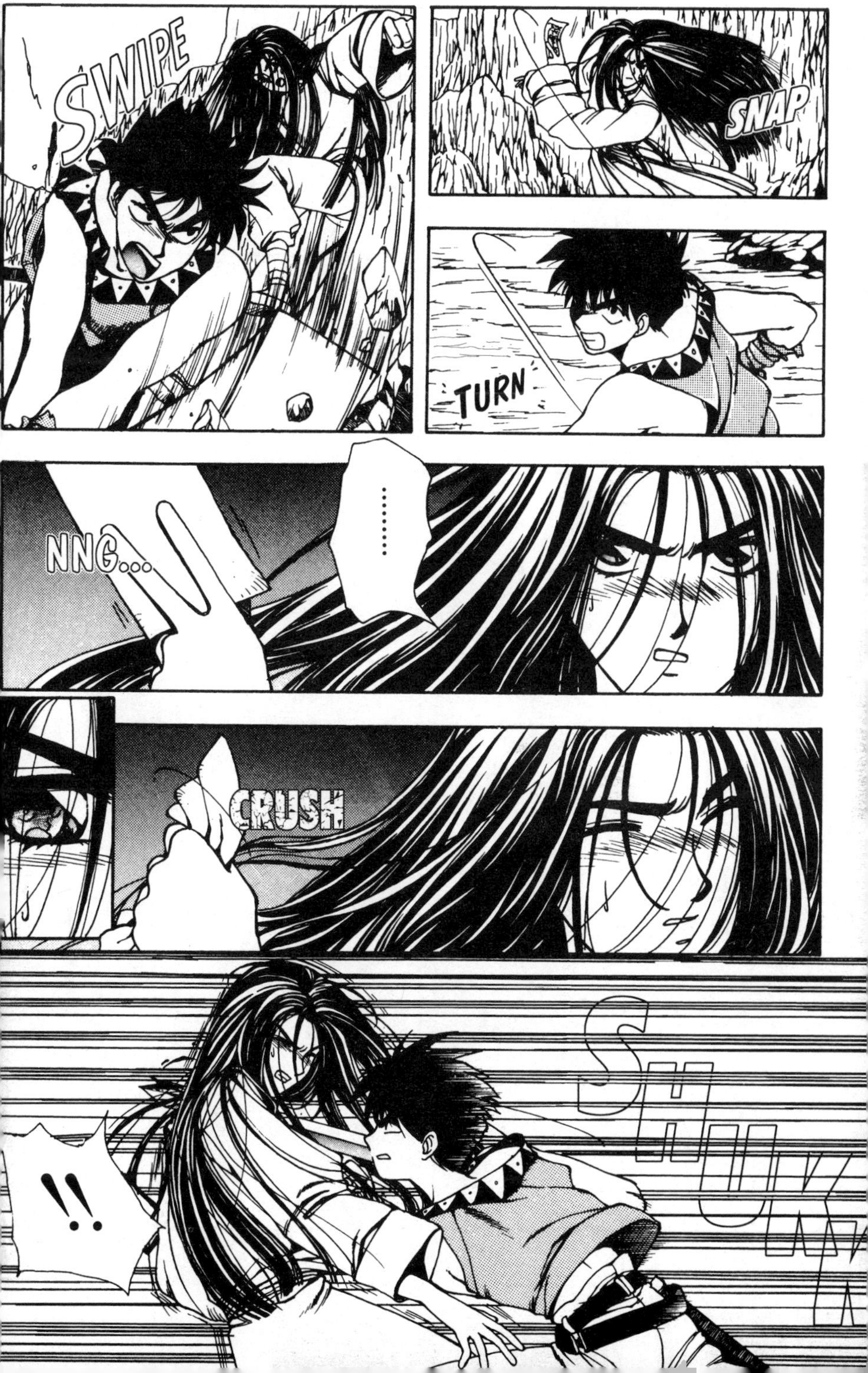
SWIPE
SNAP
TURN
NNG...
....
CRUSH
!!

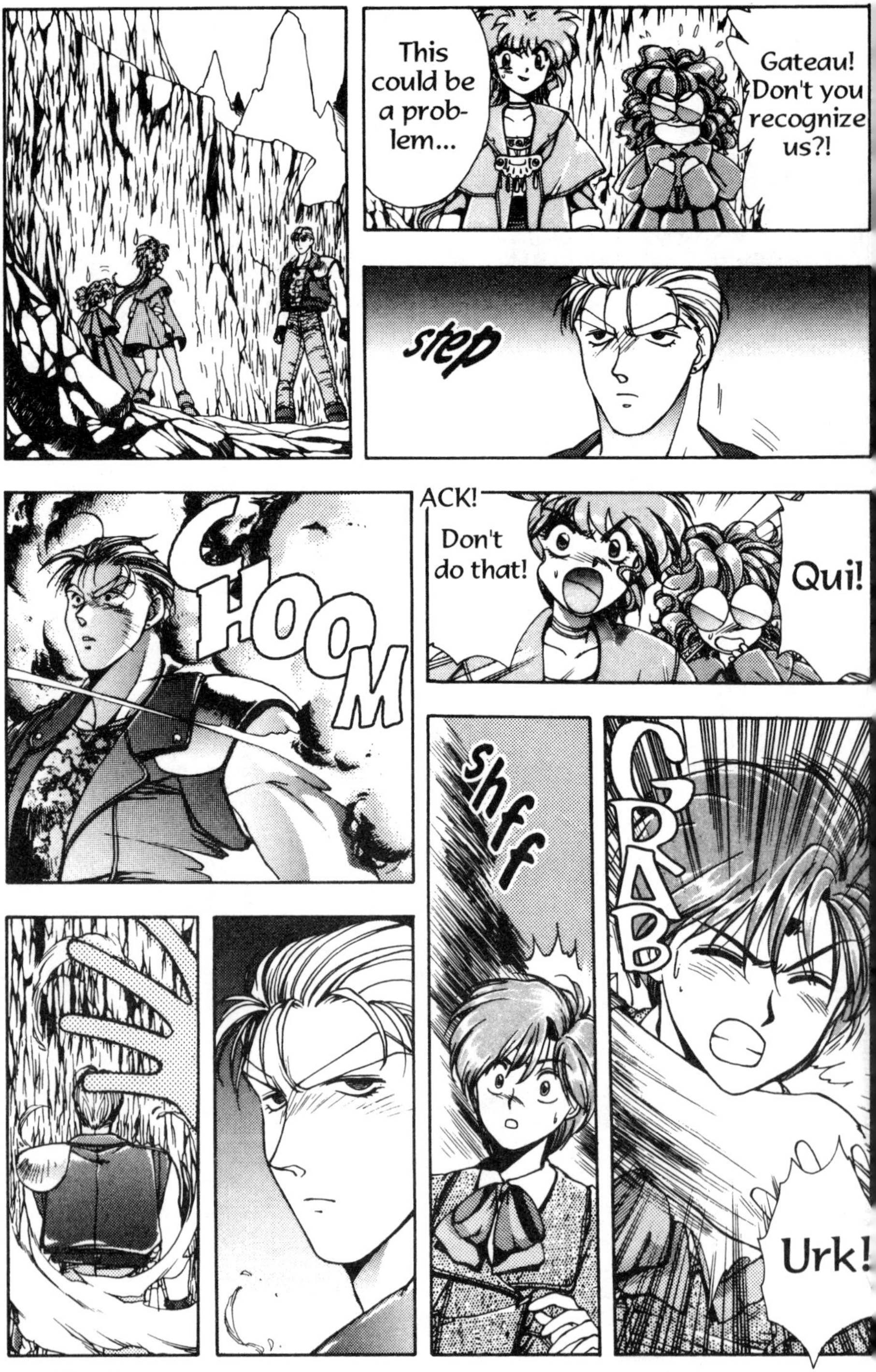
This could be a prob-lem...
Gateau! Don't you recognize us?!
step
CHOOM
ACK!
Don't do that!
Qui!
shff
GRAB
Urk!

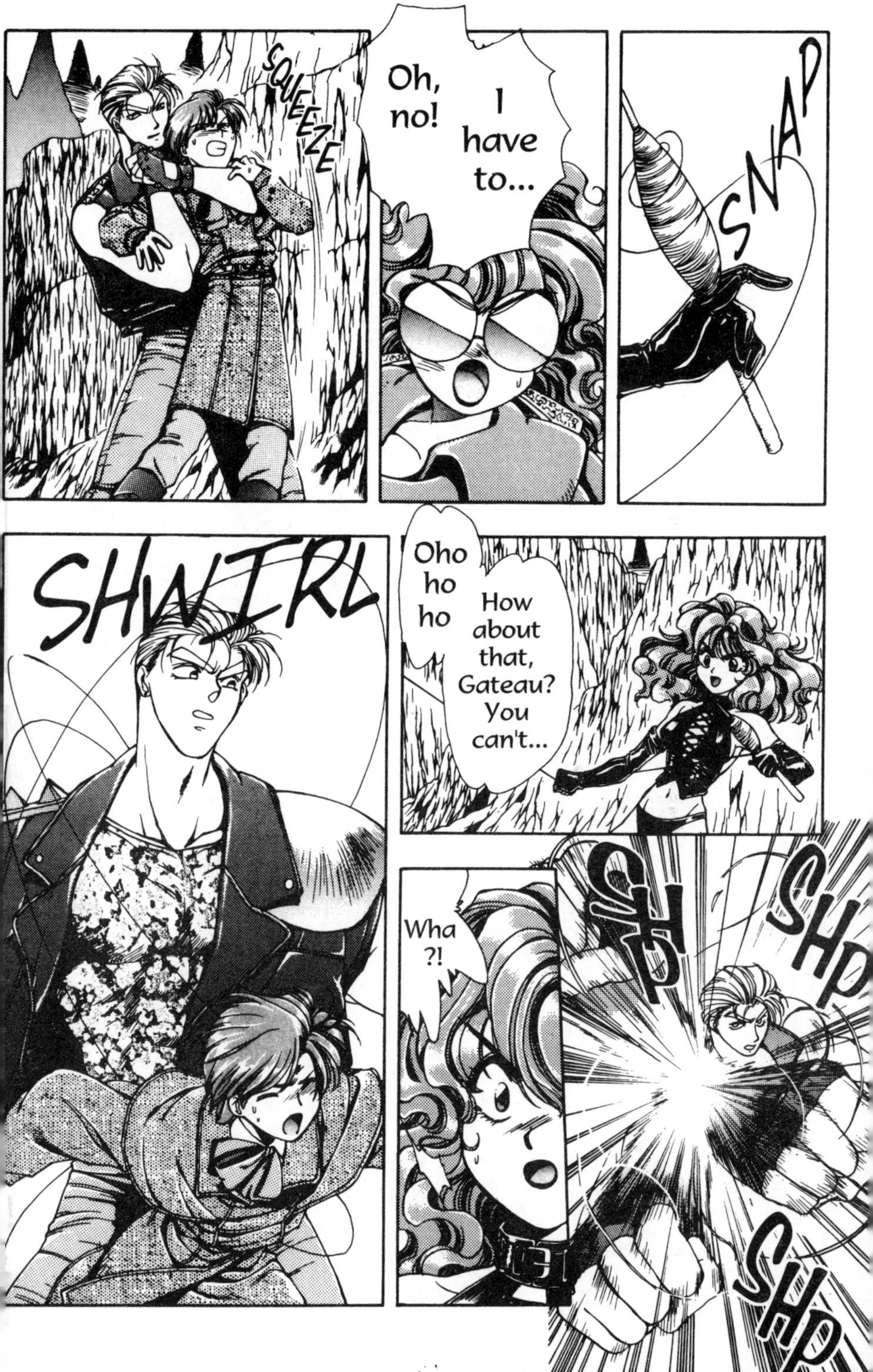
SQUEEZE
Oh, no!
I have to...
SNAP
SHWIRL
Oho ho ho
How about that, Gateau? You can't...
Wha ?!
SHP
SHP
SHP

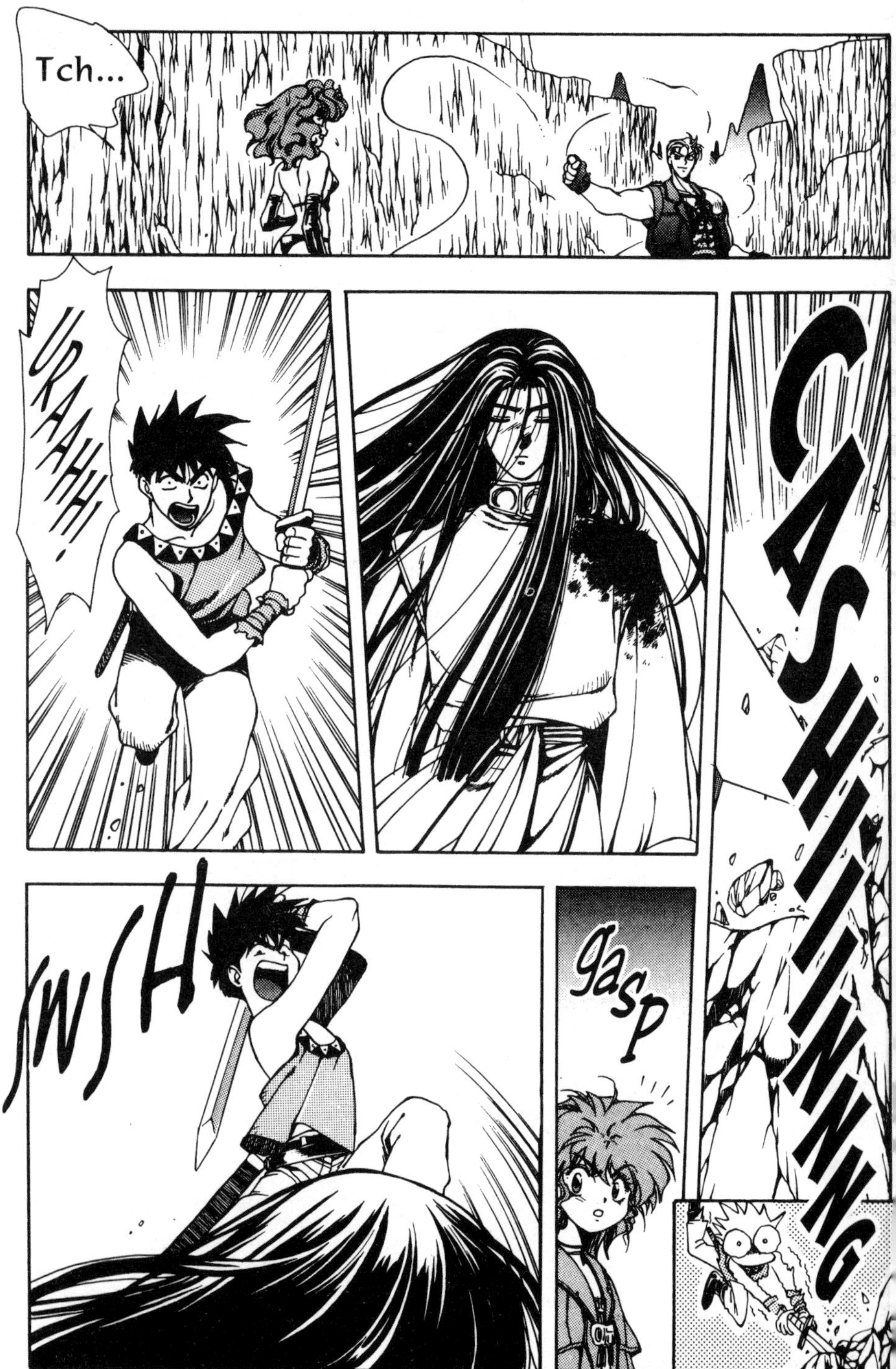
Tch...
URAAHH!!
SWSH
gasp
CASHINNNG

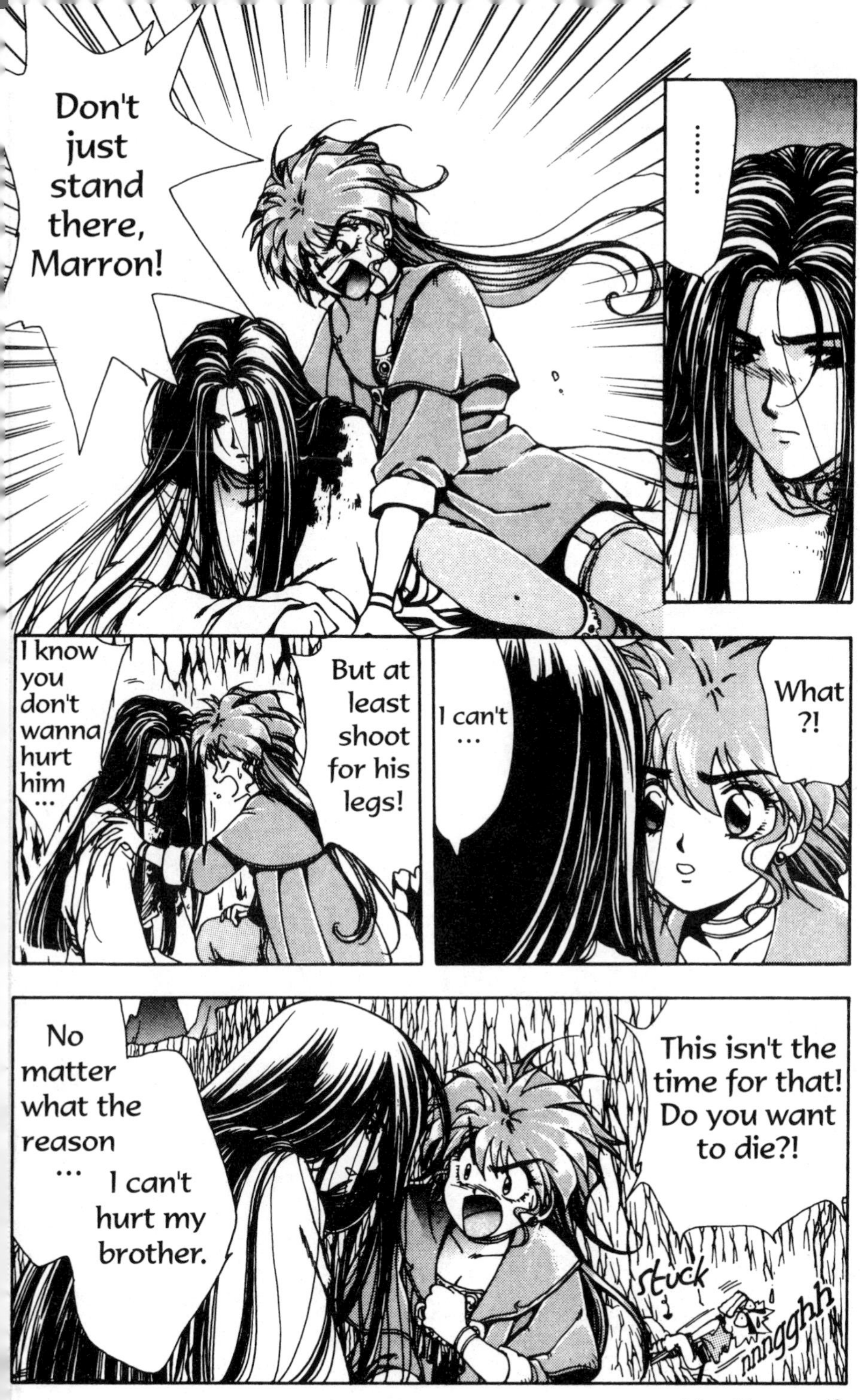
Don't just stand there, Marron!
……
I know you don't wanna hurt him ...
But at least shoot for his legs!
I can't ...
What?!
No matter what the reason ...
I can't hurt my brother.
This isn't the time for that! Do you want to die?!
stuck
nnngghh

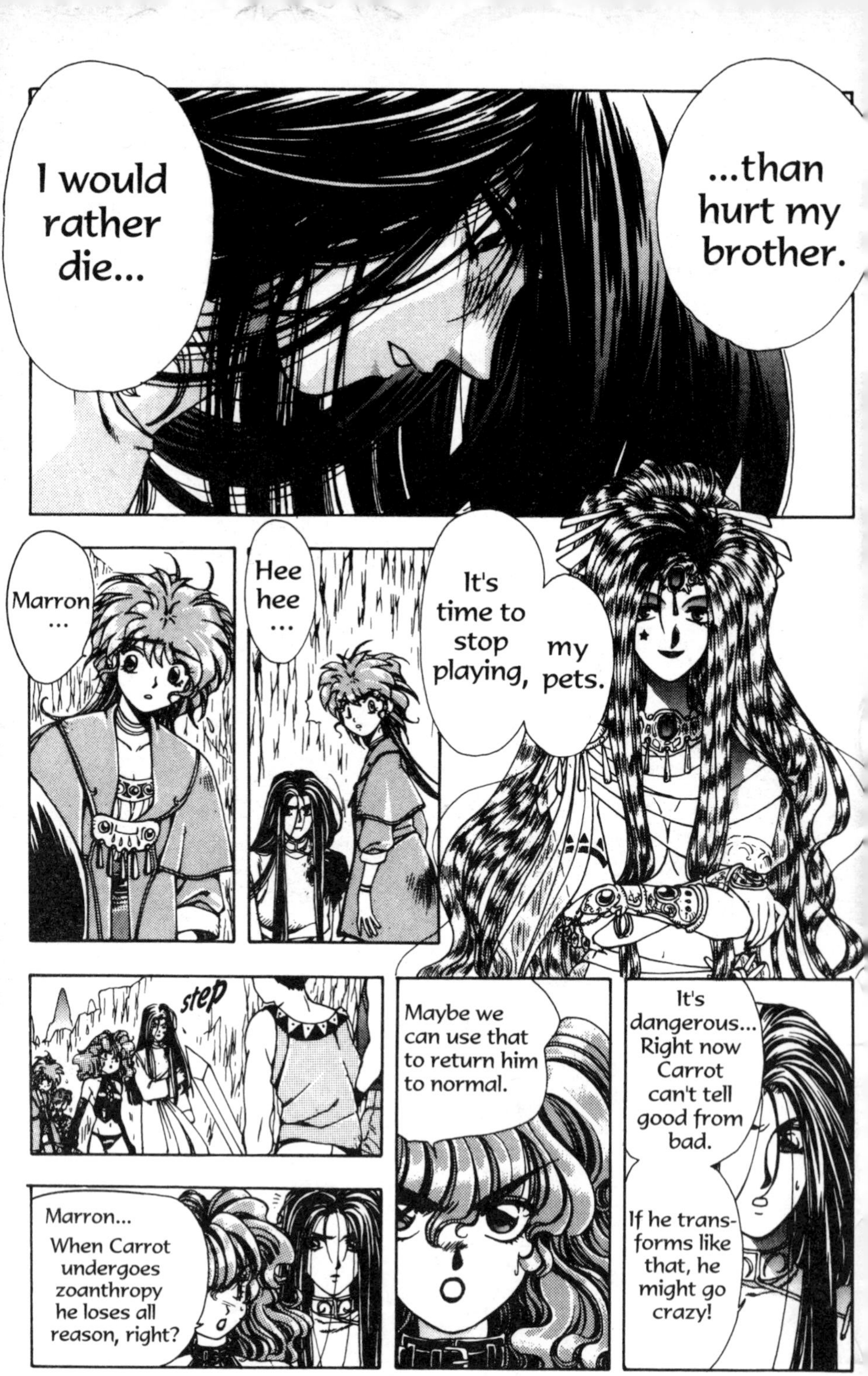
I would rather die...
...than hurt my brother.
Marron ...
Hee hee ...
It's time to stop playing, my pets.
step
Marron... When Carrot undergoes zoanthropy he loses all reason, right?
Maybe we can use that to return him to normal.
It's dangerous... Right now Carrot can't tell good from bad.
If he transforms like that, he might go crazy!

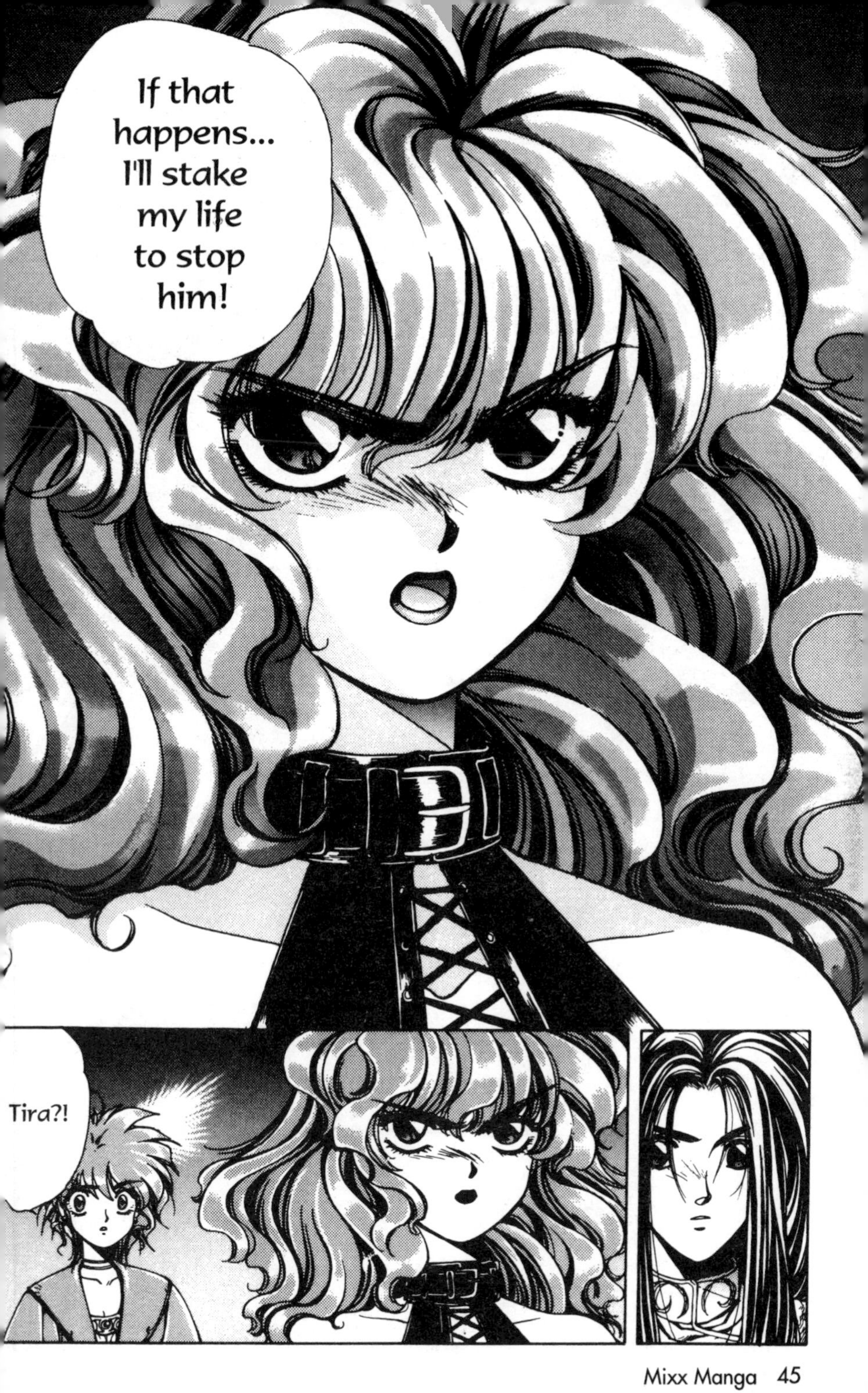
If that happens... I'll stake my life to stop him!
Tira?!

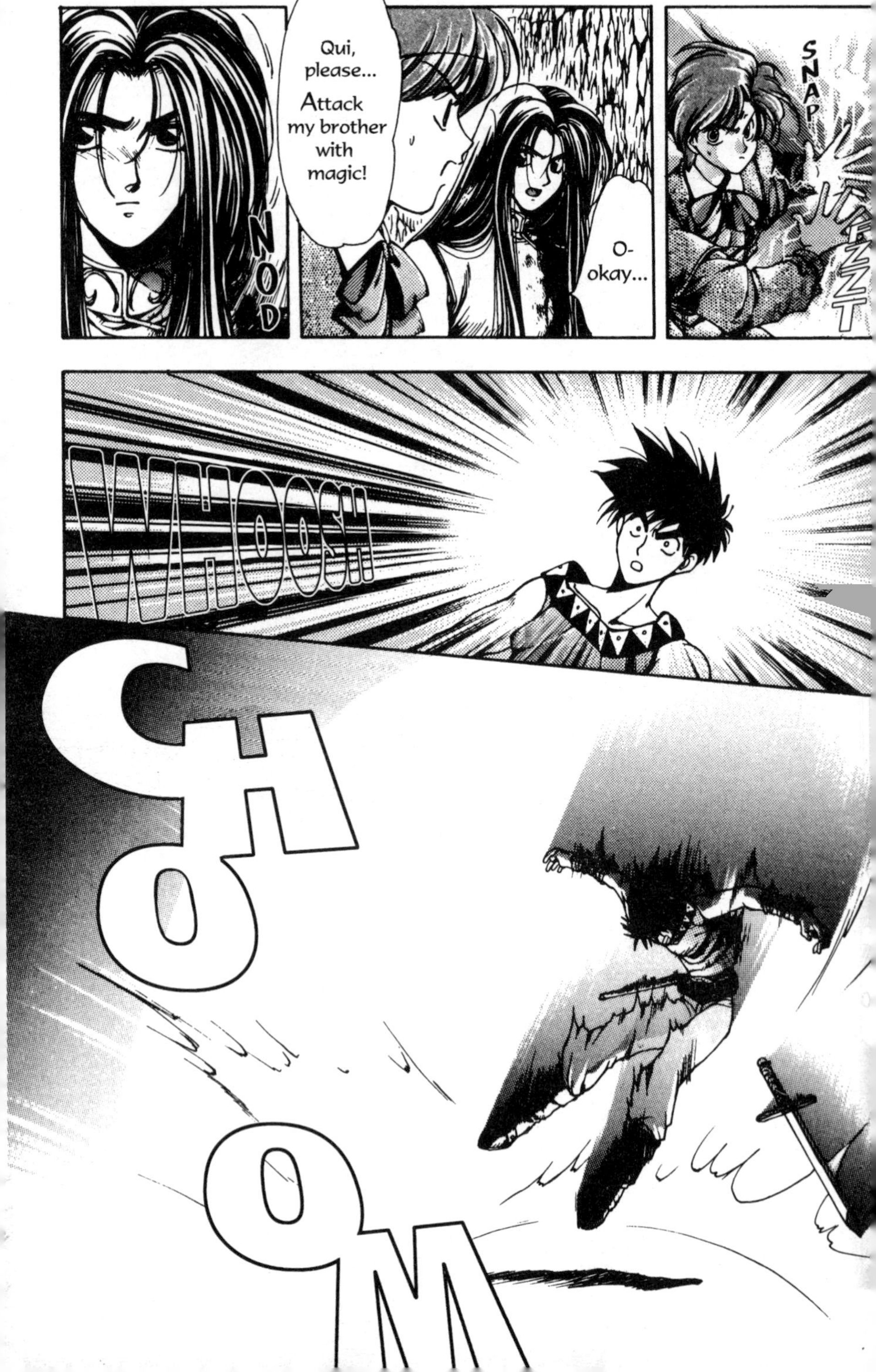

NOD
Qui, please... Attack my brother with magic!
O-okay...
SNAP
FZZT
WHOOSH
CHOOM

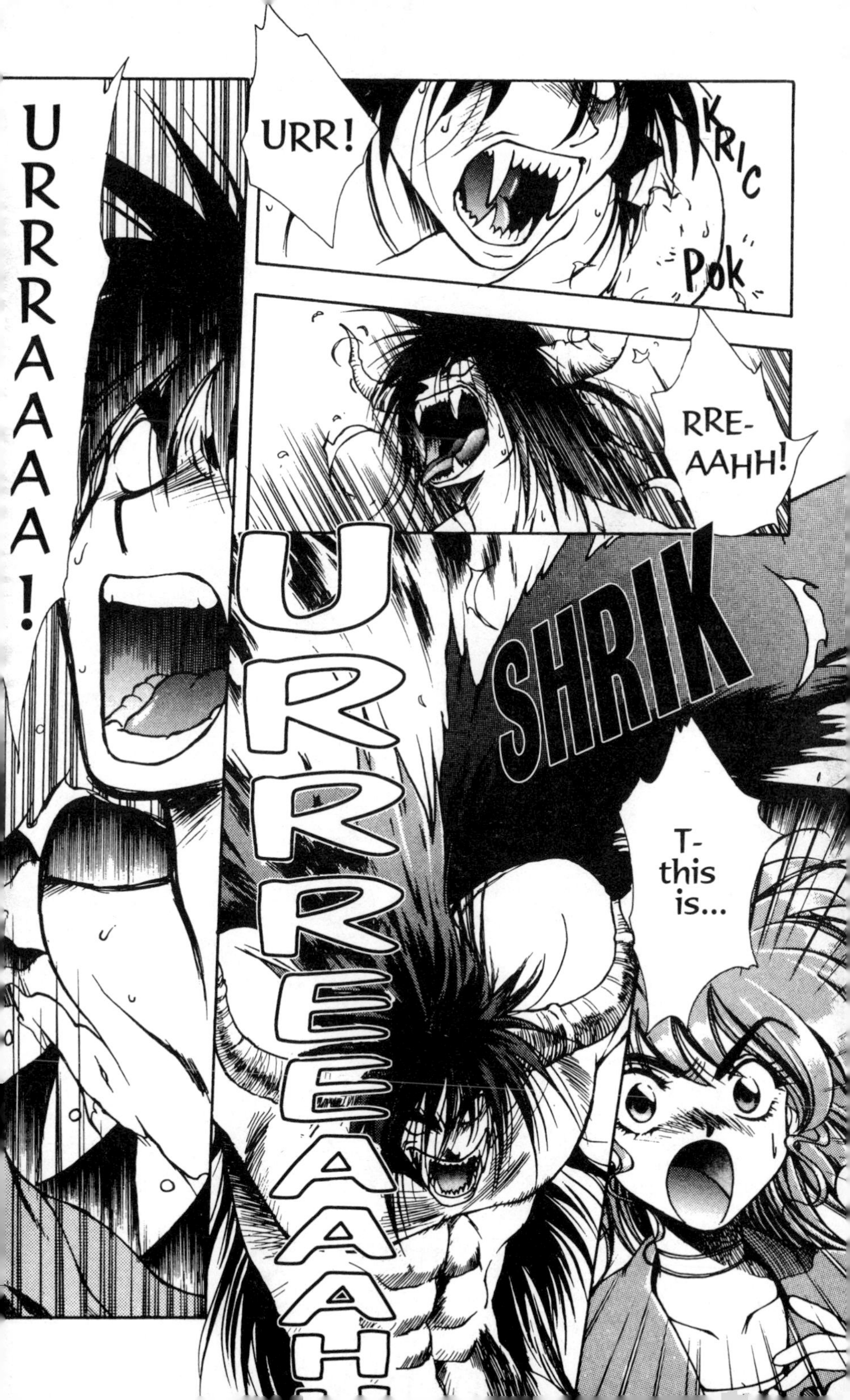
URRRAAAA!
URR!
KRIC
Pok
RRE-AAHH!
URRREEAAAH!
SHRIK
T-this is...

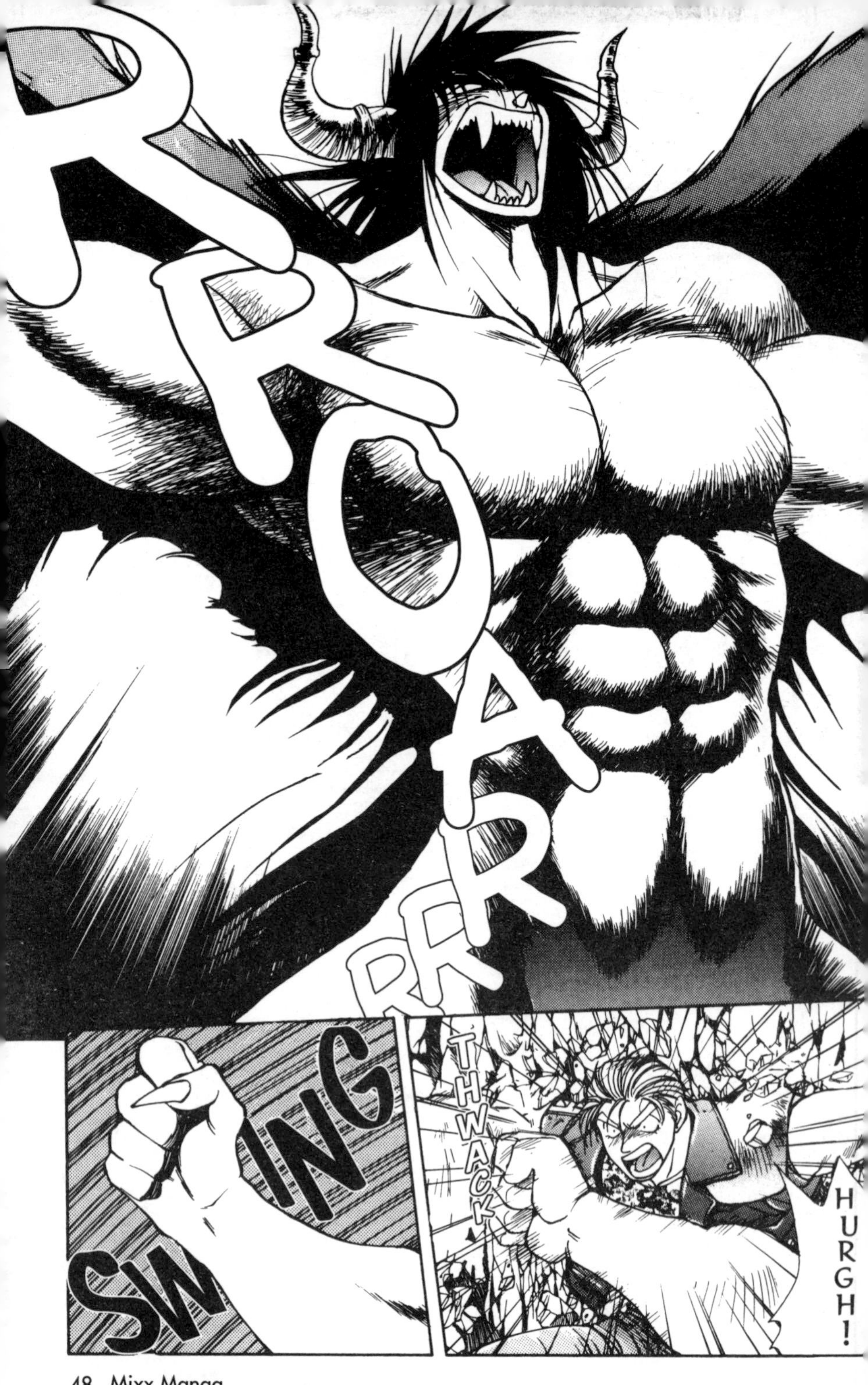
RROARRR
SWING
THWACK
HURGH!

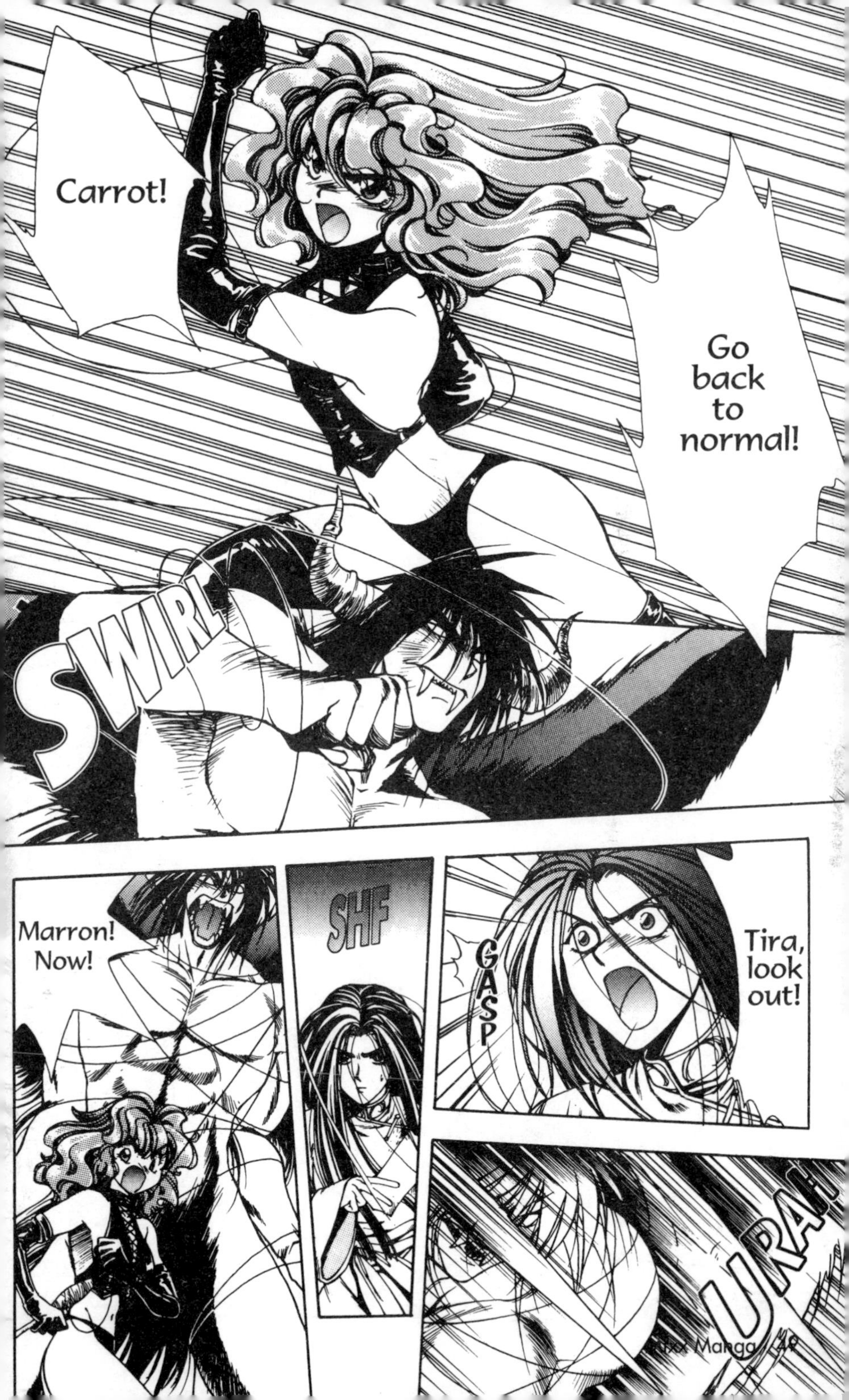
Carrot!
Go back to normal!
SWIRL
Marron! Now!
SHF
GASP
Tira, look out!
URAH!

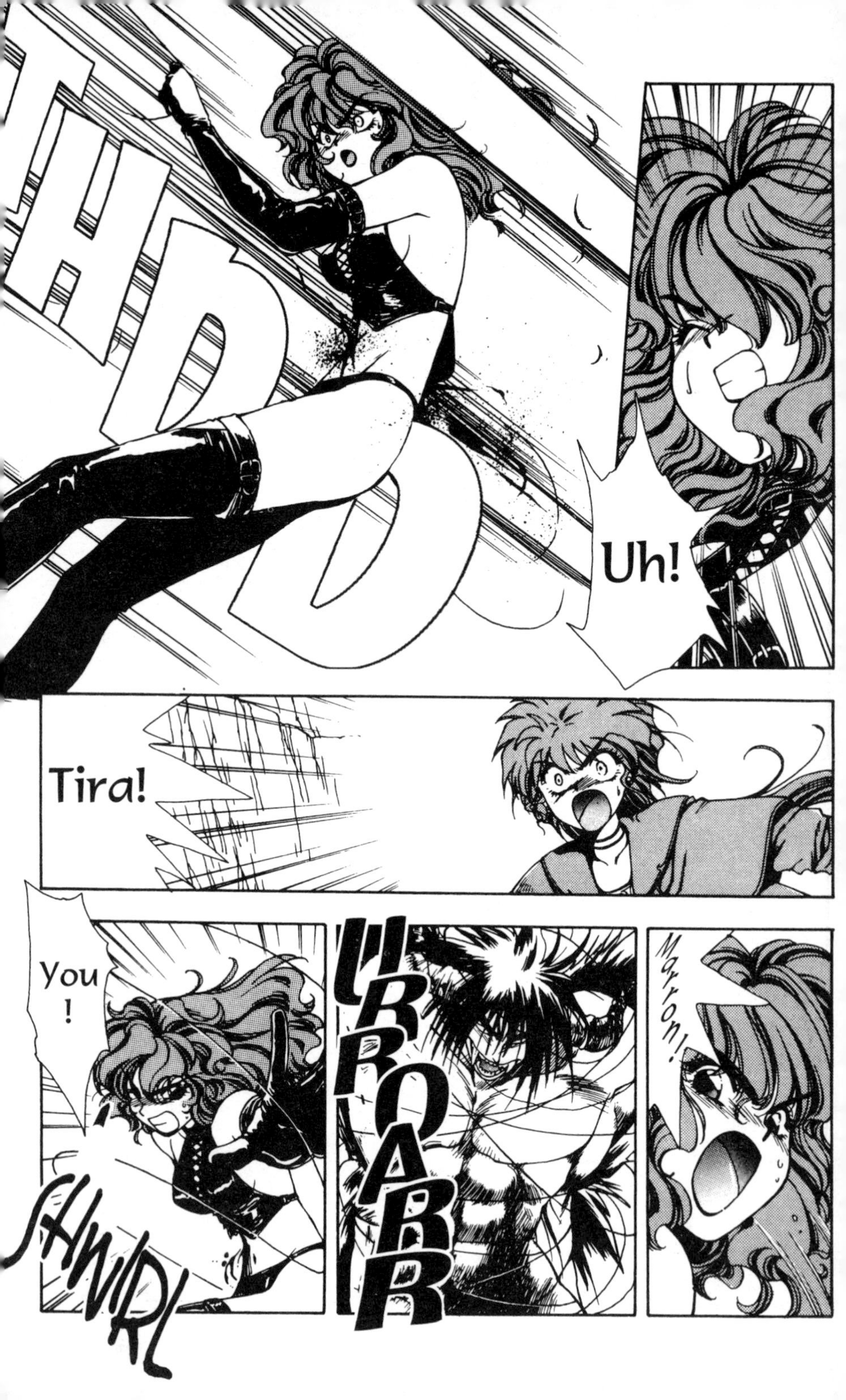
THUD
Uh!
Tira!
You!
SHWIRL
URROARR
Marron!

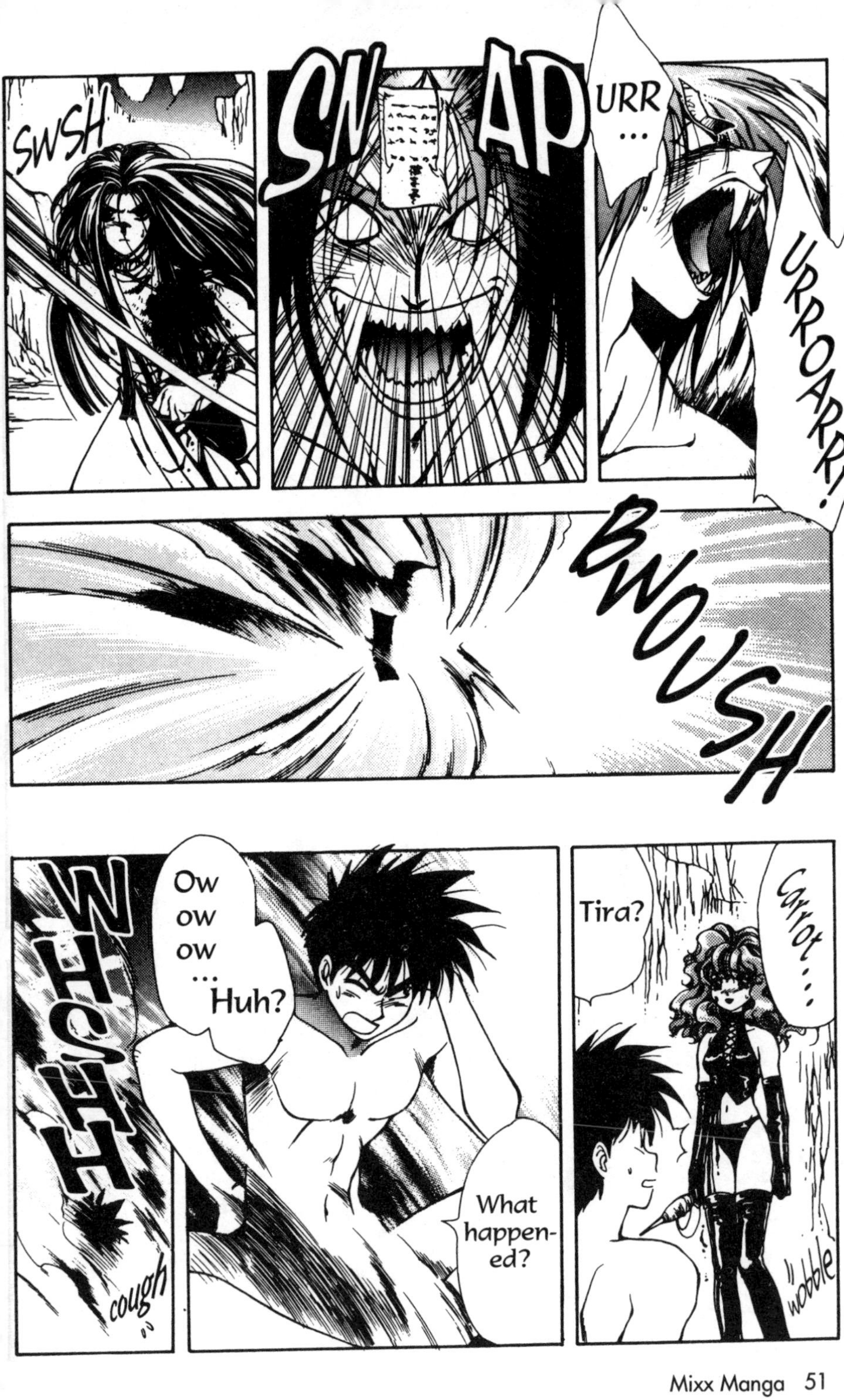
SWSH
SN AP
URR ...
URROARR!
BWOUSH
WHSHH
cough
Ow ow ow ... Huh?
What happen-ed?
Tira?
Carrot...
wobble

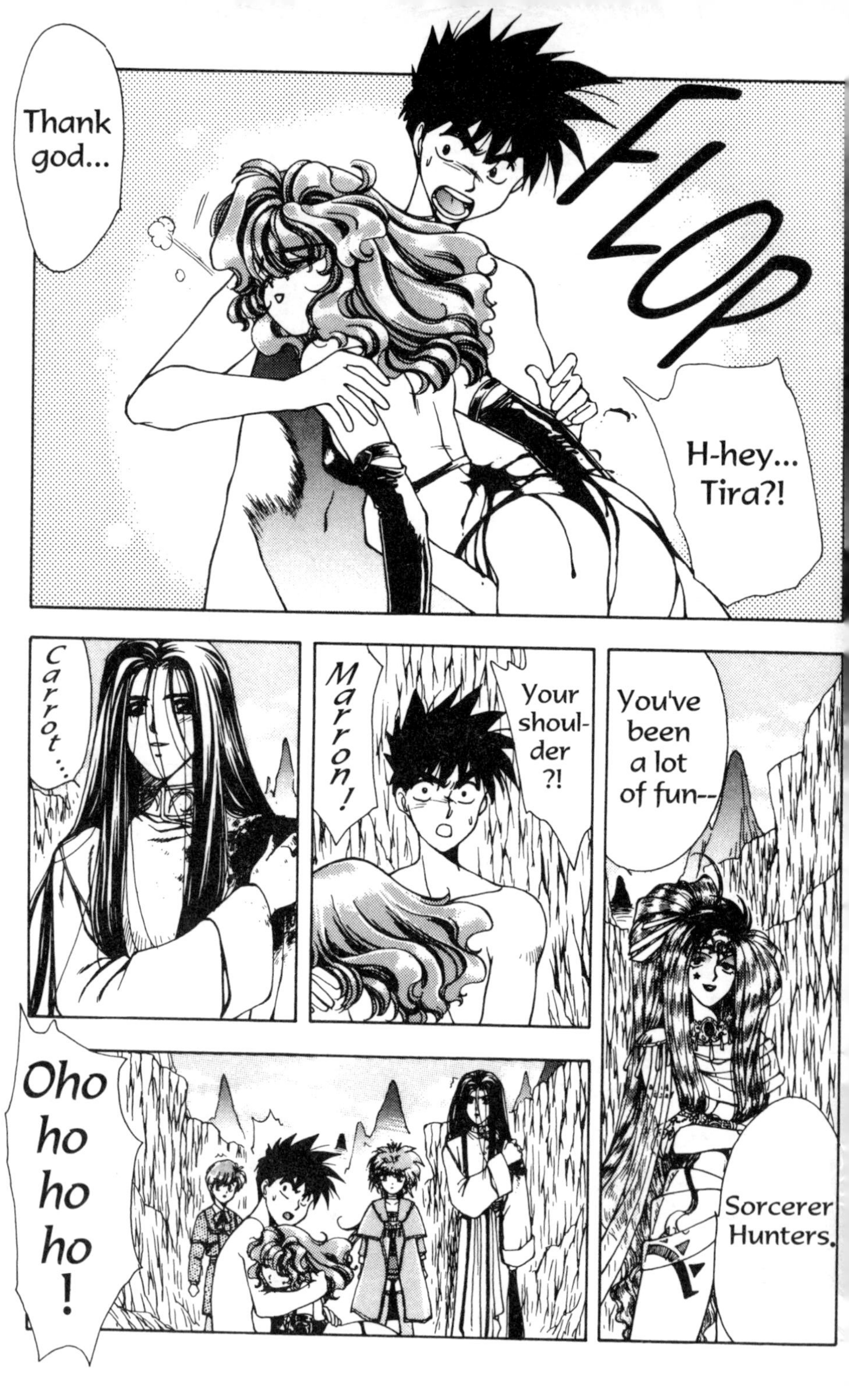

Thank god...
FLOP
H-hey... Tira?!
Carrot...
Marron!
Your shoul-der ?!
Oho ho ho ho!
You've been a lot of fun--
Sorcerer Hunters.

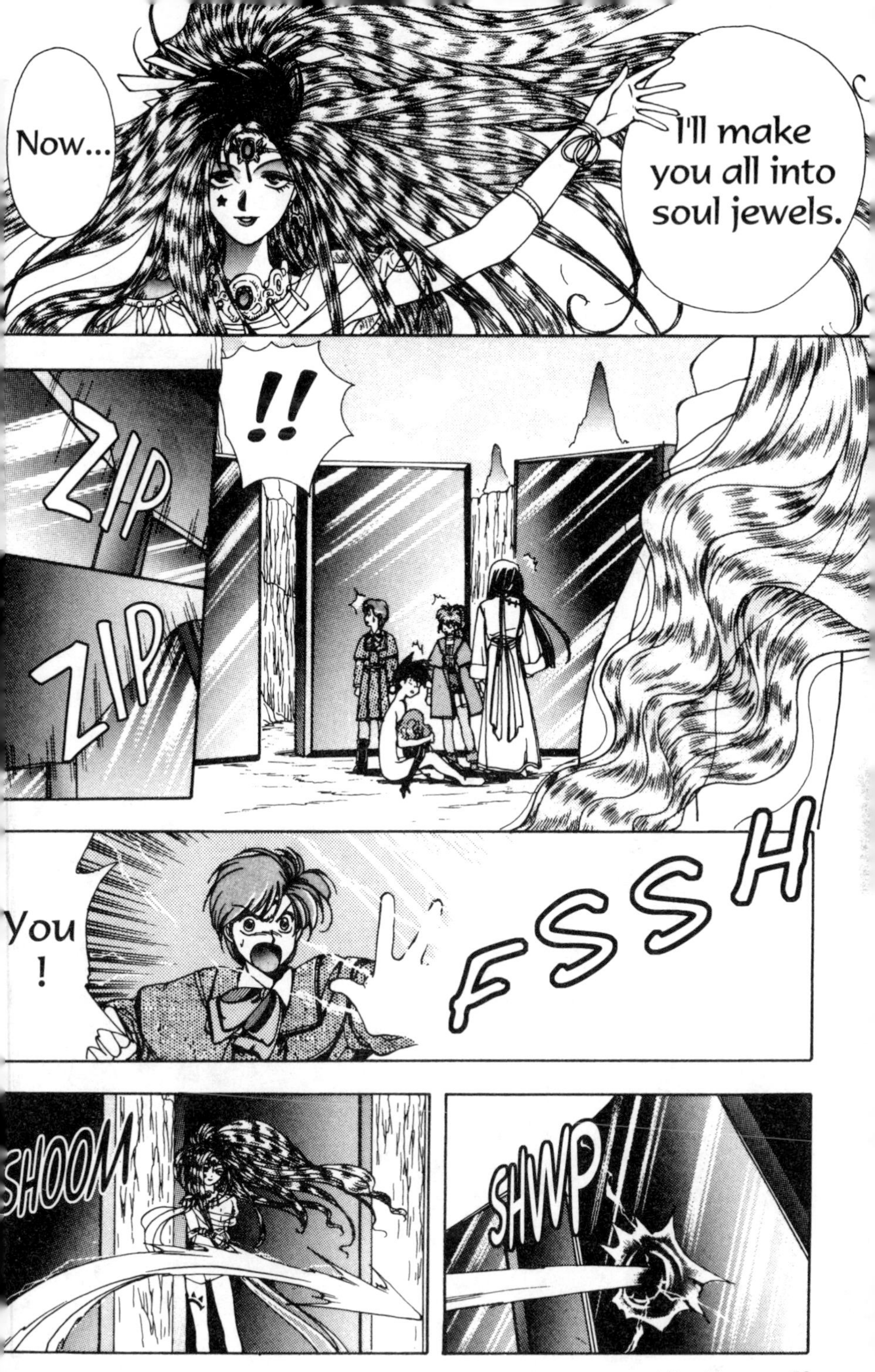
Now...
I'll make you all into soul jewels.
ZIP
!!
ZIP
You !
FSSSH
SHOOM
SHWP

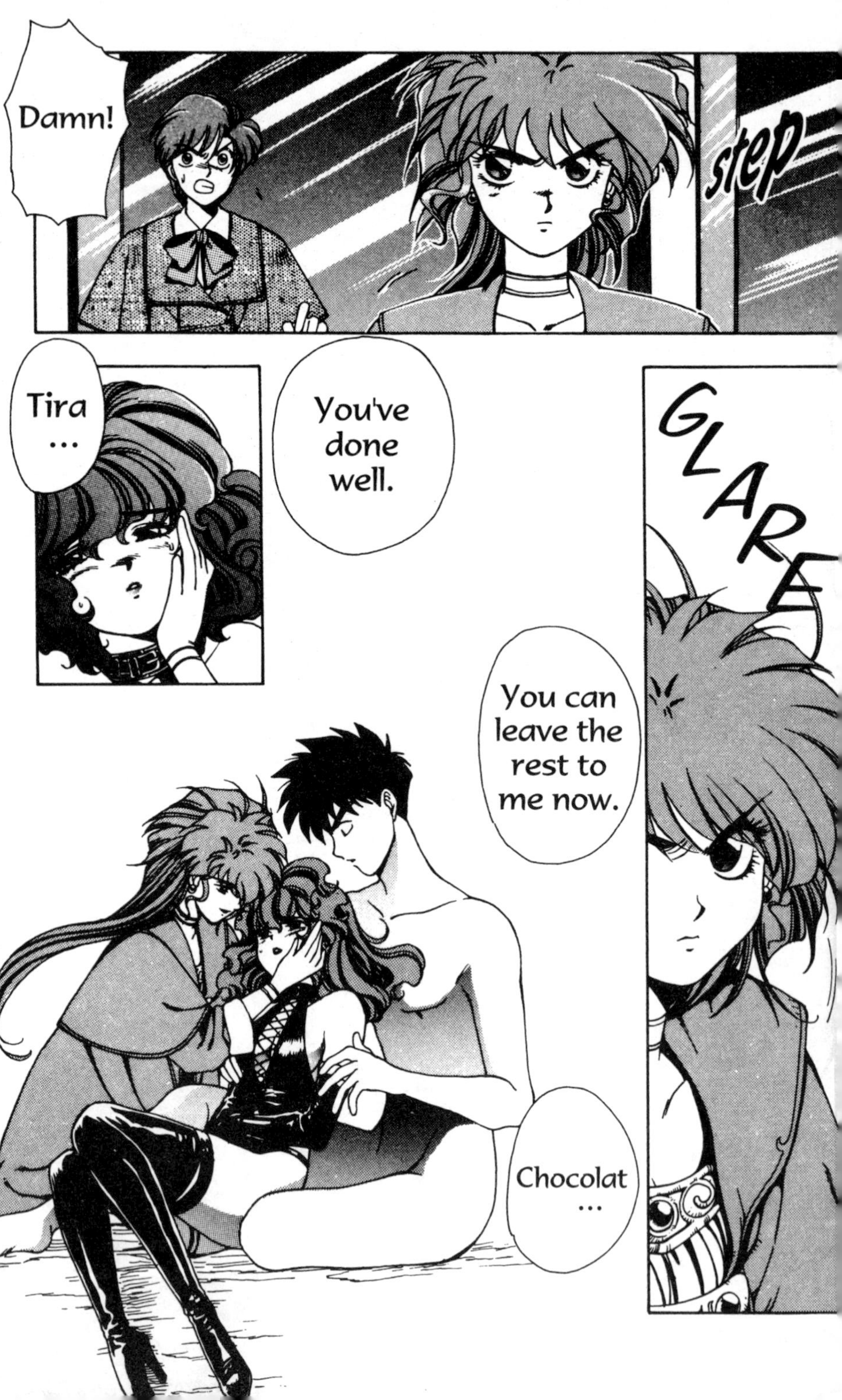
Damn!
step
Tira
...
You've done well.
You can leave the rest to me now.
Chocolat
...
GLARE

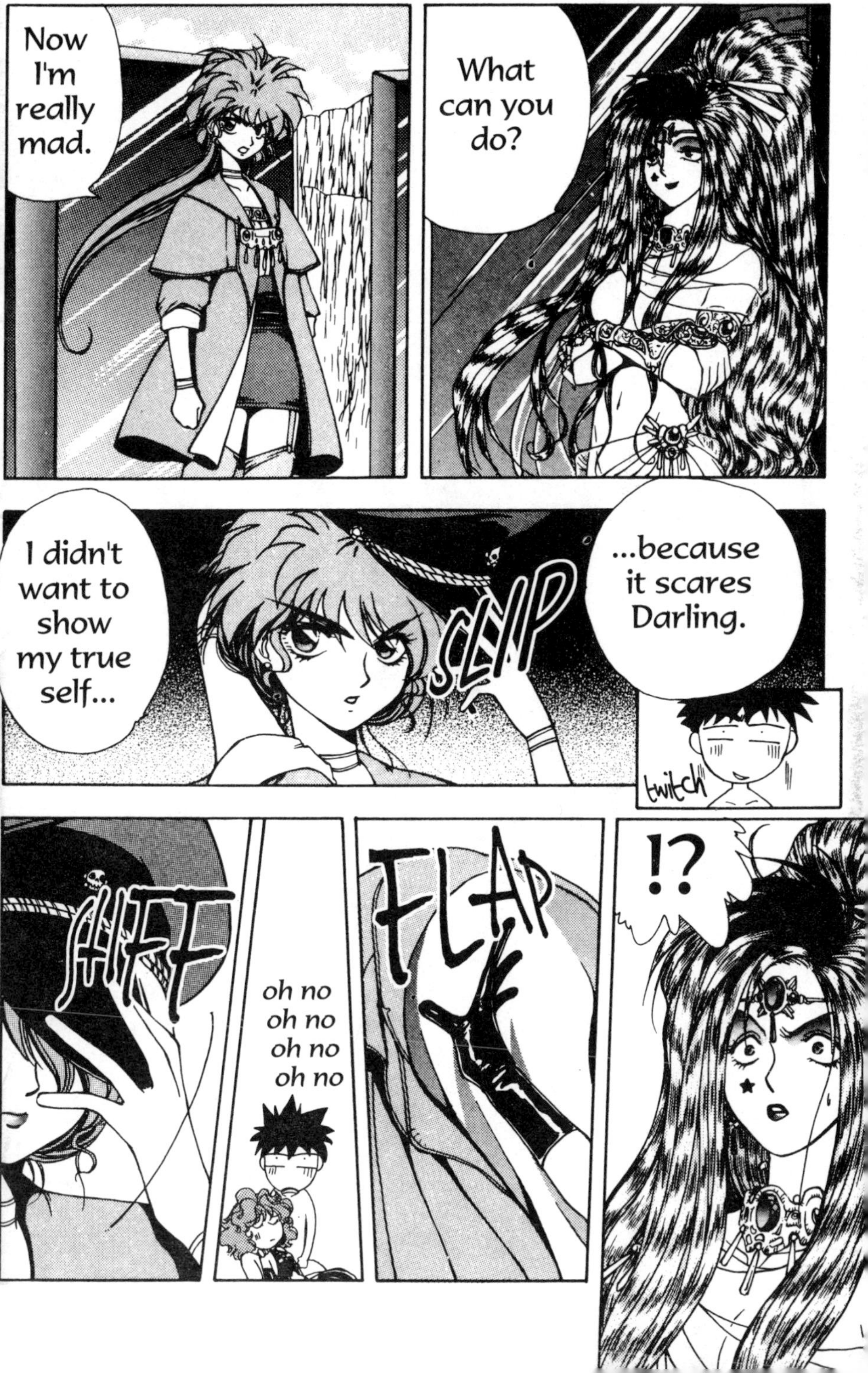
Now I'm really mad.
What can you do?
I didn't want to show my true self...
SLIP
...because it scares Darling.
twitch
oh no
oh no
oh no
oh no
FLAP
!?

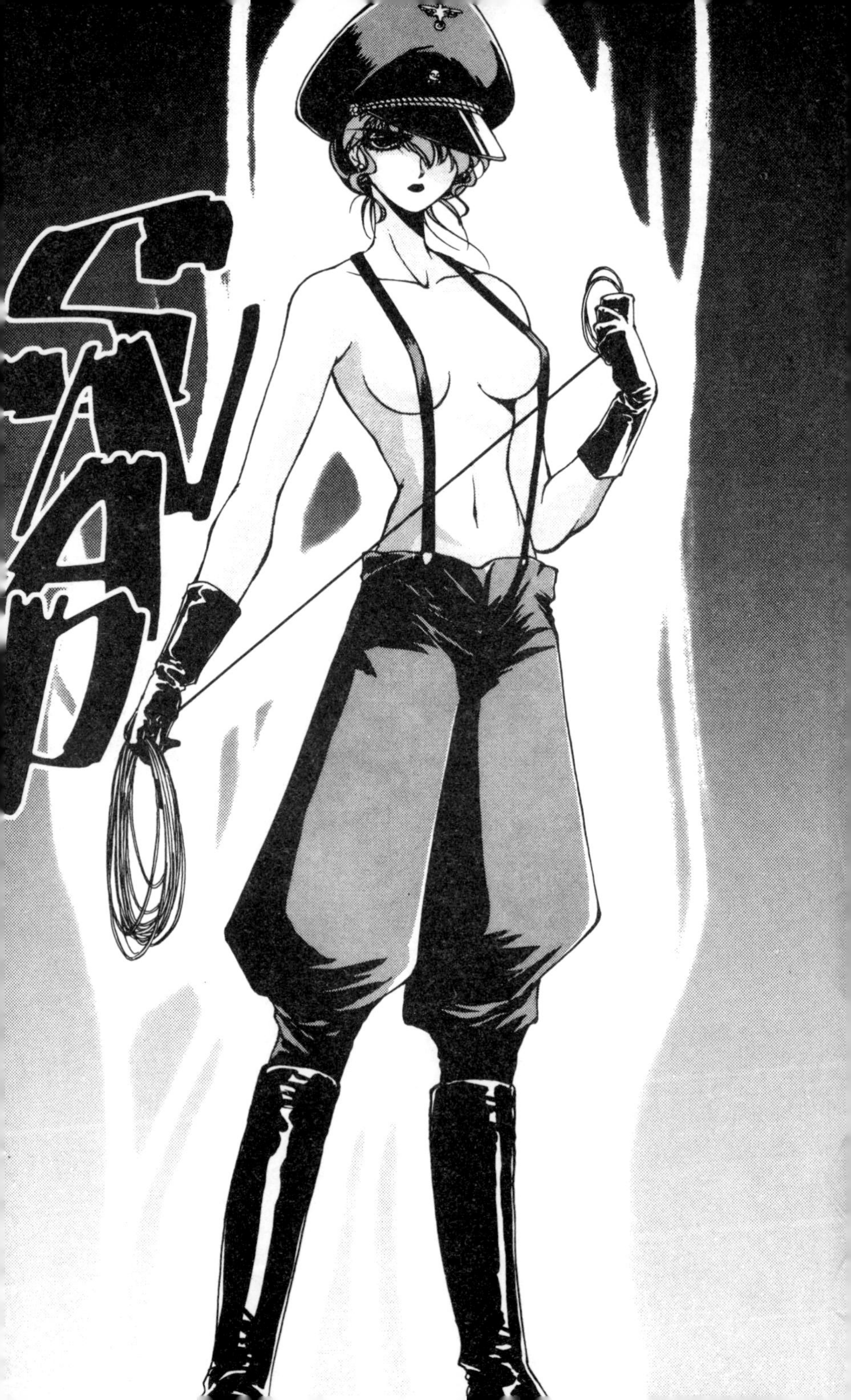

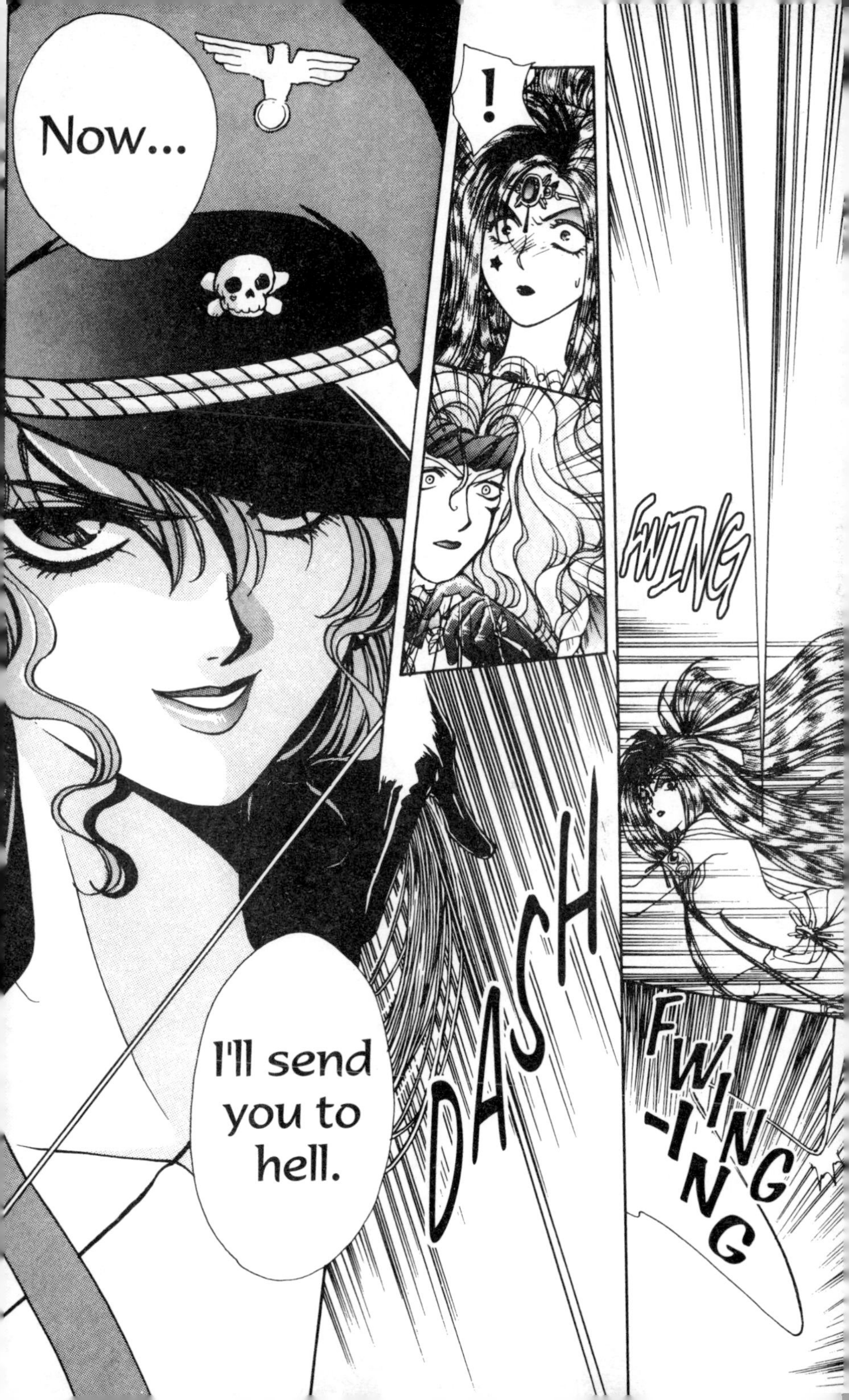
Now...
I'll send you to hell.
!
DASH
FWING
FWING-ING

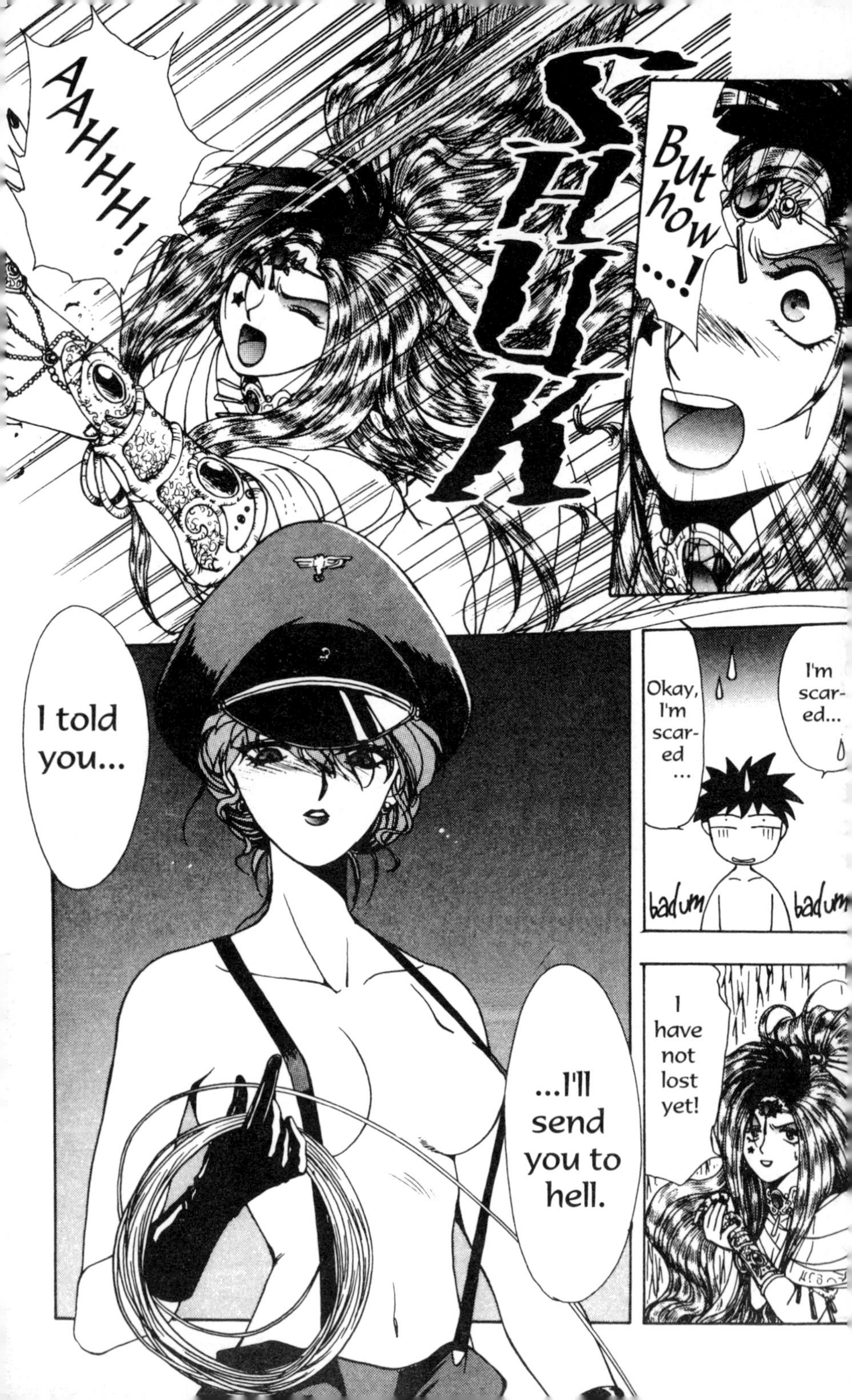
SHUK
AAHHH!
But how...!
I'm scared...
Okay, I'm scared...
badum
badum
I have not lost yet!
I told you...
...I'll send you to hell.

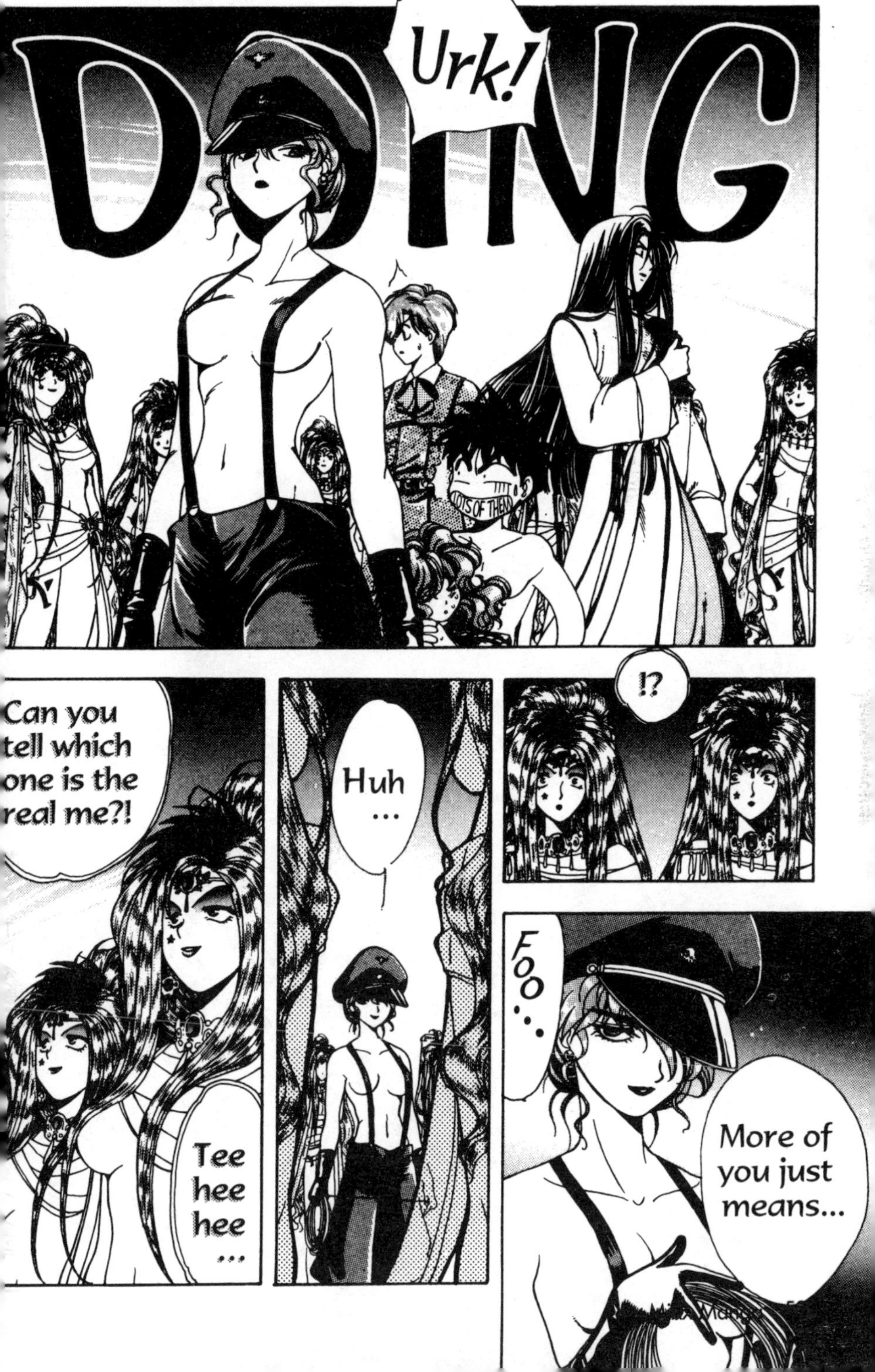
DOING
Urk!
LOTS OF THEM
Can you tell which one is the real me?!
Tee hee hee ...
Huh ...
!?
Foo...
More of you just means...

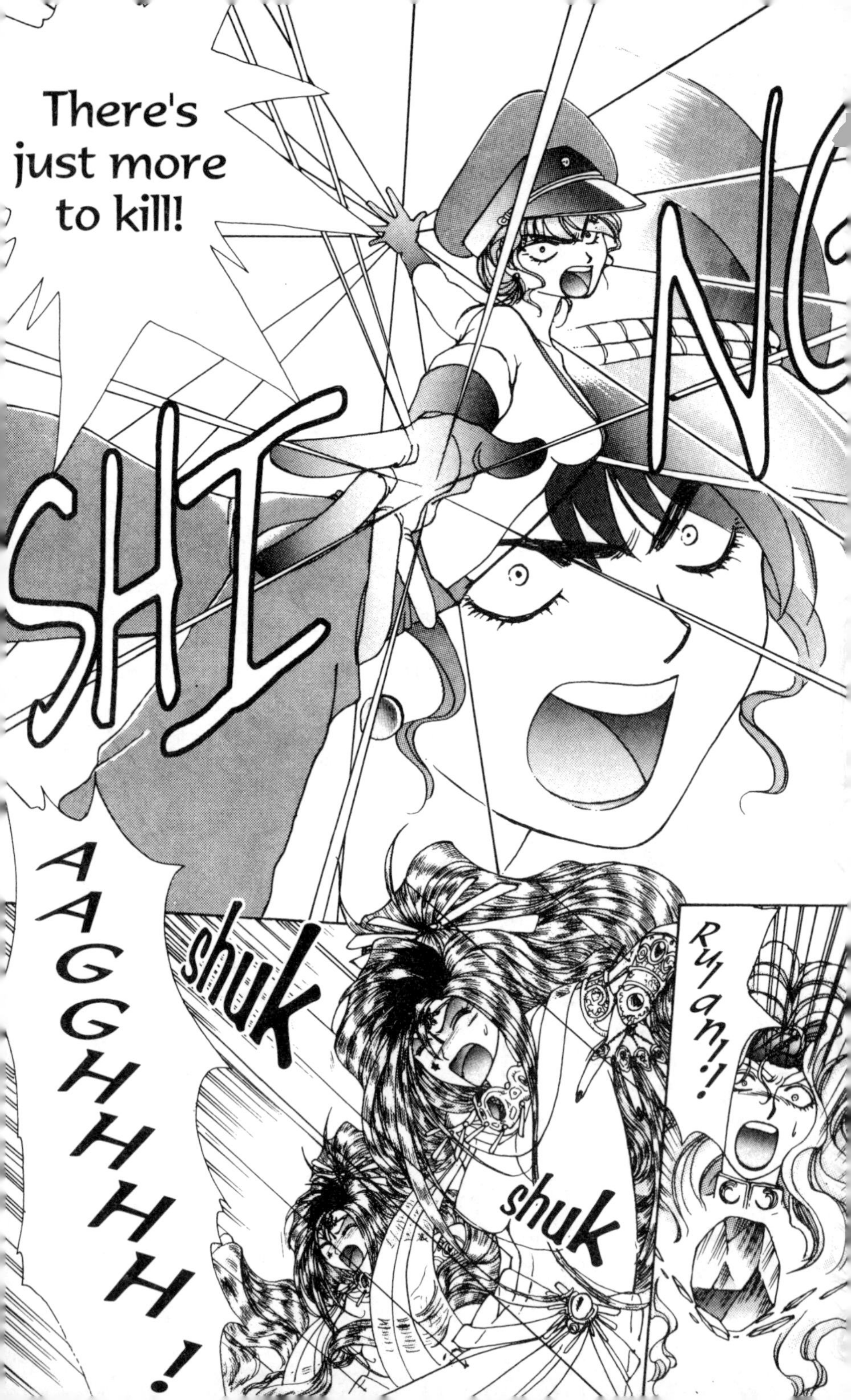
There's just more to kill!
SHI
NG
AAGGHHHHHH!
shuk
Rulan!!
shuk

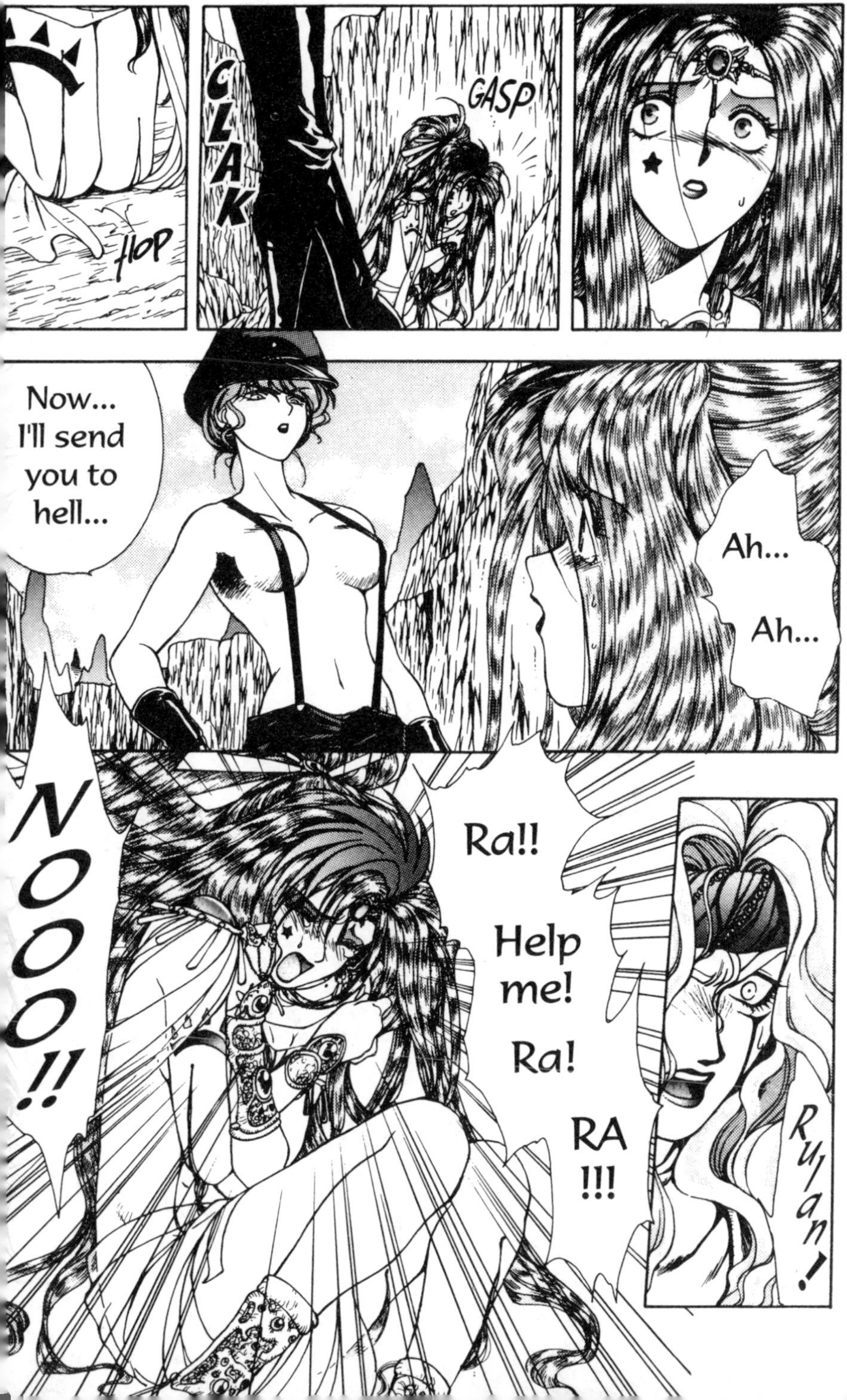
HOP
CLAK
GASP
Now... I'll send you to hell...
Ah...
Ah...
NOOOO!!
Ra!!
Help me!
Ra!
RA !!!
Rulan!

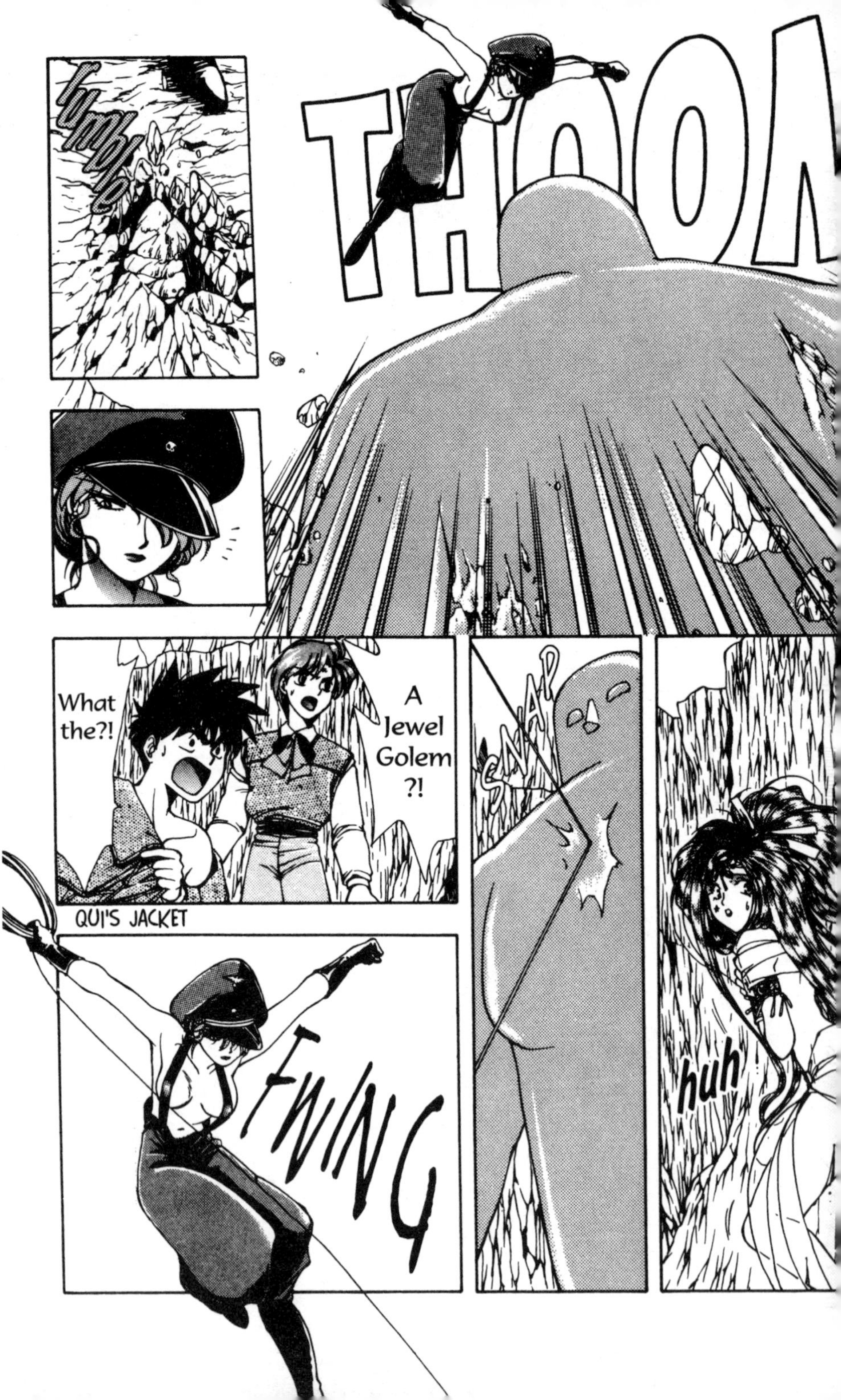
rumble
THOO
What the?!
A Jewel Golem ?!
QUI'S JACKET
FWING
SNAP
huh

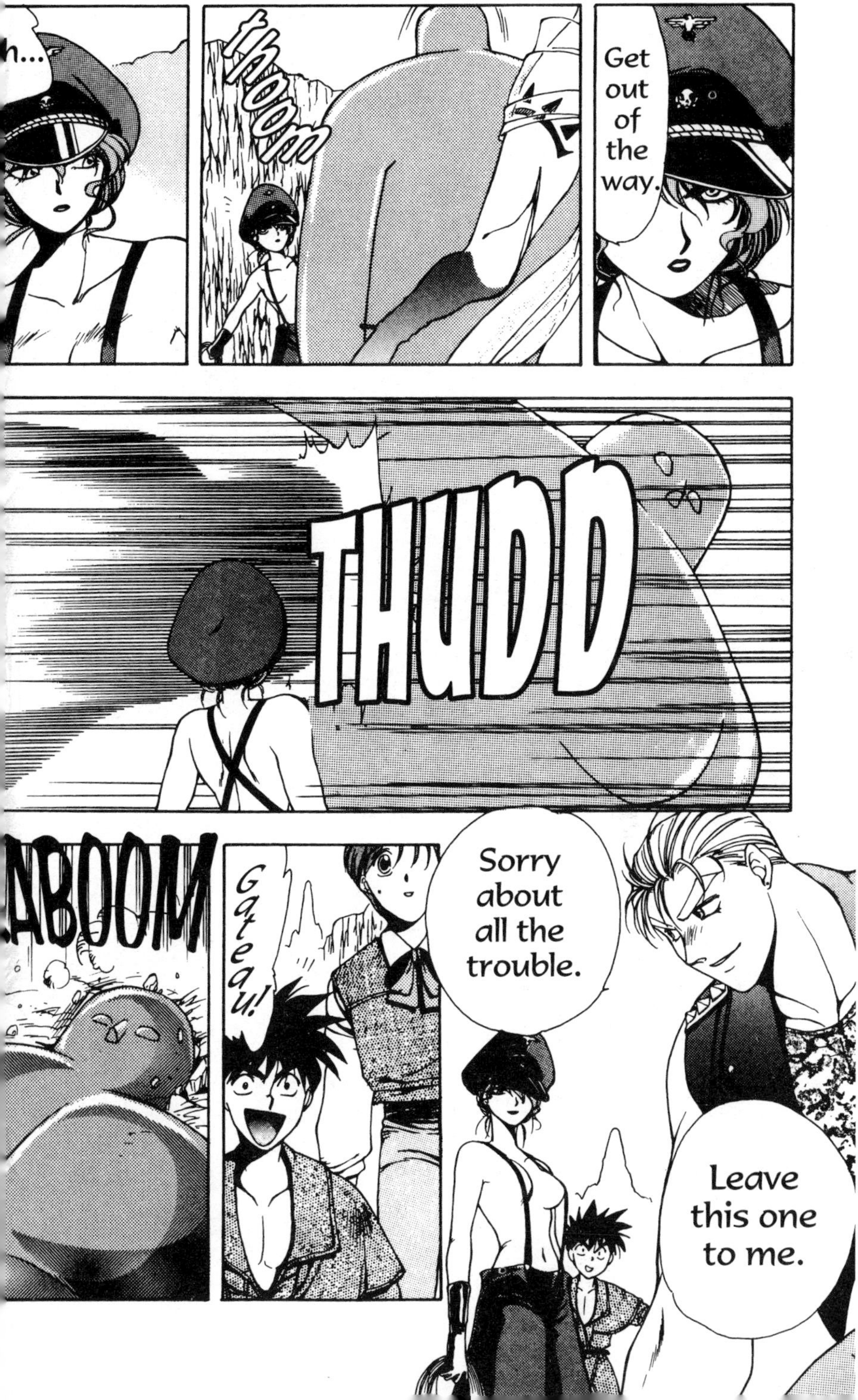

h...
thoom
Get out of the way.
THUDD
ABOOM
Gateau!
Sorry about all the trouble.
Leave this one to me.

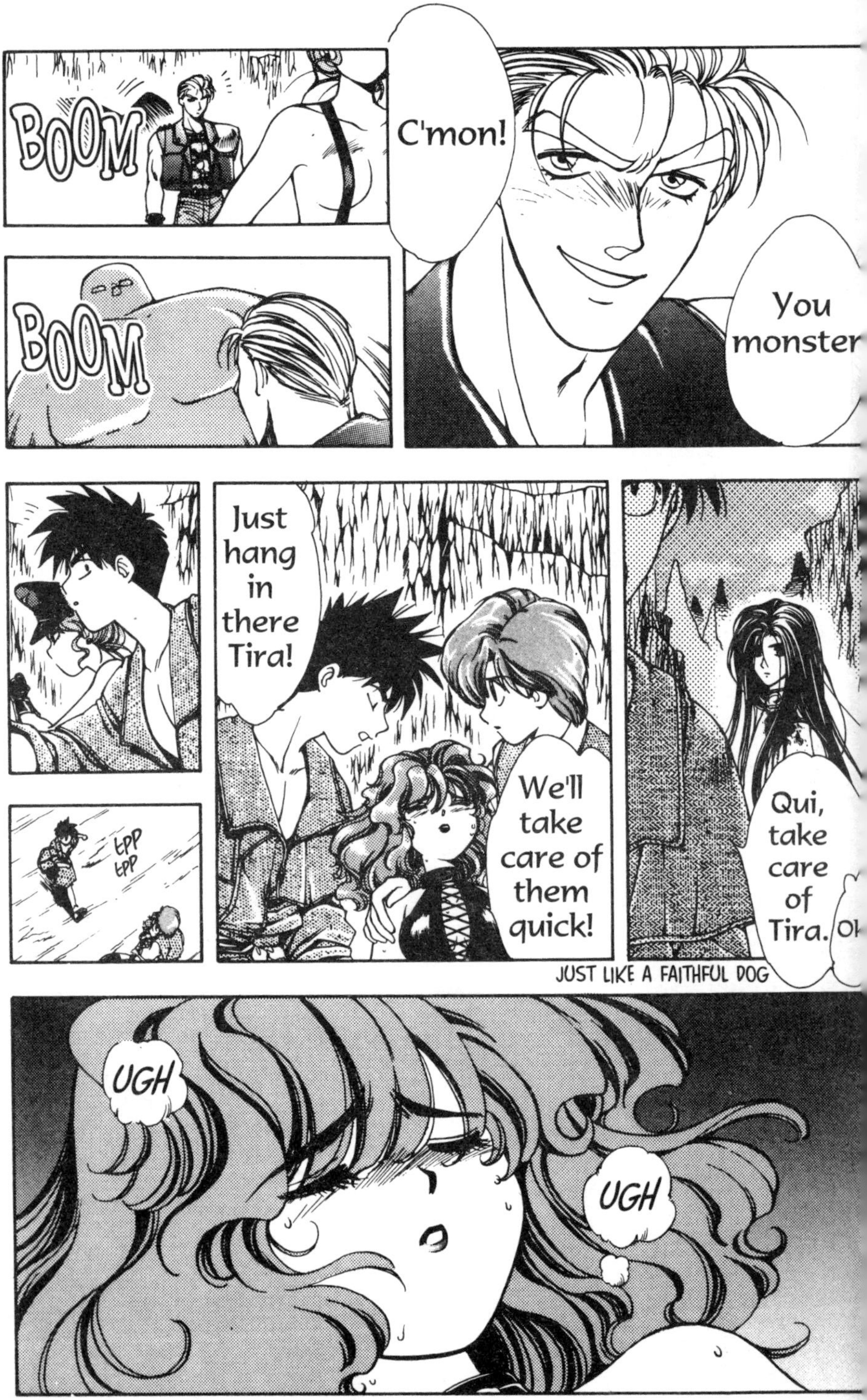
BOOM
BOOM
C'mon!
You monster
tpp tpp
Just hang in there Tira!
We'll take care of them quick!
Qui, take care of Tira.
JUST LIKE A FAITHFUL DOG
UGH
UGH

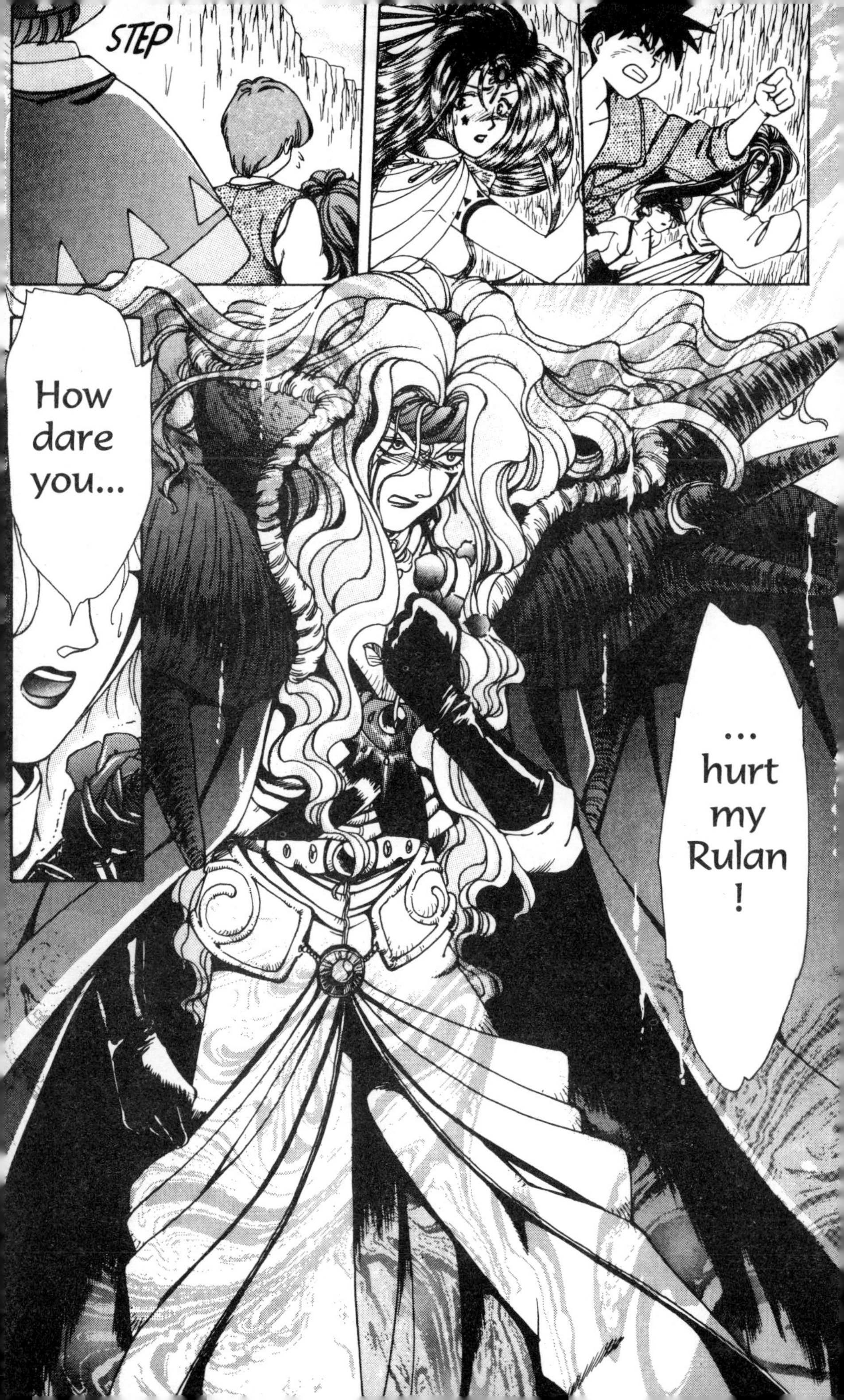
STEP
How dare you...
... hurt my Rulan !

The Terror of the Crystal Magicians - Part 4

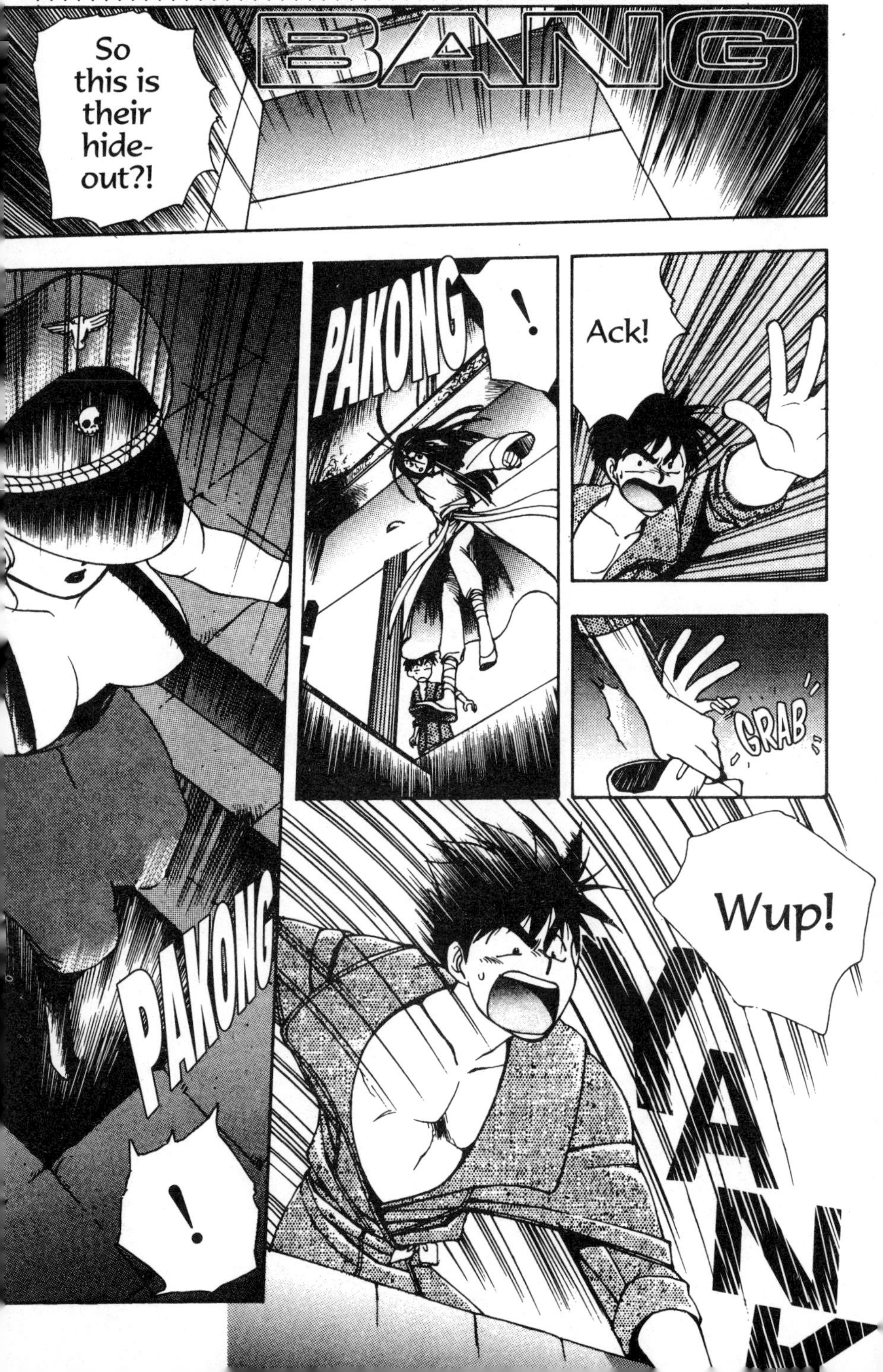

So this is their hide-out?!
BANG
PAKONG
!
PAKONG
!
Ack!
GRAB
Wup!

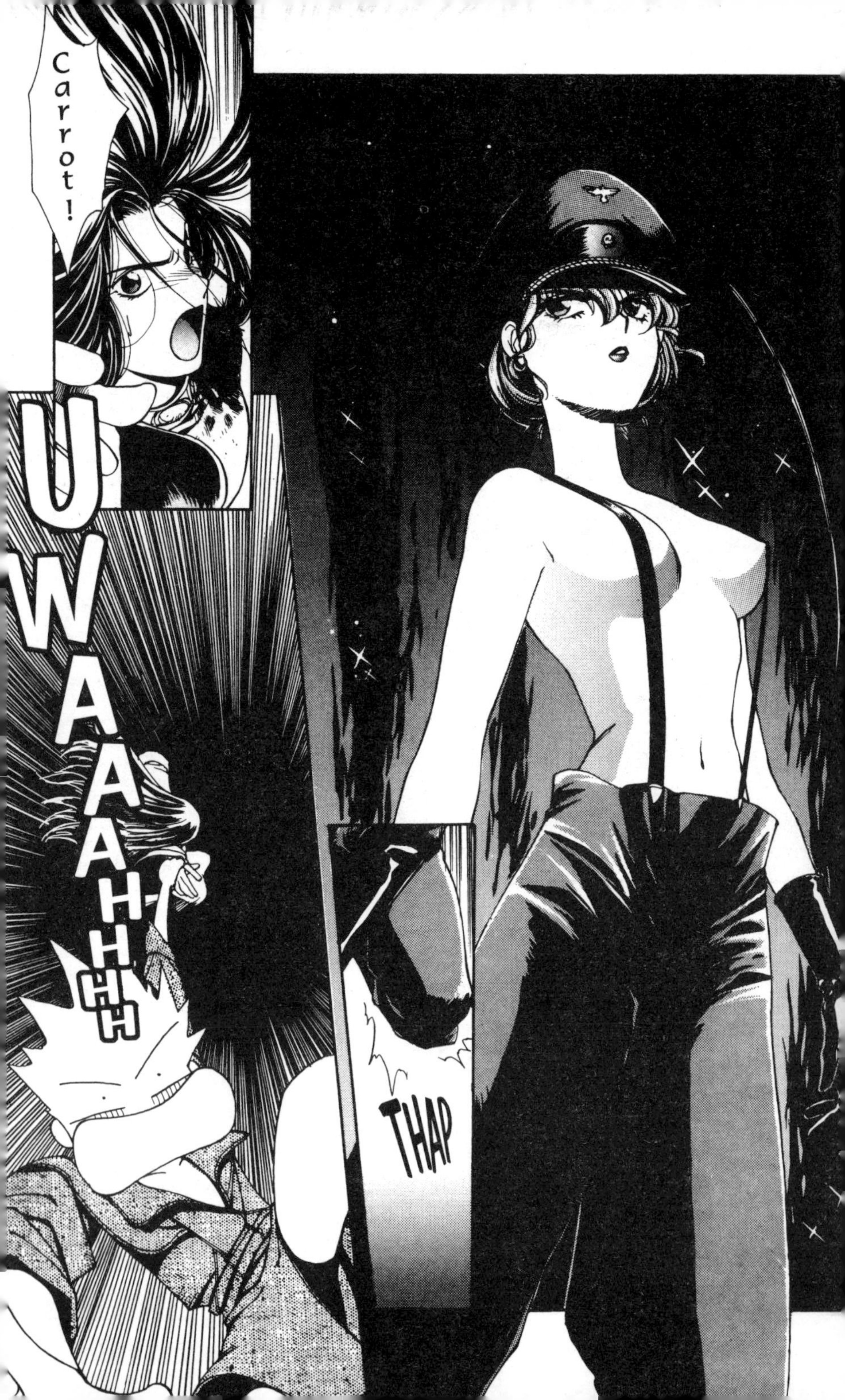
Carrot!
UWAAAHHHHH
THAP

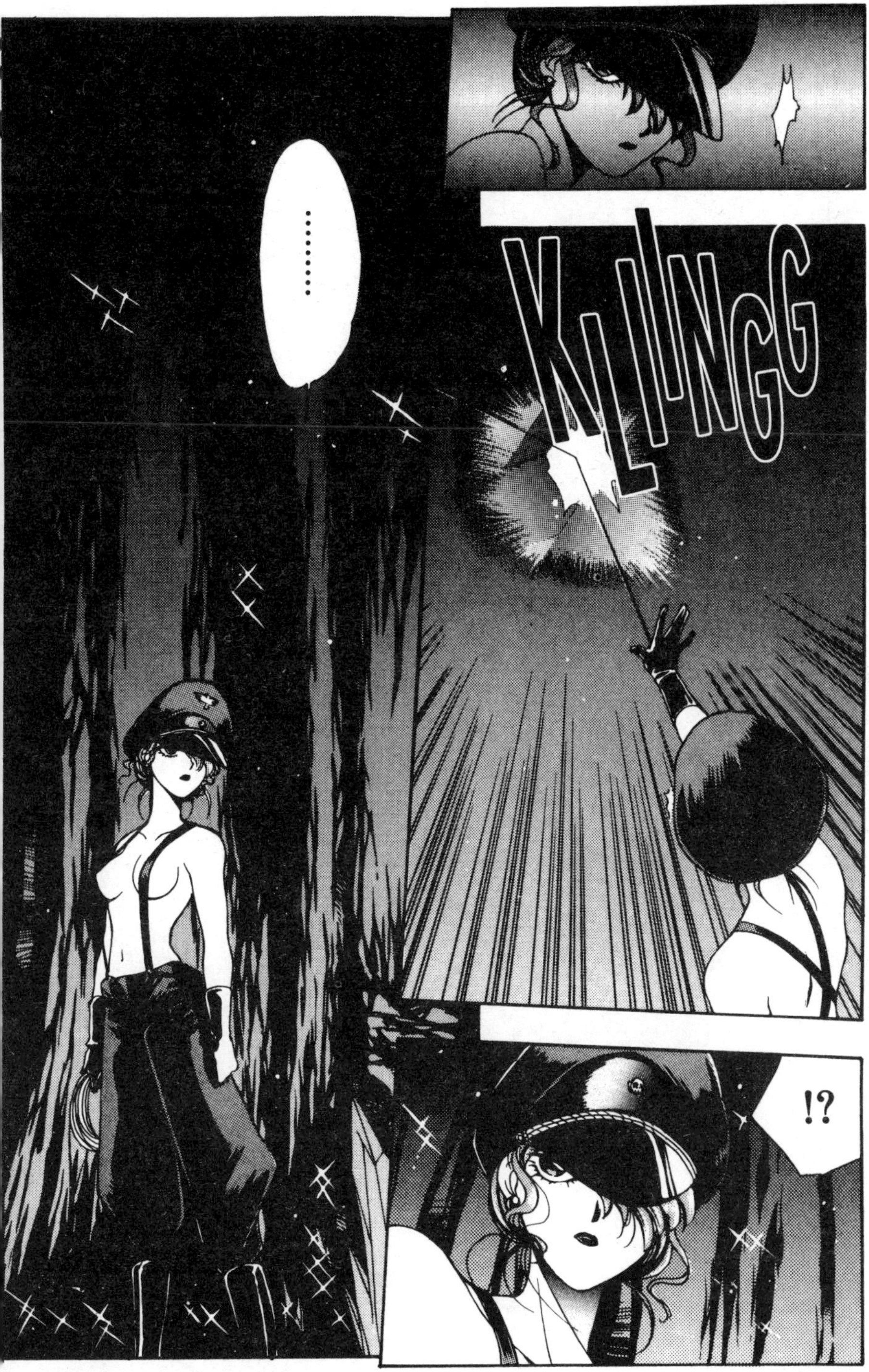

....
KLIINGG
!?

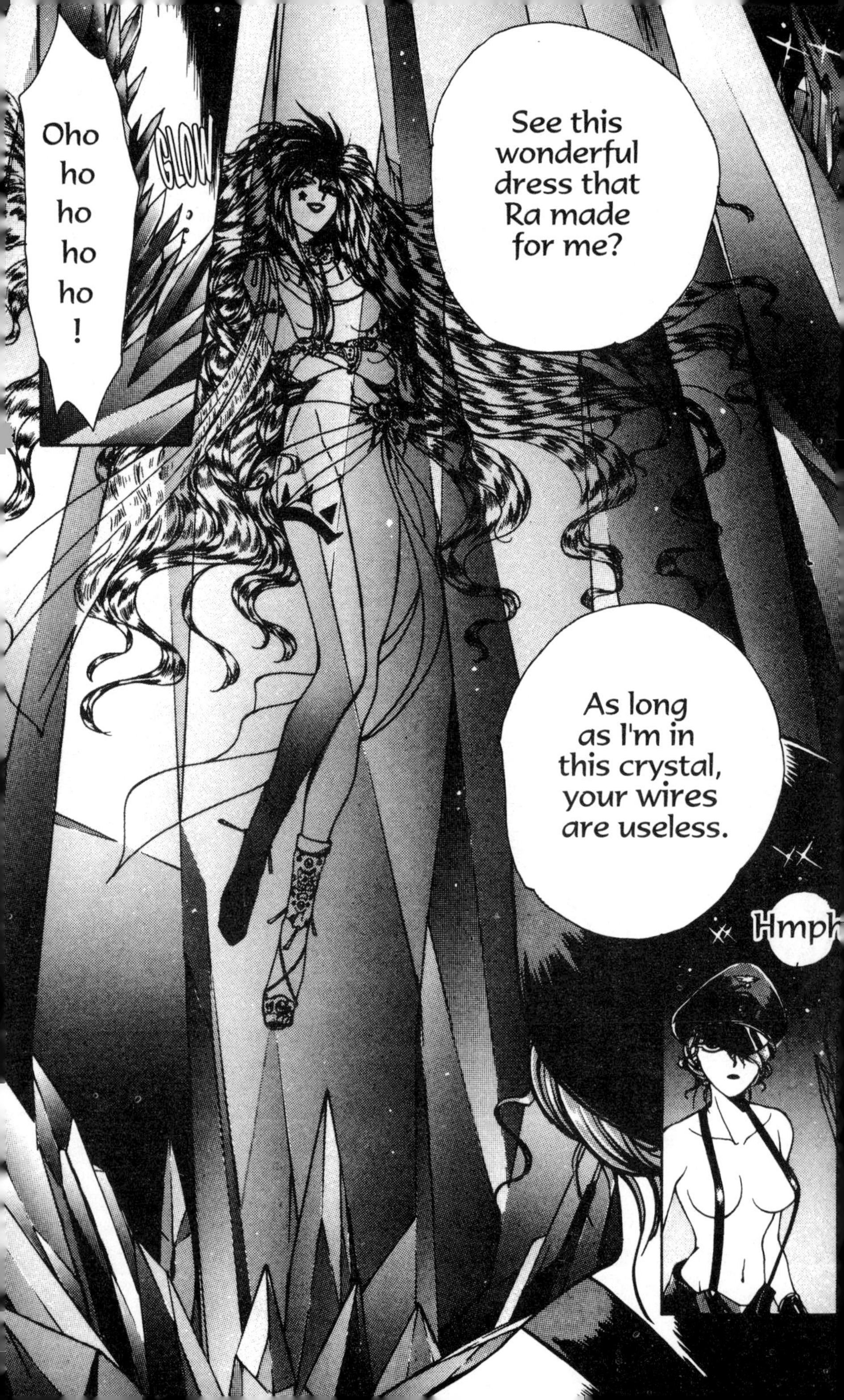
Oho ho ho ho ho !
GLOW
See this wonderful dress that Ra made for me?
As long as I'm in this crystal, your wires are useless.
Hmph

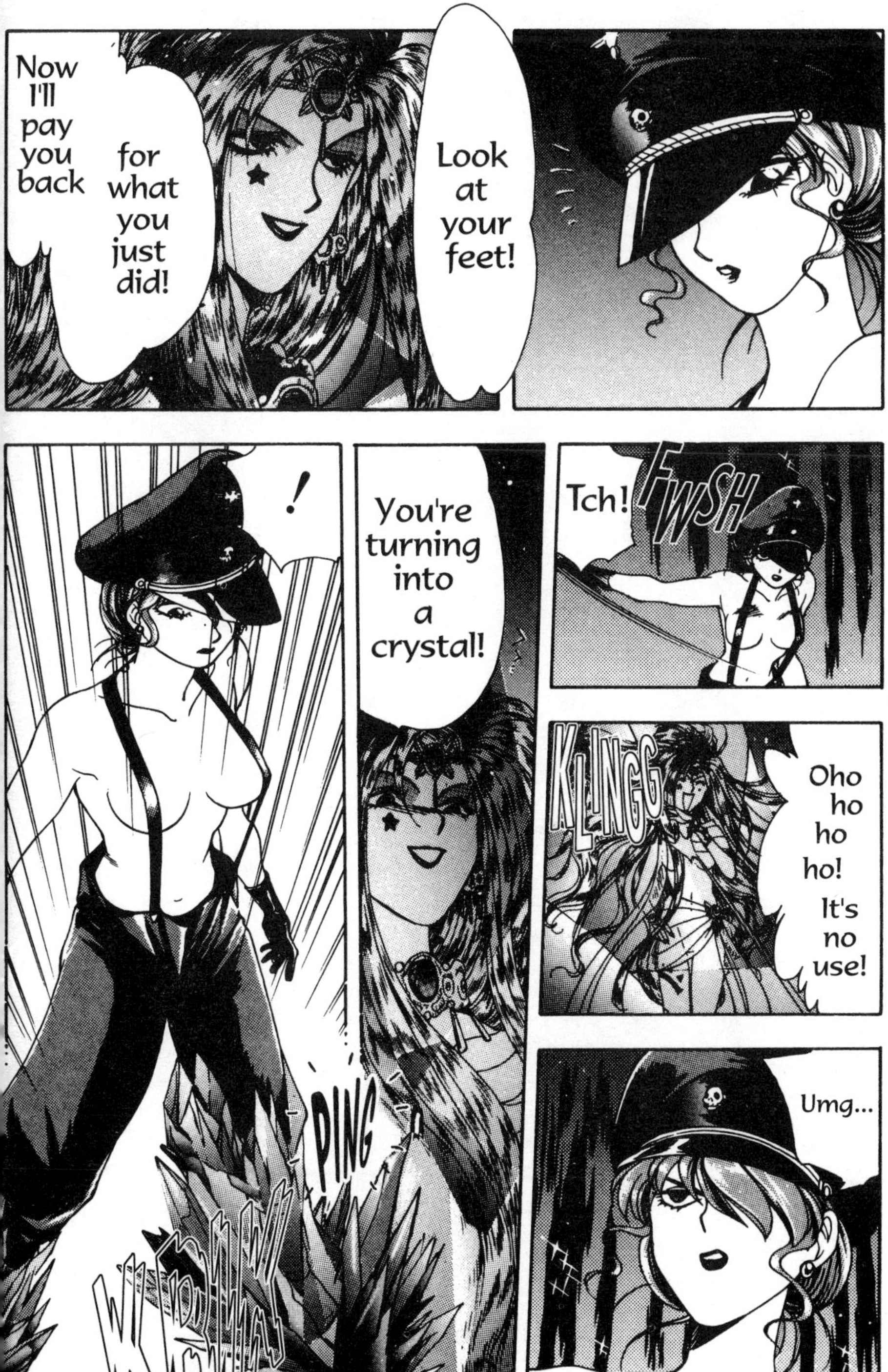
Now I'll pay you back for what you just did!
Look at your feet!
!
You're turning into a crystal!
PING
Tch!
FWSH
KLINGG
Oho ho ho ho!
It's no use!
Umg...

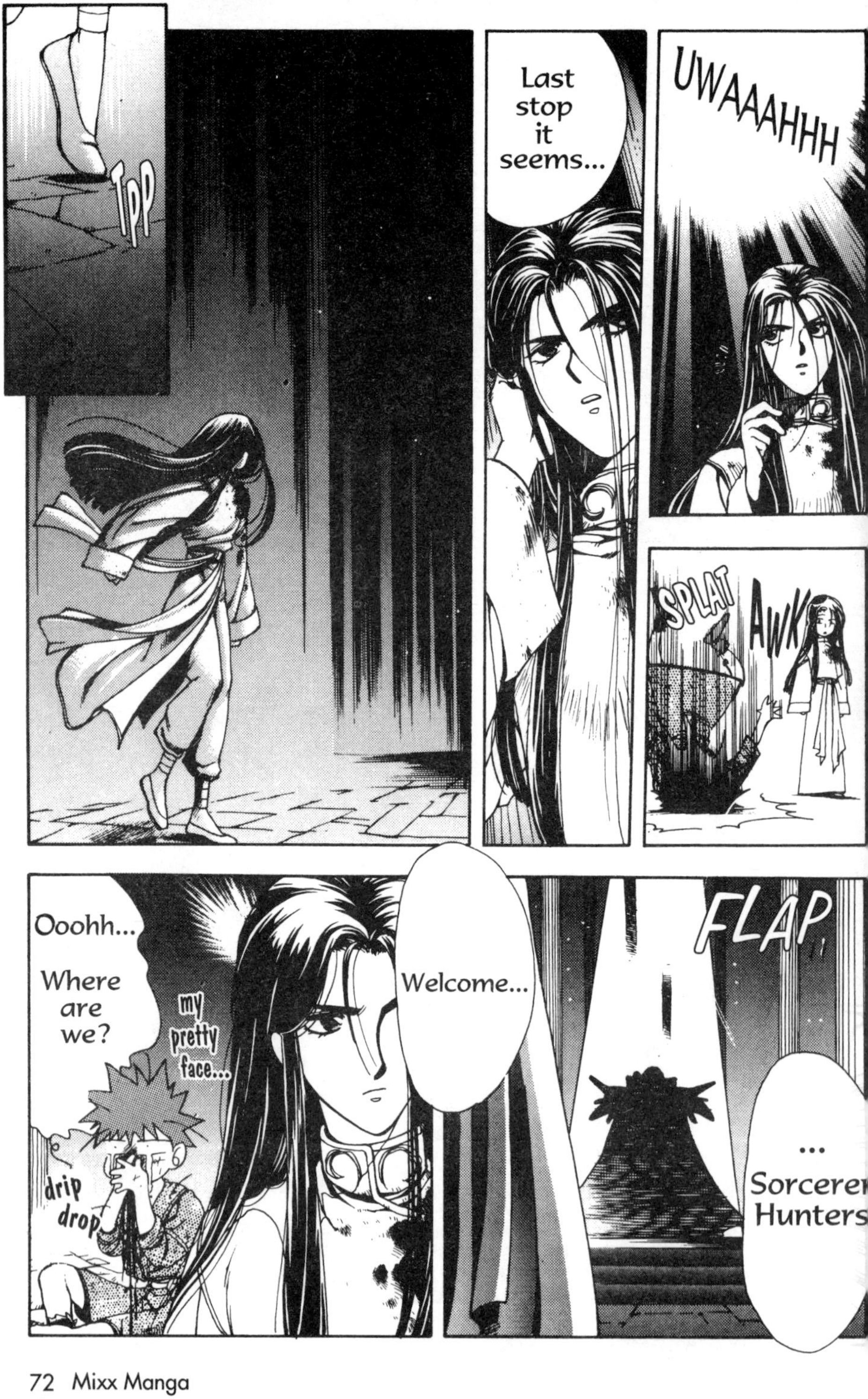
Tpp
Last stop it seems...
UWAAAHHH
SPLAT
AWK
Ooohh...
Where are we?
my pretty face...
drip drop
Welcome...
FLAP
... Sorcerer Hunters

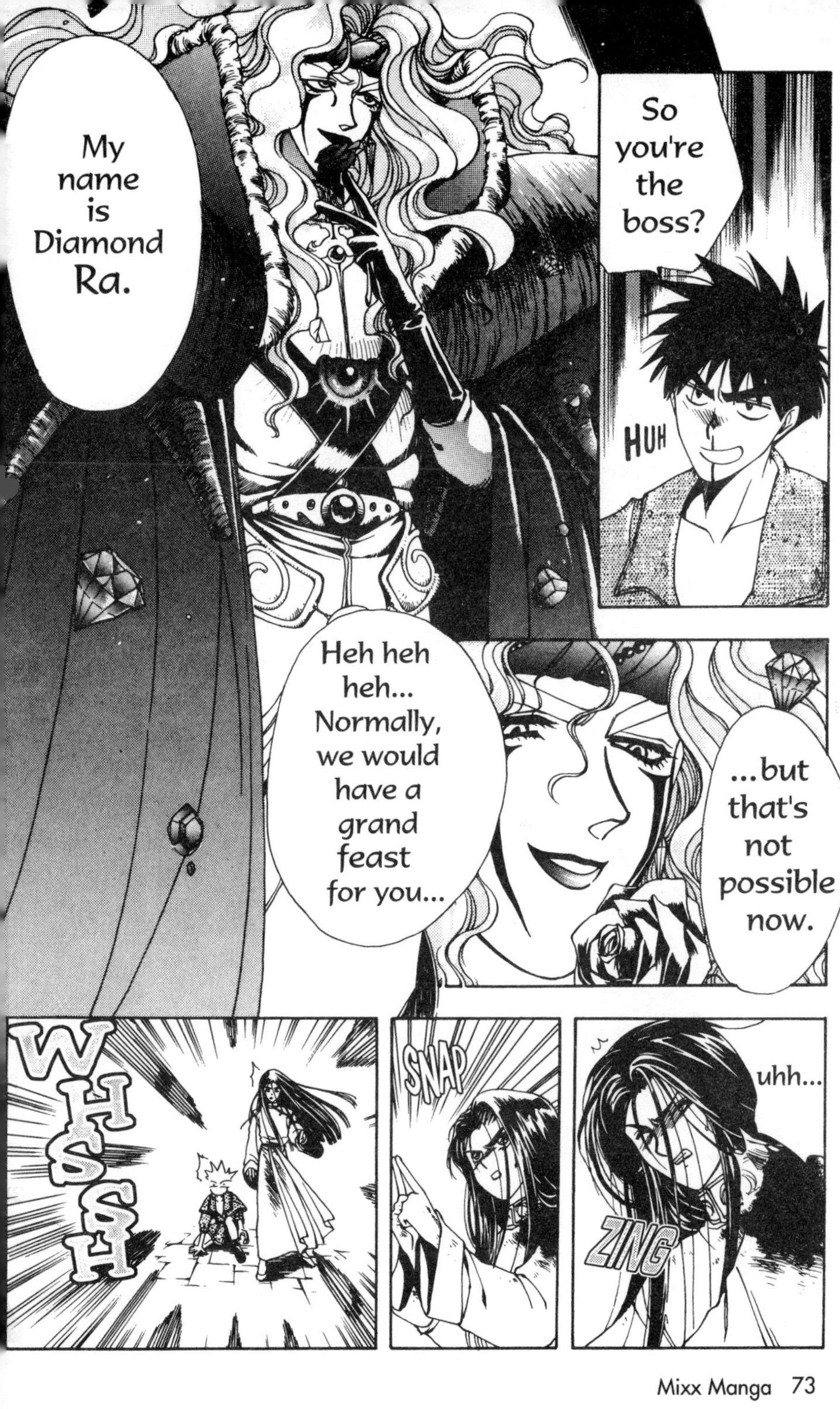
My name is Diamond Ra.
So you're the boss?
HUH
Heh heh heh... Normally, we would have a grand feast for you...
...but that's not possible now.
WHSH
SNAP
uhh...
ZING

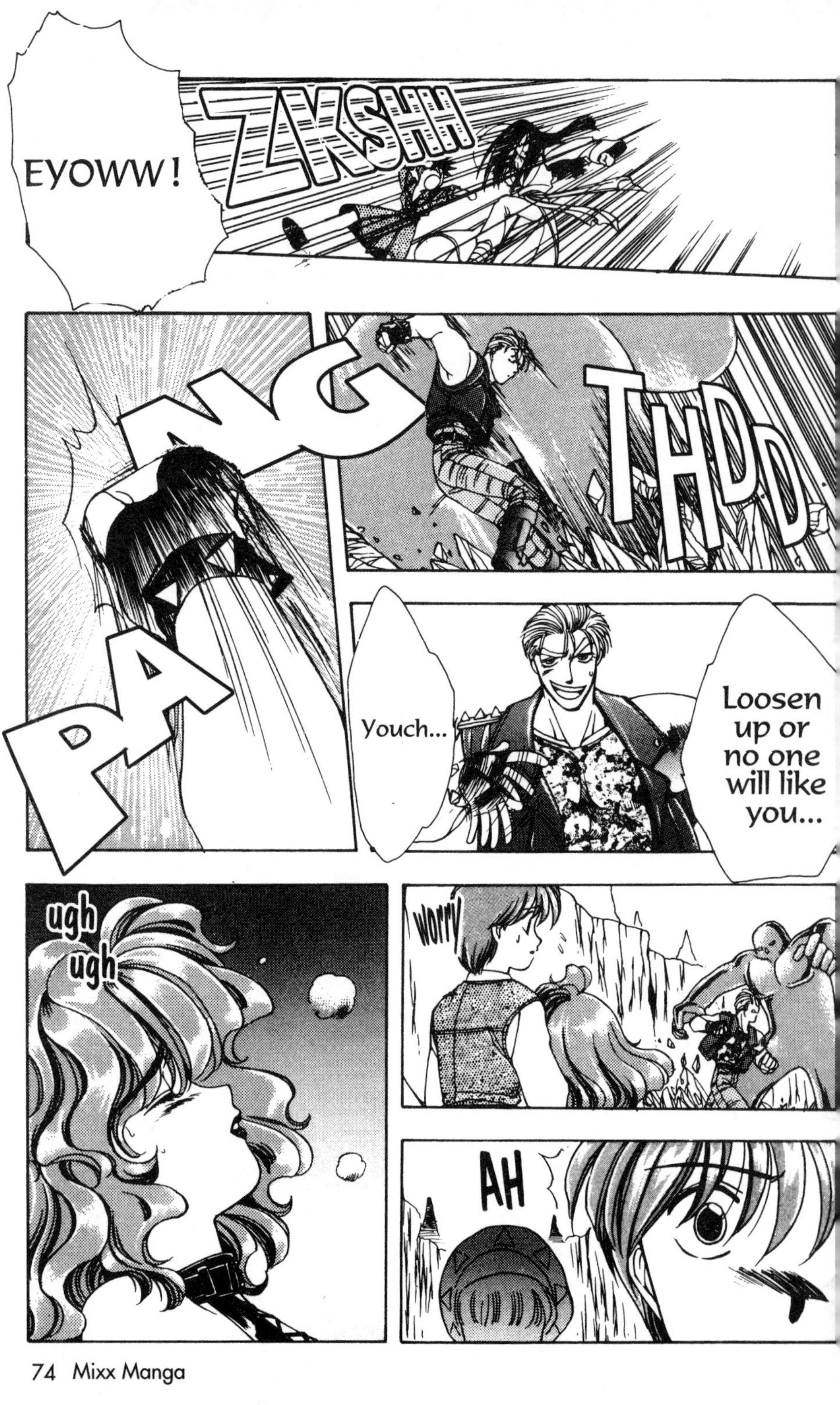
EYOWW!
ZKSHH
PANG
THDD
Youch...
Loosen up or no one will like you...
ugh
ugh
worry
AH

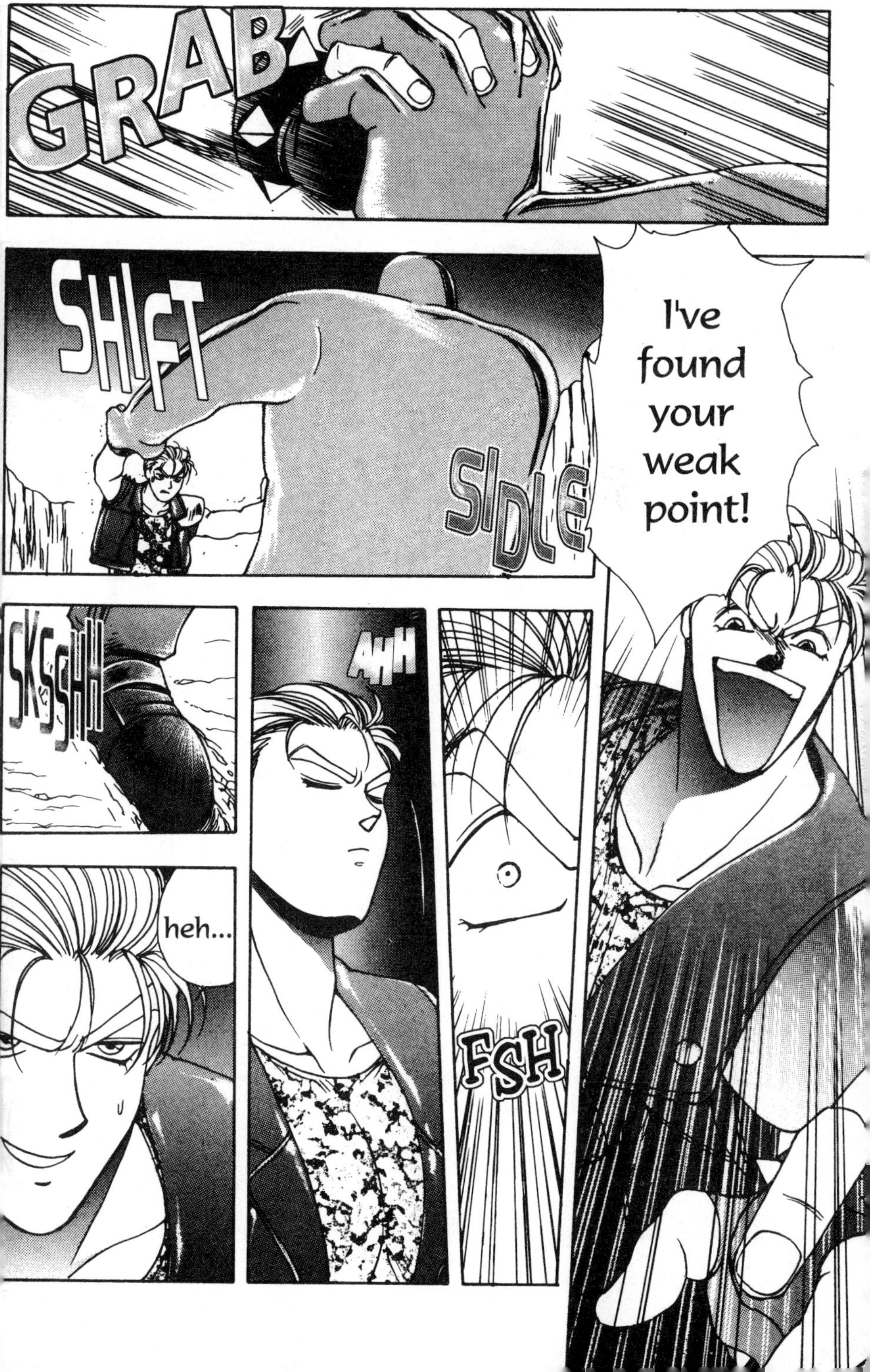
GRAB
SHIFT
SIDLE
SKSSHH
heh...
AHH
FSH
I've found your weak point!

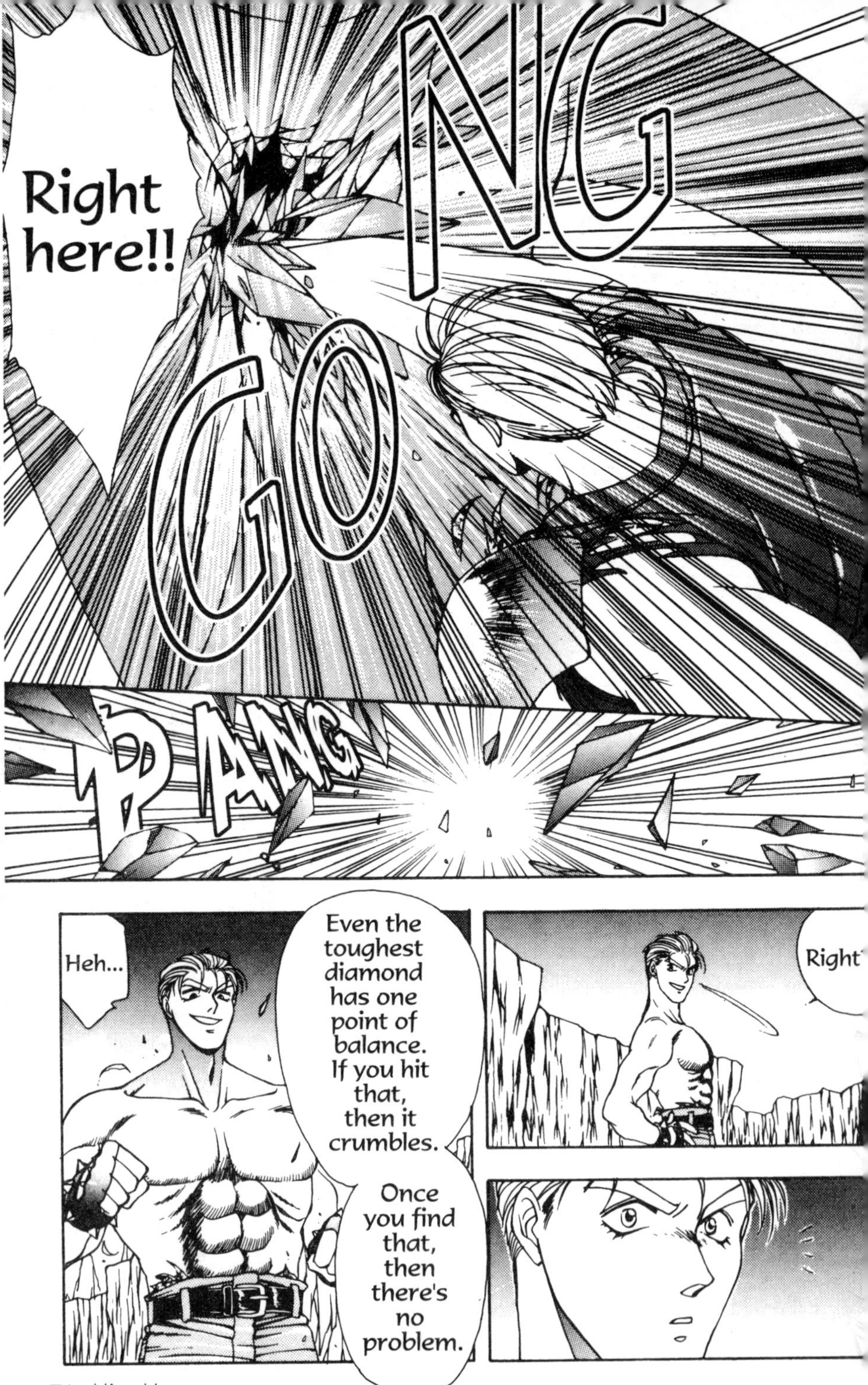
Right here!!
NG
GO
PANG
Heh...
Even the toughest diamond has one point of balance. If you hit that, then it crumbles.
Once you find that, then there's no problem.
Right

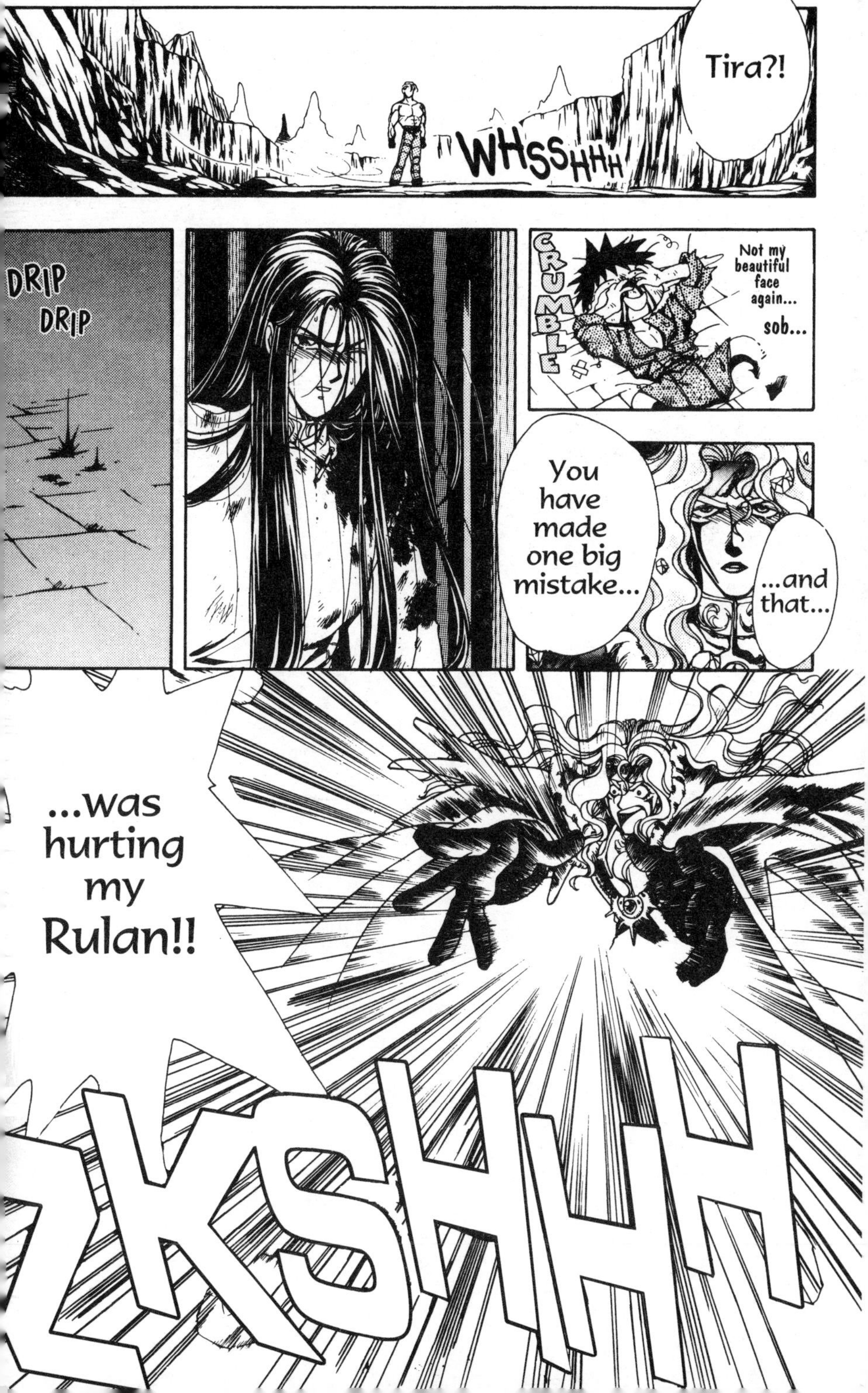
WHSSHHH
Tira?!
DRIP
DRIP
CRUMBLE
Not my beautiful face again...
sob...
You have made one big mistake...
...and that...
...was hurting my Rulan!!
ZKSHHH

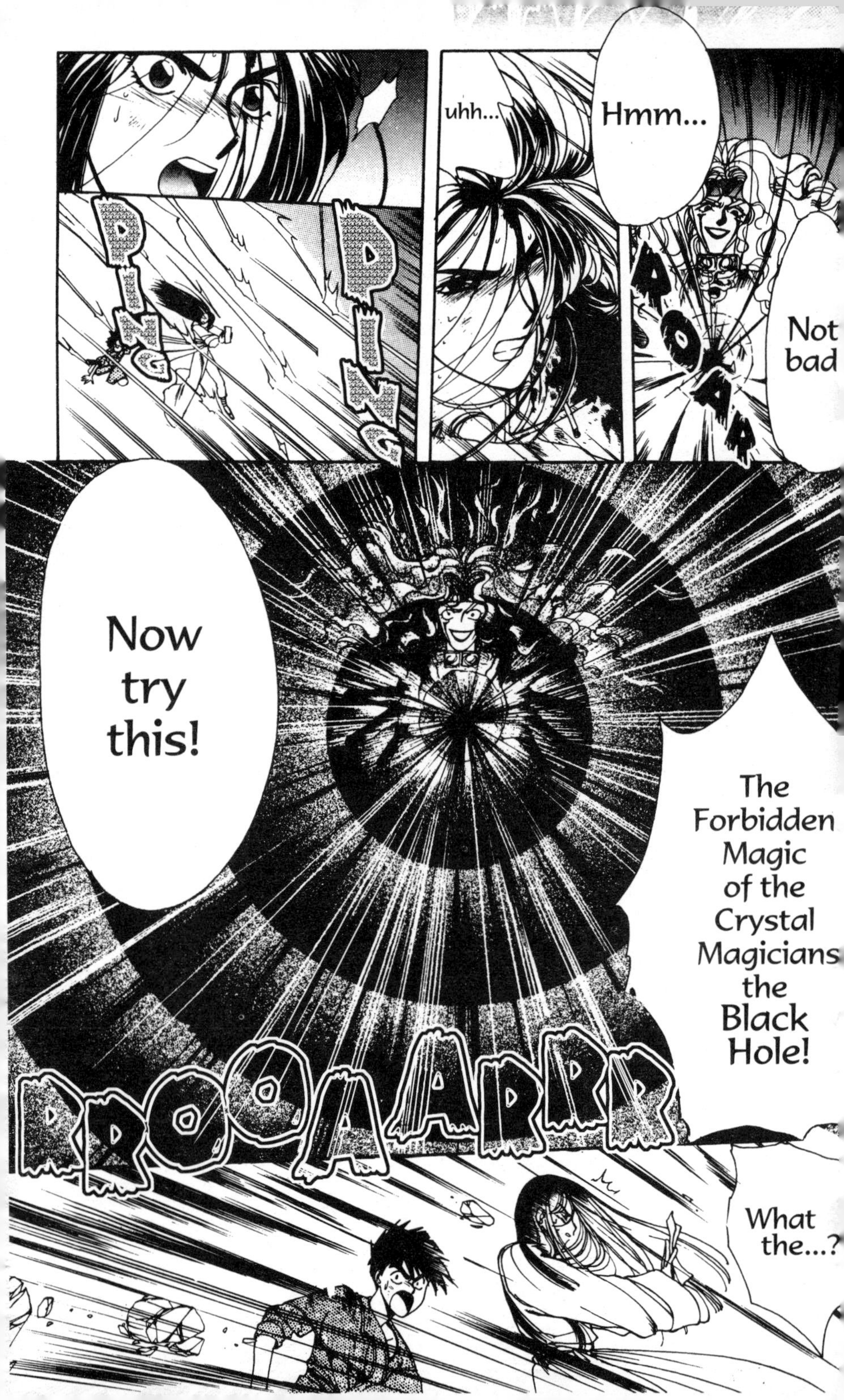
PING
PING
uhh...
Hmm...
ROAR
Not bad
Now try this!
RROOAARRR
The Forbidden Magic of the Crystal Magicians the Black Hole!
What the...?

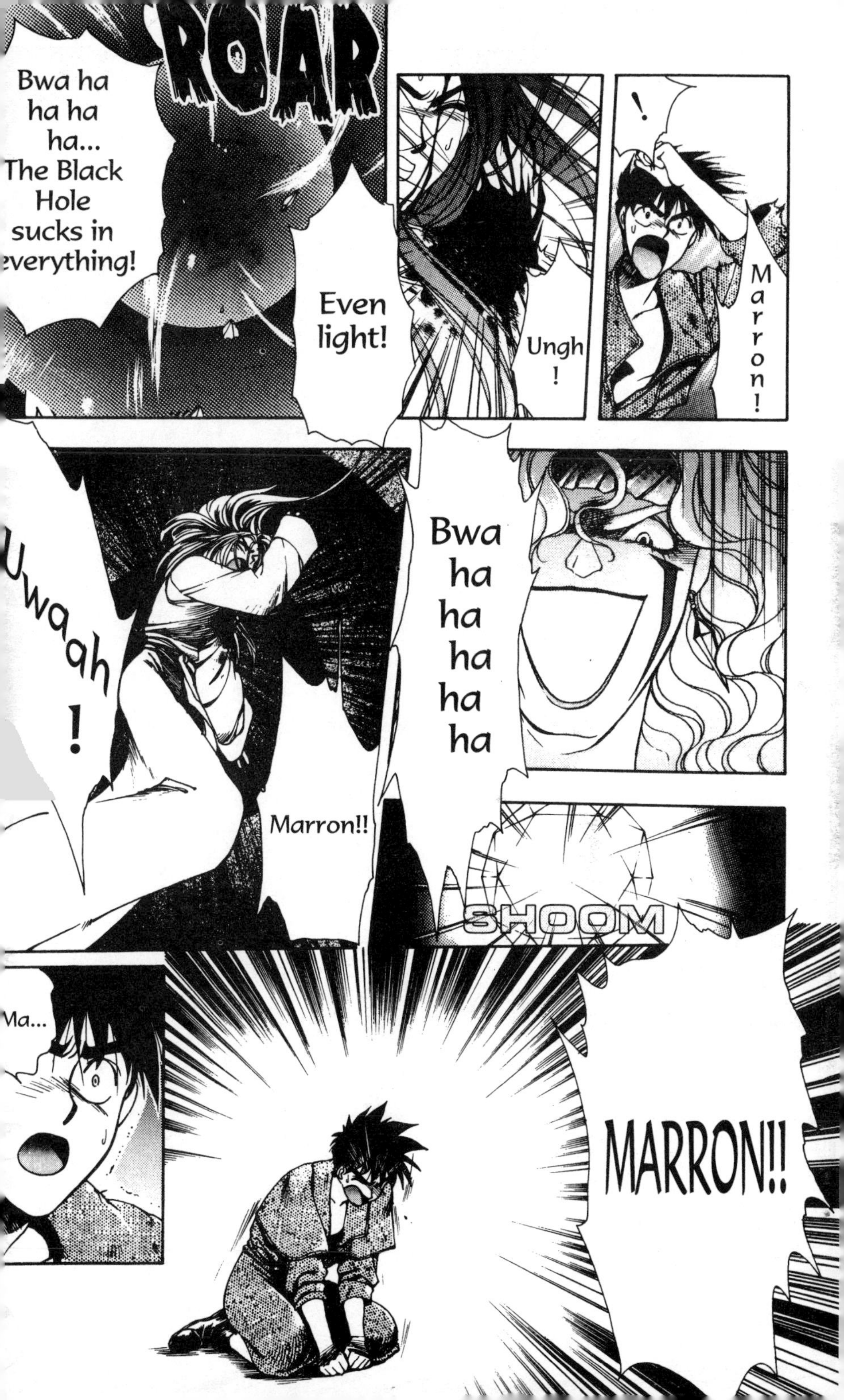
ROAR
Bwa ha ha ha ha... The Black Hole sucks in everything!
Even light!
Ungh!
!
Marron!
Uwaah!
Marron!!
Bwa ha ha ha ha ha
SHOOM
Ma...
MARRON!!

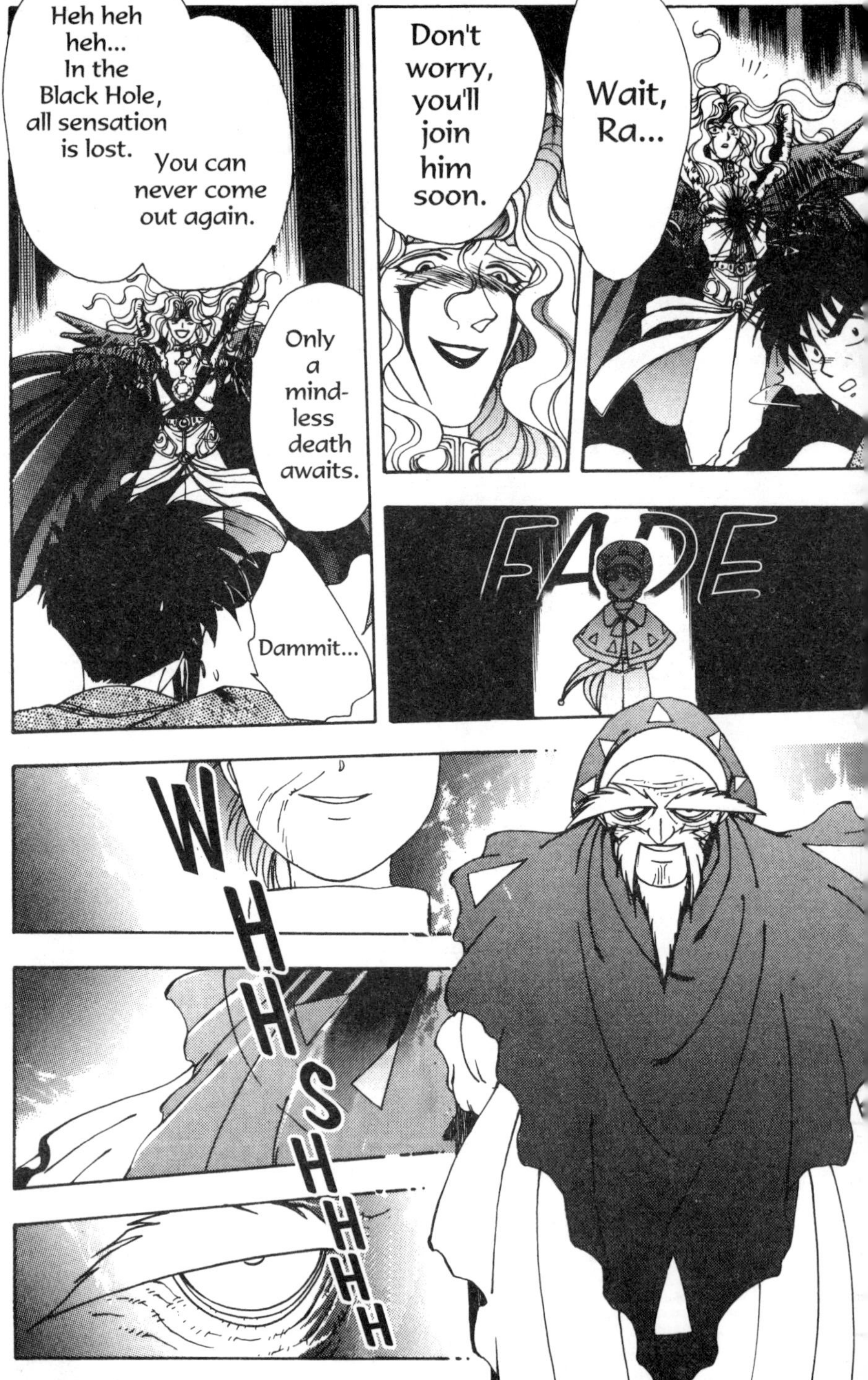
Heh heh heh... In the Black Hole, all sensation is lost.
You can never come out again.
Only a mindless death awaits.
Dammit...
Don't worry, you'll join him soon.
Wait, Ra...
FADE
WHHHSHHHH

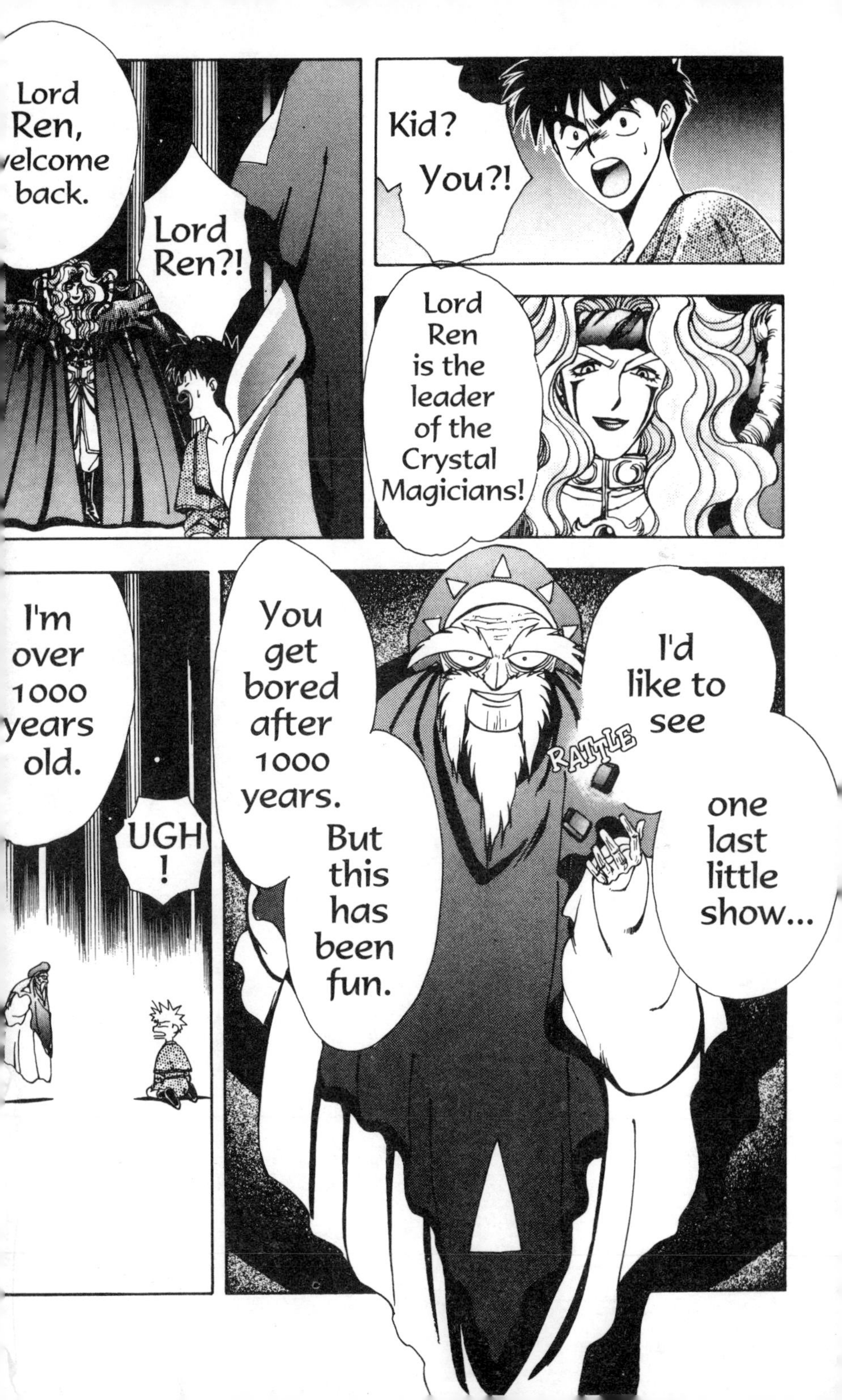
Lord Ren, elcome back.
Lord Ren?!
Kid? You?!
Lord Ren is the leader of the Crystal Magicians!
I'm over 1000 years old.
UGH!
You get bored after 1000 years.
But this has been fun.
RATTLE
I'd like to see
one last little show...

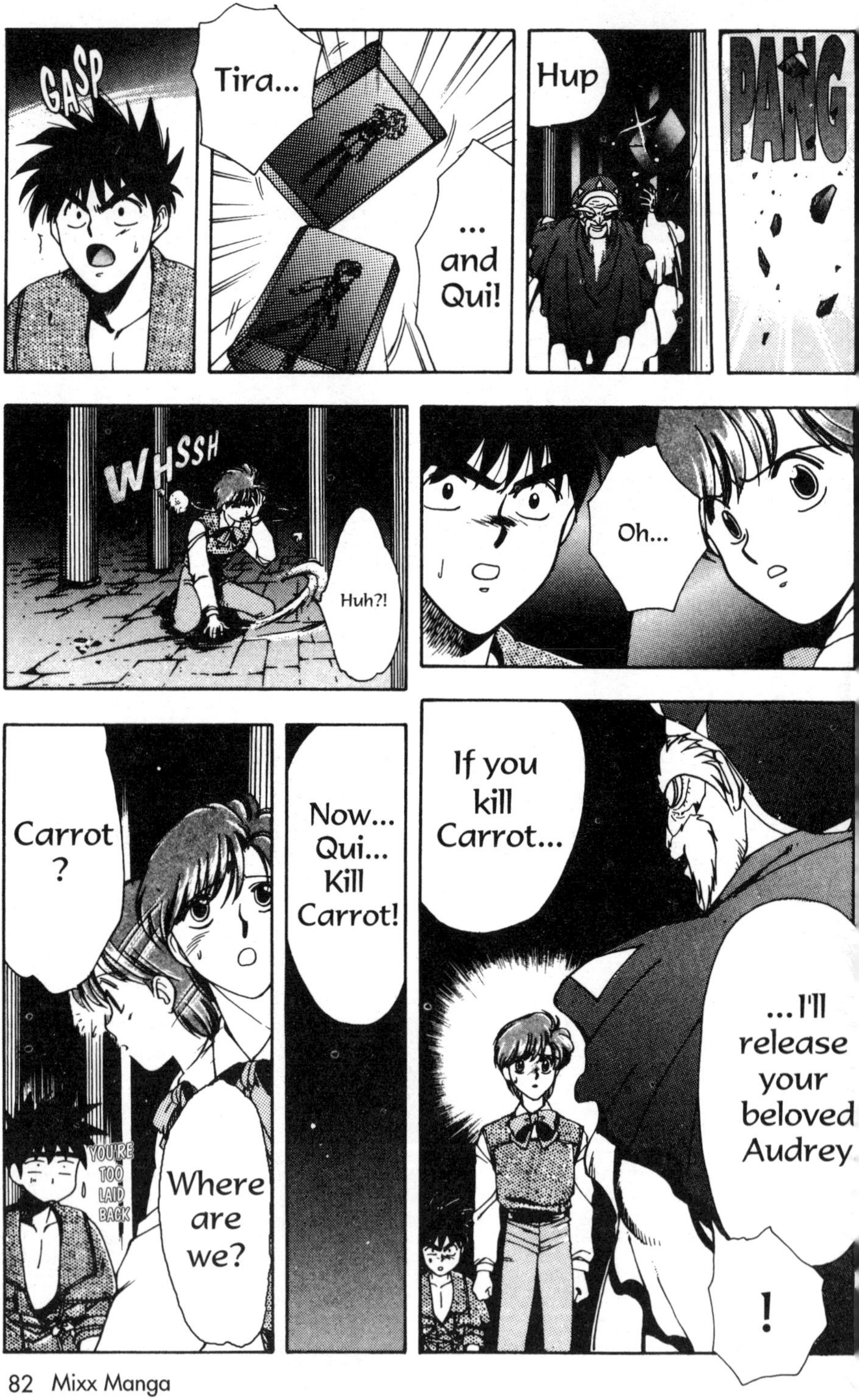

GASP
Tira...
... and Qui!
Hup
PANG
WHSSH
Huh?!
Oh...
Carrot ?
YOU'RE TOO LAID BACK
Where are we?
Now... Qui... Kill Carrot!
If you kill Carrot...
...I'll release your beloved Audrey
!

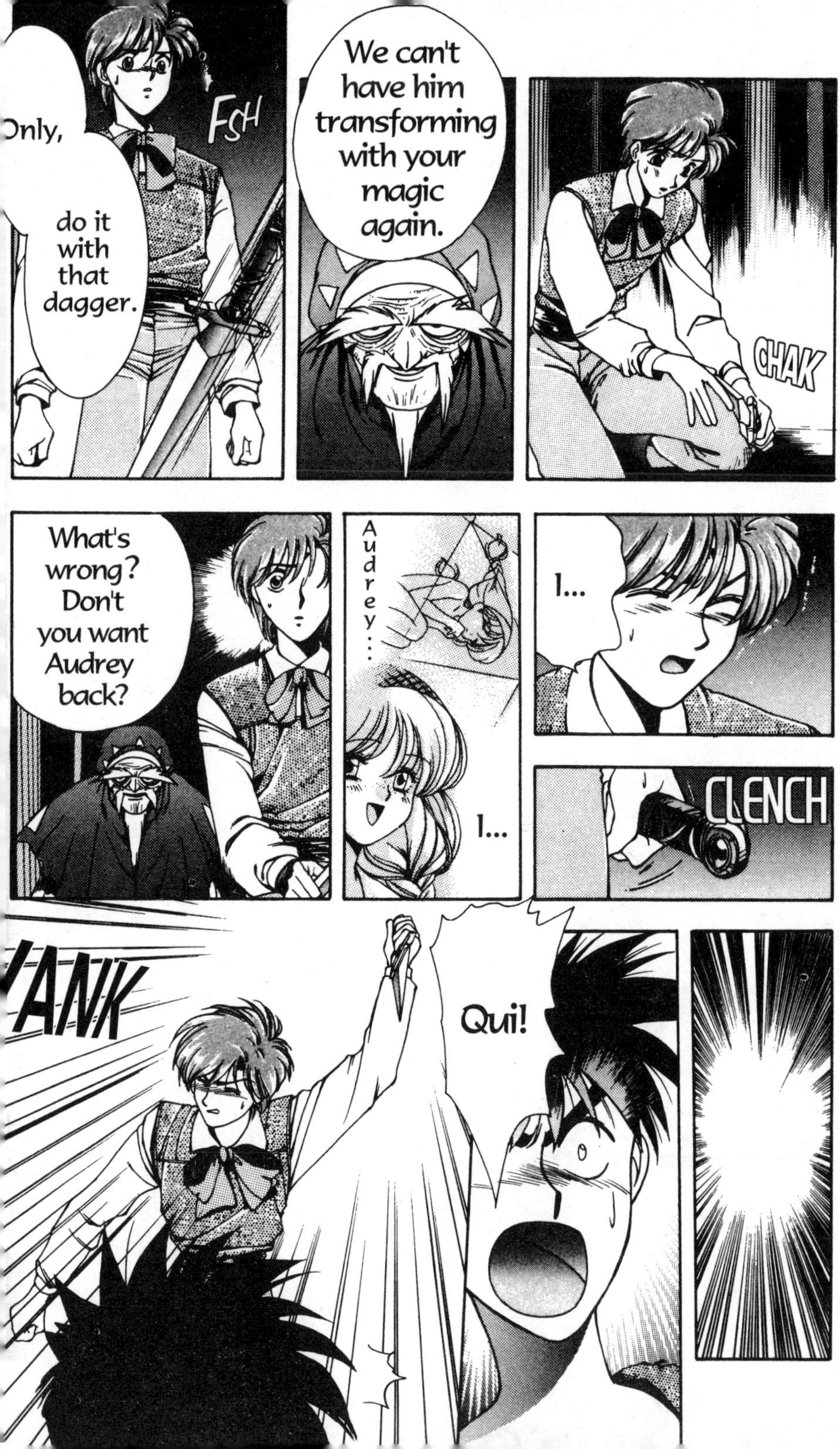
Only,
do it with that dagger.
FSH
We can't have him transforming with your magic again.
CHAK
What's wrong? Don't you want Audrey back?
Audrey...
I...
I...
CLENCH
YANK
Qui!

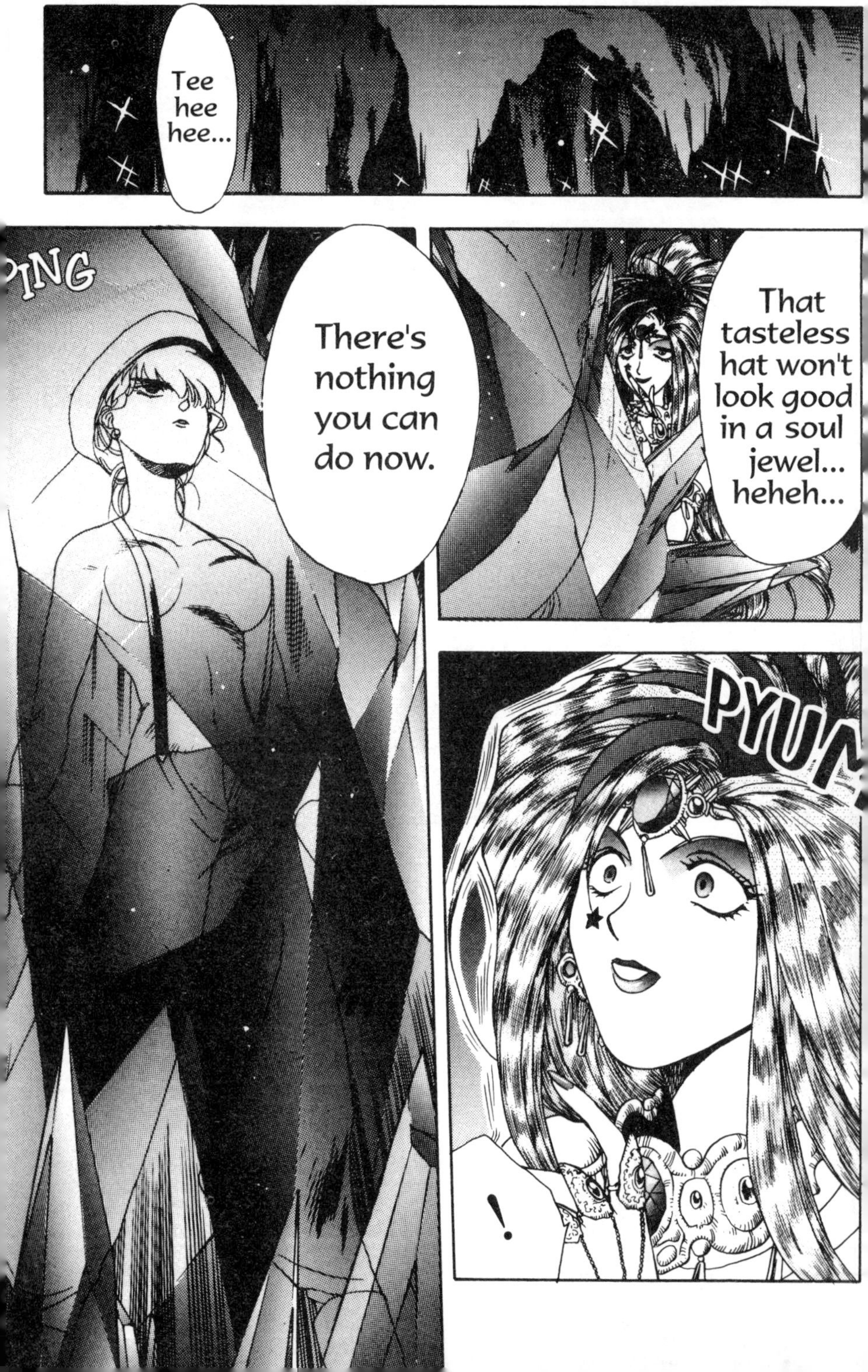
Tee hee hee...
PING
There's nothing you can do now.
That tasteless hat won't look good in a soul jewel... heheh...
PYUN
!

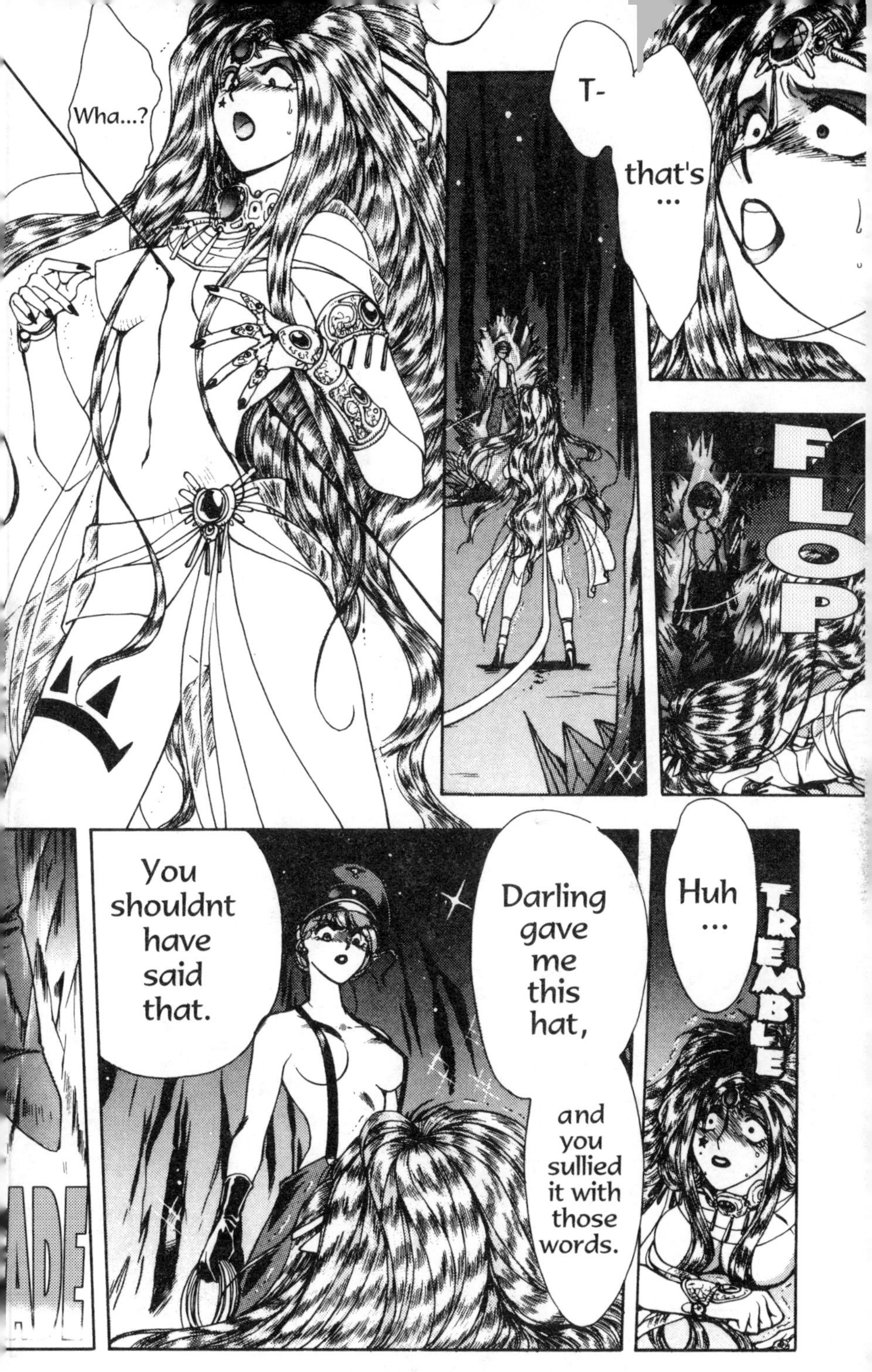
Wha...?
T- that's ...
FLOP
ADE
You shouldnt have said that.
Darling gave me this hat,
and you sullied it with those words.
Huh ...
TREMBLE

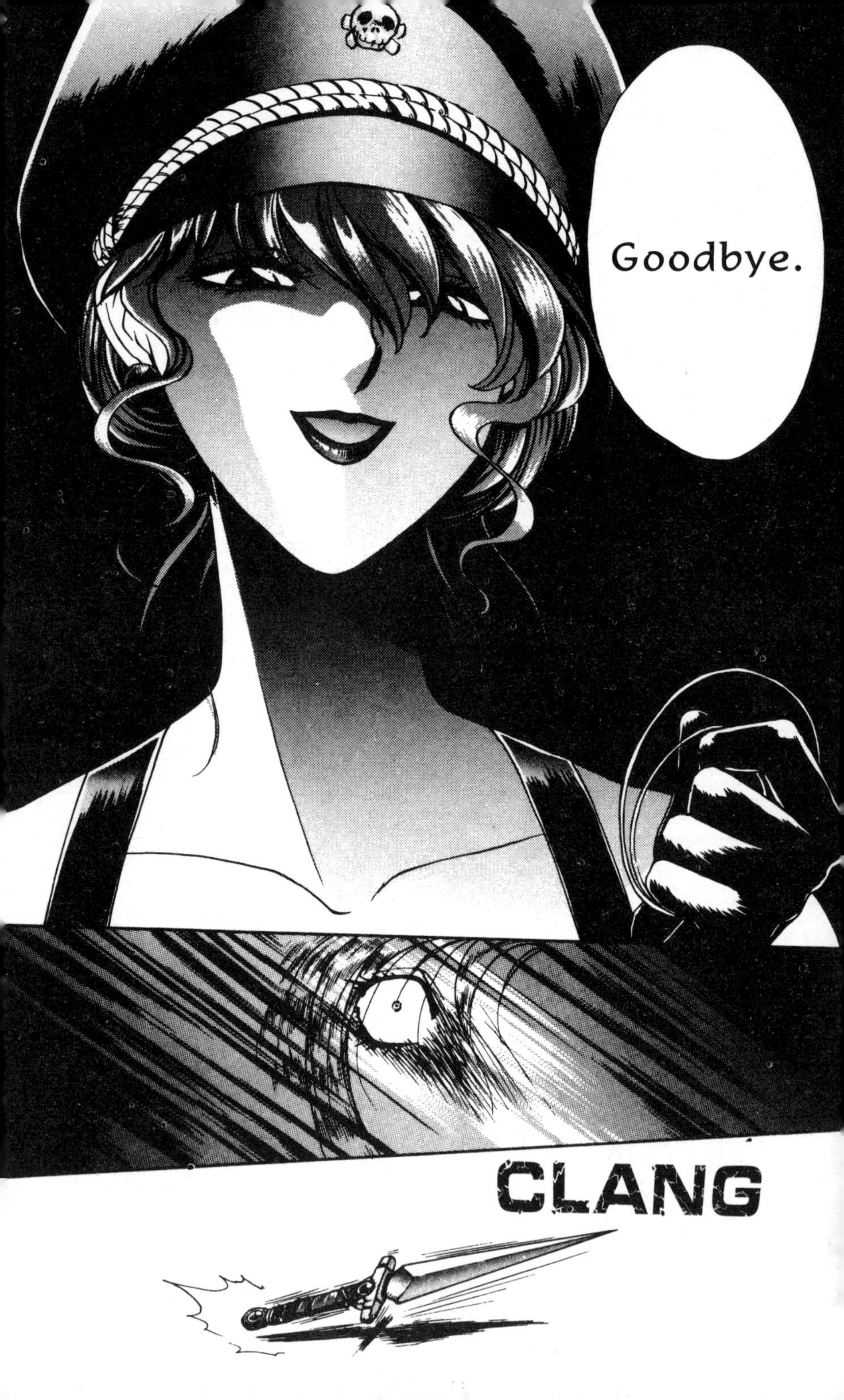
Goodbye.
CLANG

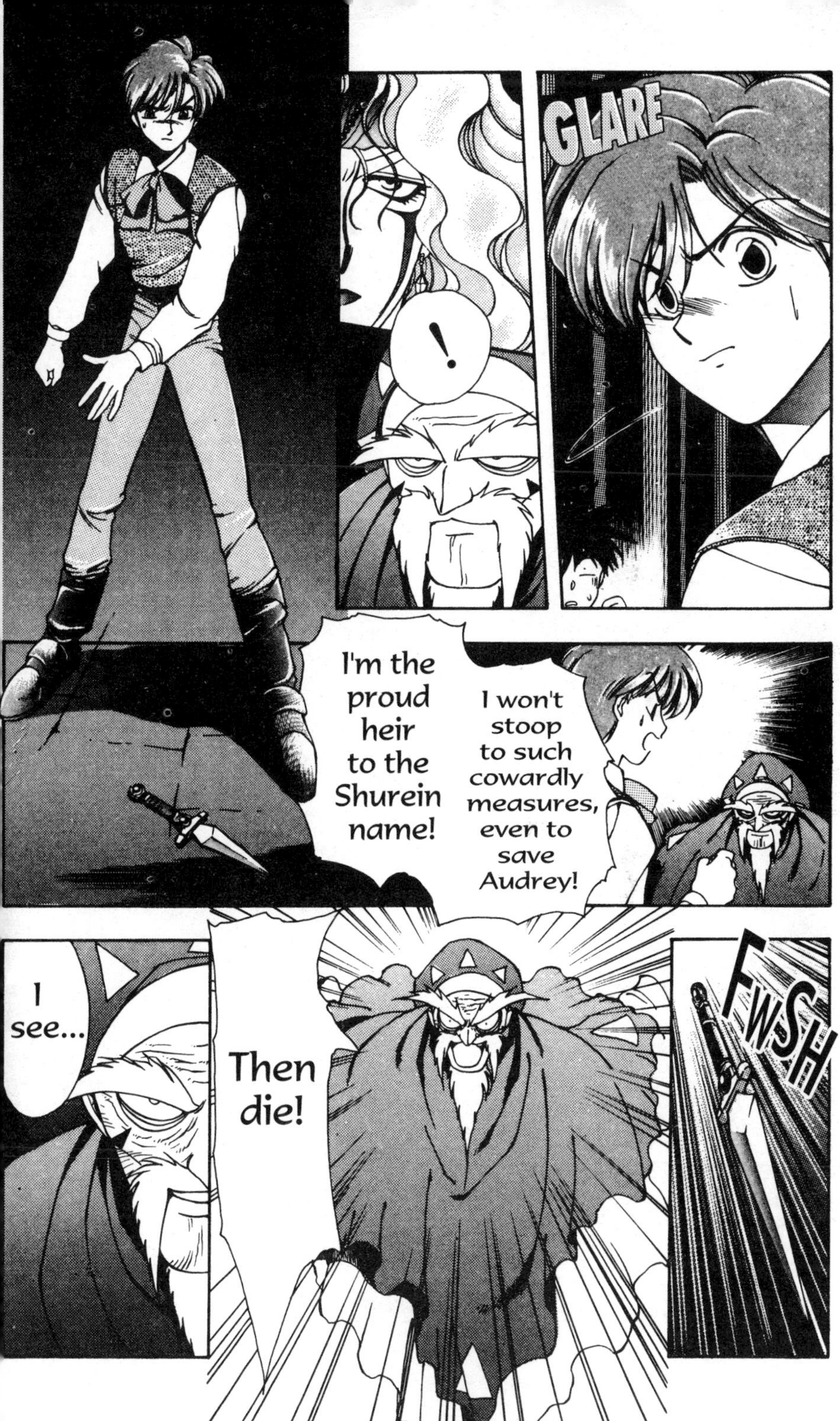
!
GLARE
I'm the proud heir to the Shurein name!
I won't stoop to such cowardly measures, even to save Audrey!
I see...
Then die!
FWSH

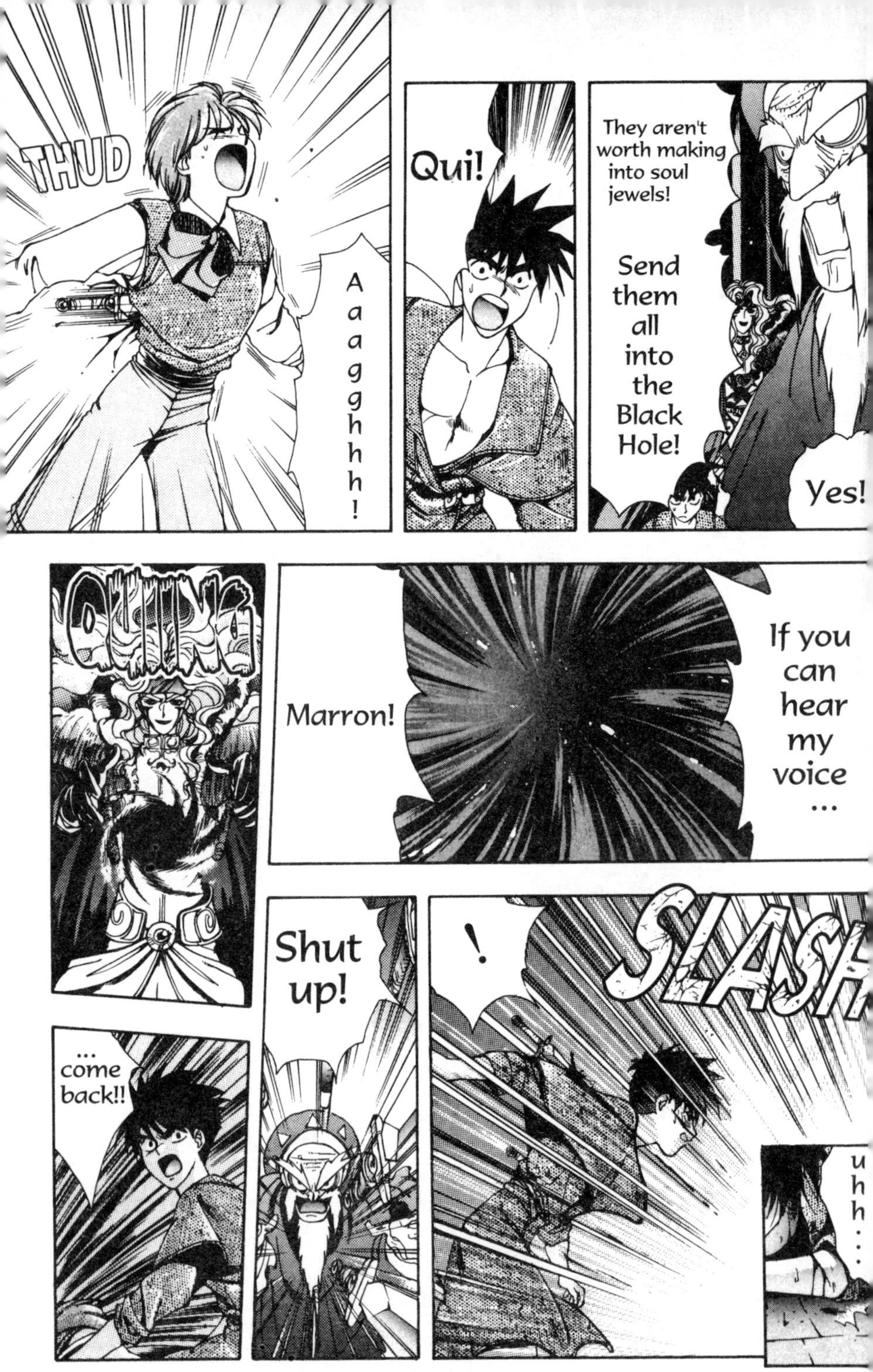
THUD
Aaagghhhh!
Qui!
They aren't worth making into soul jewels!
Send them all into the Black Hole!
Yes!
Marron!
If you can hear my voice ...
... come back!!
Shut up!
!
SLASH
uhh...

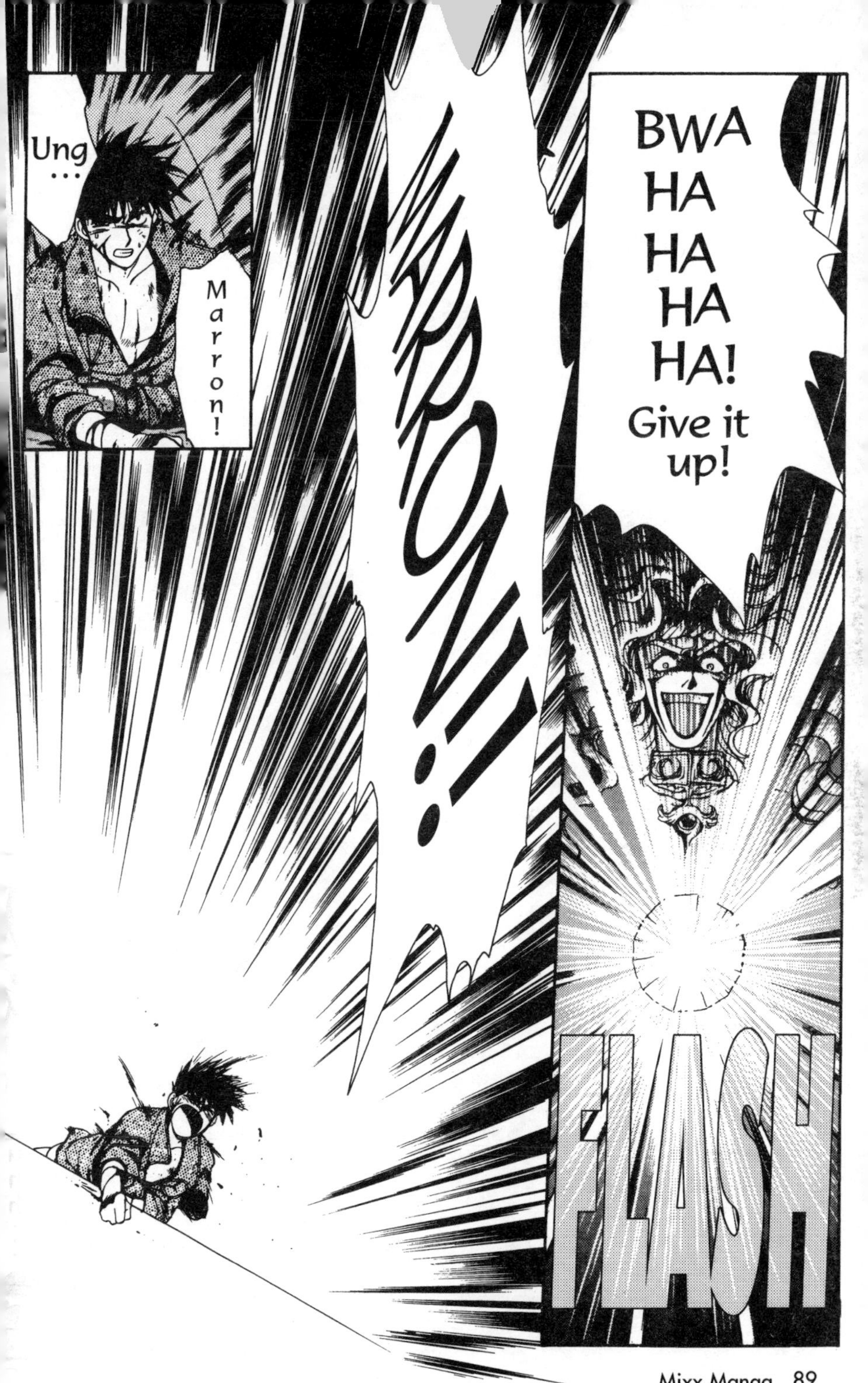
Ung...
Marron!
MARRON!!!
BWA HA HA HA HA!
Give it up!
FLASH

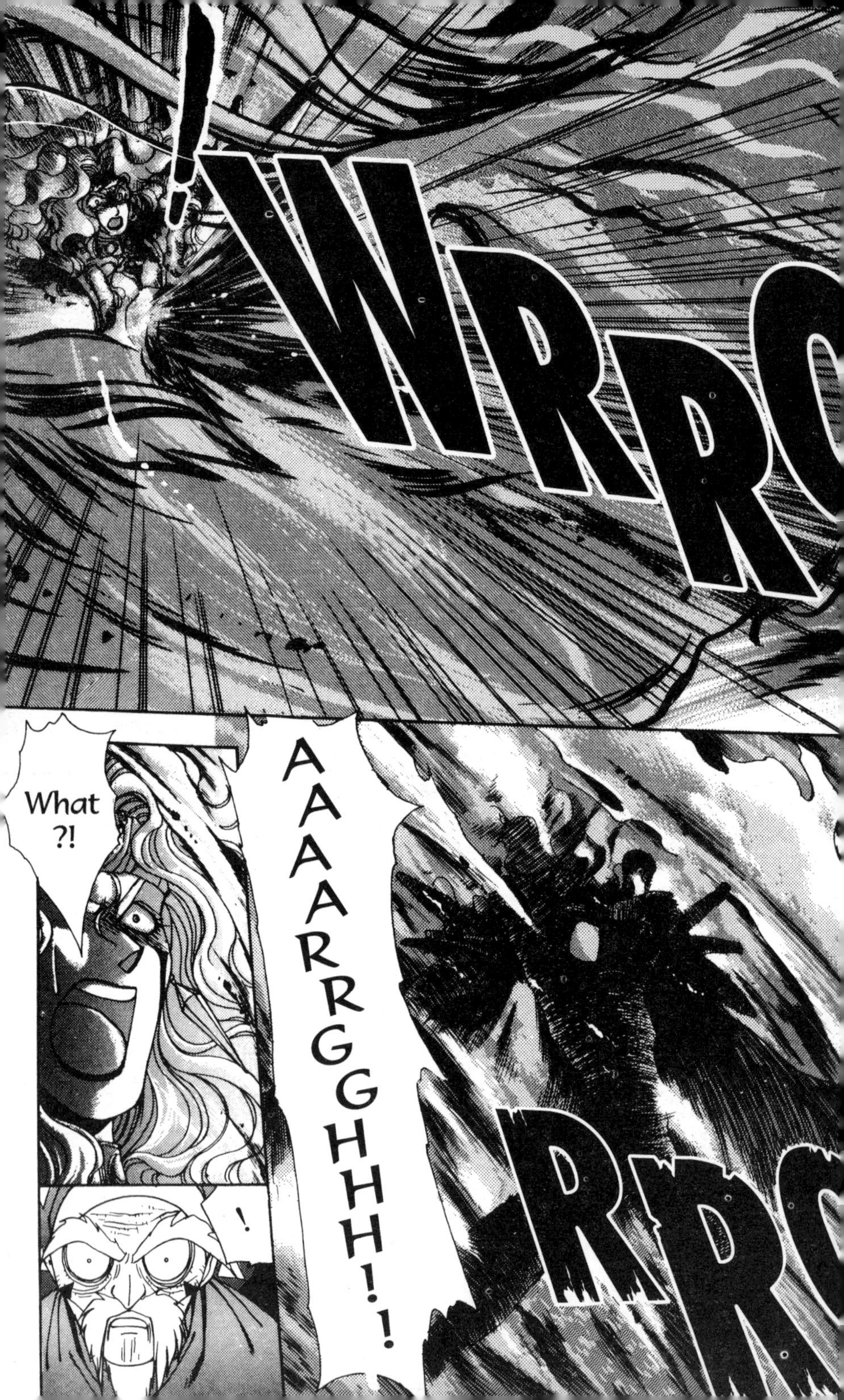
!
WRRO
What ?!
!
AAAARRGGHHH!!!
RRO

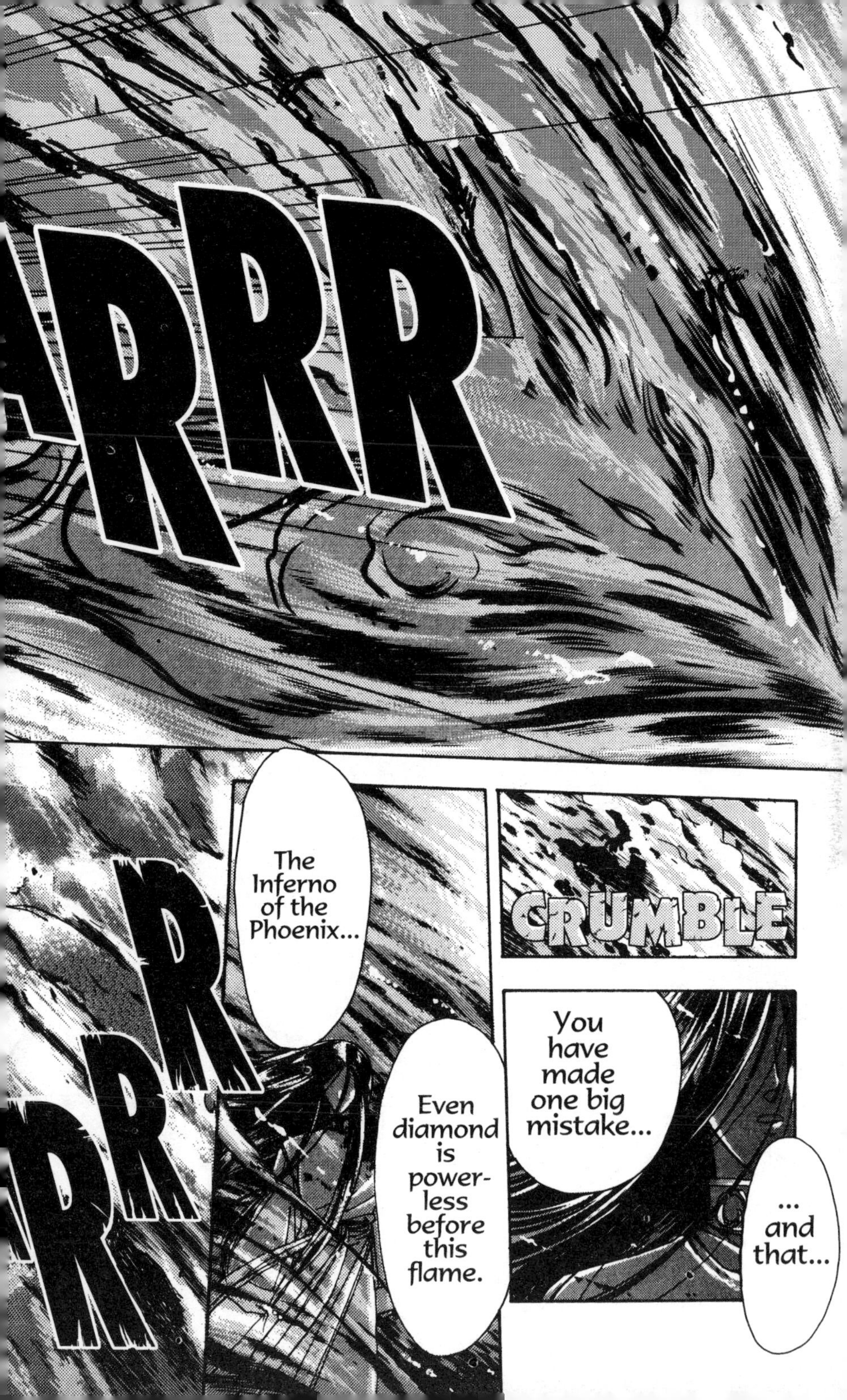
RRR
The Inferno of the Phoenix...
Even diamond is powerless before this flame.
CRUMBLE
You have made one big mistake...
... and that...

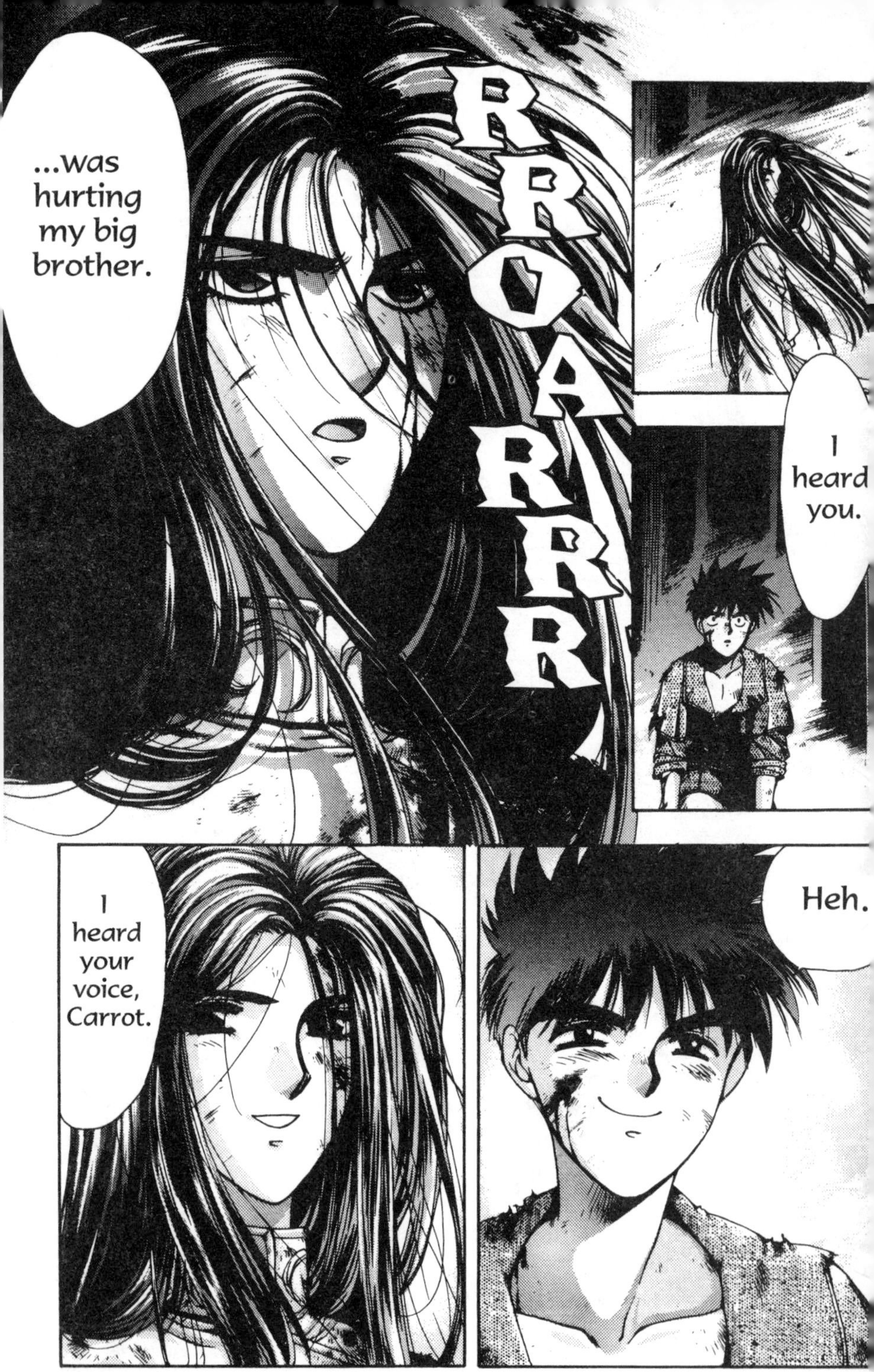
...was hurting my big brother.
RROARRR
I heard you.
I heard your voice, Carrot.
Heh.

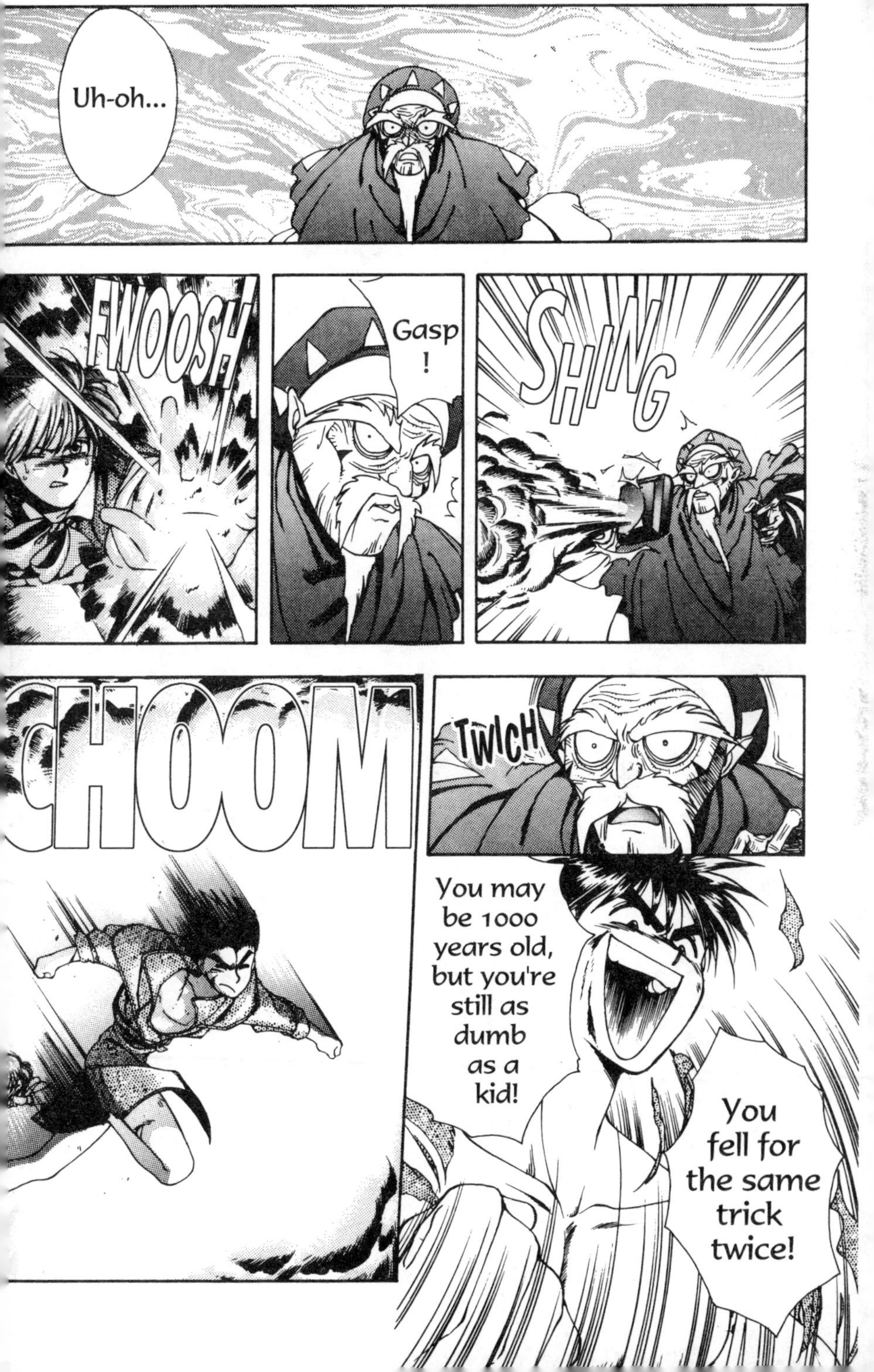
Uh-oh...
FWOOSH
Gasp!
SHING
CHOOM
TWICH
You may be 1000 years old, but you're still as dumb as a kid!
You fell for the same trick twice!

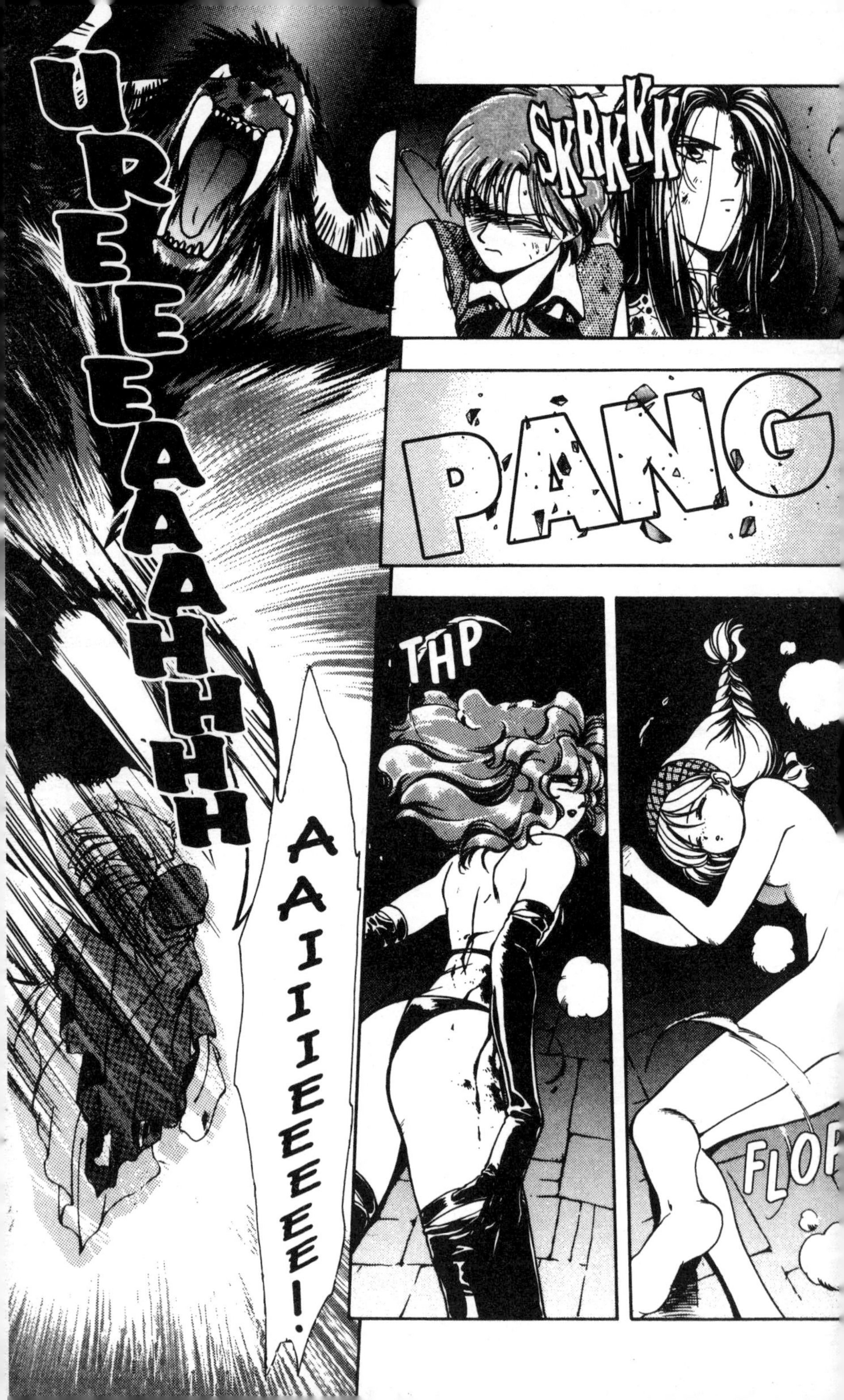
UREEEAAAHHHH
AAIIEEEEE!
SKRKKK
PANG
THP
FLOP

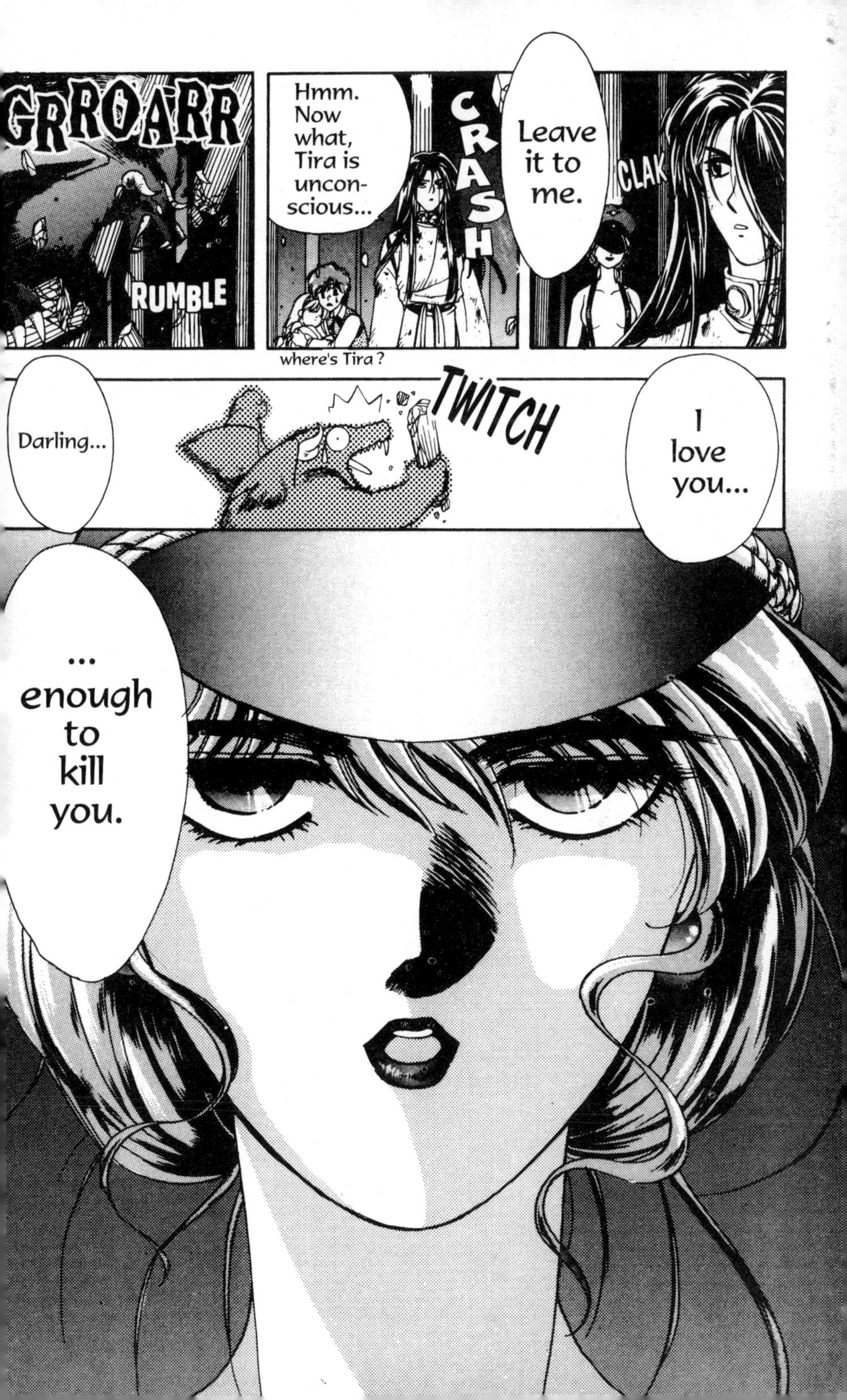
GRROARR
RUMBLE
Hmm. Now what, Tira is unconscious...
CRASH
where's Tira?
Leave it to me.
CLAK
Darling...
TWITCH
I love you...
... enough to kill you.

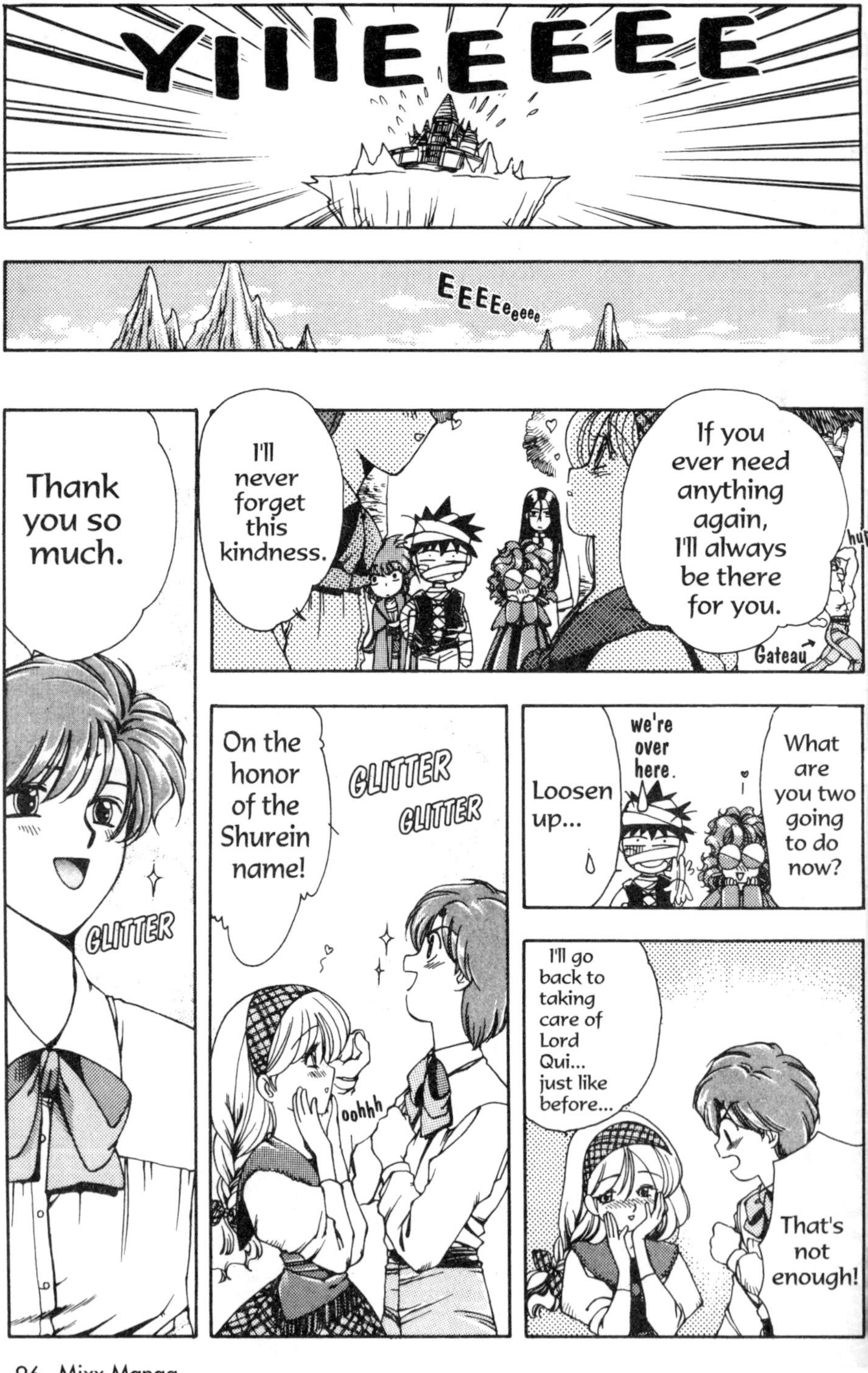
YIIIEEEEE
EEEEeeee
Thank you so much.
GLITTER
I'll never forget this kindness.
If you ever need anything again, I'll always be there for you.
hup
Gateau
On the honor of the Shurein name!
GLITTER
GLITTER
oohhh
Loosen up...
we're over here.
What are you two going to do now?
I'll go back to taking care of Lord Qui... just like before...
That's not enough!

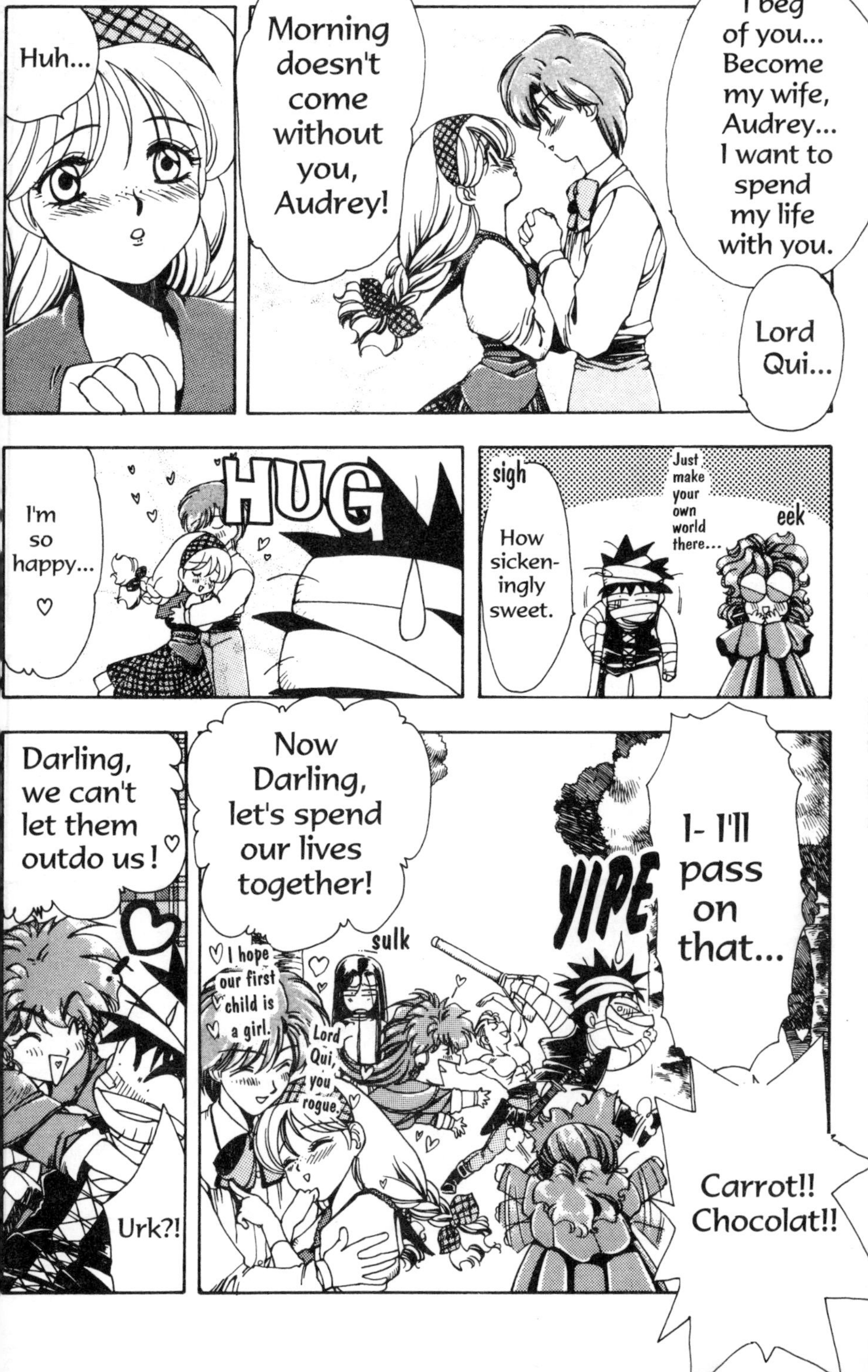
Huh...
Morning doesn't come without you, Audrey!
I beg of you... Become my wife, Audrey... I want to spend my life with you.
Lord Qui...
I'm so happy... ♡
HUG
sigh
How sicken-ingly sweet.
Just make your own world there...
eek
Darling, we can't let them outdo us! ♡
Urk?!
Now Darling, let's spend our lives together!
I hope our first child is a girl.
sulk
Lord Qui, you rogue.
YIPE
I- I'll pass on that...
Carrot!! Chocolat!!

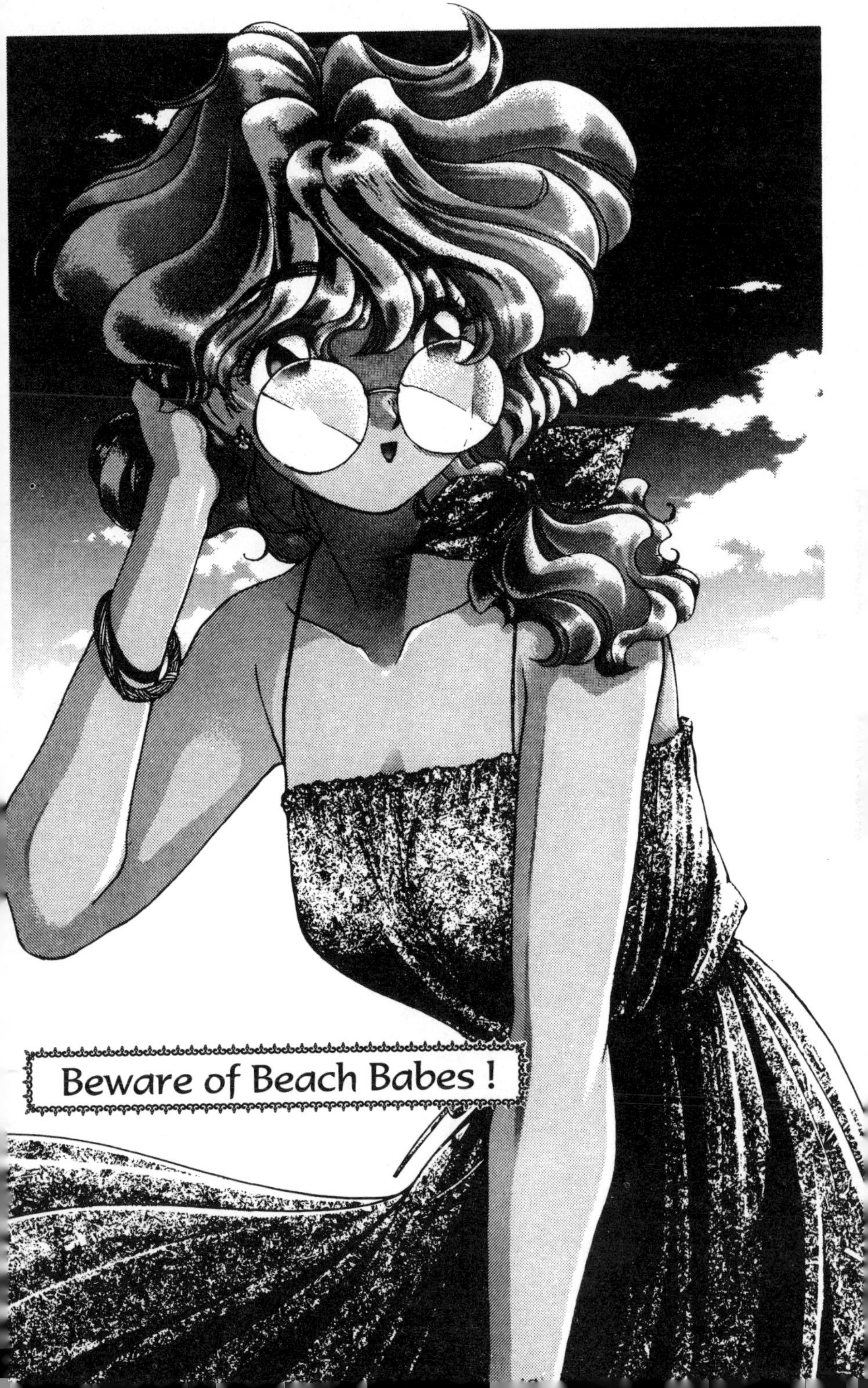
Beware of Beach Babes !

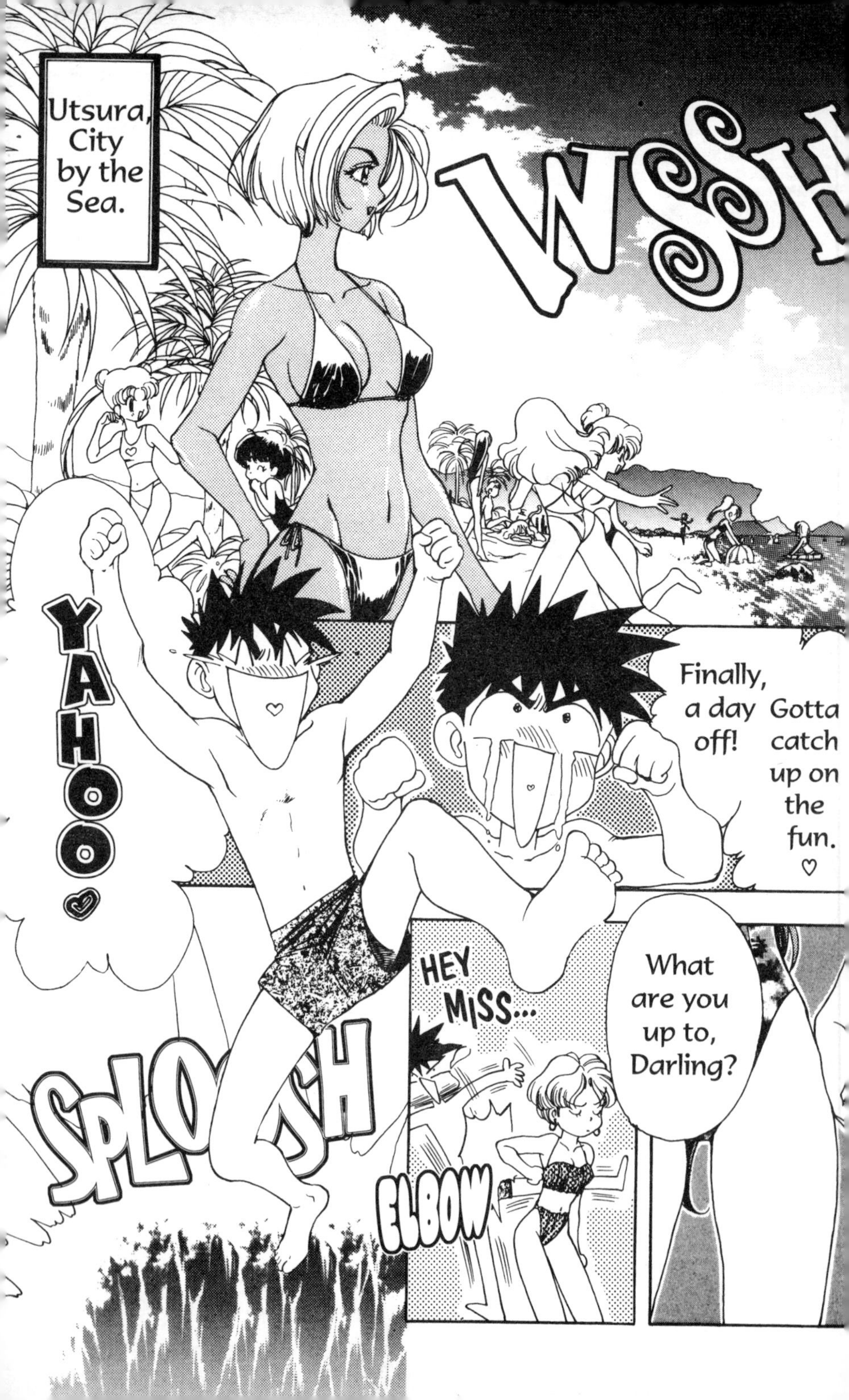

Utsura, City by the Sea.
WSSH
YAHOO
Finally, a day off!
Gotta catch up on the fun. ♡
SPLOSH
HEY MISS...
ELBOW
What are you up to, Darling?

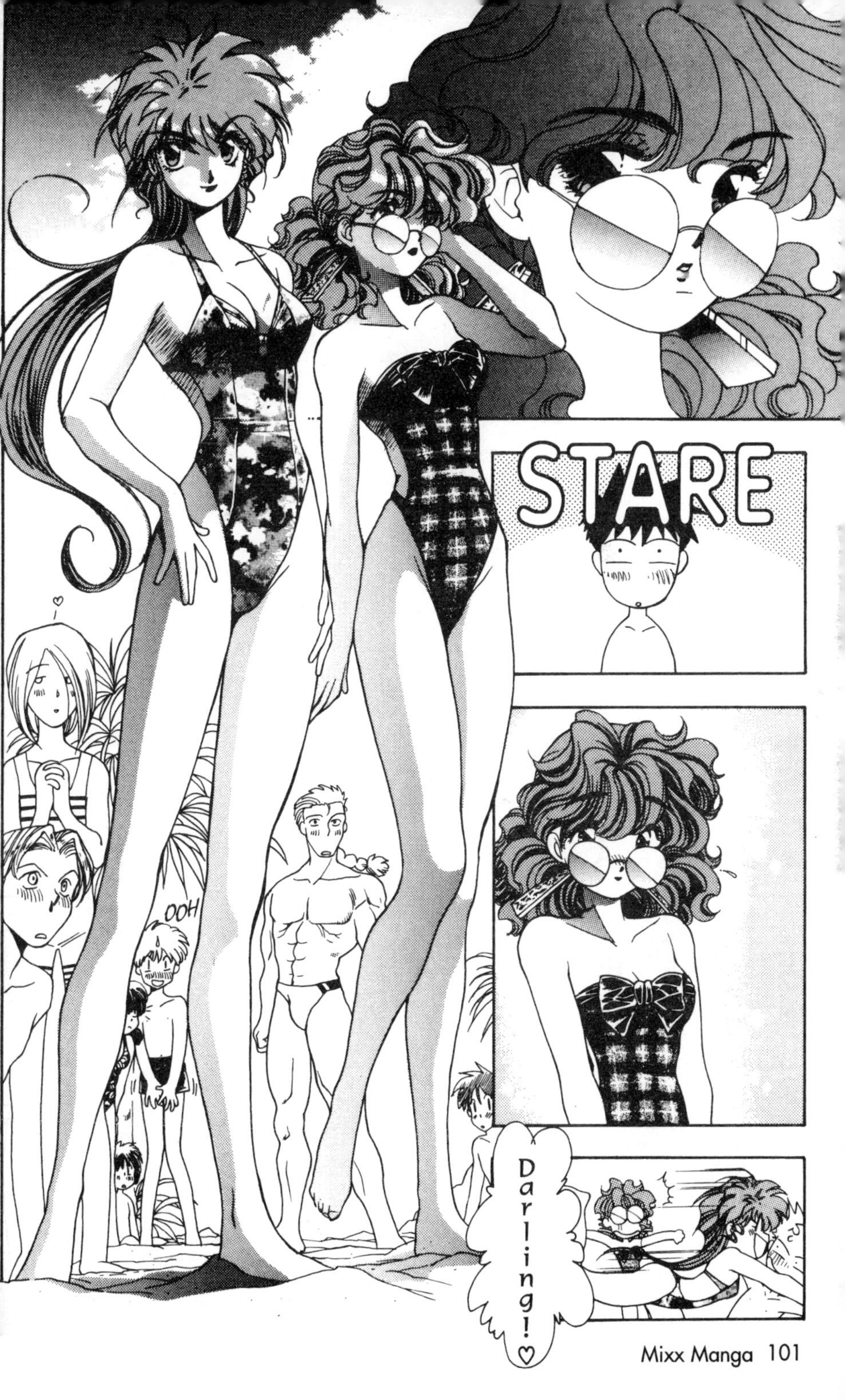
OOH
STARE
Darling!♡

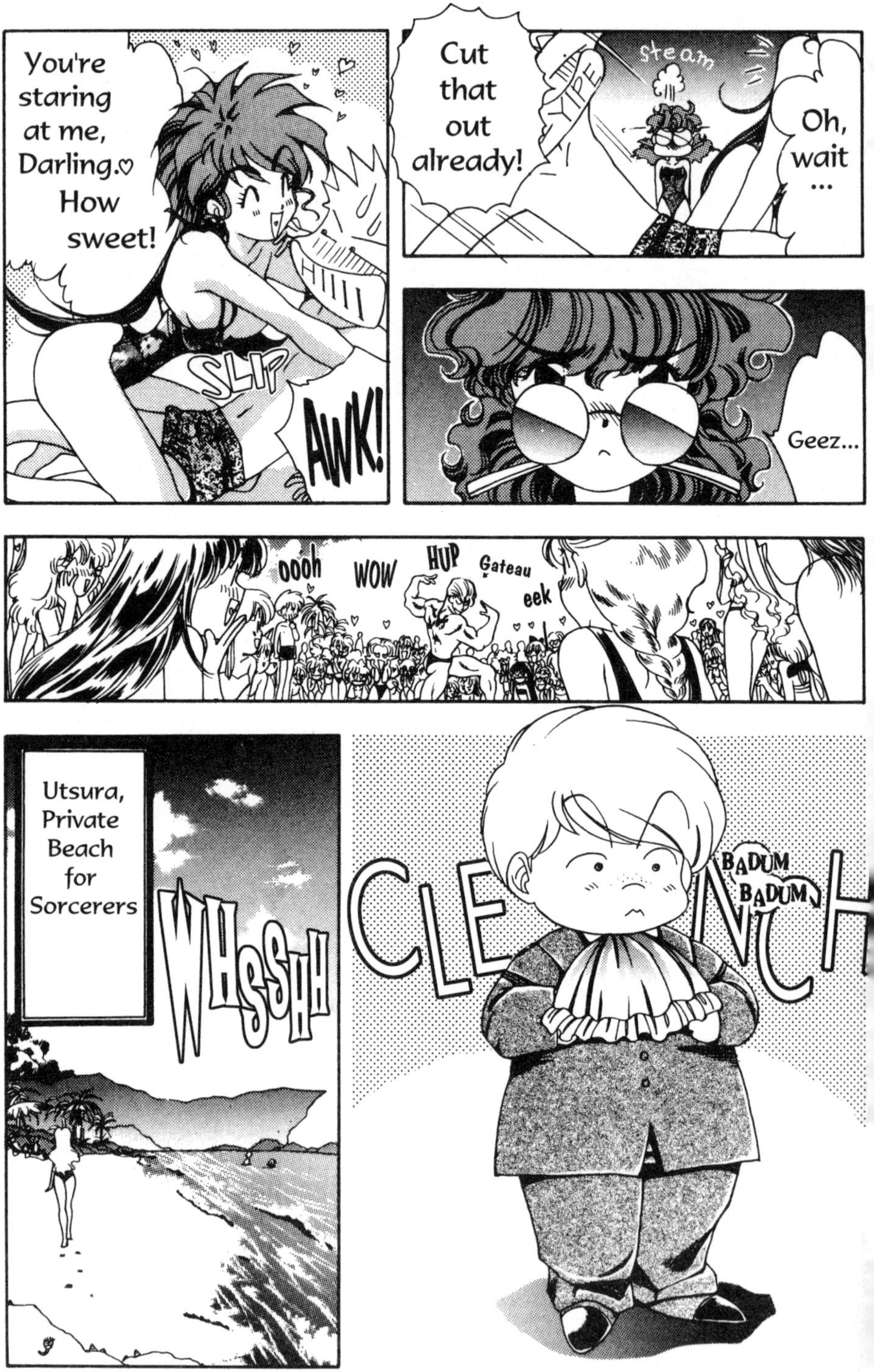
You're staring at me, Darling.♡ How sweet!
HIIII
SLIP
AWK!
Cut that out already!
YIPE
steam
Oh, wait ...
Geez...
oooh
WOW
HUP
Gateau
eek
Utsura, Private Beach for Sorcerers
WHSSHH
CLENCH
BADUM
BADUM

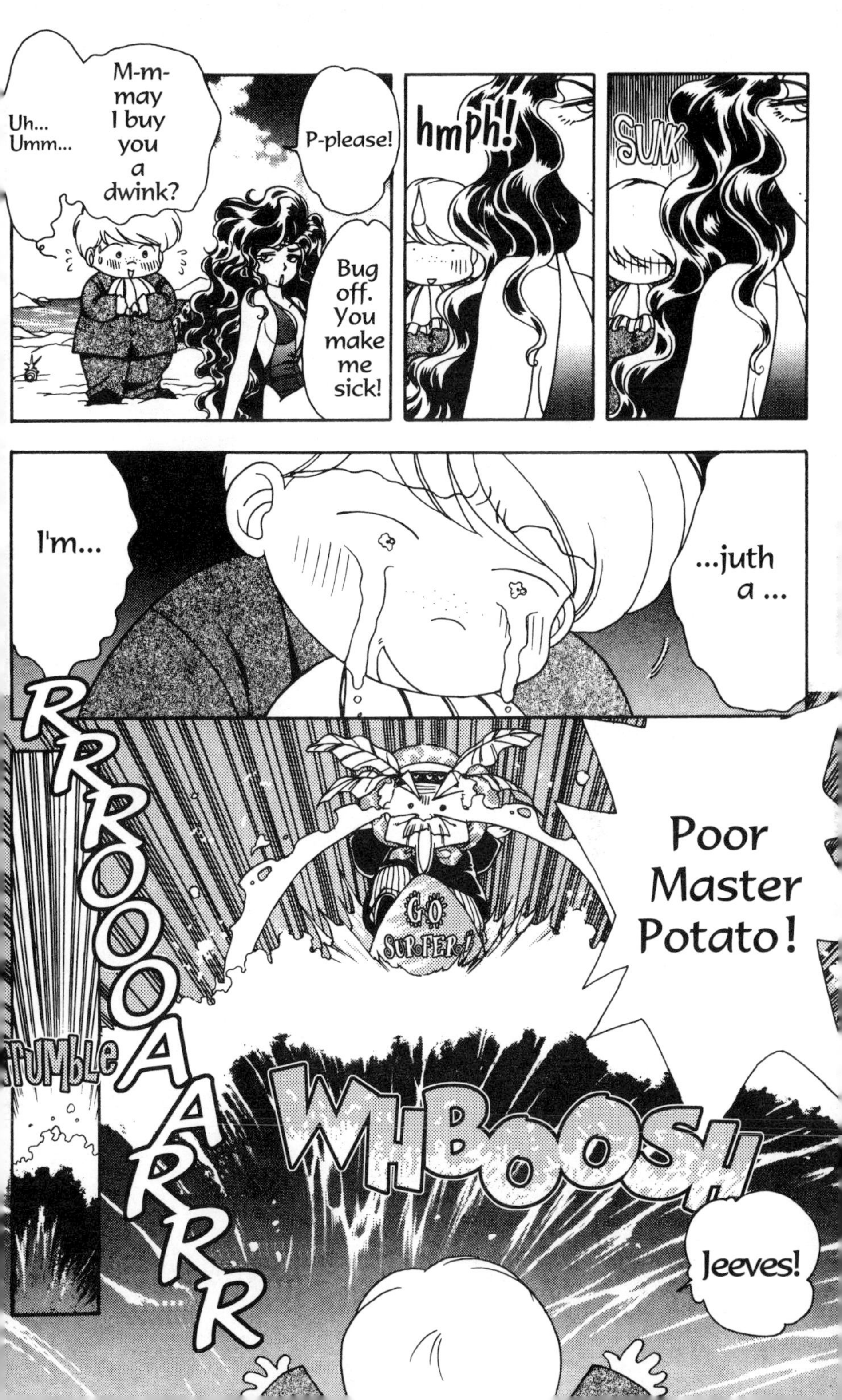

Uh... Umm...
M-m-may I buy you a dwink?
P-please!
Bug off. You make me sick!
hmph!
SUNK
I'm...
...juth a ...
RRROOOAARRR
TUMBLE
GO SURFER
Poor Master Potato!
WHOOSH
Jeeves!

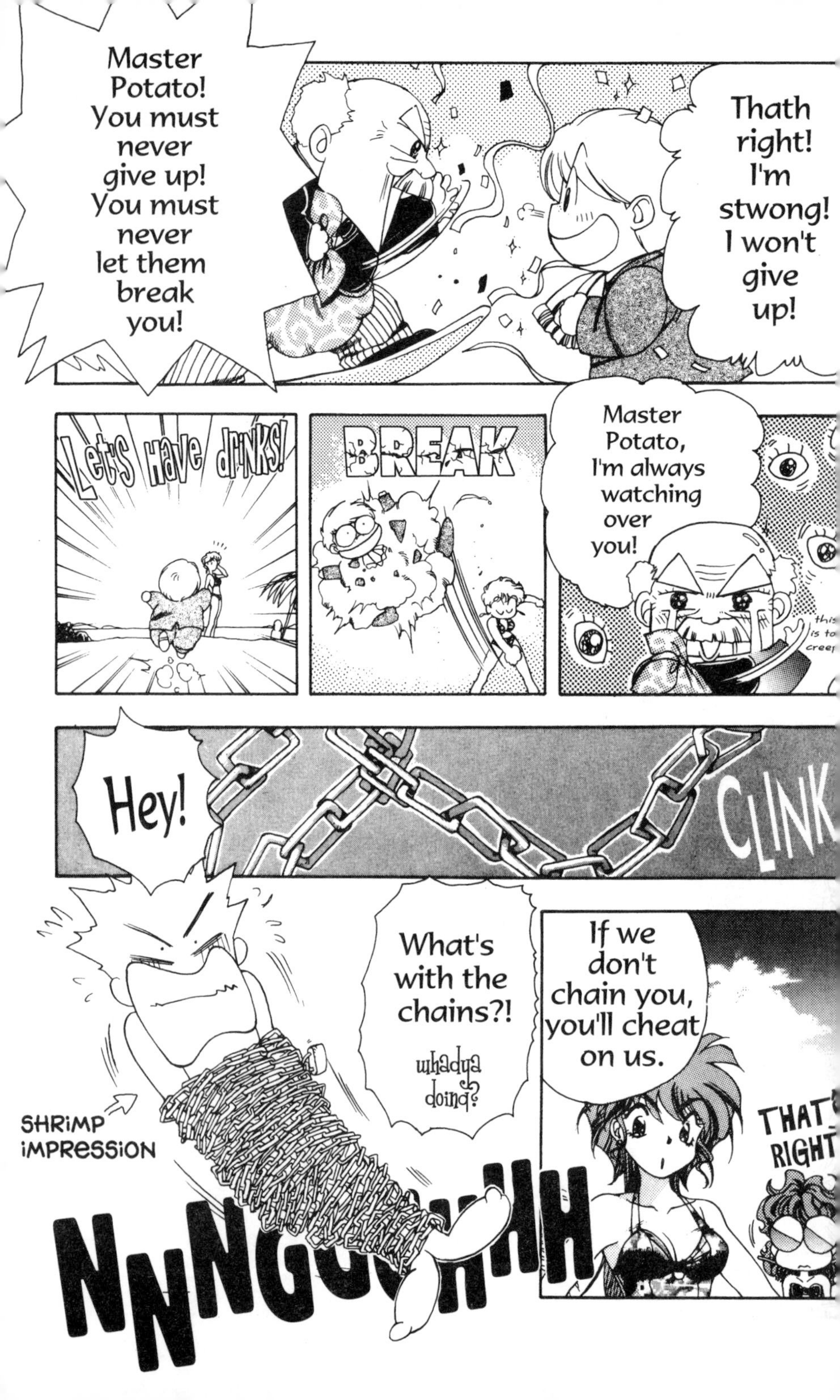
Master Potato! You must never give up! You must never let them break you!
Thath right! I'm stwong! I won't give up!
Let's have drinks!
BREAK
Master Potato, I'm always watching over you!
this is to creep
Hey!
CLINK
SHRIMP IMPRESSION
What's with the chains?!
whadya doing?
NNNGOOHHHH
If we don't chain you, you'll cheat on us.
THAT'S RIGHT

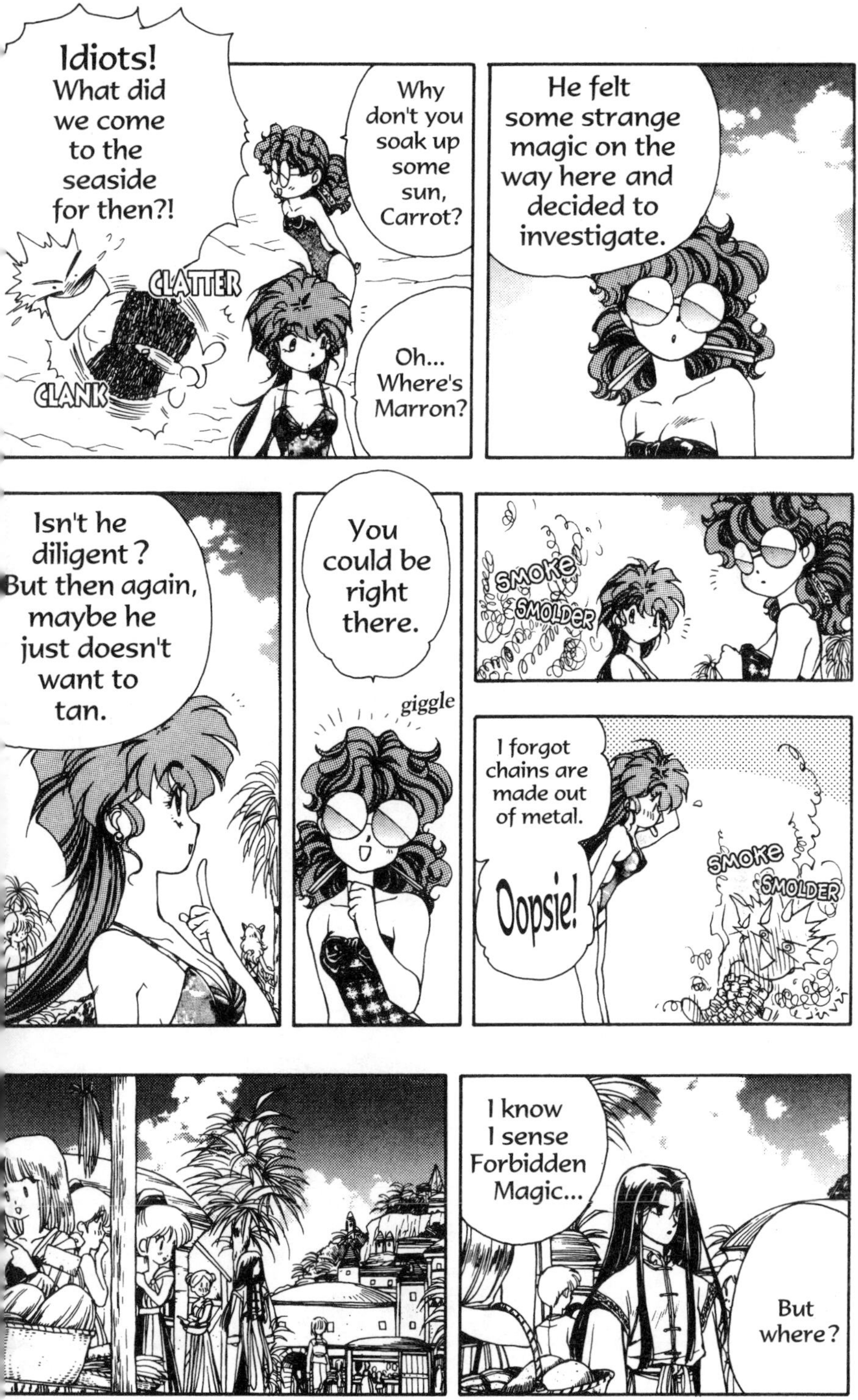
Idiots! What did we come to the seaside for then?!
CLATTER
CLANK
Why don't you soak up some sun, Carrot?
Oh... Where's Marron?
He felt some strange magic on the way here and decided to investigate.
Isn't he diligent? But then again, maybe he just doesn't want to tan.
You could be right there.
giggle
SMOKE
SMOLDER
I forgot chains are made out of metal.
Oopsie!
SMOKE
SMOLDER
I know I sense Forbidden Magic...
But where?

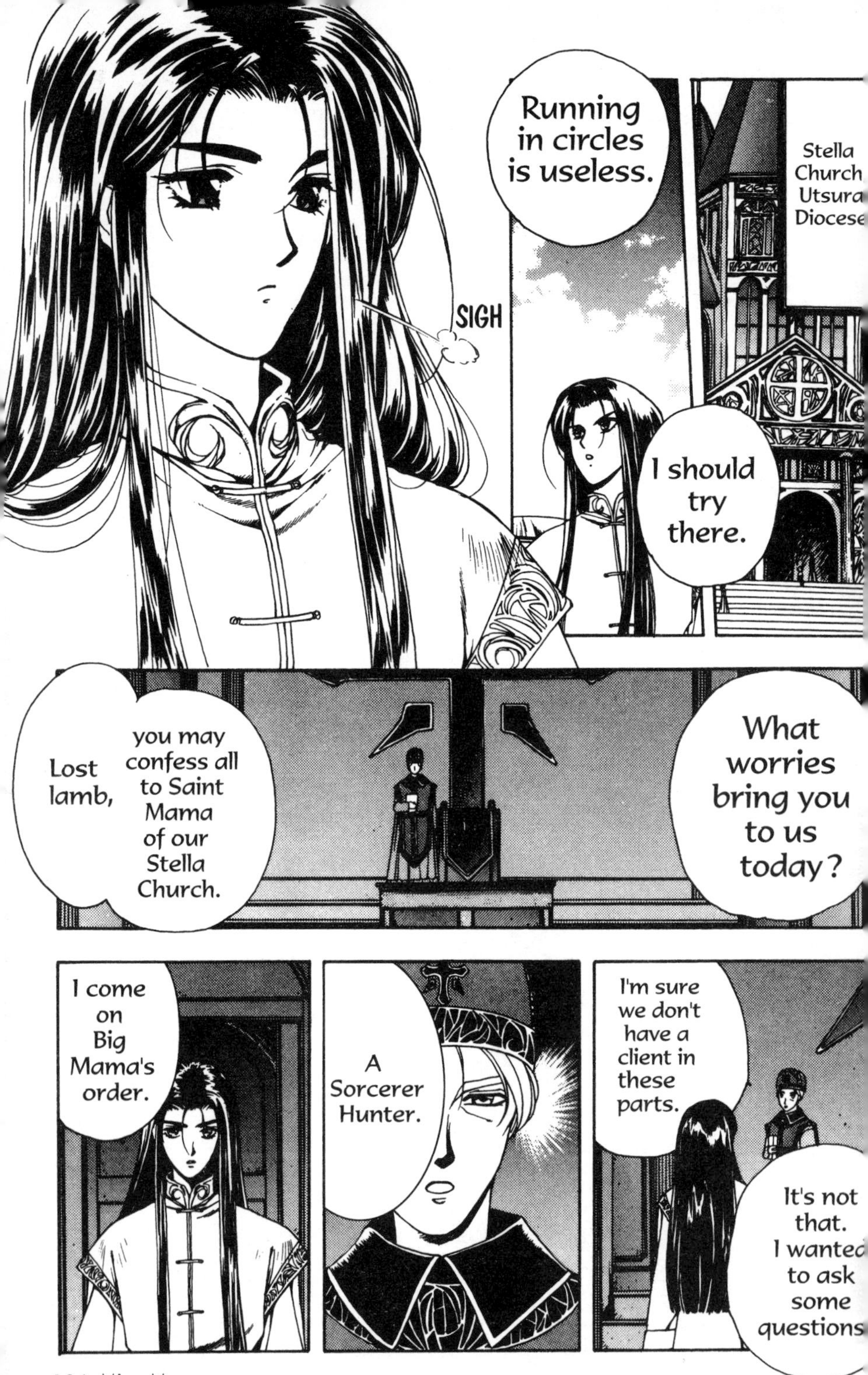
SIGH
Running in circles is useless.
Stella Church Utsura Diocese
I should try there.
Lost lamb, you may confess all to Saint Mama of our Stella Church.
What worries bring you to us today?
I come on Big Mama's order.
A Sorcerer Hunter.
I'm sure we don't have a client in these parts.
It's not that. I wanted to ask some questions.

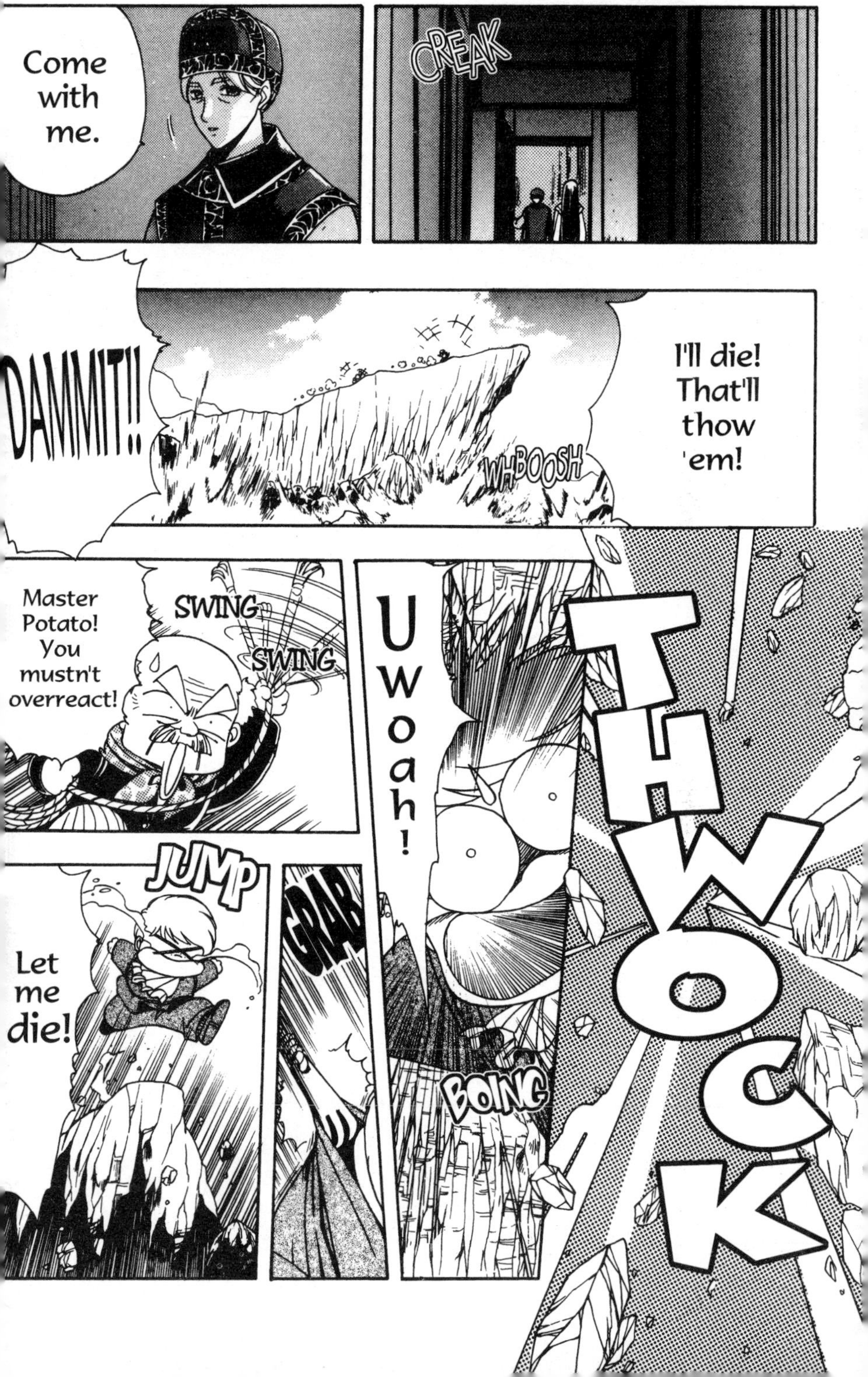
Come with me.
CREAK
DAMMIT!!
WHBOOSH
I'll die! That'll thow 'em!
Master Potato! You mustn't overreact!
SWING
SWING
Uwoah!
THWOCK
JUMP
Let me die!
GRAB
BOING

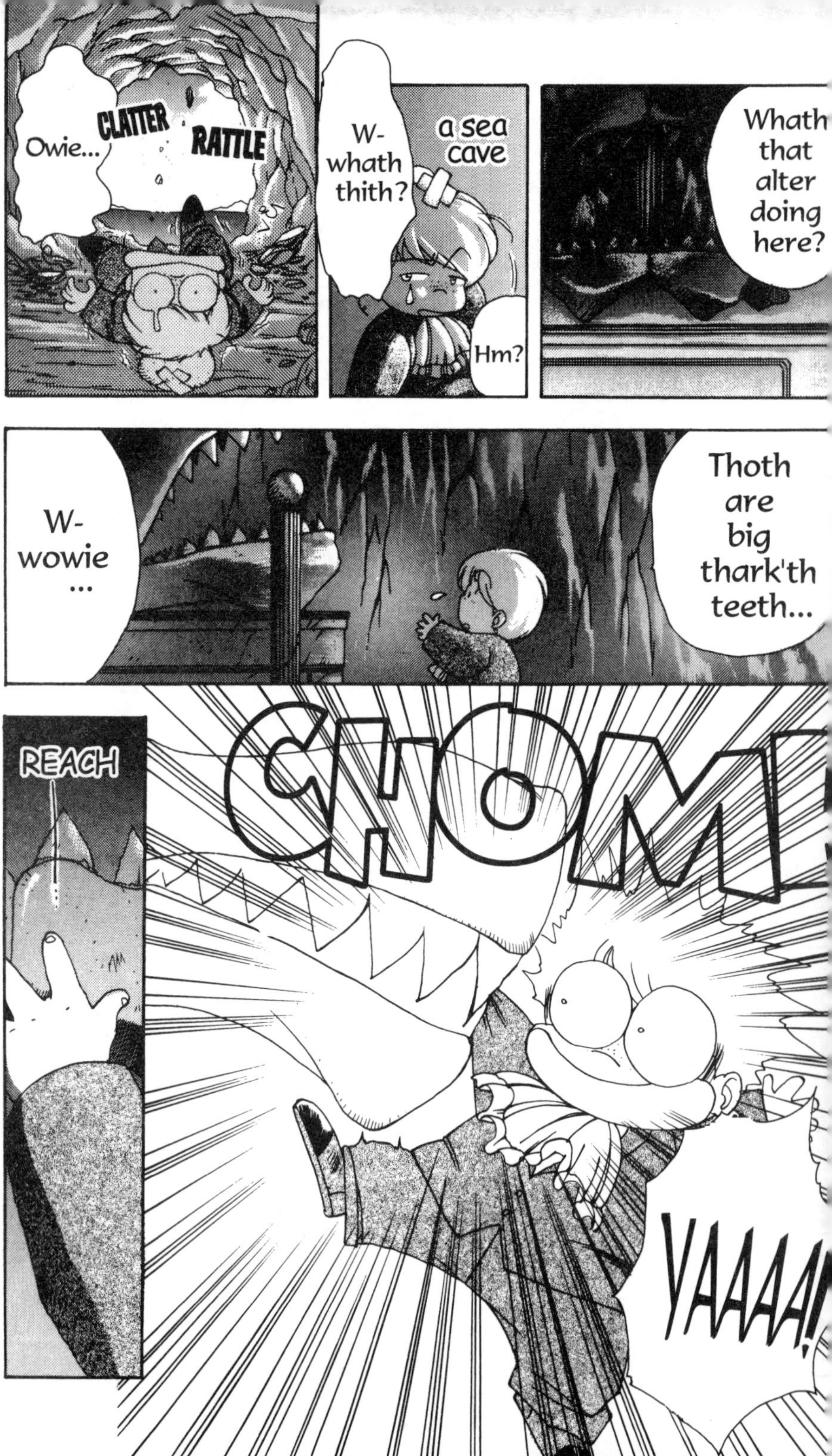

Owie...
CLATTER
RATTLE
W- whath thith?
a sea cave
Hm?
Whath that alter doing here?
W- wowie ...
Thoth are big thark'th teeth...
REACH
CHOM
YAAAA!

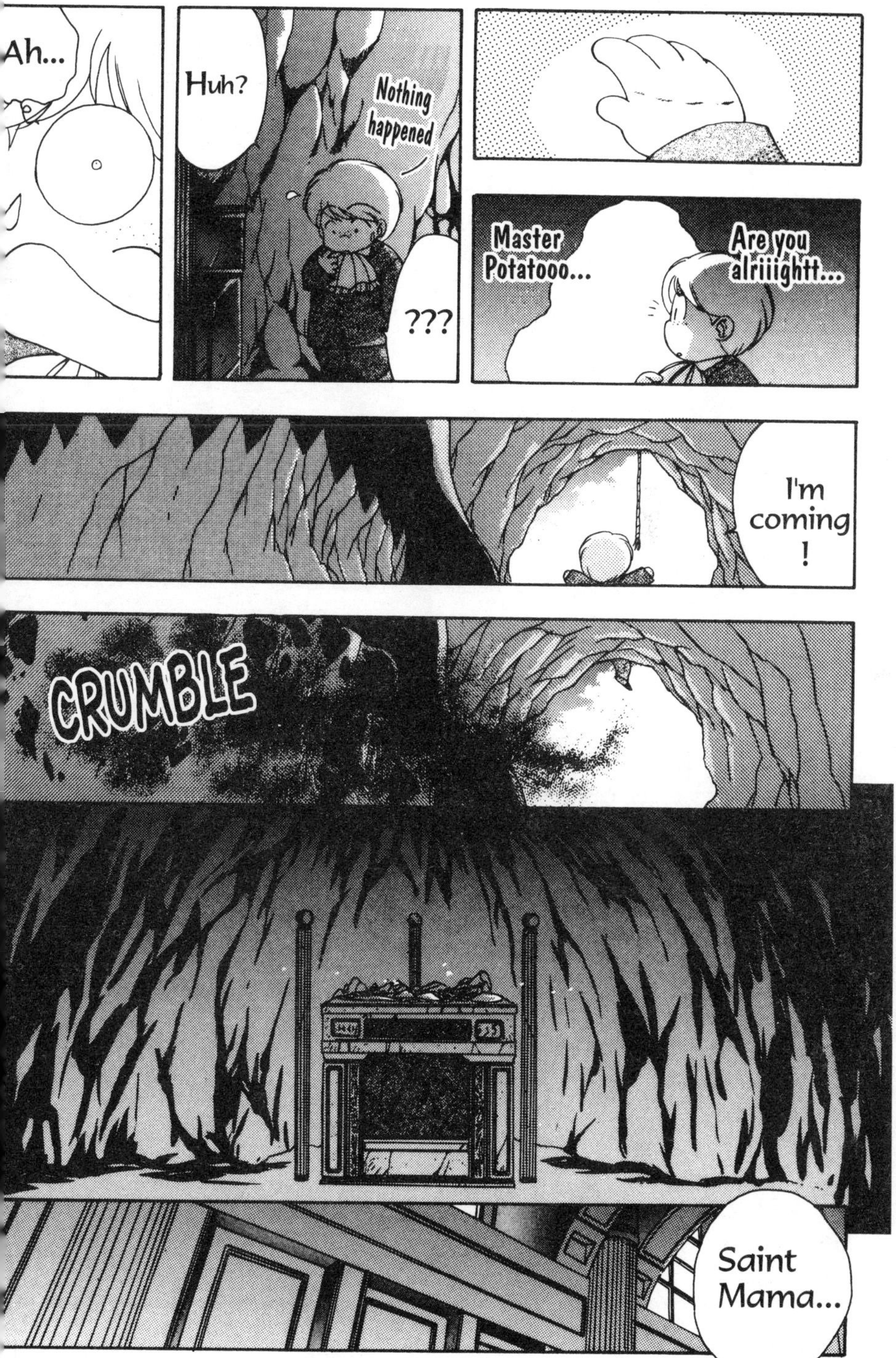
Ah...
Huh?
Nothing happened
???
Master Potatooo...
Are you alriiightt...
I'm coming !
CRUMBLE
Saint Mama...

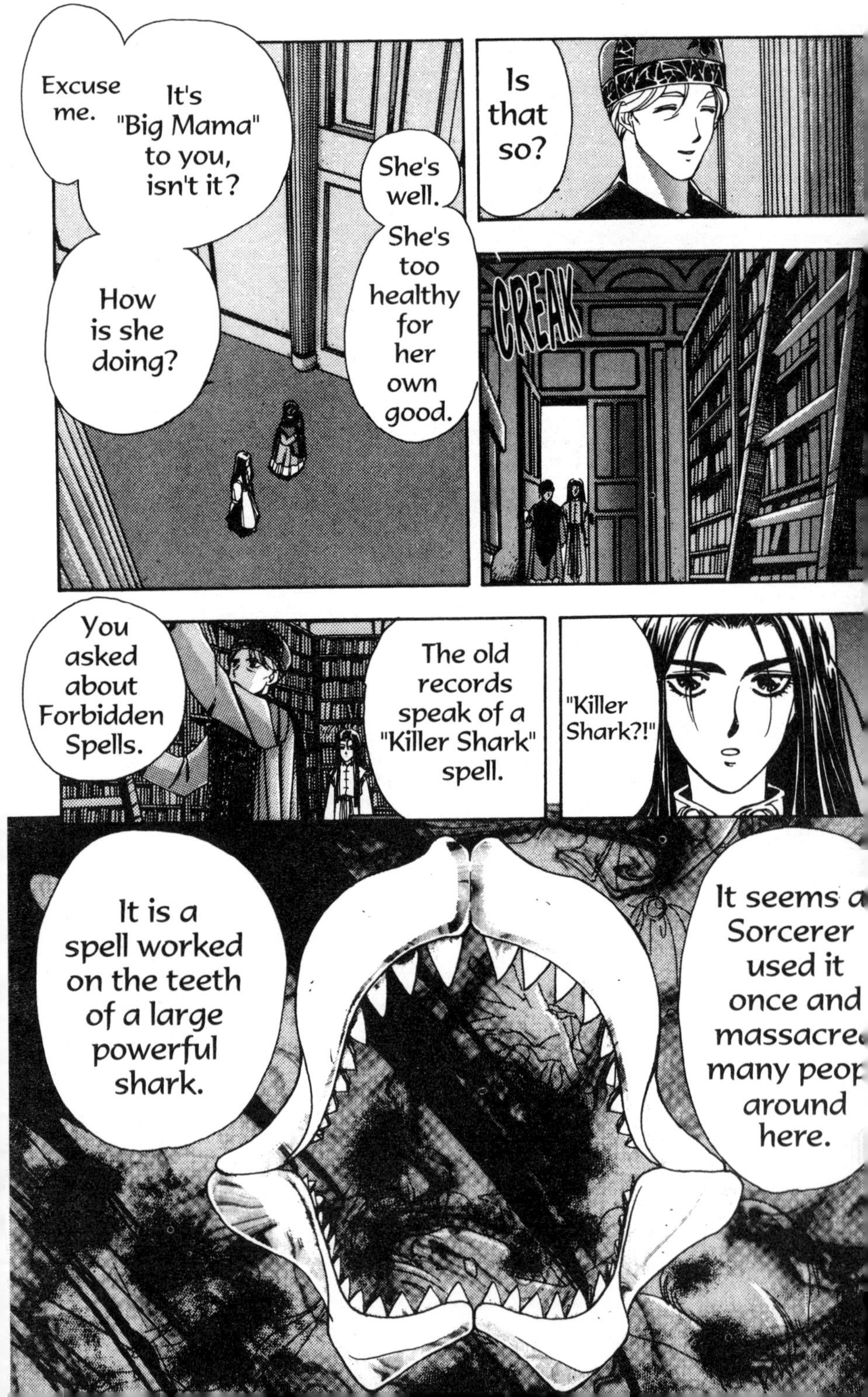
Excuse me.
It's "Big Mama" to you, isn't it?
How is she doing?
She's well.
She's too healthy for her own good.
Is that so?
CREAK
You asked about Forbidden Spells.
The old records speak of a "Killer Shark" spell.
"Killer Shark?!"
It is a spell worked on the teeth of a large powerful shark.
It seems a Sorcerer used it once and massacre many peop around here.

What's worse, it is a form of Creet Magic.

Creet Magic?

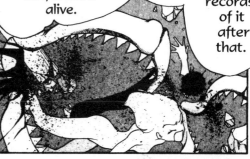

When activated by a weak magician, it gains a will of its own and rages out of control, as if it were alive.

That's why it was sealed away 200 years ago.

I'm afraid there are no records of it after that.

hat's all ight.

It's enough to know there is a Forbidden Spell in this vicinity.

But... Why would a Sorcerer Hunter be concerned with Forbidden Spells?

You wouldn't know, being on the official side...

...but we Sorcerer Hunters have two missions.

One is to punish criminal Sorcerers.

And the other...

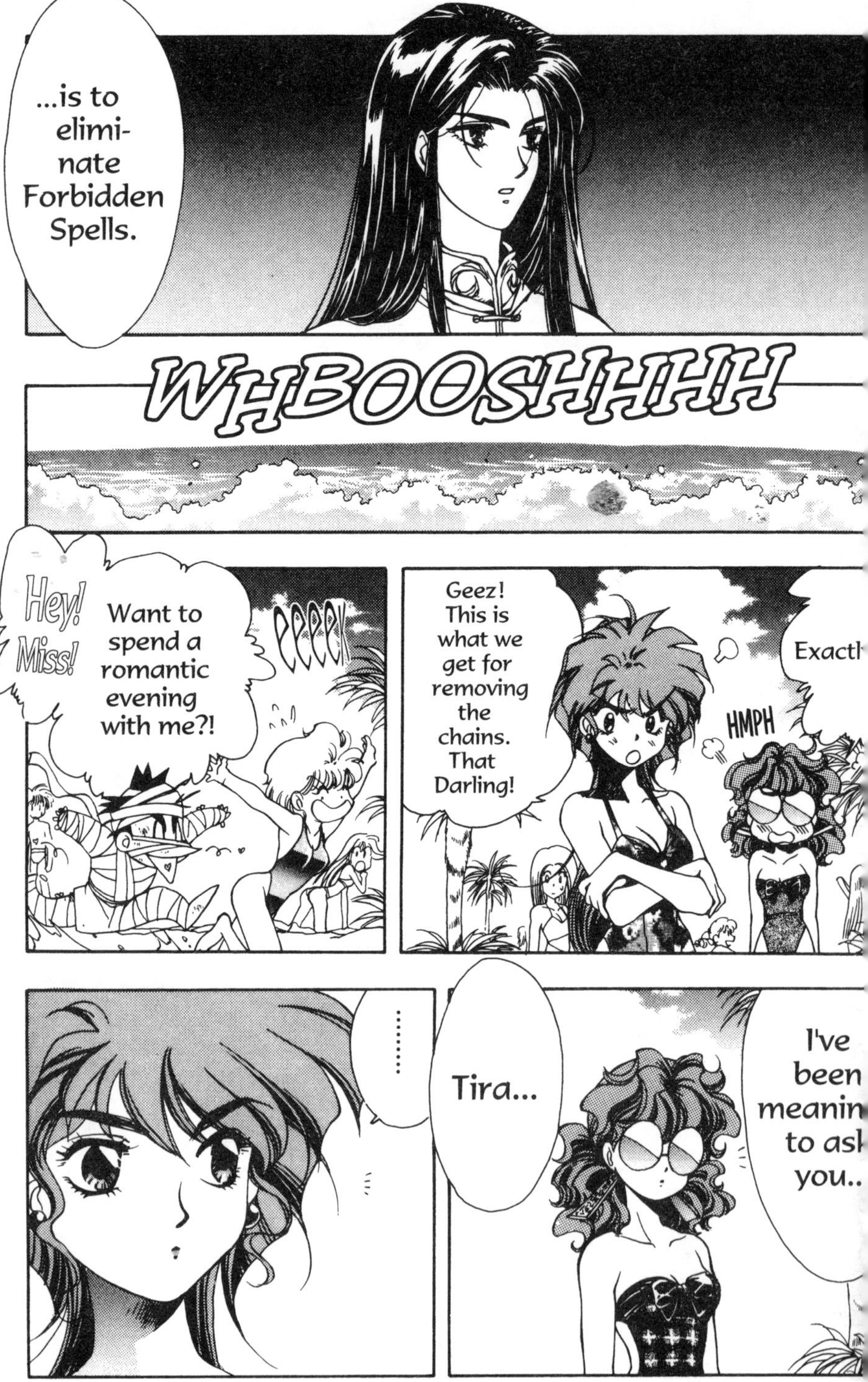

...is to elimi- nate Forbidden Spells.
WHBOOSHHHH
Hey! Miss!
Want to spend a romantic evening with me?!
eeeek
Geez! This is what we get for removing the chains. That Darling!
HMPH
Exactl
....
Tira...
I've been meanin to as you..

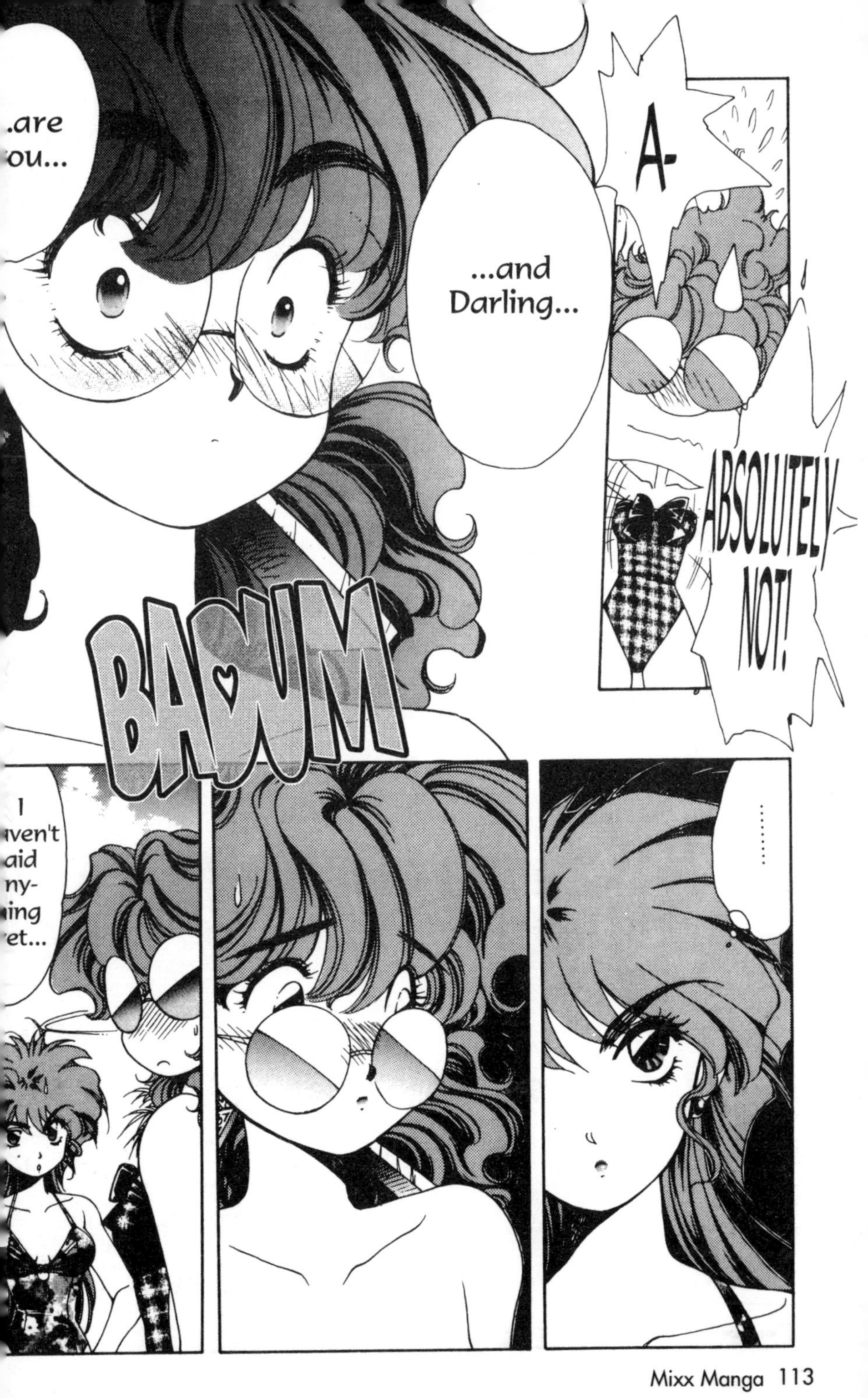
.are
ou...
...and Darling...
BADUM
A-
ABSOLUTELY NOT!
I iven't aid ny- ing et...
......

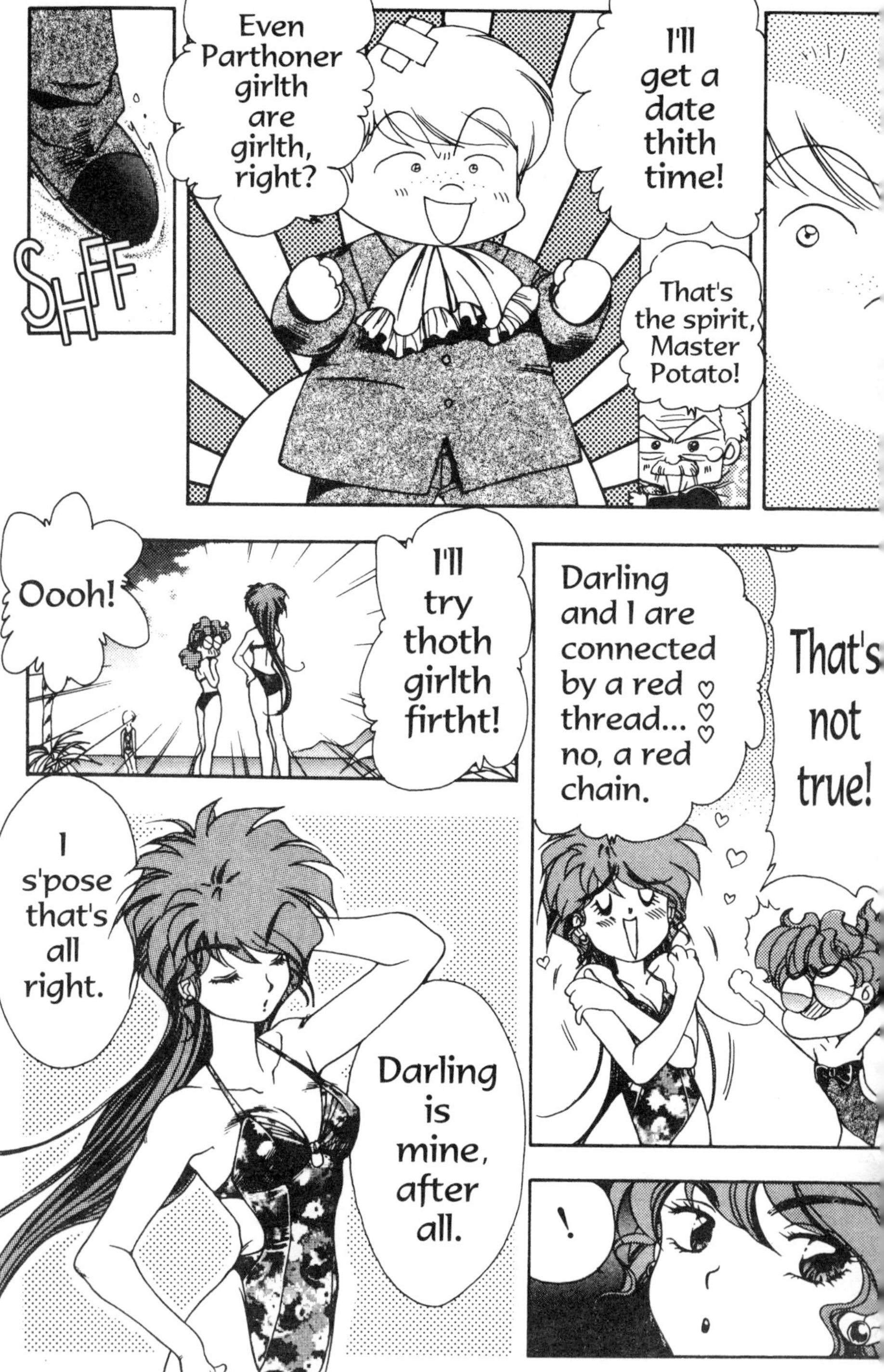
SHFF
Even Parthoner girlth are girlth, right?
I'll get a date thith time!
That's the spirit, Master Potato!
Oooh!
I'll try thoth girlth firtht!
Darling and I are connected by a red thread... ♡♡♡ no, a red chain.
That's not true!
I s'pose that's all right.
Darling is mine, after all.
!

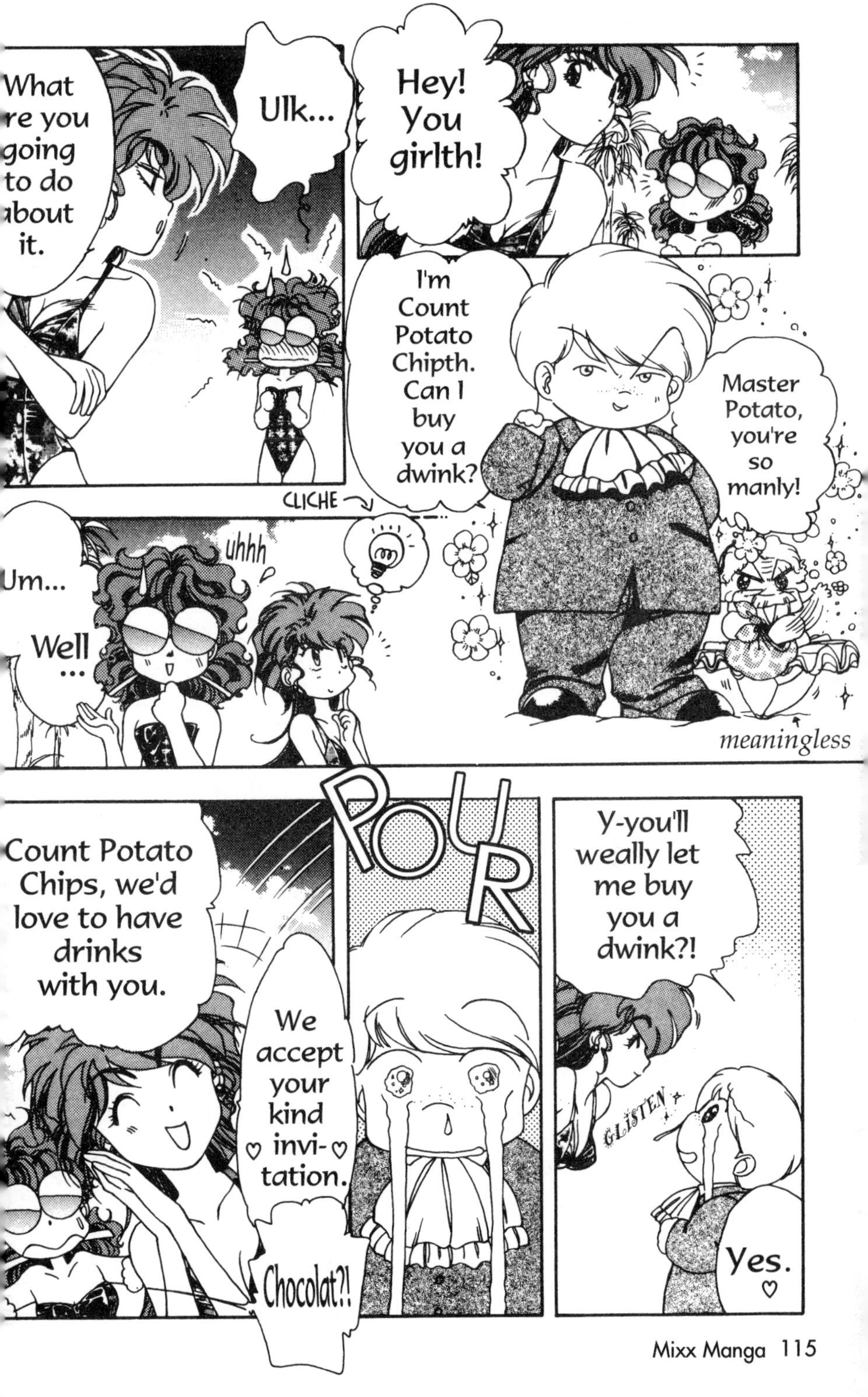

What re you going to do about it.
Ulk...
Hey! You girlth!
I'm Count Potato Chipth. Can I buy you a dwink?
Master Potato, you're so manly!
meaningless
CLICHE
Um...
Well ...
uhhh
Count Potato Chips, we'd love to have drinks with you.
We accept your kind ♡ invi- ♡ tation.
Chocolat?!
POUR
Y-you'll weally let me buy you a dwink?!
GLISTEN
Yes. ♡

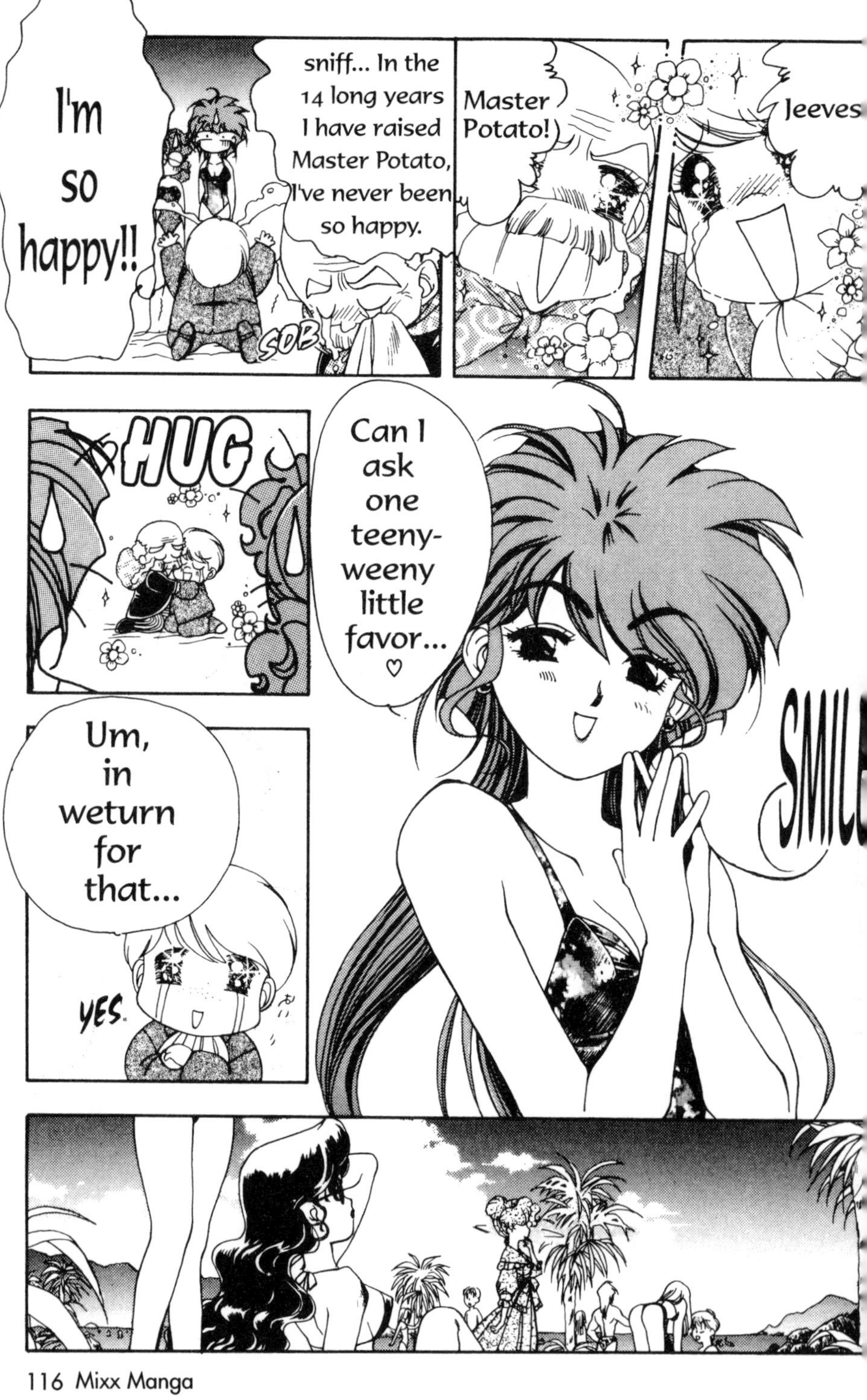
I'm so happy!!
sniff... In the 14 long years I have raised Master Potato, I've never been so happy.
SOB
Master Potato!
Jeeves
HUG
Um, in weturn for that...
YES
Can I ask one teeny-weeny little favor... ♡
SMIL

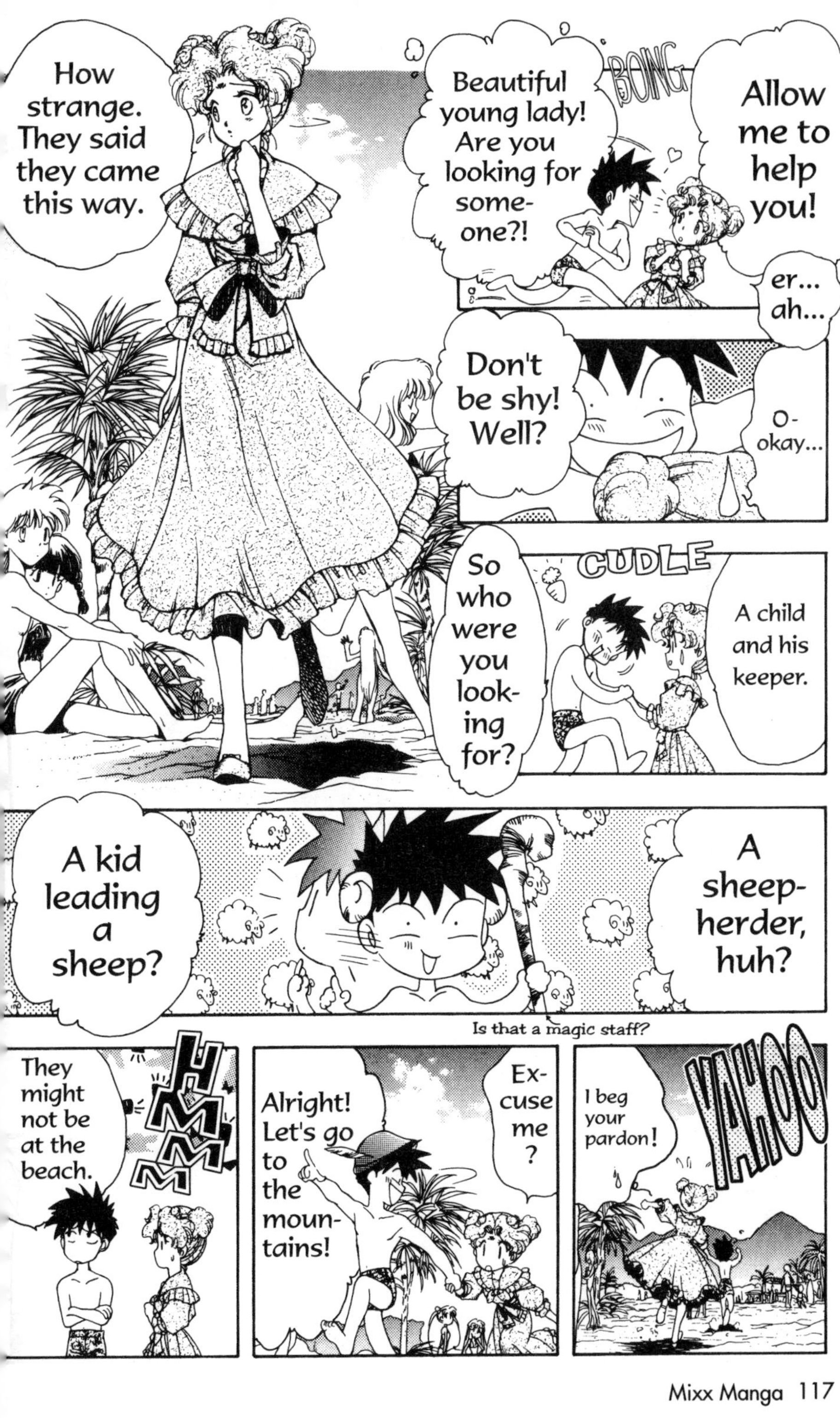
How strange. They said they came this way.
Beautiful young lady! Are you looking for some-one?!
BONG
Allow me to help you!
er... ah...
Don't be shy! Well?
O-okay...
So who were you look-ing for?
CUDLE
A child and his keeper.
A kid leading a sheep?
A sheep-herder, huh?
Is that a magic staff?
They might not be at the beach.
HMMM
Alright! Let's go to the moun-tains!
Ex-cuse me ?
I beg your pardon!
YAHOO

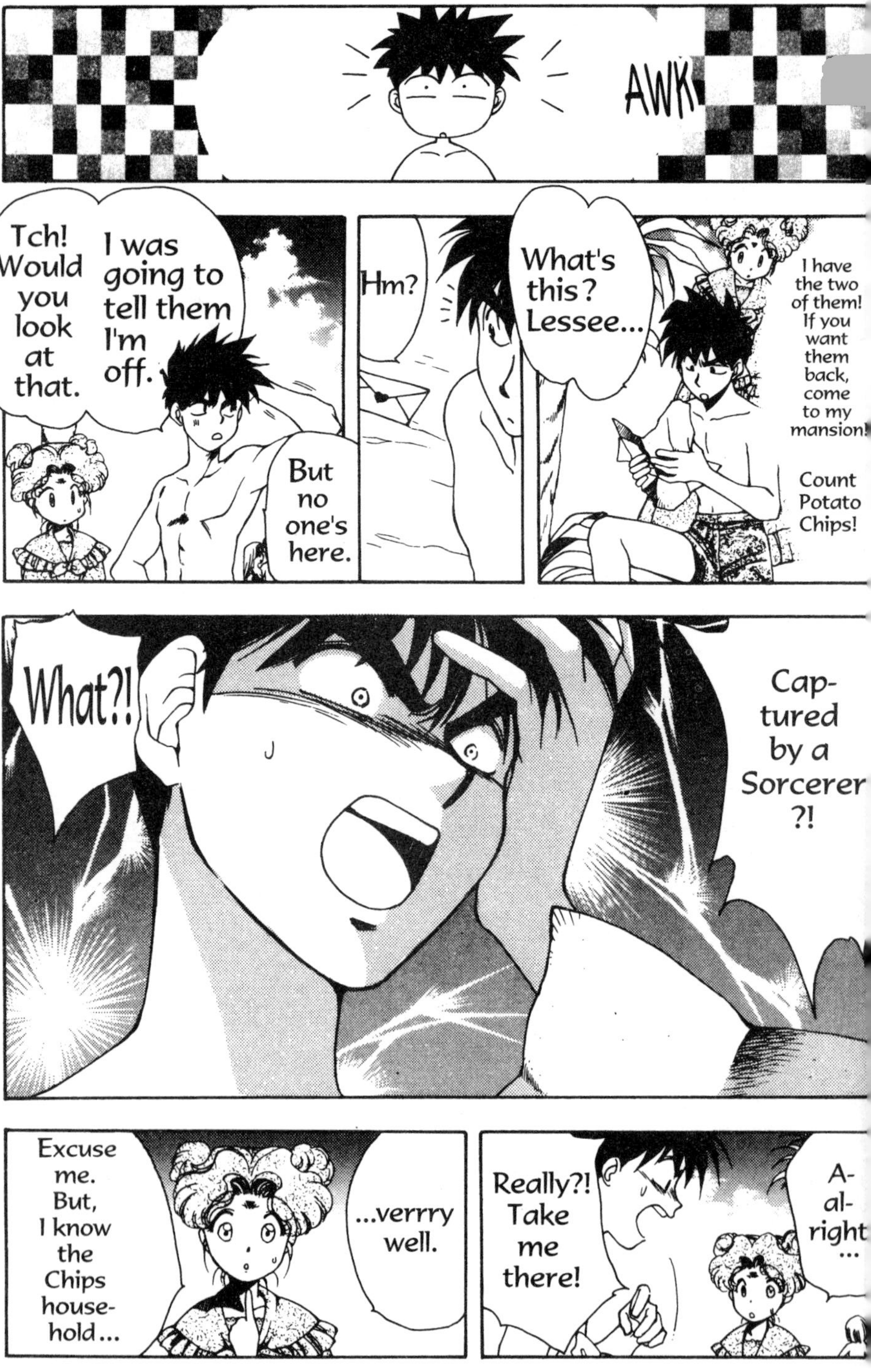
AWK
Tch! Would you look at that.
I was going to tell them I'm off.
But no one's here.
Hm?
What's this? Lessee...
I have the two of them! If you want them back, come to my mansion!
Count Potato Chips!
What?!
Cap-tured by a Sorcerer ?!
Excuse me. But, I know the Chips house-hold...
...verrry well.
Really?! Take me there!
A-al-right...

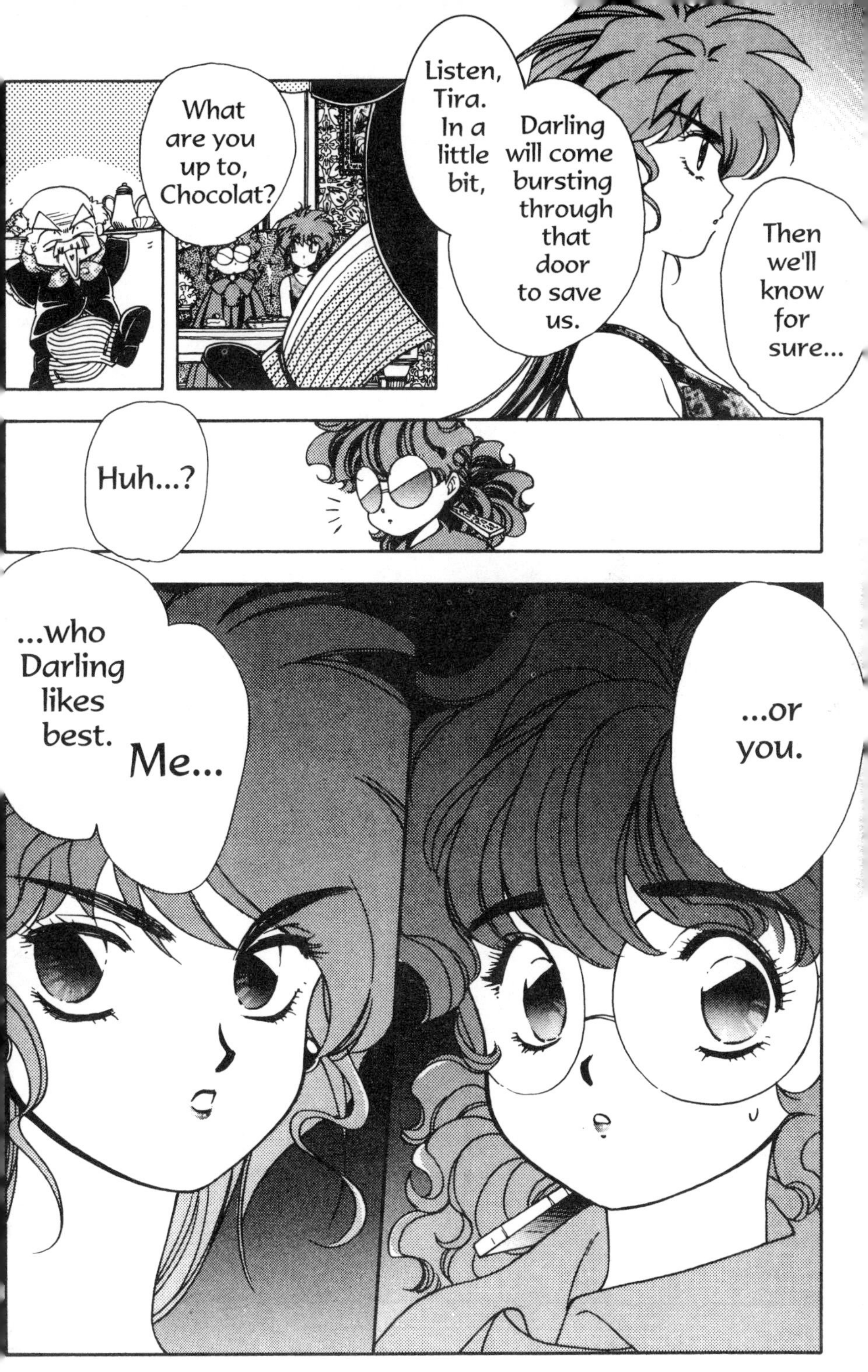
What are you up to, Chocolat?
Listen, Tira. In a little bit,
Darling will come bursting through that door to save us.
Then we'll know for sure...
Huh...?
...who Darling likes best.
Me...
...or you.

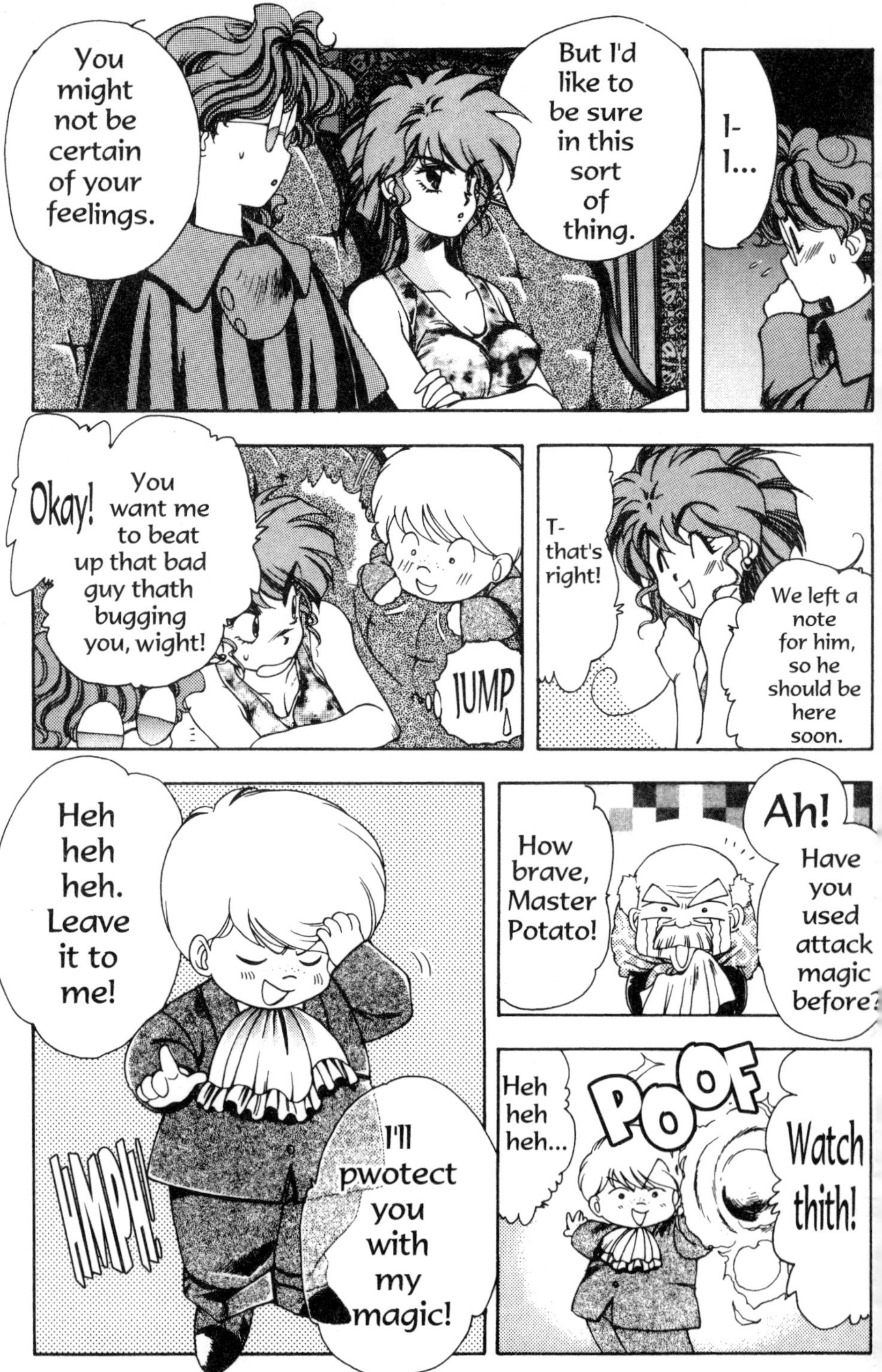
You might not be certain of your feelings.
But I'd like to be sure in this sort of thing.
I- I...
Okay!
You want me to beat up that bad guy thath bugging you, wight!
JUMP
T- that's right!
We left a note for him, so he should be here soon.
Heh heh heh. Leave it to me!
HMPH!
I'll pwotect you with my magic!
How brave, Master Potato!
Ah!
Have you used attack magic before?
Heh heh heh...
POOF
Watch thith!

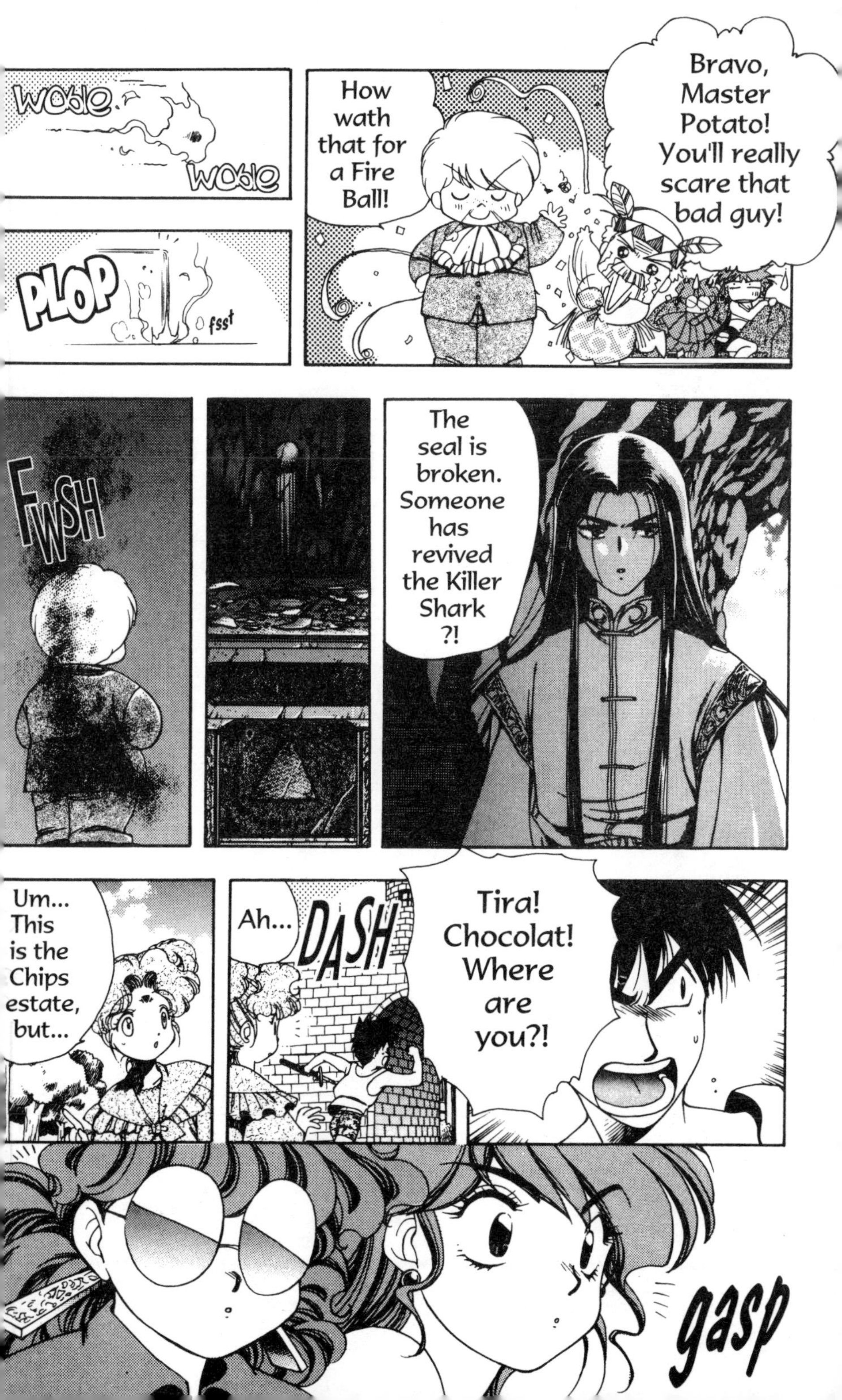
WOBLE
WOBLE
PLOP
fsst
How wath that for a Fire Ball!
Bravo, Master Potato! You'll really scare that bad guy!
FWSH
The seal is broken. Someone has revived the Killer Shark ?!
Um... This is the Chips estate, but...
Ah...
DASH
Tira! Chocolat! Where are you?!
gasp

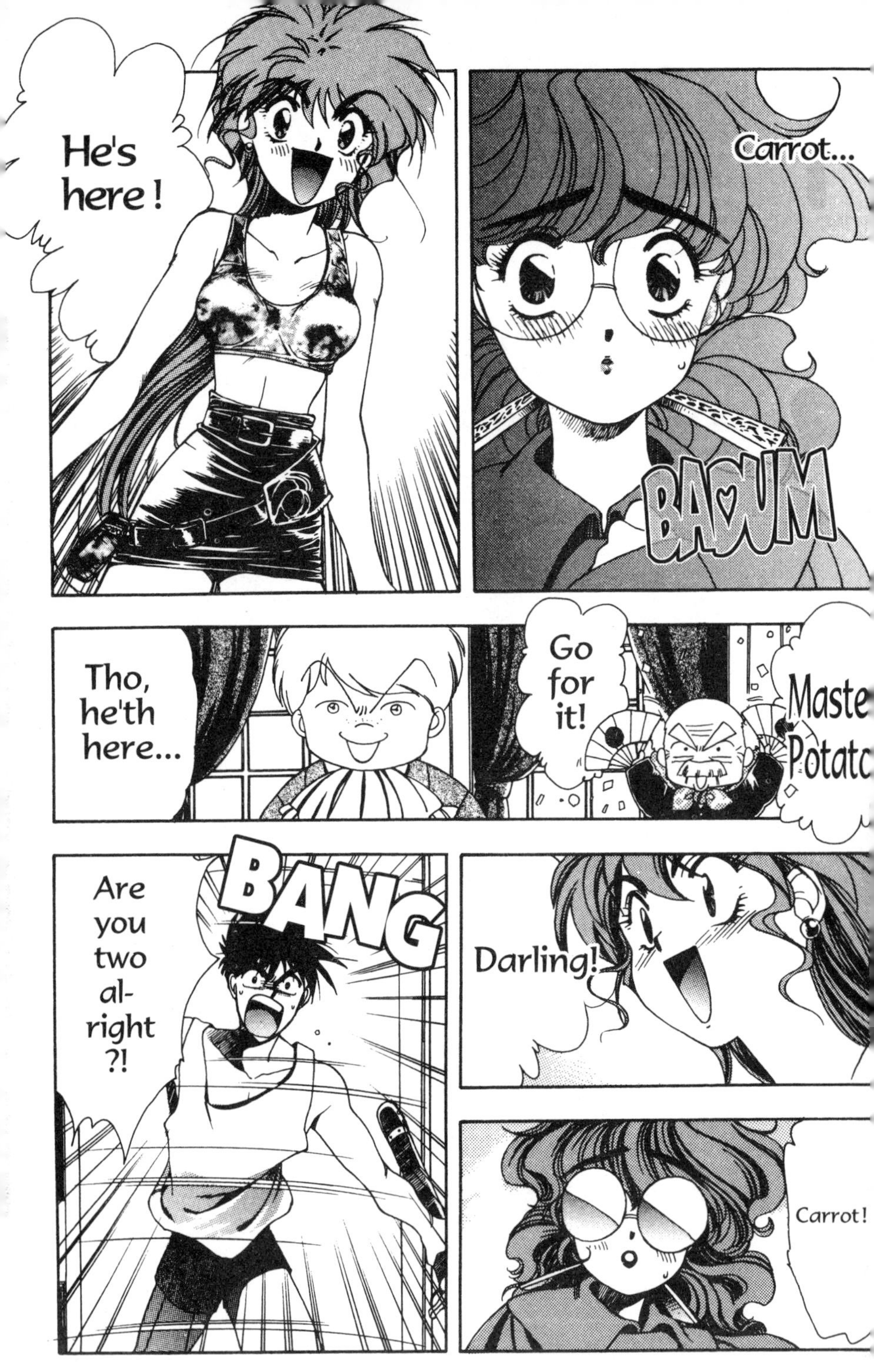

He's here!
Carrot...
BADUM
Tho, he'th here...
Go for it!
Maste
Potatc
BANG
Are you two al-right?!
Darling!
Carrot!

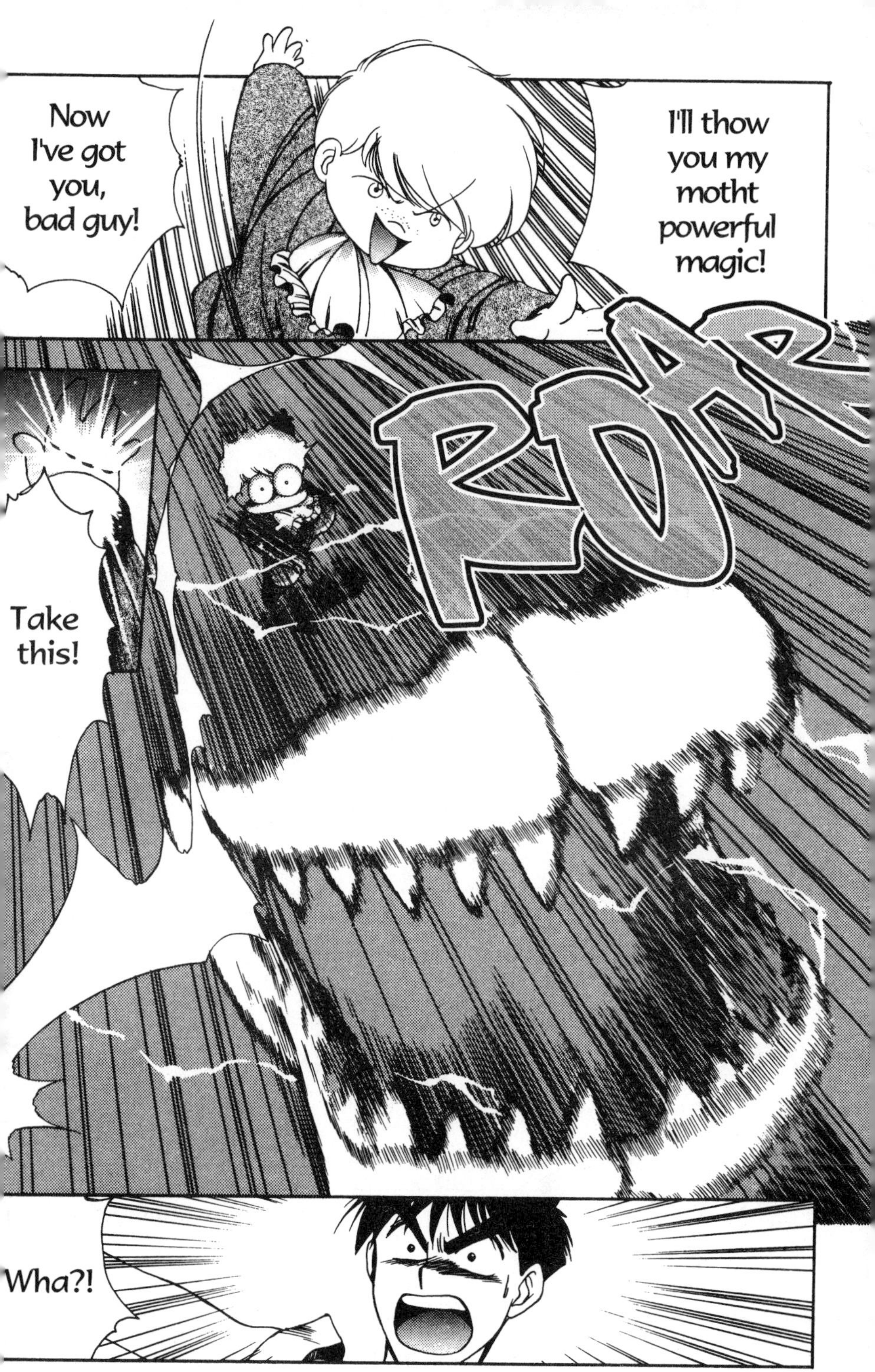
Now I've got you, bad guy!
I'll thow you my motht powerful magic!
ROAR
Take this!
Wha?!

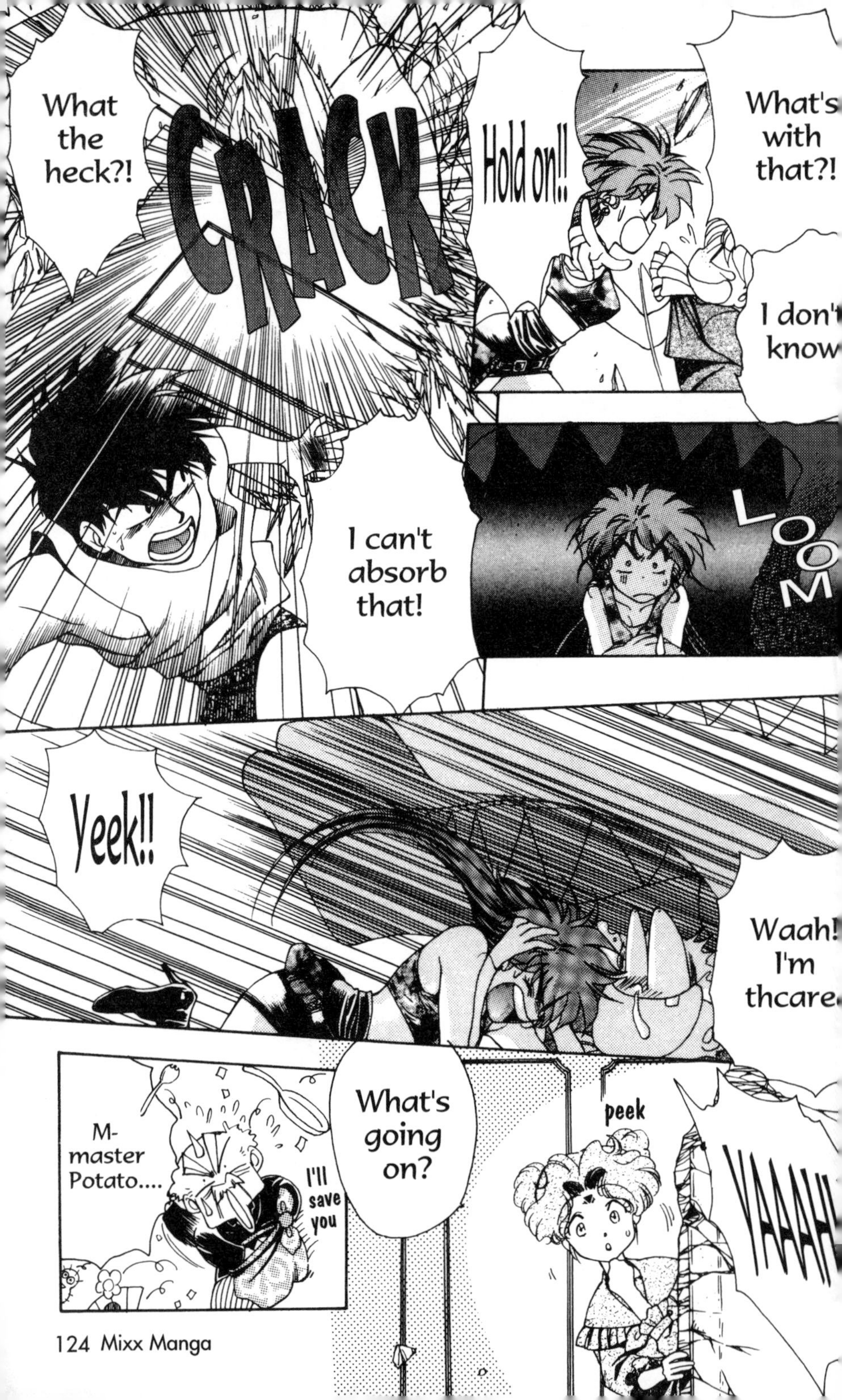

What the heck?!
CRACK
Hold on!!
What's with that?!
I don't know
I can't absorb that!
LOOOM
Yeek!!
Waah! I'm thcare
M-master Potato....
I'll save you
What's going on?
peek
YAAAH

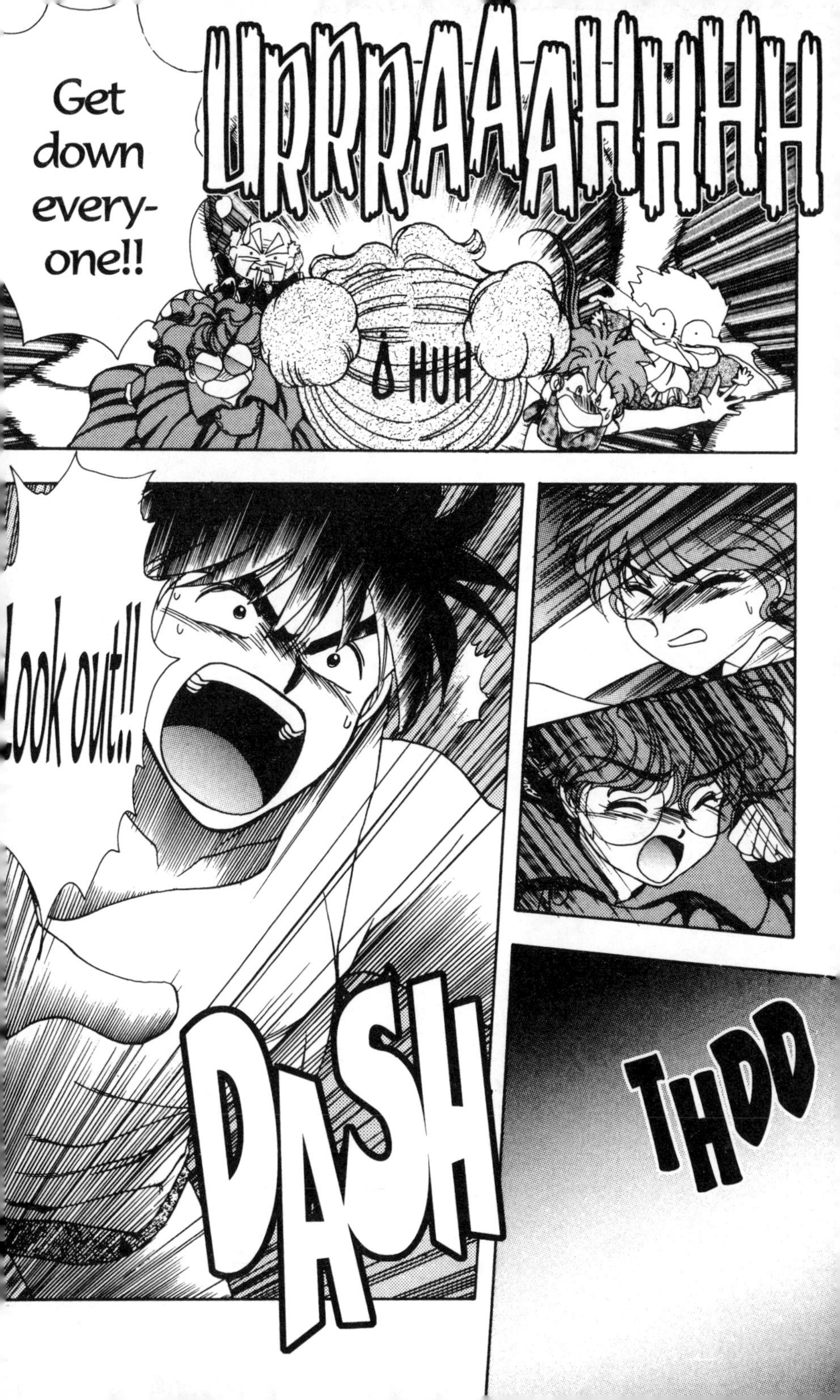
Get down every-one!!
URRRAAAHHHH
HUH
Look out!!
DASH
THDD

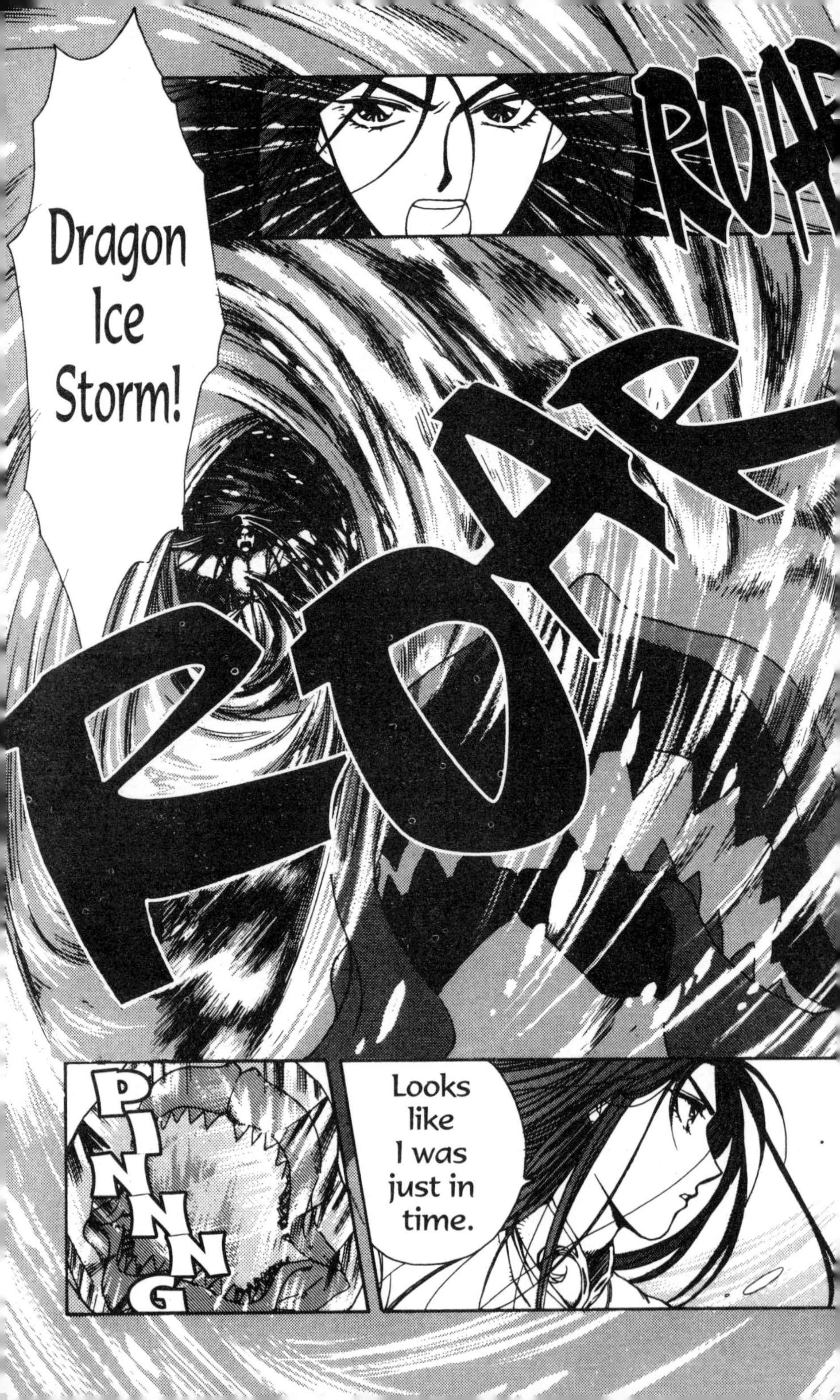
Dragon Ice Storm!
ROAR
ROAR
PINNNG
Looks like I was just in time.

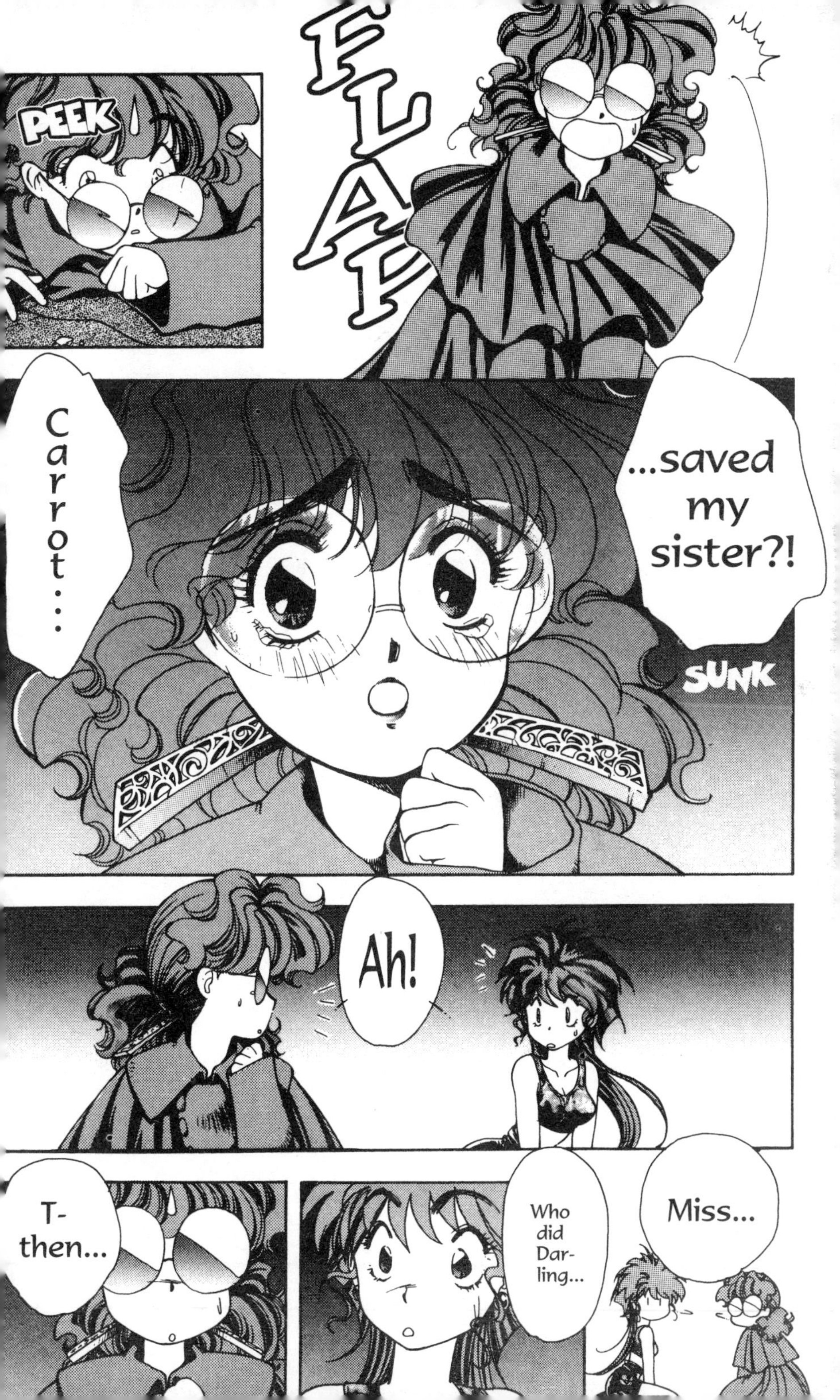
PEEK
FLAP
Carrot...
...saved my sister?!
SUNK
Ah!
T-then...
Who did Dar-ling...
Miss...

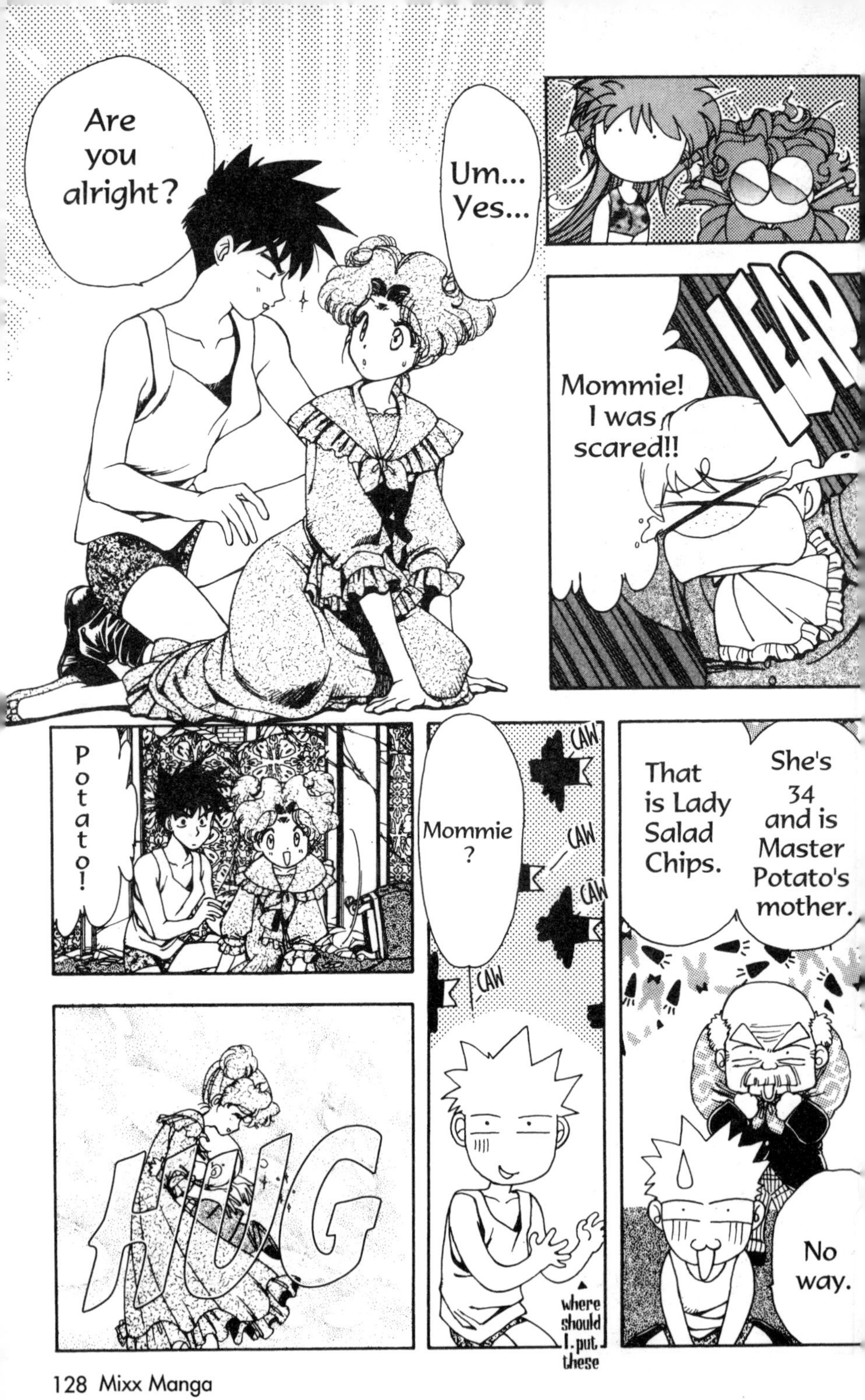

Are you alright?
Um... Yes...
LEAP
Mommie! I was scared!!
Potato!
HUG
Mommie?
CAW
CAW
CAW
CAW
where should I put these
That is Lady Salad Chips.
She's 34 and is Master Potato's mother.
No way.

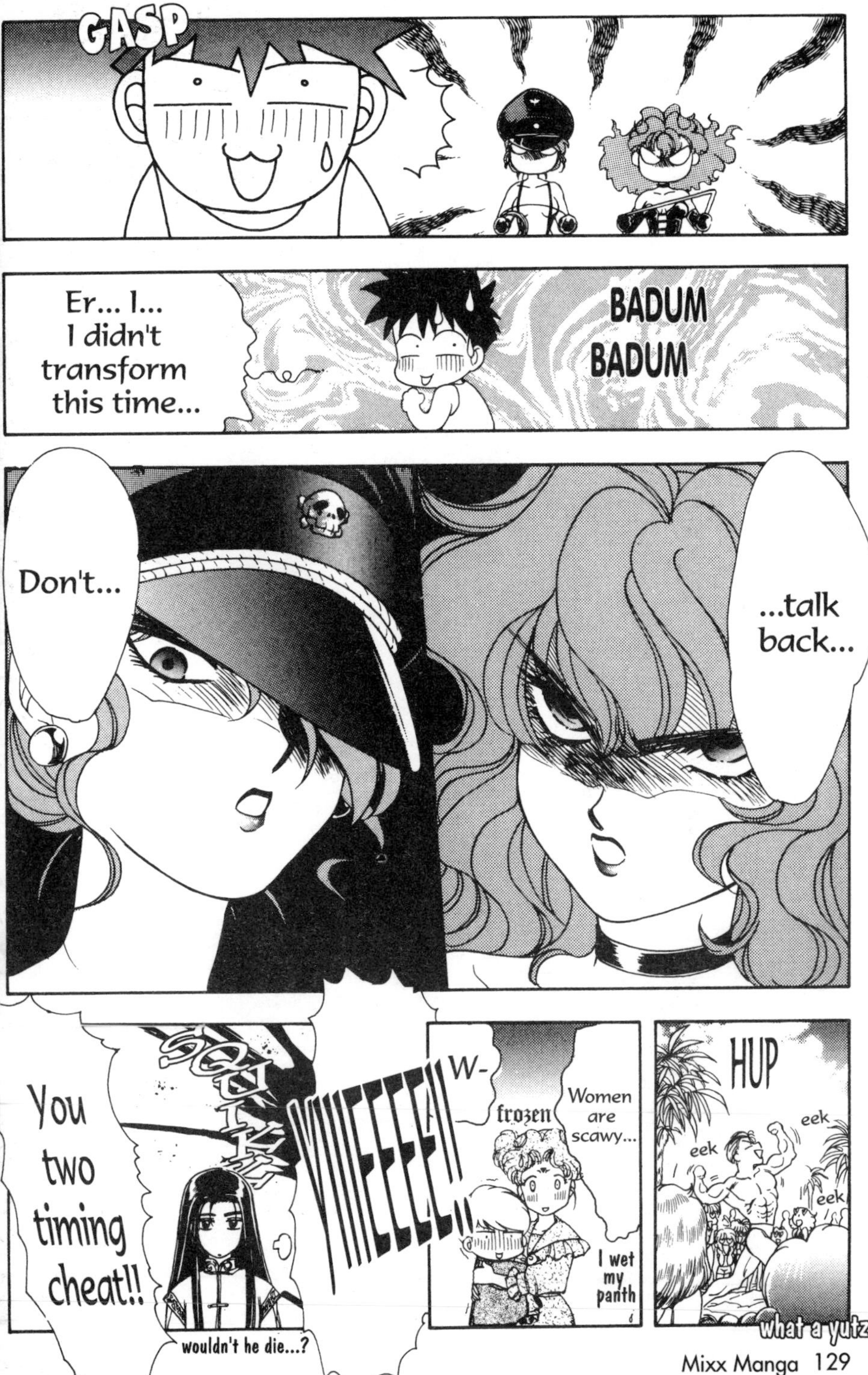
GASP
Er... I...
I didn't
transform
this time...
BADUM
BADUM
Don't...
...talk
back...
You
two
timing
cheat!!
wouldn't he die...?
W-
frozen
Women
are
scawy...
I wet
my
panth
HUP
eek
eek
eek
what a yutz

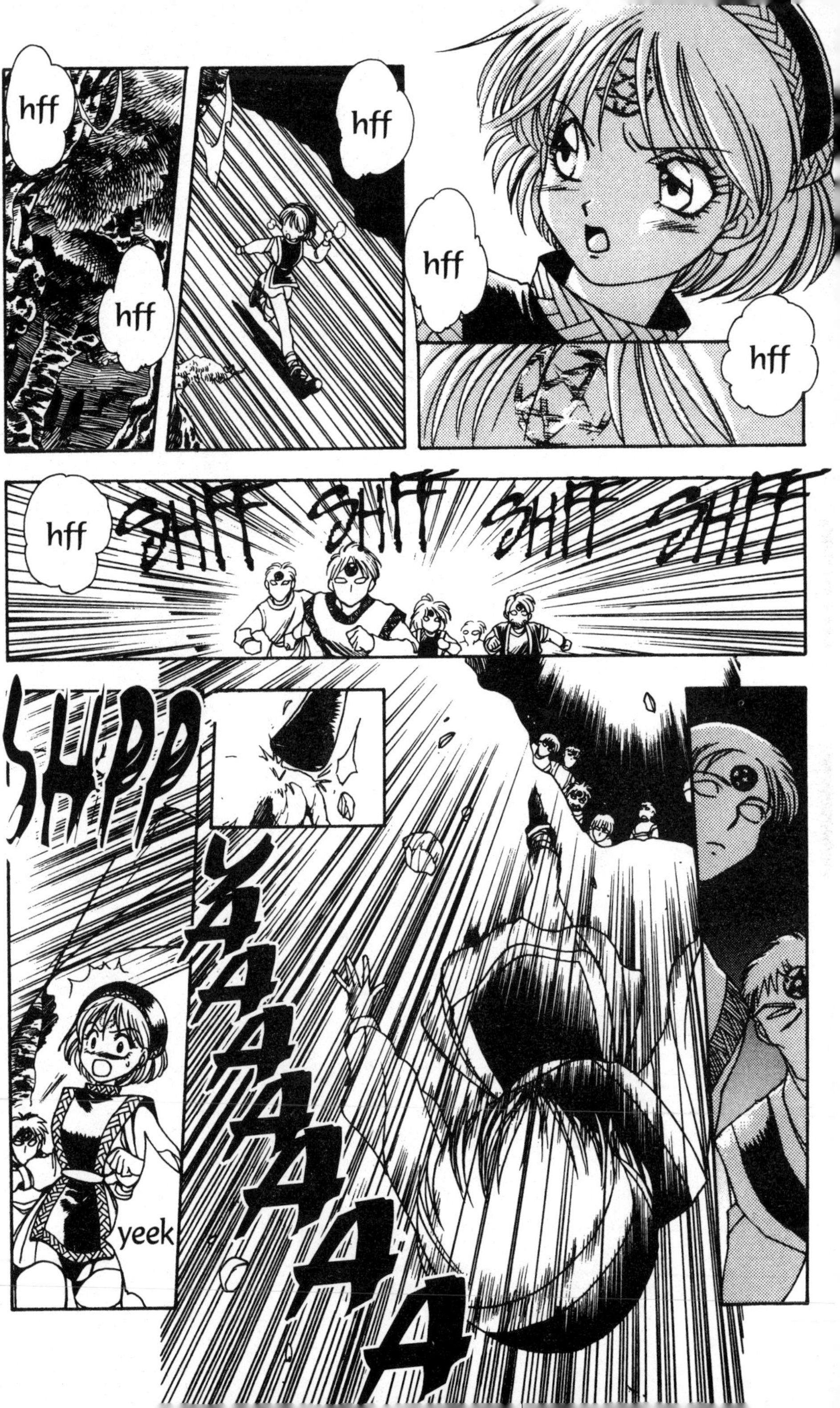
hff
hff
hff
hff
hff
hff
SHFF SHFF SHFF SHFF
SHPP
yeek

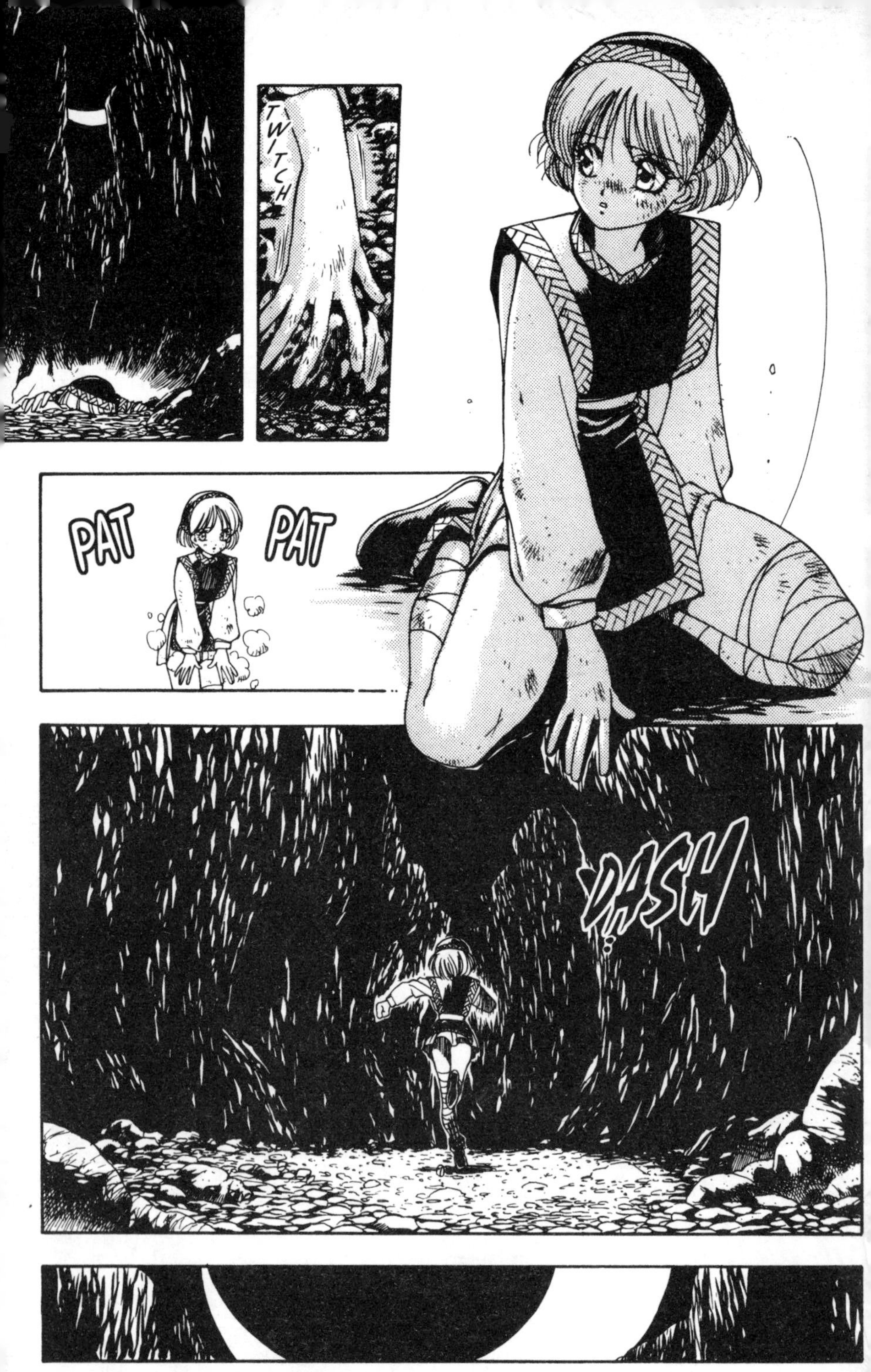
TWITCH
PAT
PAT
DASH

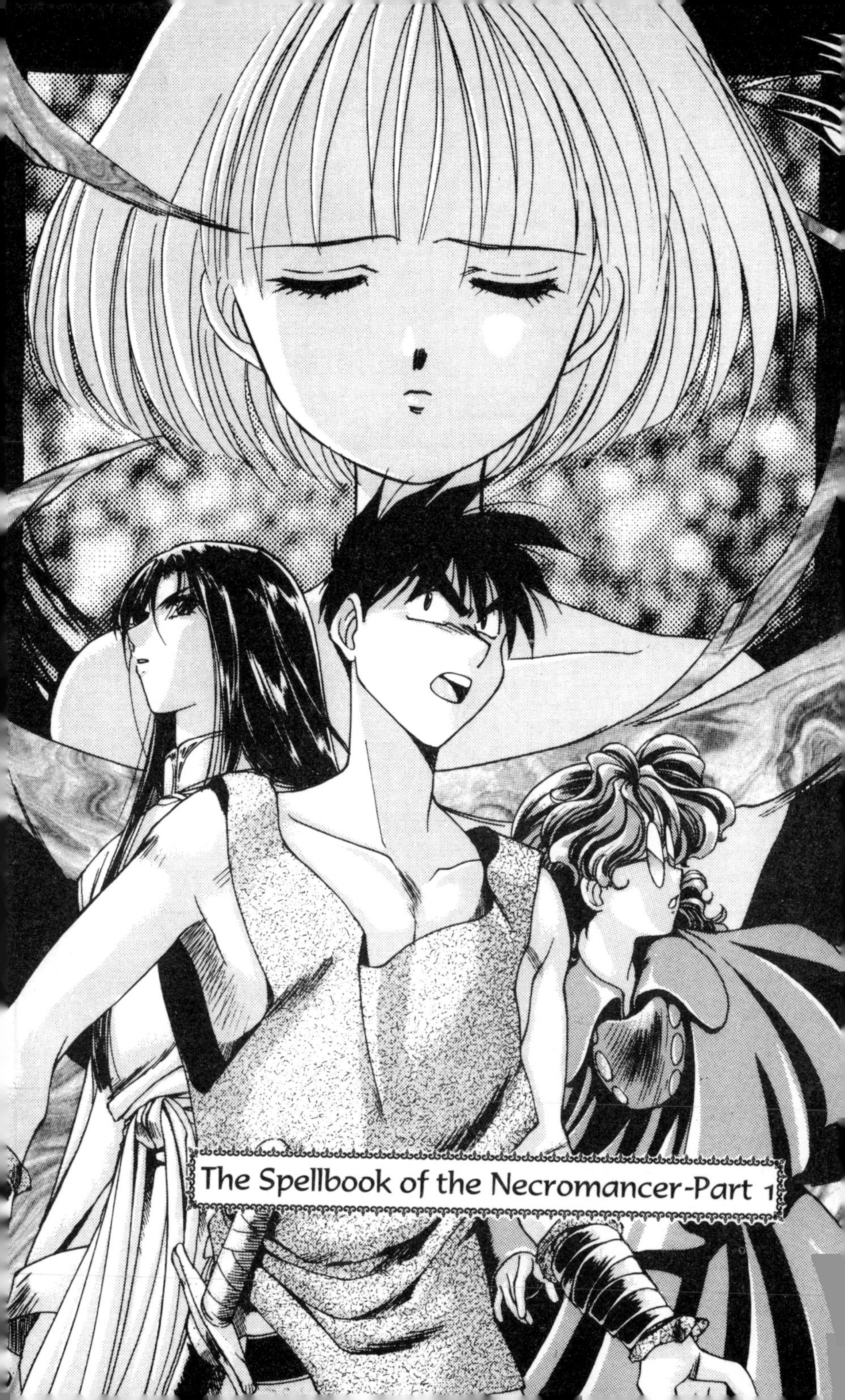
The Spellbook of the Necromancer-Part 1

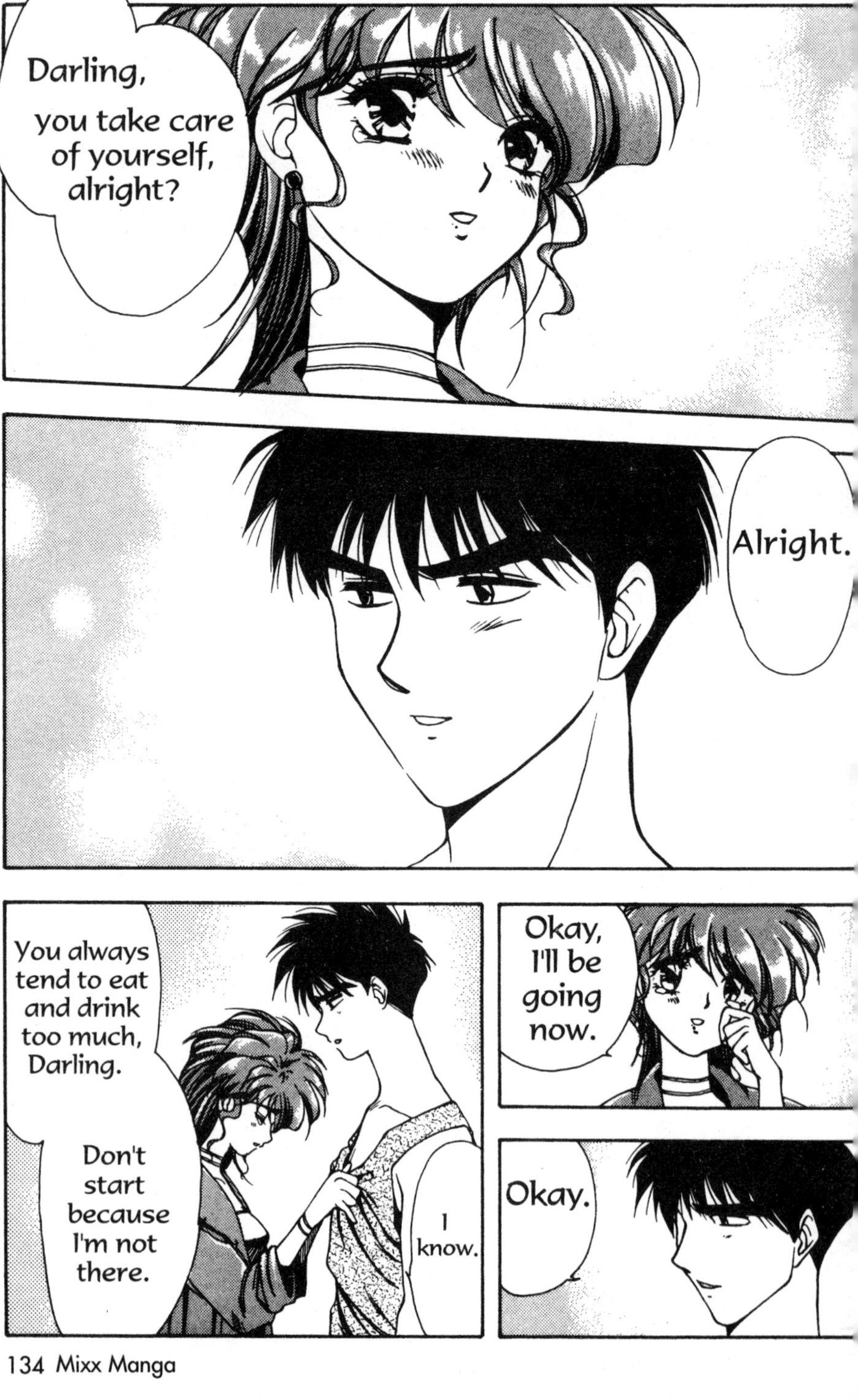
Darling, you take care of yourself, alright?
Alright.
You always tend to eat and drink too much, Darling.
Don't start because I'm not there.
I know.
Okay, I'll be going now.
Okay.

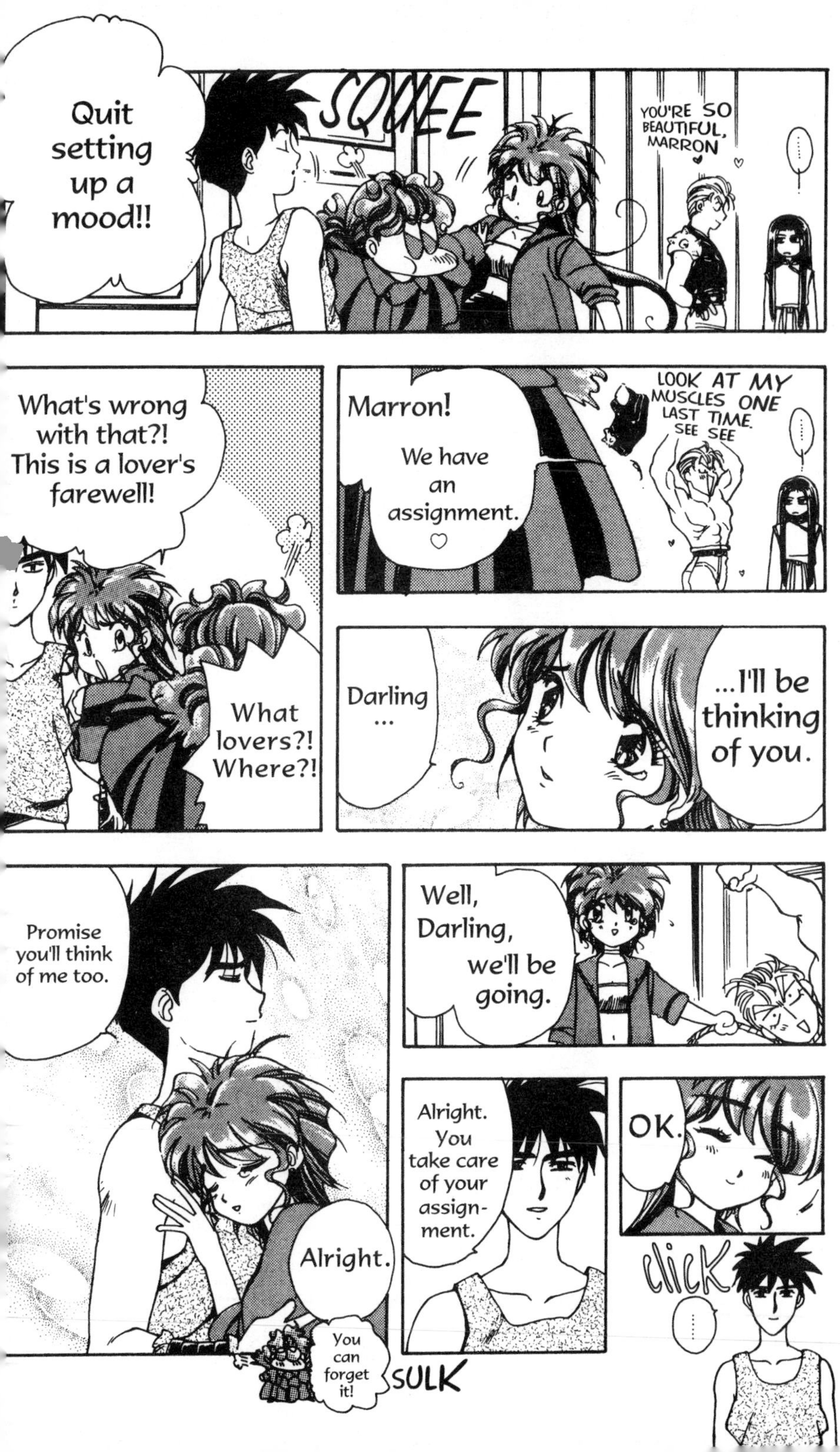
Quit setting up a mood!!
SQUEE
YOU'RE SO BEAUTIFUL, MARRON
......
What's wrong with that?! This is a lover's farewell!
What lovers?! Where?!
Marron!
We have an assignment.
LOOK AT MY MUSCLES ONE LAST TIME. SEE SEE
......
Darling ...
...I'll be thinking of you.
Promise you'll think of me too.
Alright.
You can forget it!
SULK
Well, Darling, we'll be going.
Alright. You take care of your assign-ment.
OK.
click
......

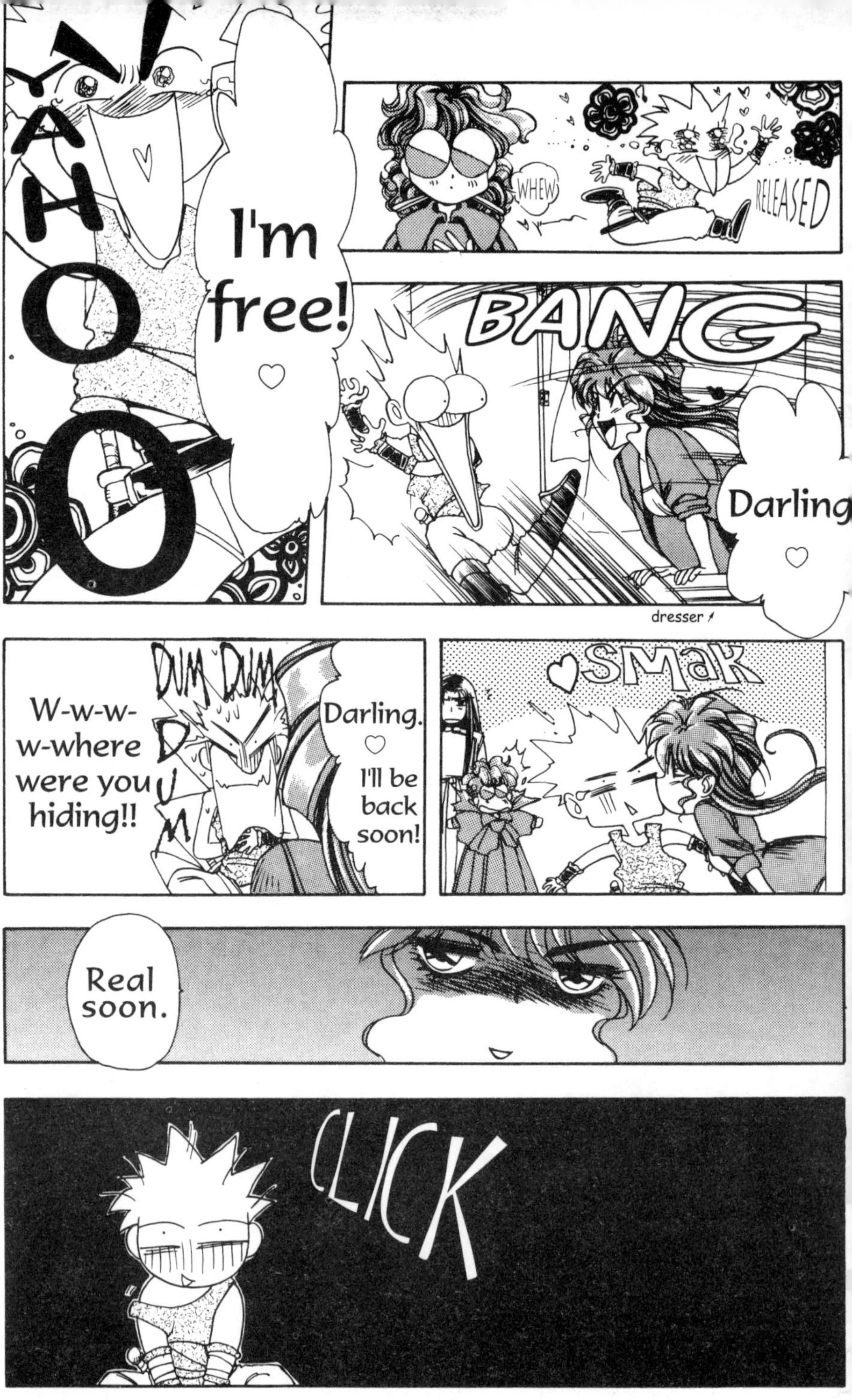
YAHOOO
I'm free!
WHEW
RELEASED
BANG
Darling
dresser
DUM DUM DUM
W-w-w-w-where were you hiding!!
Darling.
I'll be back soon!
SMAK
Real soon.
CLICK

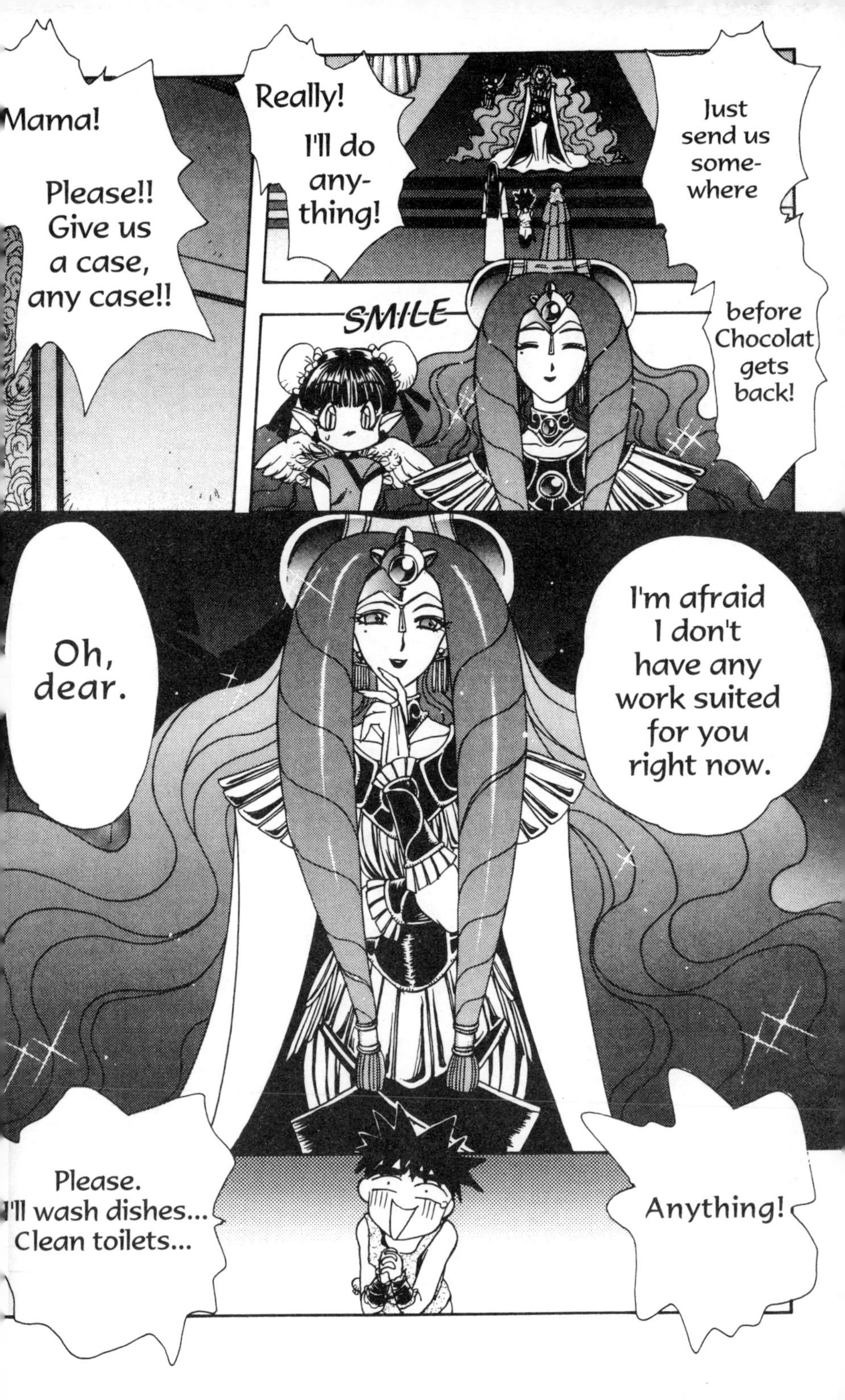
Mama!
Please!! Give us a case, any case!!
Really!
I'll do any-thing!
Just send us some-where
SMILE
before Chocolat gets back!
Oh, dear.
I'm afraid I don't have any work suited for you right now.
Please. I'll wash dishes... Clean toilets...
Anything!

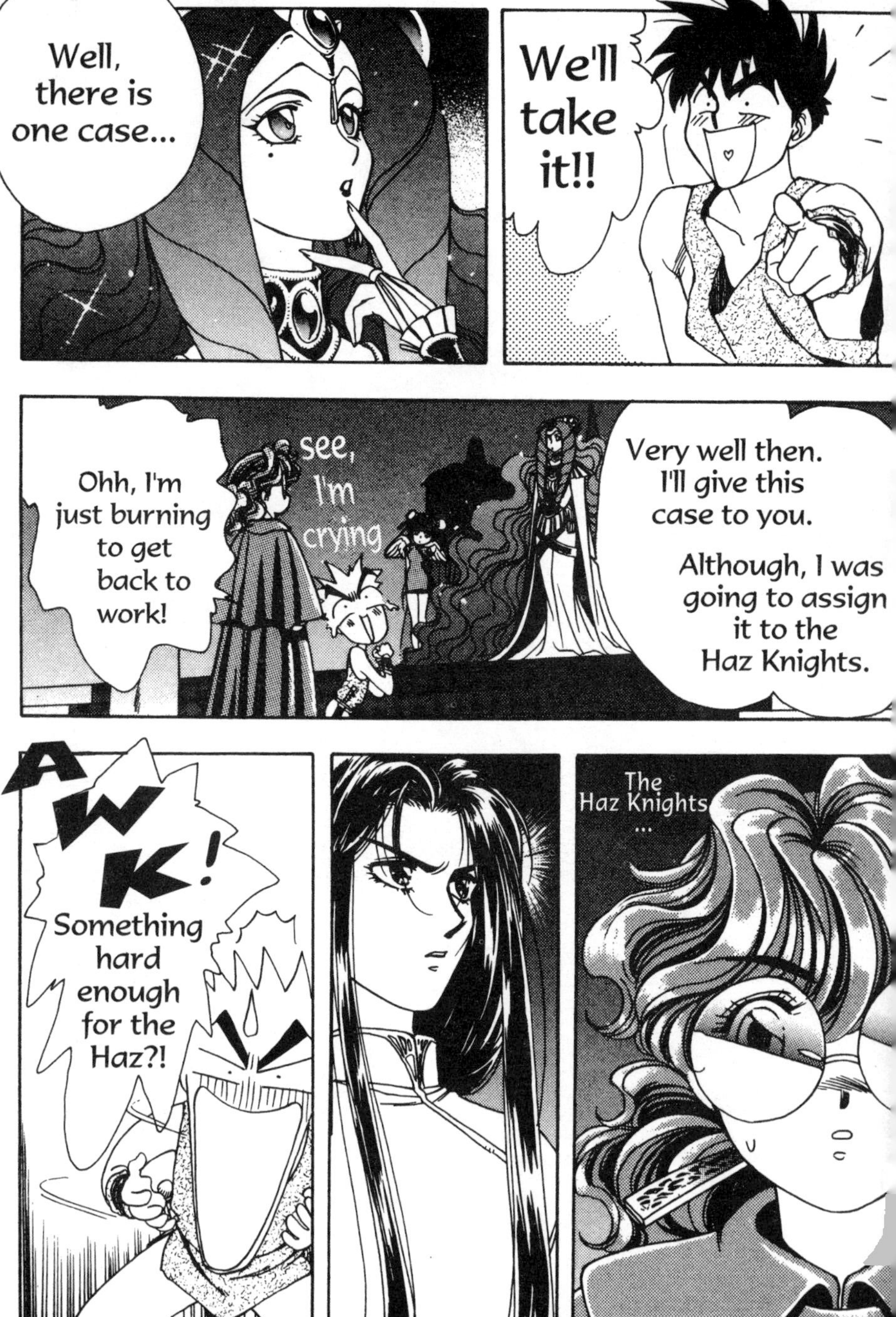
Well, there is one case...
We'll take it!!
Ohh, I'm just burning to get back to work!
see, I'm crying
Very well then. I'll give this case to you.
Although, I was going to assign it to the Haz Knights.
AWK!
Something hard enough for the Haz?!
The Haz Knights ...

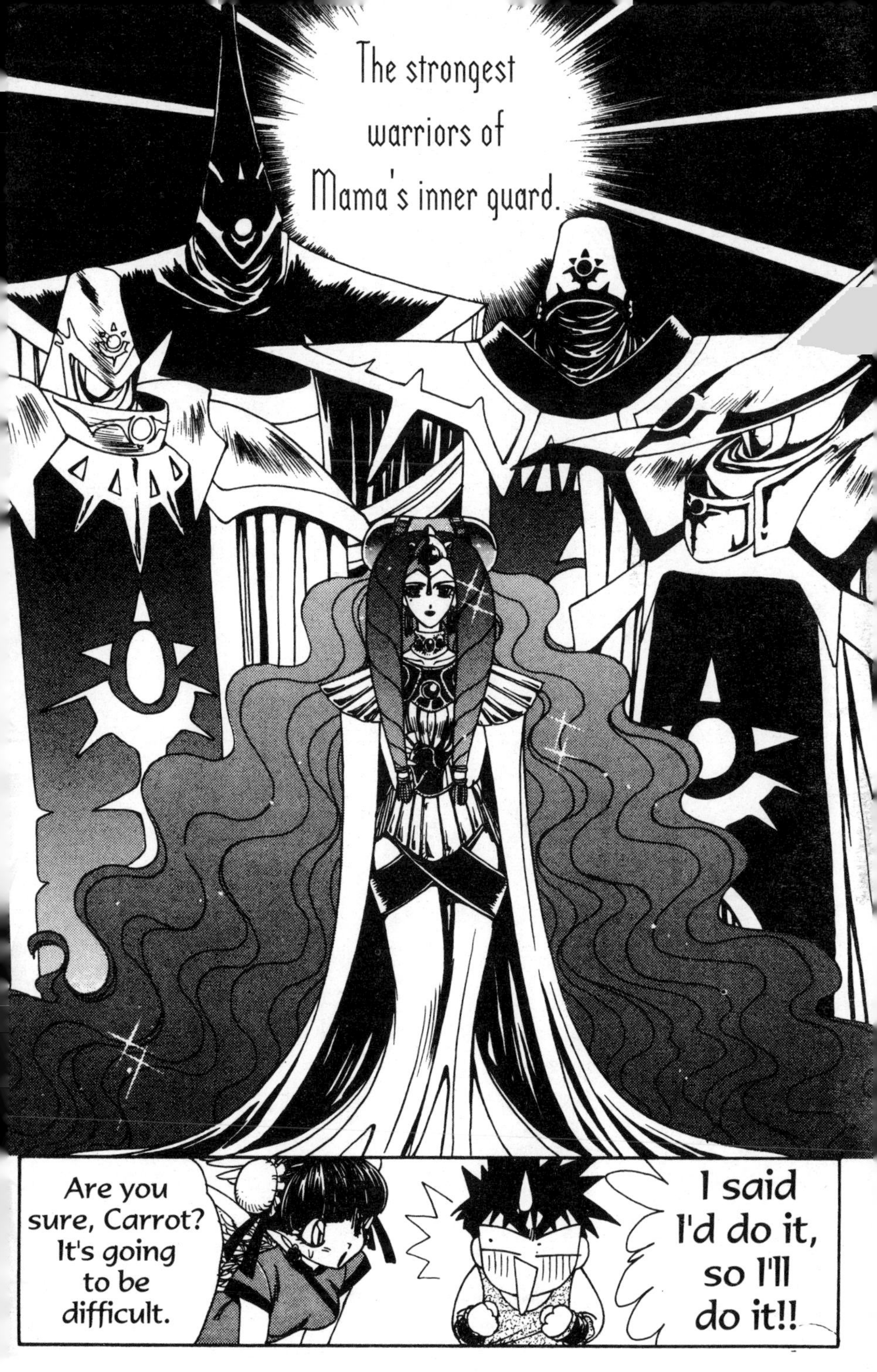
The strongest warriors of Mama's inner guard.
Are you sure, Carrot? It's going to be difficult.
I said I'd do it, so I'll do it!!

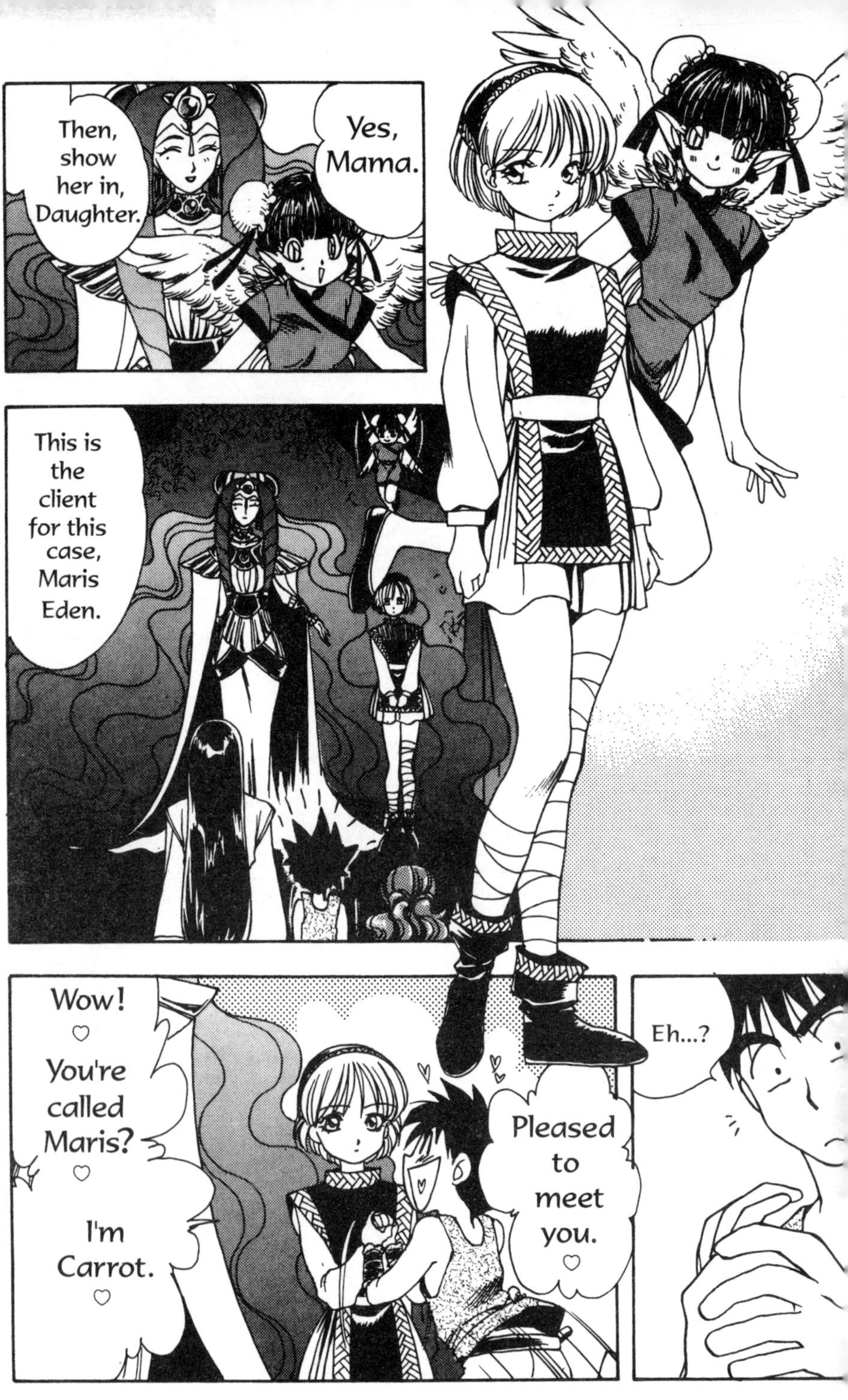
Then, show her in, Daughter.
Yes, Mama.
This is the client for this case, Maris Eden.
Wow! ♡ You're called Maris? ♡
I'm Carrot. ♡
Pleased to meet you. ♡
Eh...?

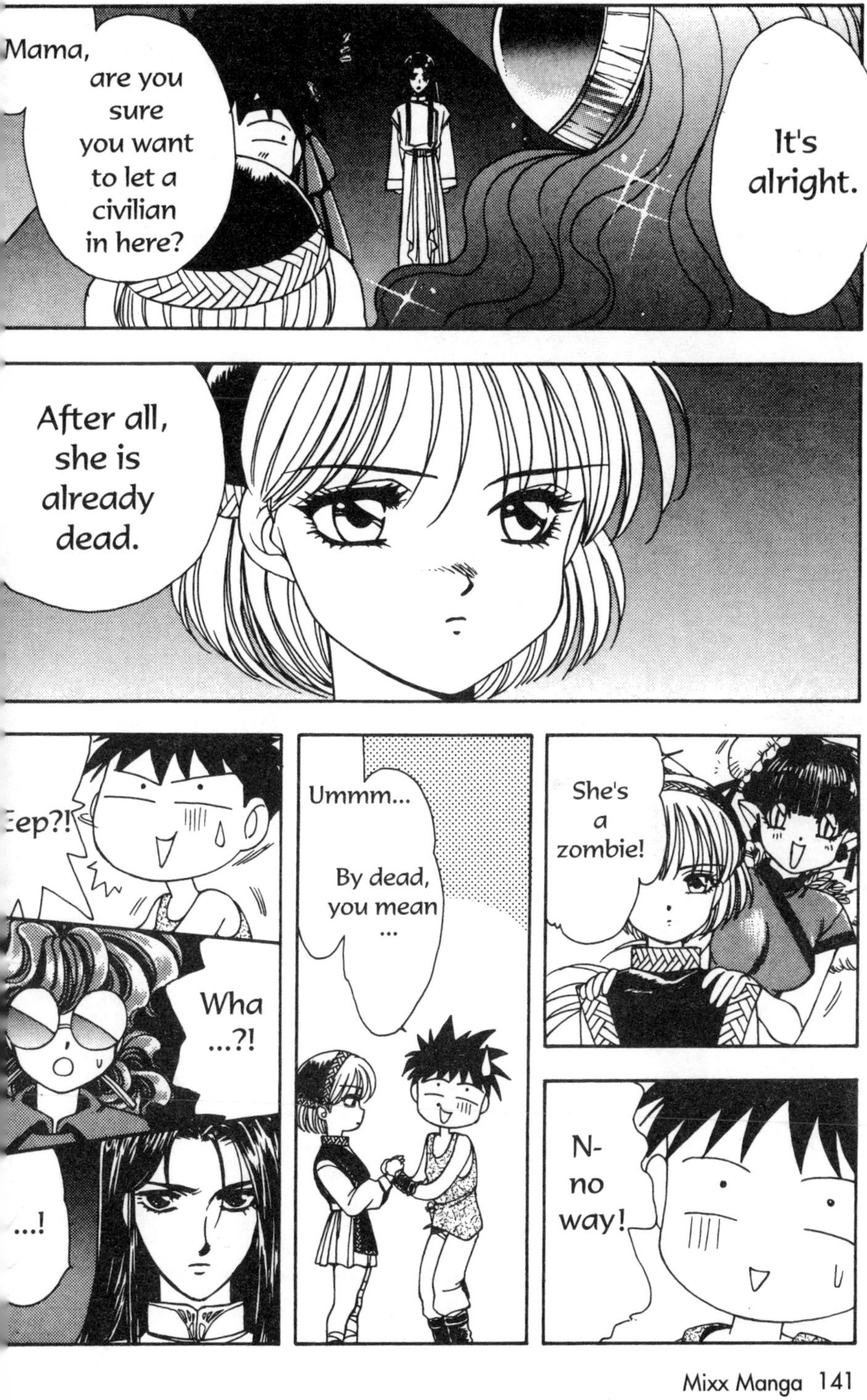
Mama, are you sure you want to let a civilian in here?
It's alright.
After all, she is already dead.
Eep?!
Wha ...?!
...!
Ummm...
By dead, you mean ...
She's a zombie!
N- no way!

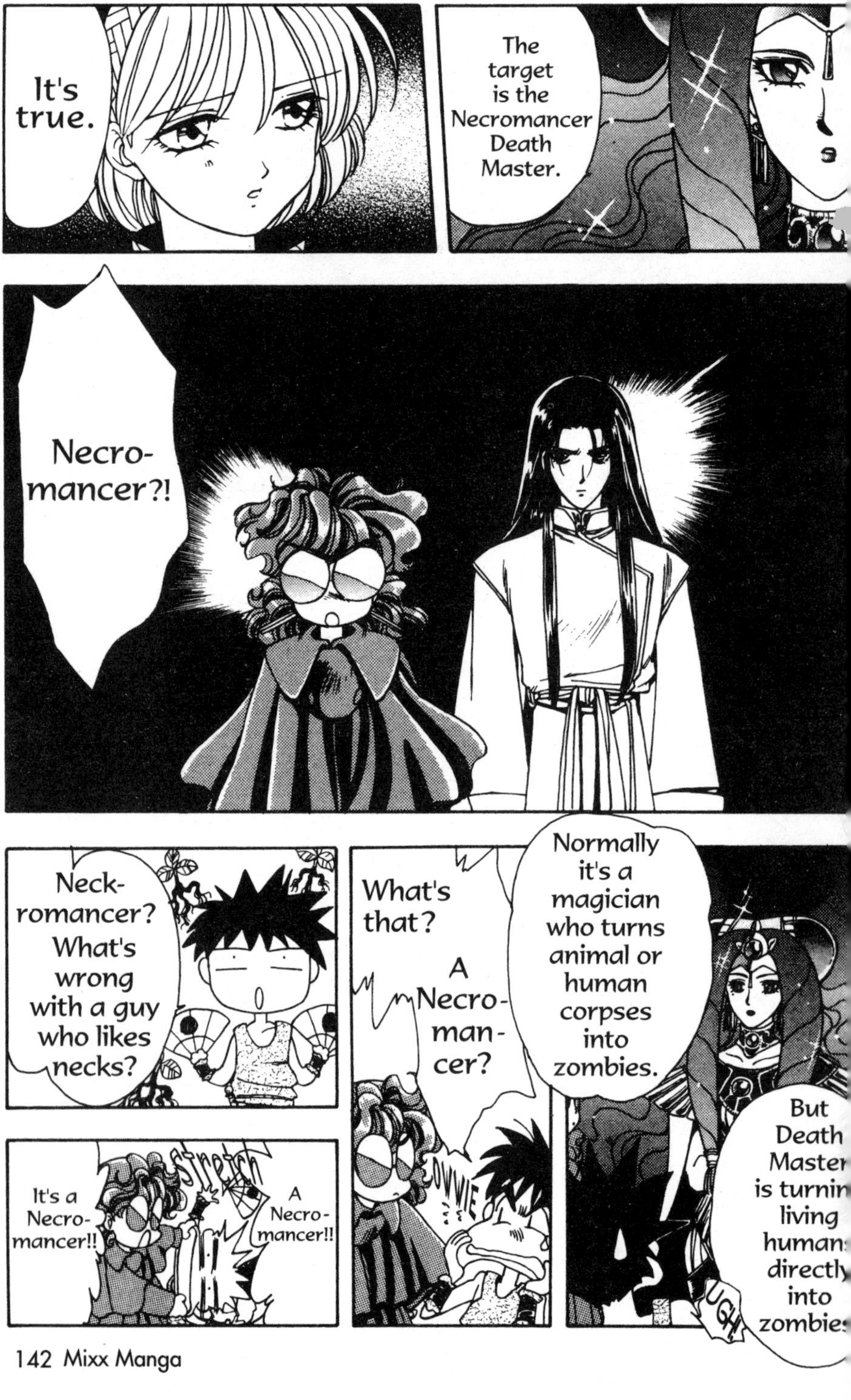
It's true.
The target is the Necromancer Death Master.
Necro-mancer?!
Neck-romancer? What's wrong with a guy who likes necks?
Stretch
It's a Necro-mancer!!
A Necro-mancer!!
What's that?
A Necro-man-cer?
Normally it's a magician who turns animal or human corpses into zombies.
But Death Maste is turnin living human directl into zombie
UGH!

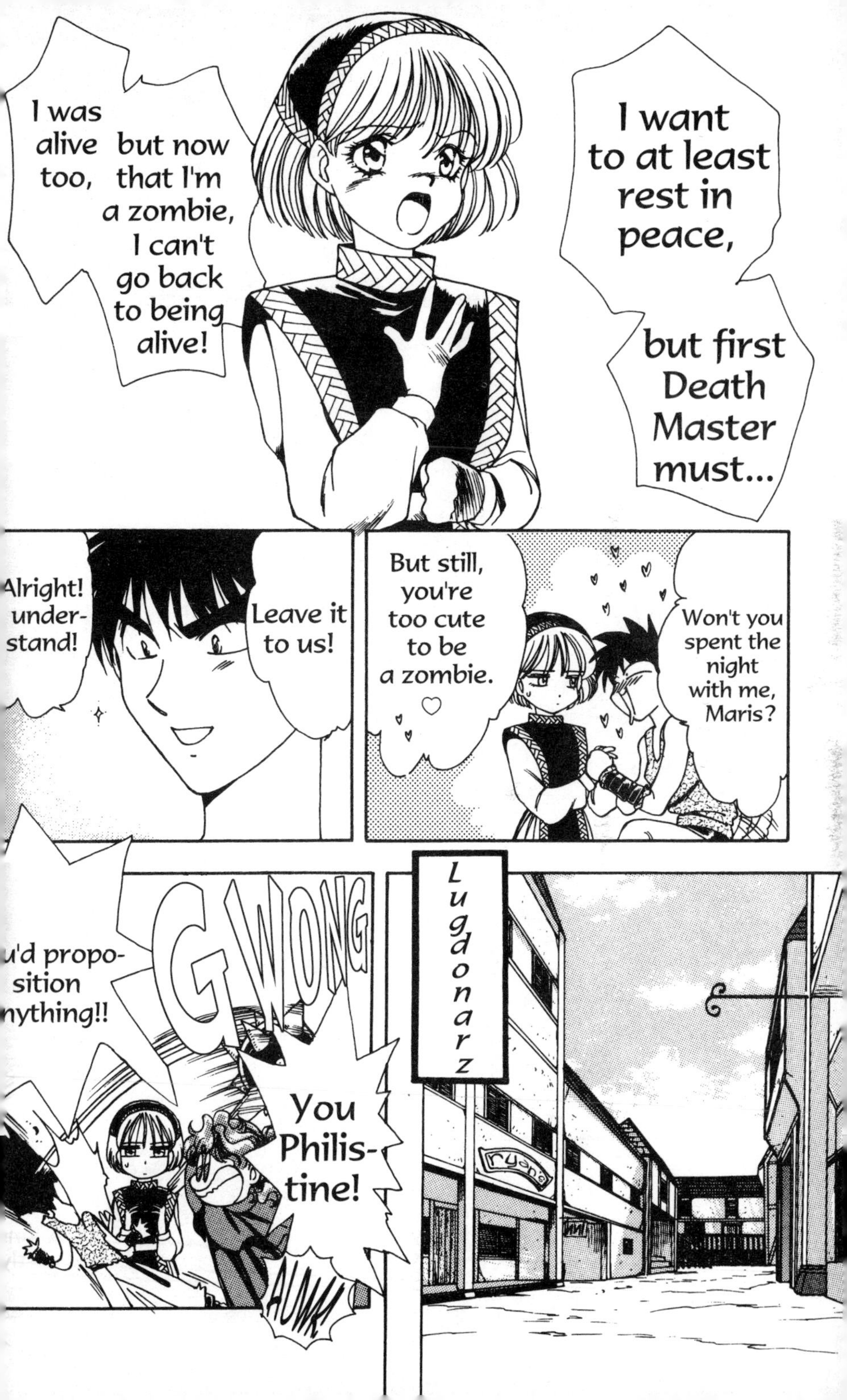

I was alive too,
but now that I'm a zombie, I can't go back to being alive!
I want to at least rest in peace,
but first Death Master must...
Alright! under-stand!
Leave it to us!
But still, you're too cute to be a zombie.
Won't you spent the night with me, Maris?
u'd propo-sition nything!!
GWONG
You Philis-tine!
AUWK
Lugdonarz
ryan's

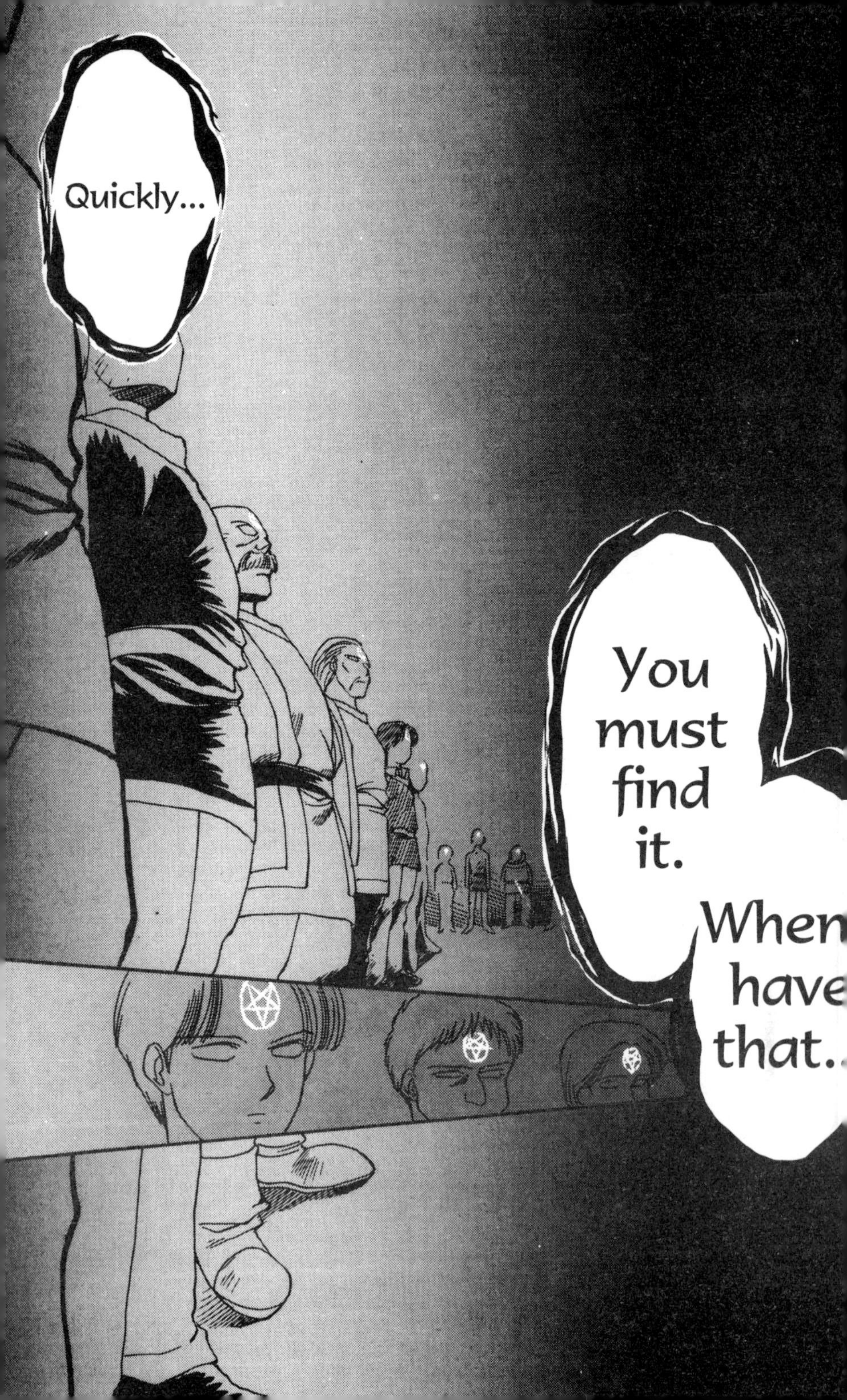
Quickly...
You must find it.
When have that..

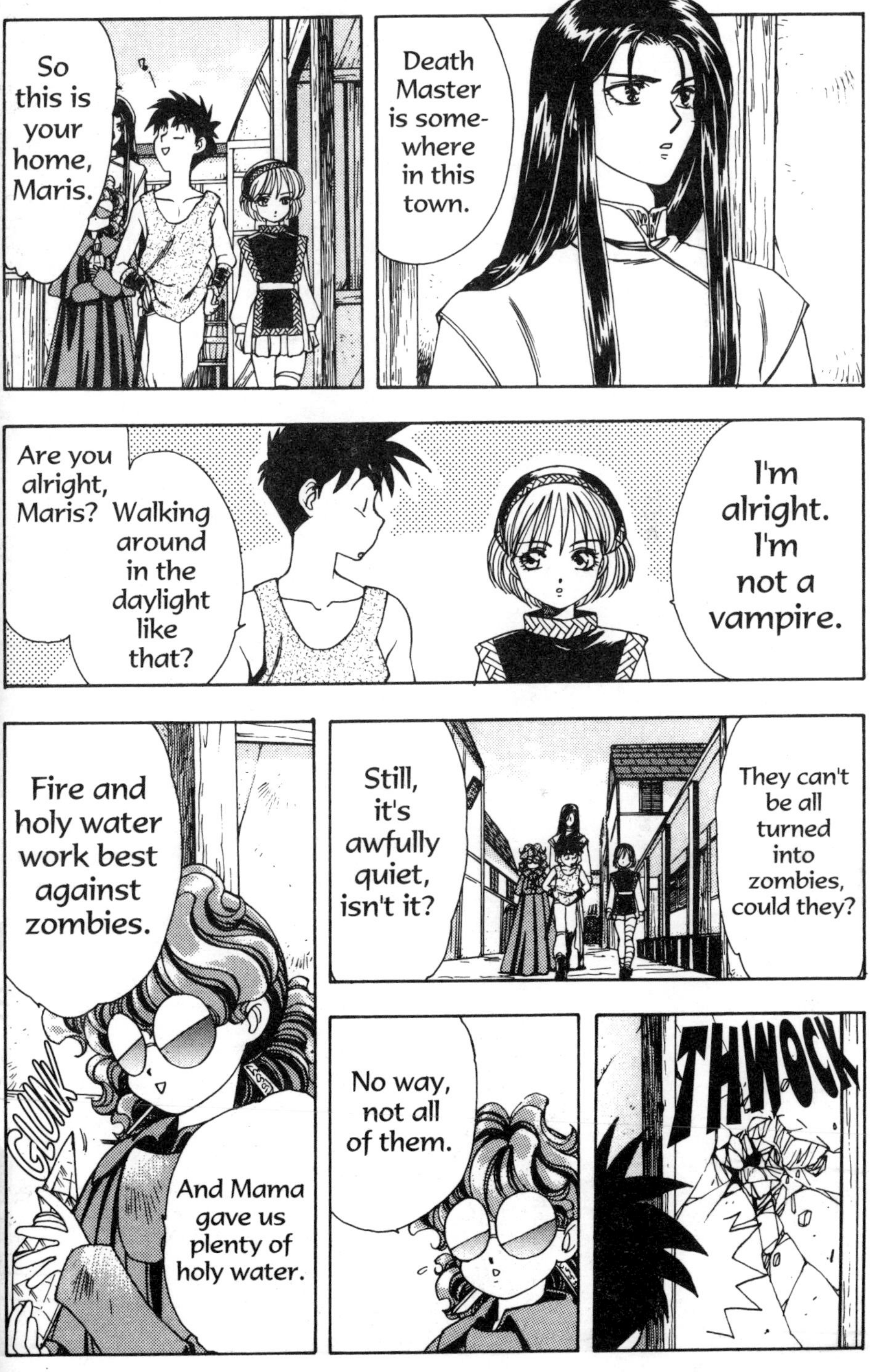
So this is your home, Maris.
Death Master is somewhere in this town.
Are you alright, Maris? Walking around in the daylight like that?
I'm alright. I'm not a vampire.
Fire and holy water work best against zombies.
GLUNK
And Mama gave us plenty of holy water.
Still, it's awfully quiet, isn't it?
They can't be all turned into zombies, could they?
No way, not all of them.
THWOCK

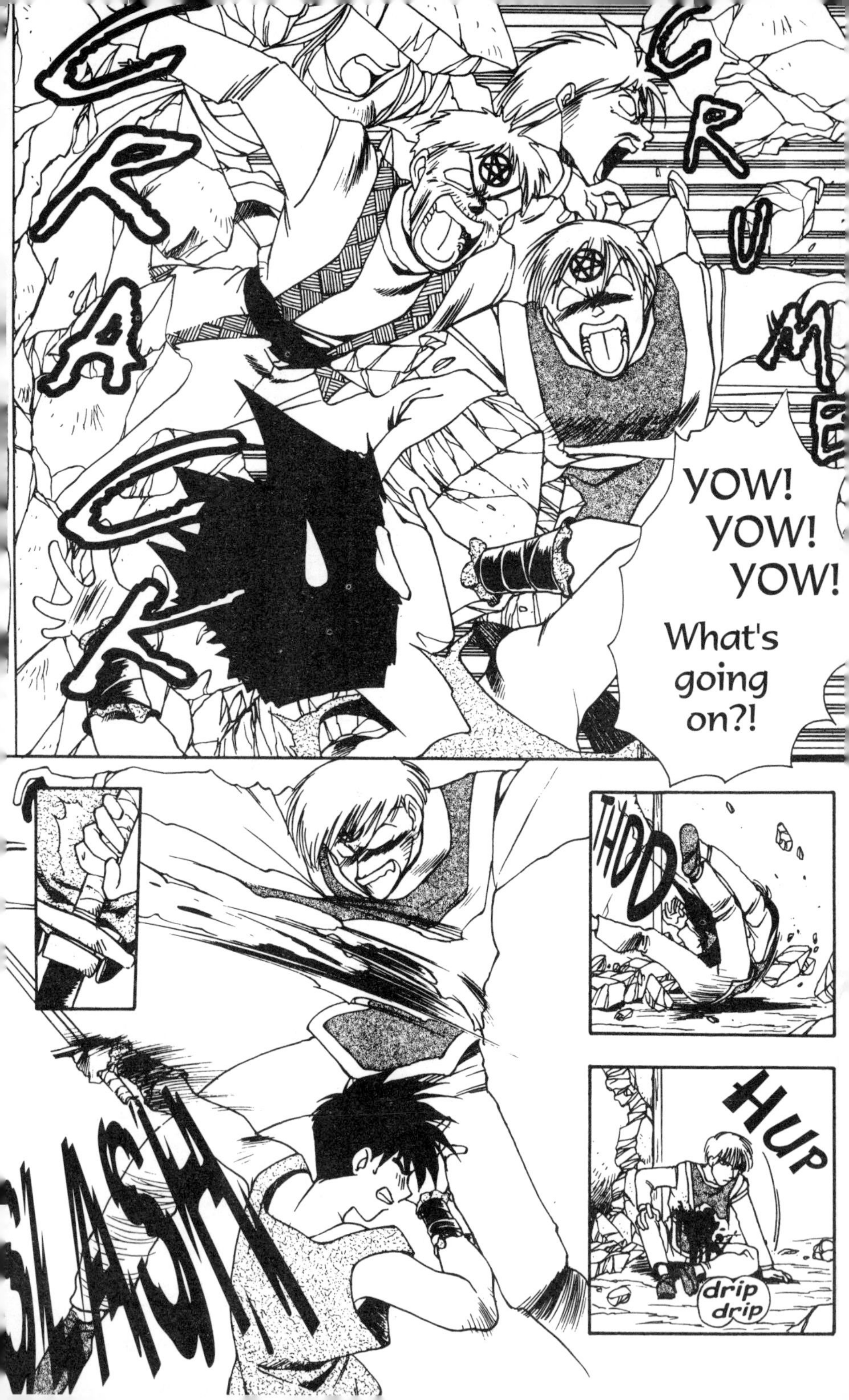
CRACK
CRUMBLE
YOW! YOW! YOW!
What's going on?!
THDD
SLASH
HUP
drip drip

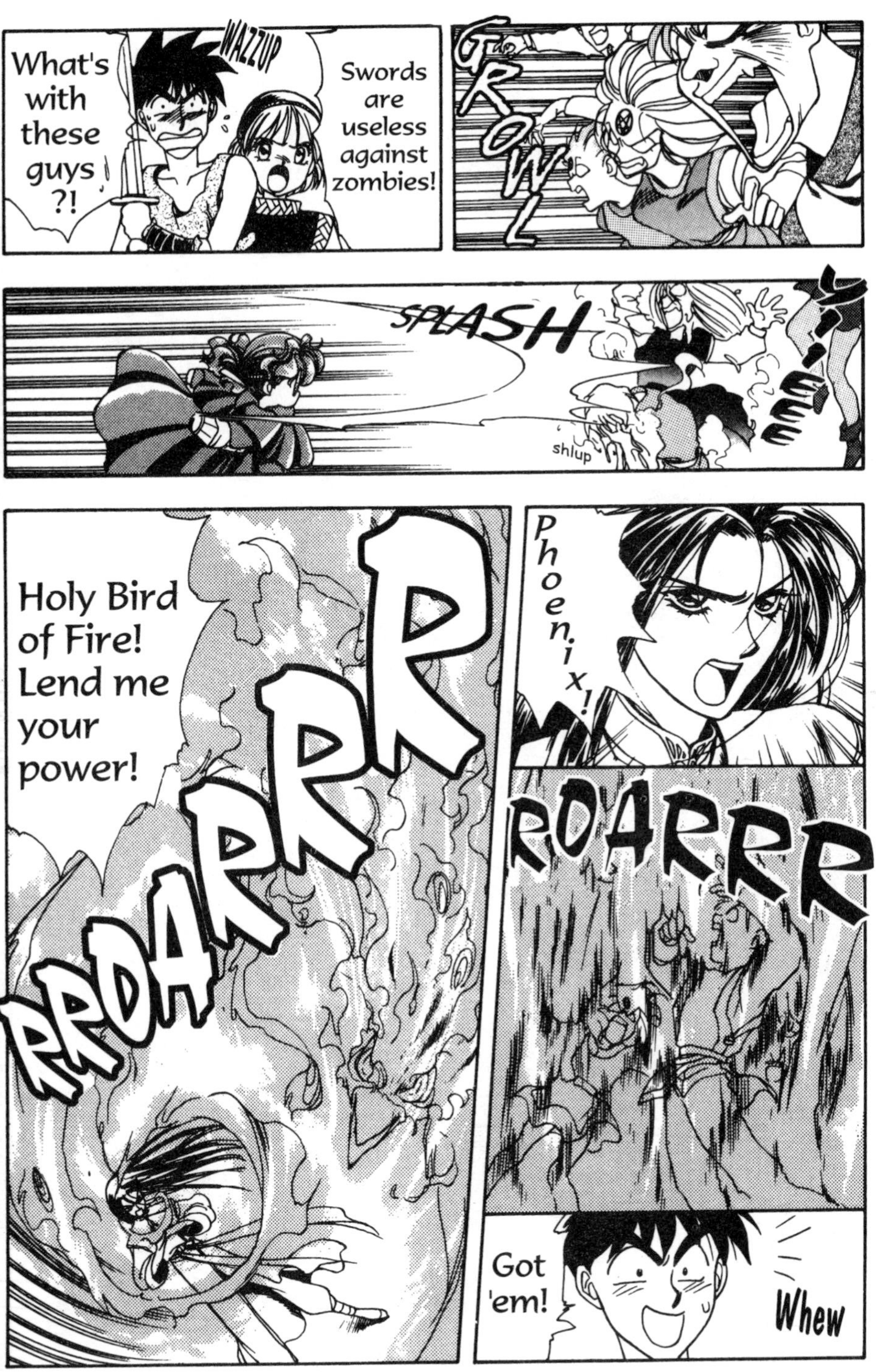
What's with these guys ?!
WAZZUP
Swords are useless against zombies!
GROWL
SPLASH
shlup
Holy Bird of Fire! Lend me your power!
RROARRR
Phoenix!
ROARRR
Got 'em!
Whew

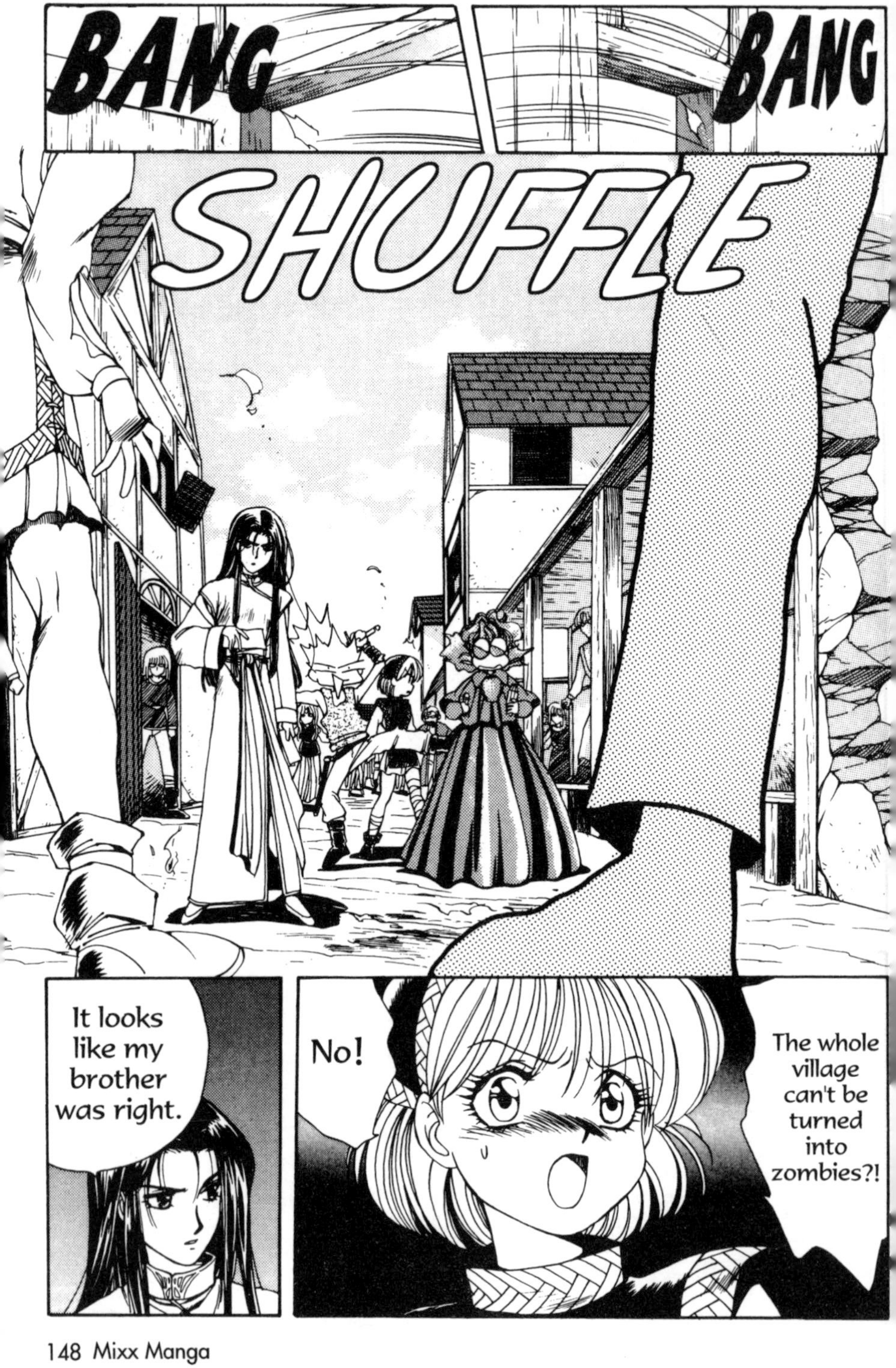
BANG
BANG
SHUFFLE
It looks like my brother was right.
No!
The whole village can't be turned into zombies?!

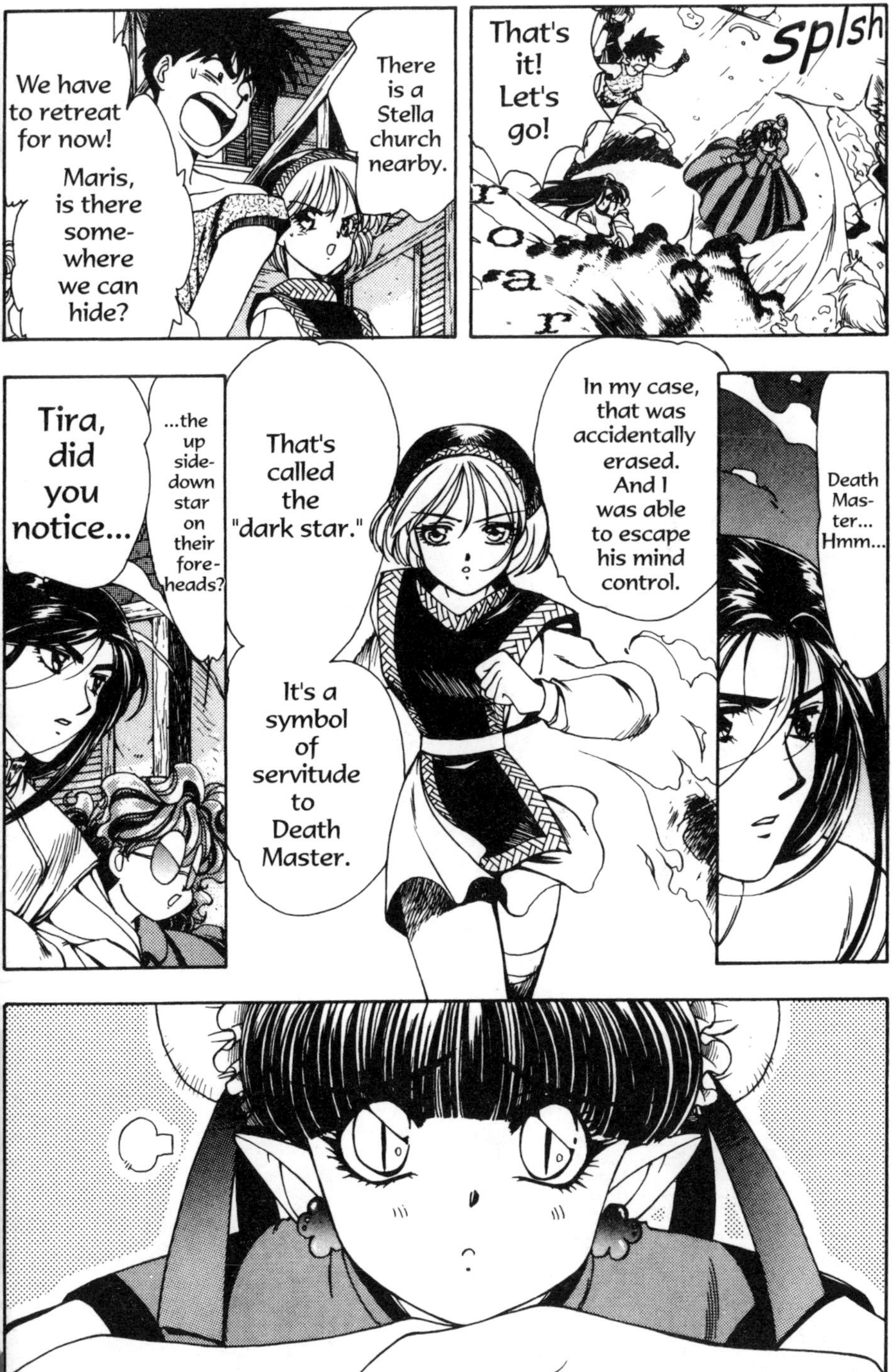
We have to retreat for now!
Maris, is there somewhere we can hide?
There is a Stella church nearby.
That's it! Let's go!
Splsh
roar
Tira, did you notice...
...the upside-down star on their foreheads?
That's called the "dark star."
It's a symbol of servitude to Death Master.
In my case, that was accidentally erased. And I was able to escape his mind control.
Death Master... Hmm...

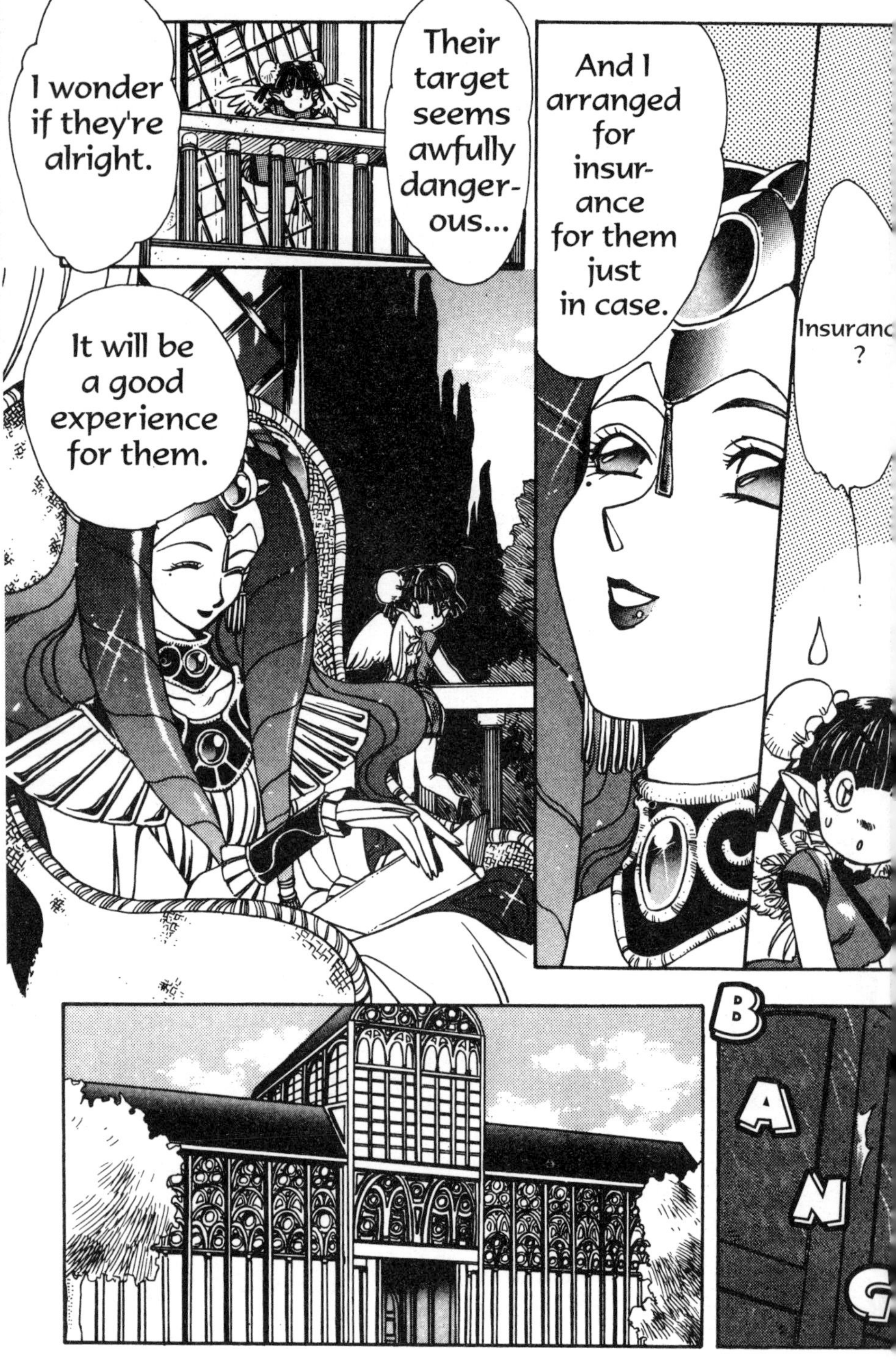
I wonder if they're alright.
Their target seems awfully danger-ous...
It will be a good experience for them.
And I arranged for insur-ance for them just in case.
Insuranc ?
BANG

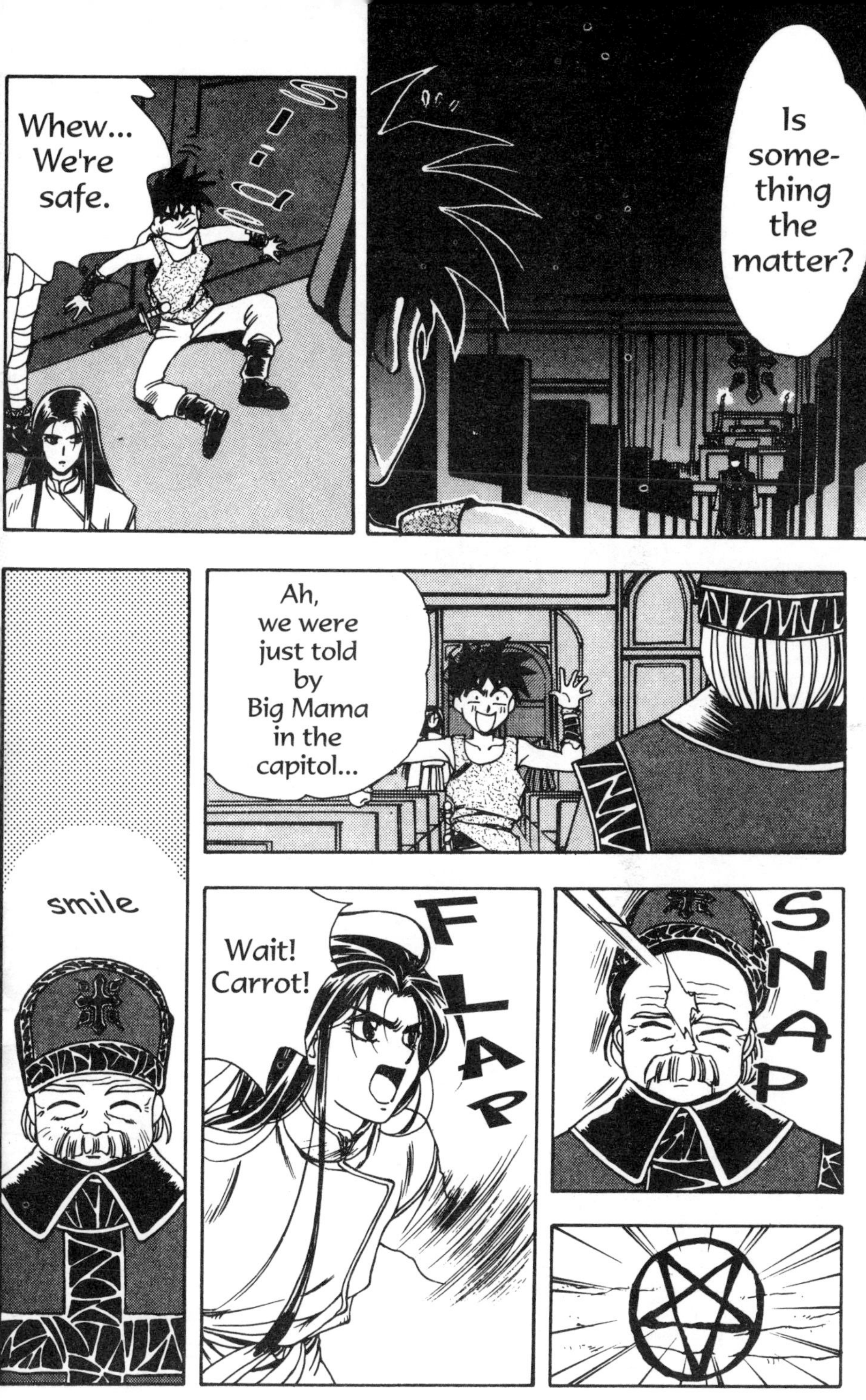
Whew... We're safe.
Is something the matter?
Ah, we were just told by Big Mama in the capitol...
smile
Wait! Carrot!
FLAP
SNAP

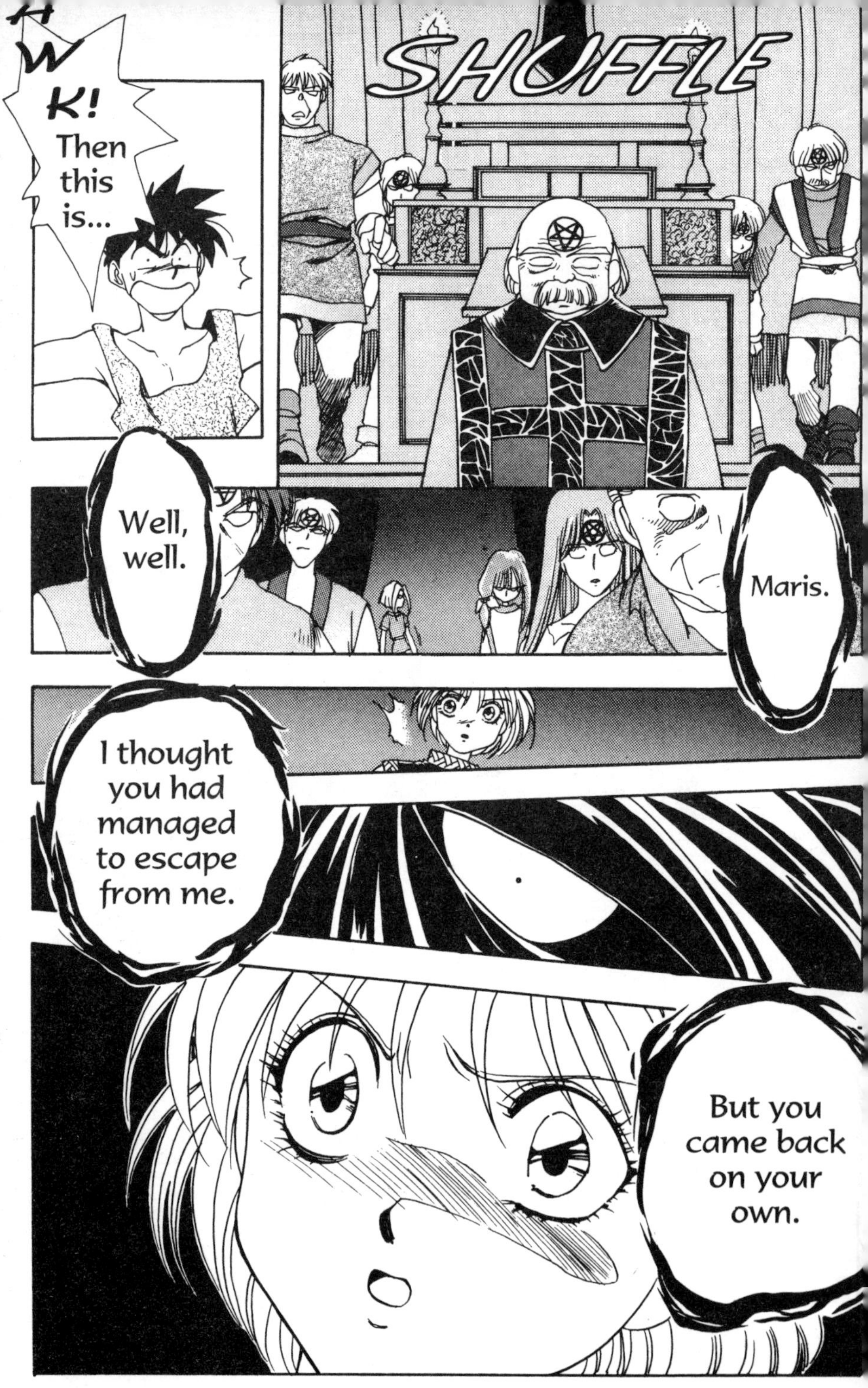
HWK!
Then this is...
SHUFFLE
Well, well.
Maris.
I thought you had managed to escape from me.
But you came back on your own.

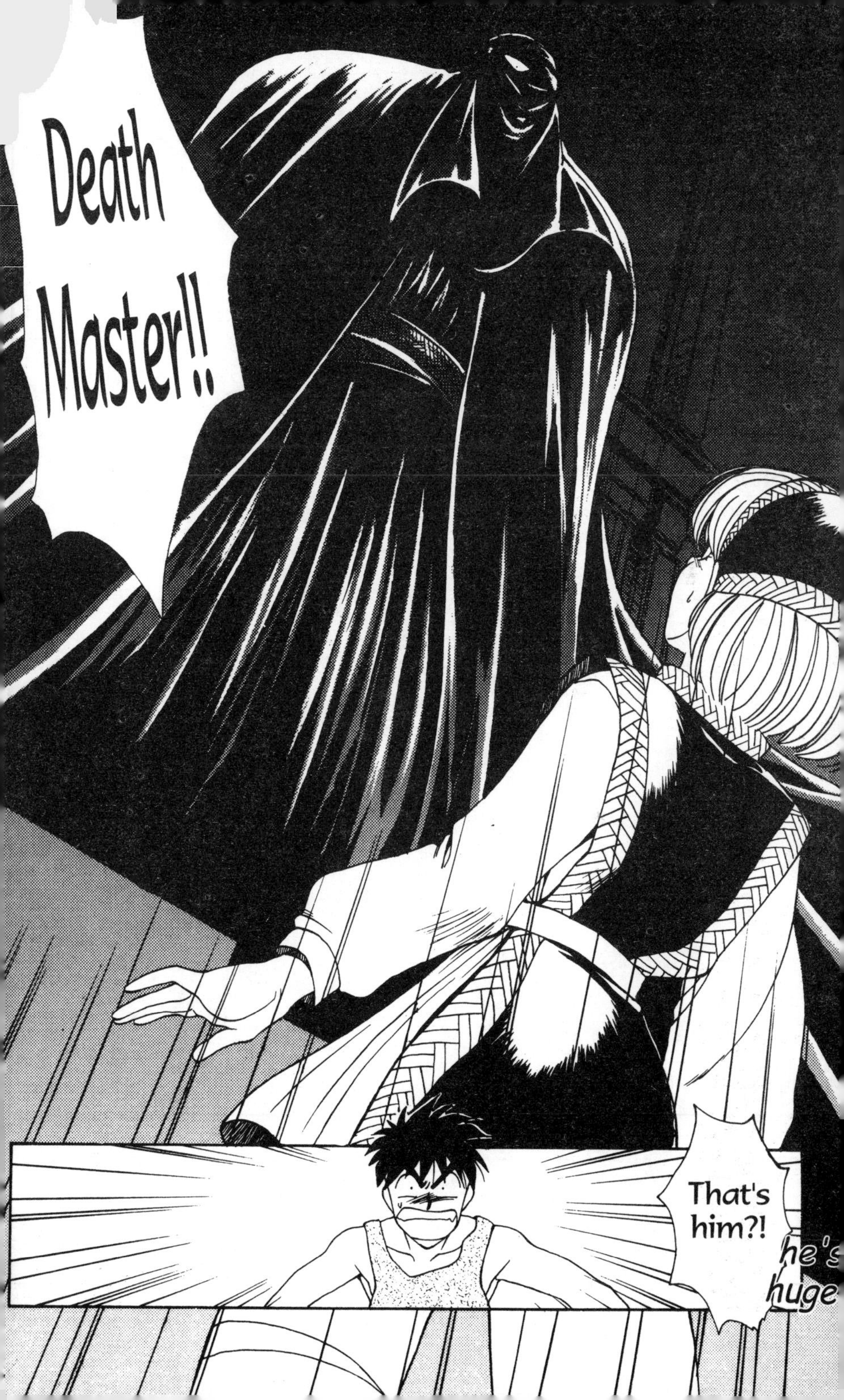
Death Master!!
That's him?!
he's huge

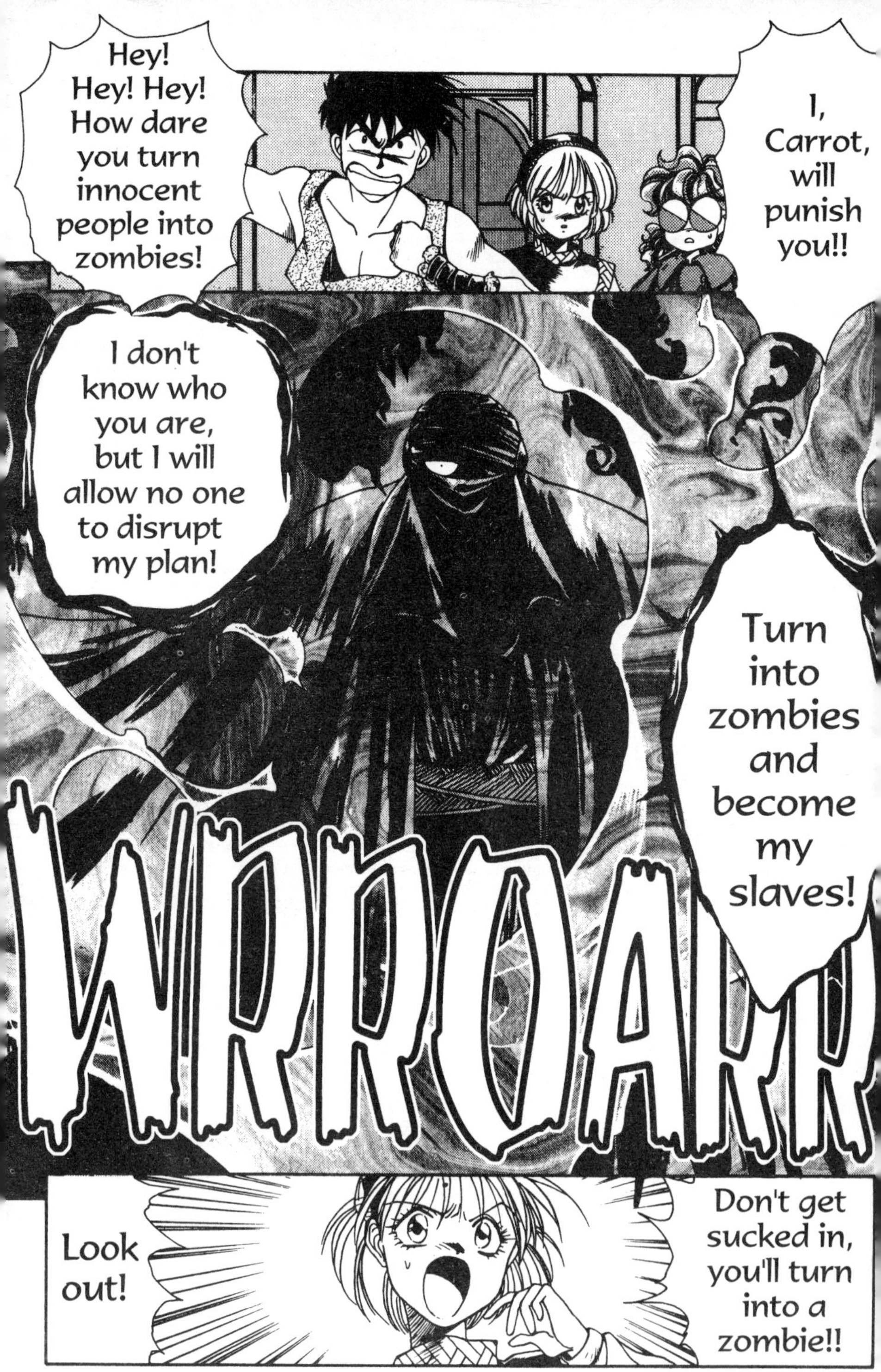
Hey! Hey! Hey! How dare you turn innocent people into zombies!
I, Carrot, will punish you!!
I don't know who you are, but I will allow no one to disrupt my plan!
Turn into zombies and become my slaves!
WRROARR
Look out!
Don't get sucked in, you'll turn into a zombie!!

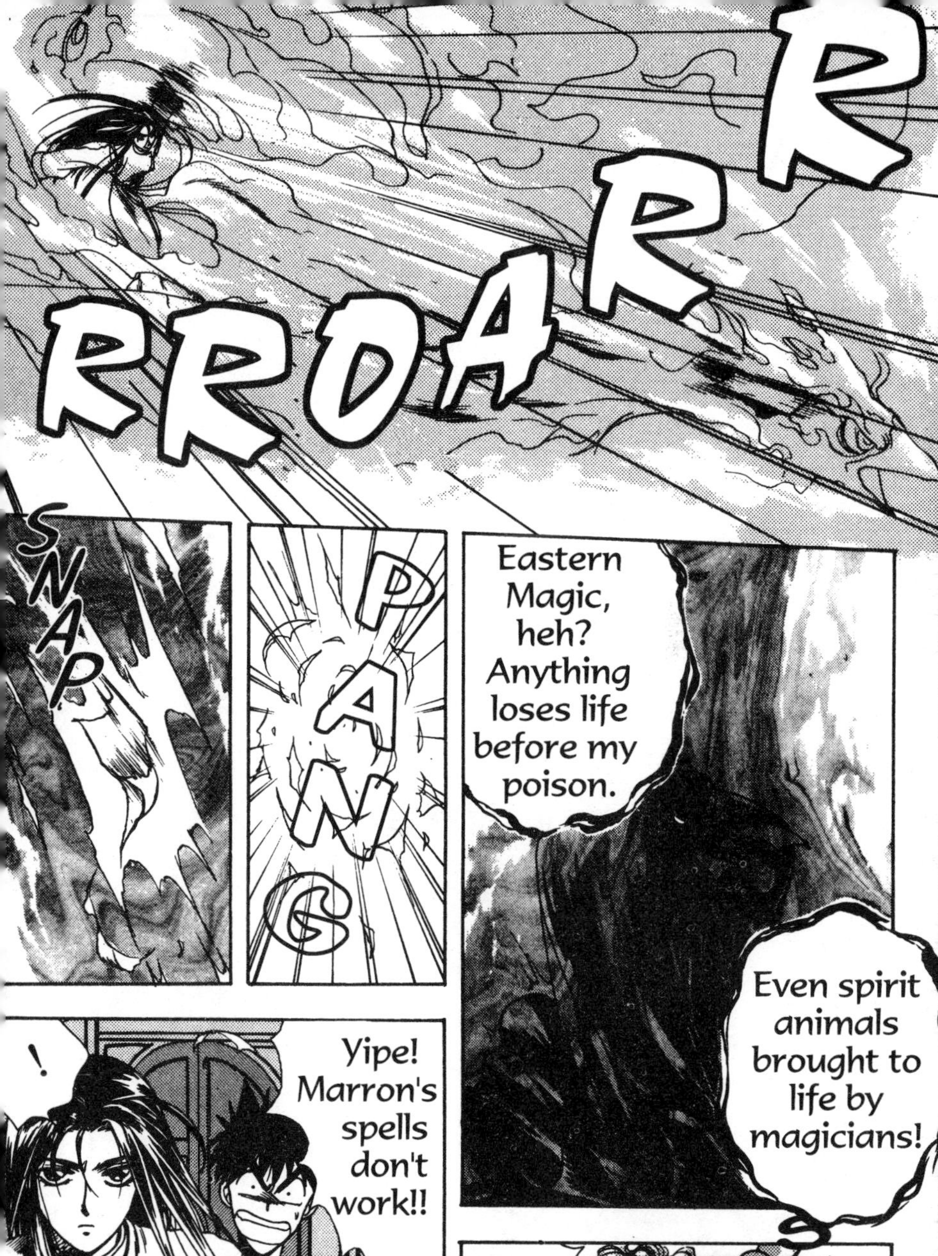
RROARRR
SNAP
PANG
!
Yipe! Marron's spells don't work!!
Eastern Magic, heh? Anything loses life before my poison.
Even spirit animals brought to life by magicians!
Then how about this!
SPLISH

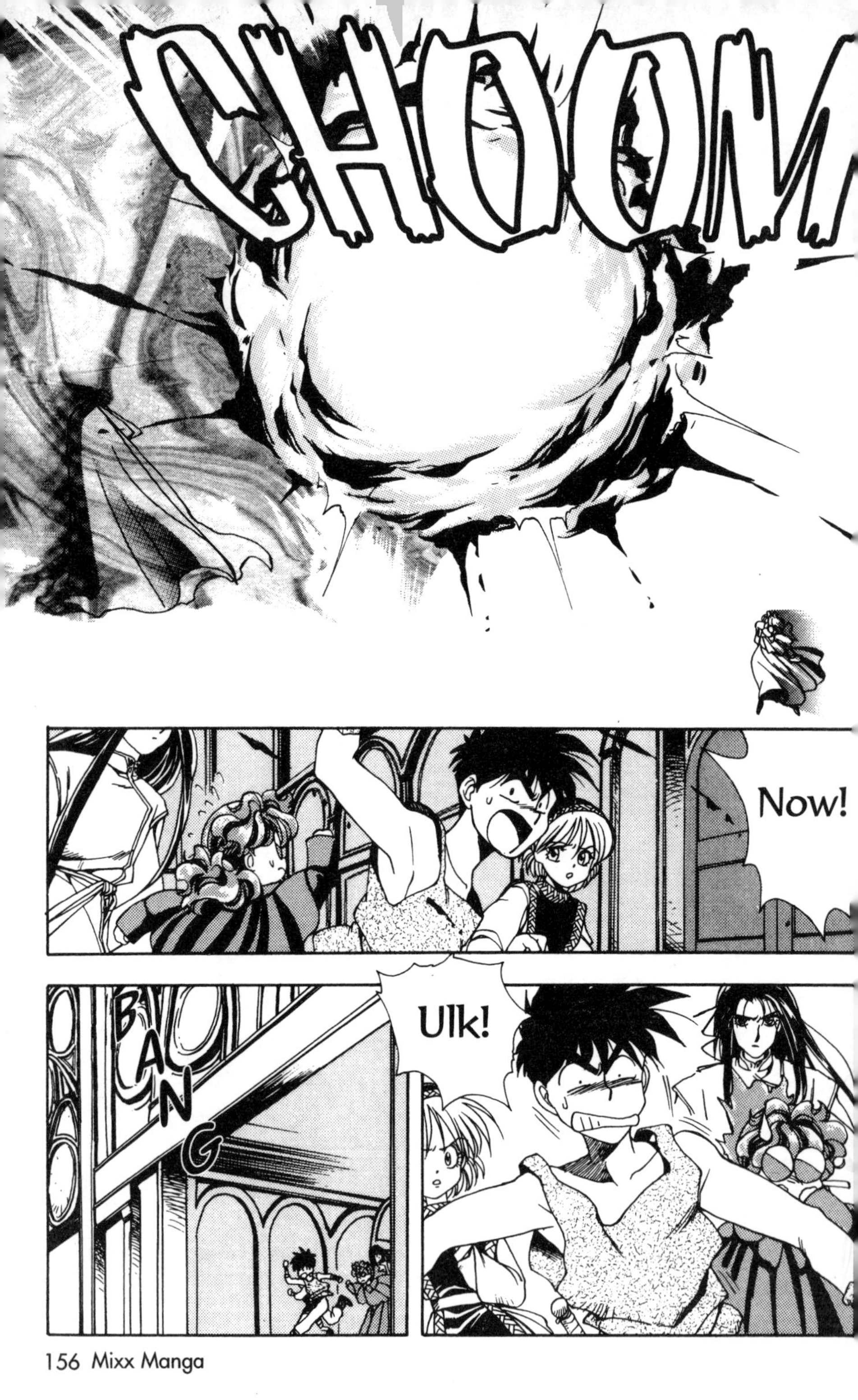
CHOOM
Now!
Ulk!
BANG

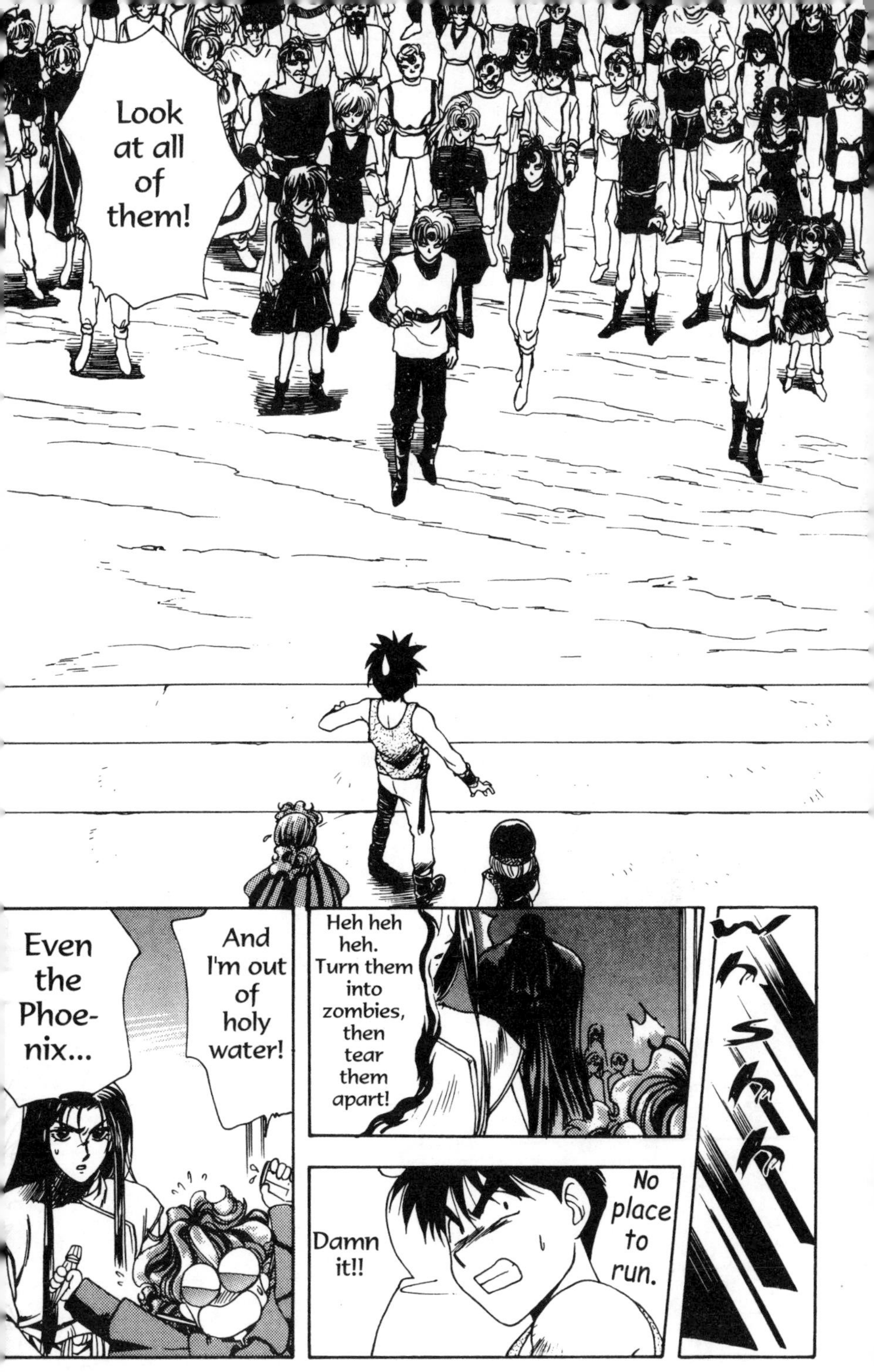
Look at all of them!
Even the Phoenix...
And I'm out of holy water!
Heh heh heh. Turn them into zombies, then tear them apart!
Damn it!!
No place to run.

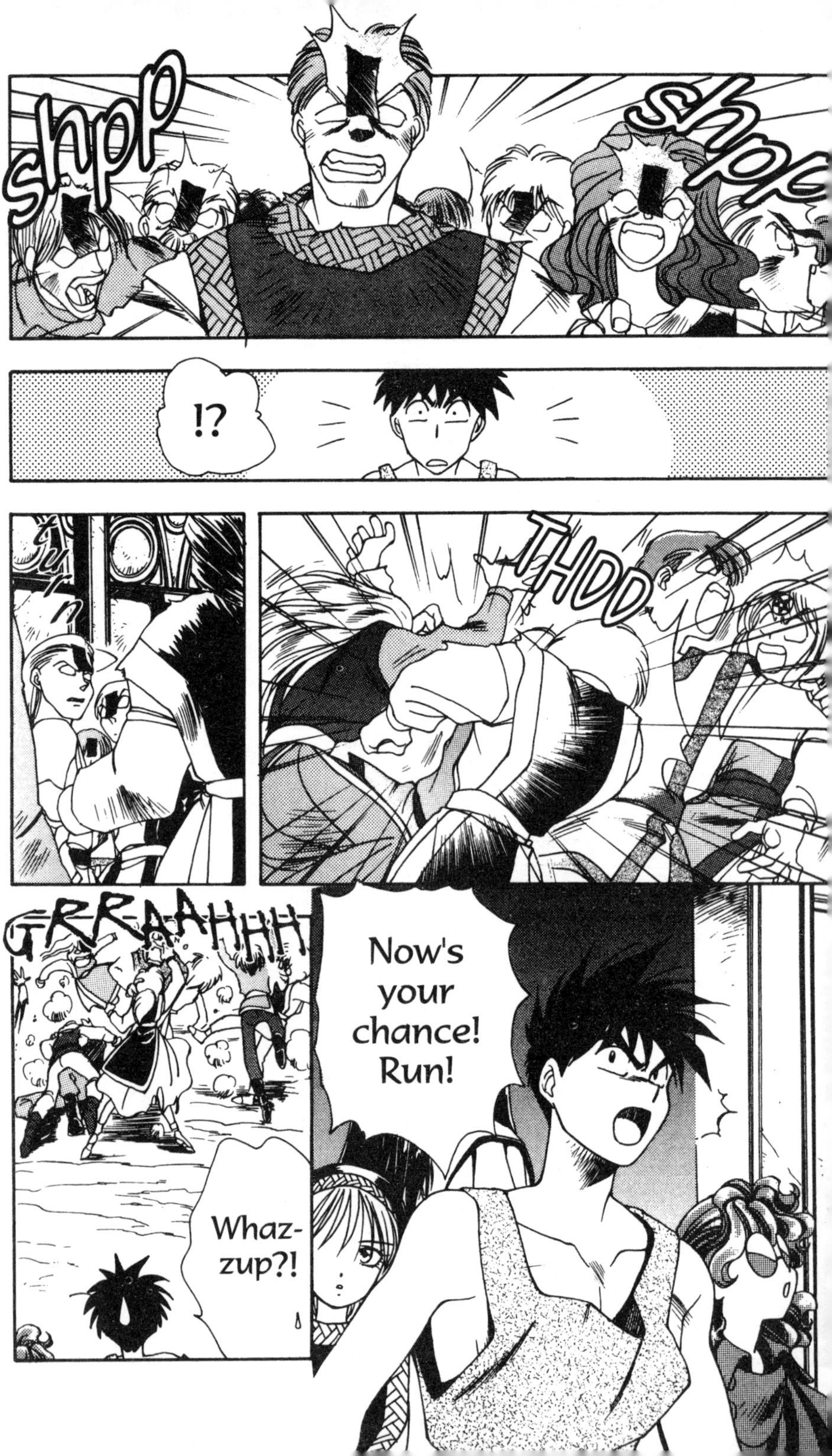
shpp
shpp
!?
turn
THDD
GRRAAHHH
Now's your chance! Run!
Whaz-zup?!

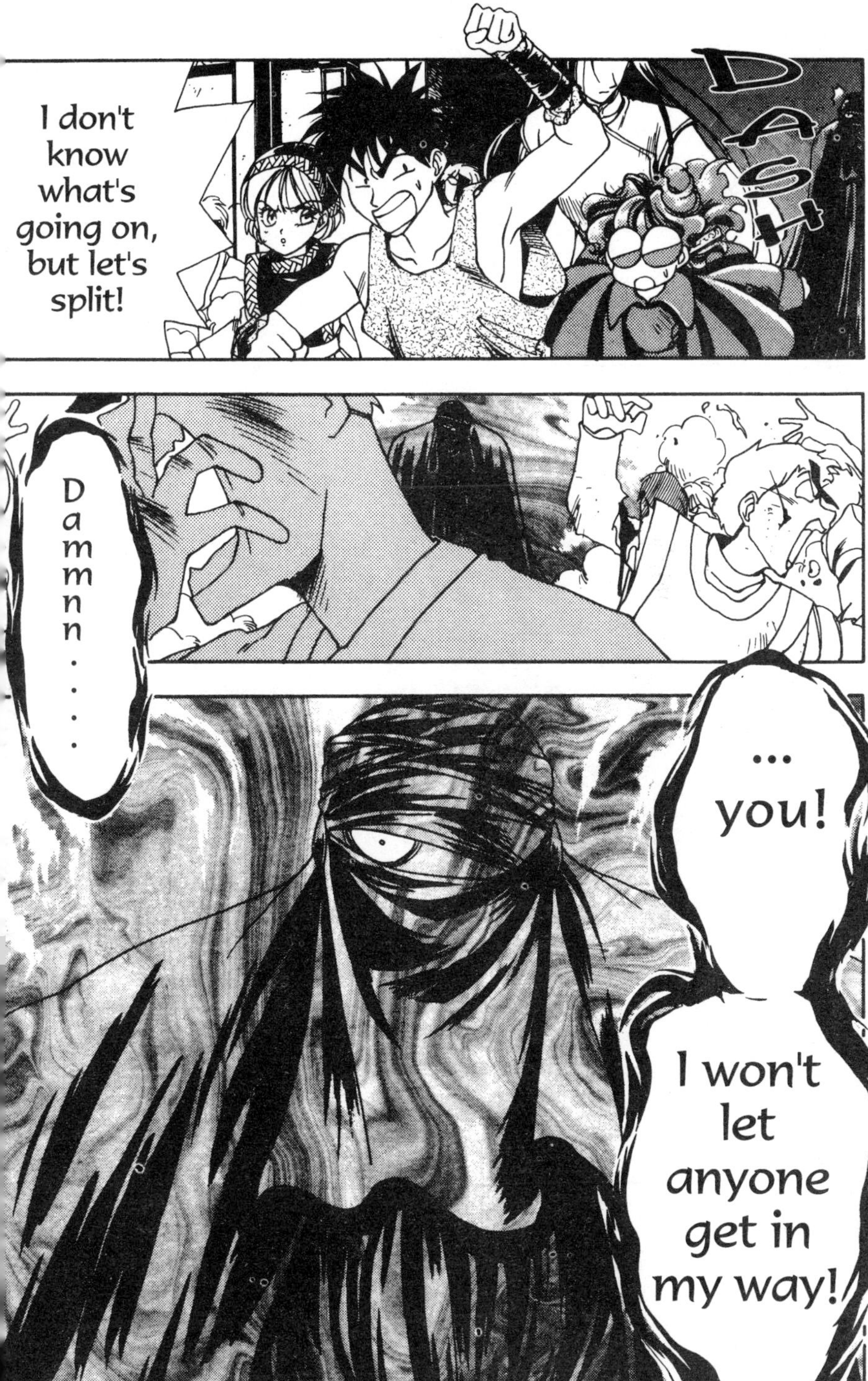

I don't know what's going on, but let's split!
DASH
Dammnn.....
... you!
I won't let anyone get in my way!

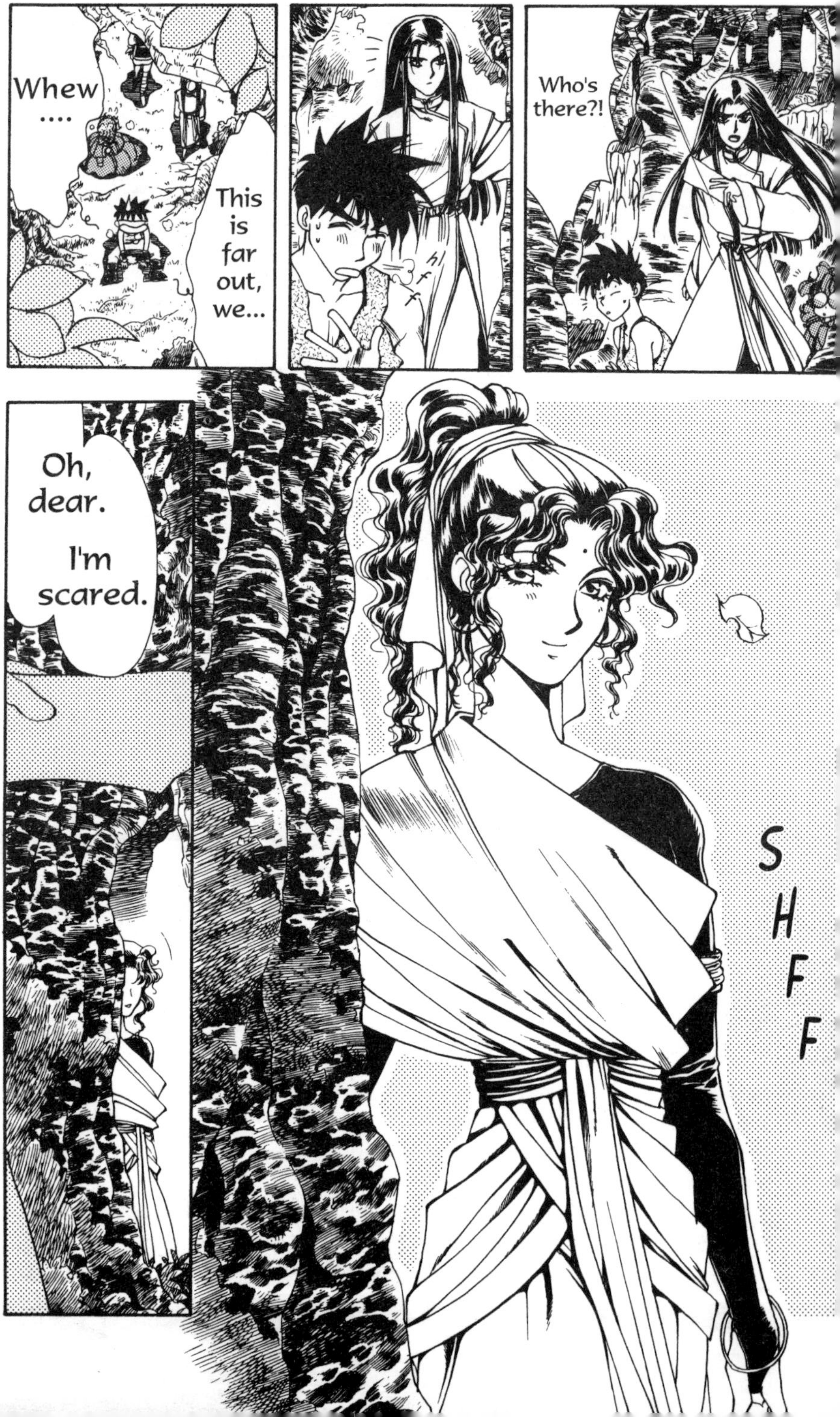
Whew ....
This is far out, we...
Who's there?!
Oh, dear.
I'm scared.
SHFF

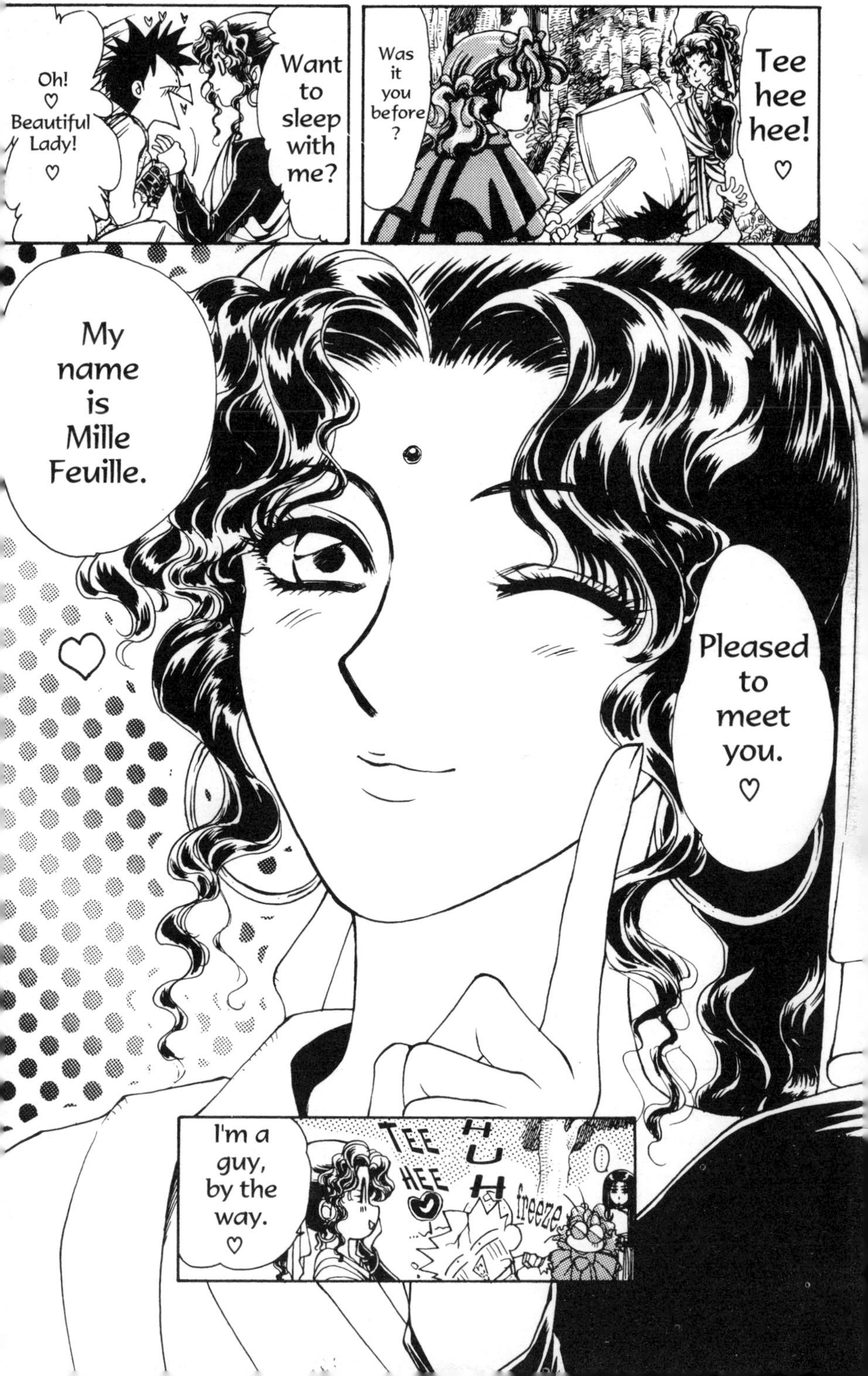
Oh! ♡ Beautiful Lady! ♡
Want to sleep with me?
Was it you before ?
Tee hee hee! ♡
My name is Mille Feuille.
Pleased to meet you. ♡
I'm a guy, by the way. ♡
TEE HEE
HUH
freeze

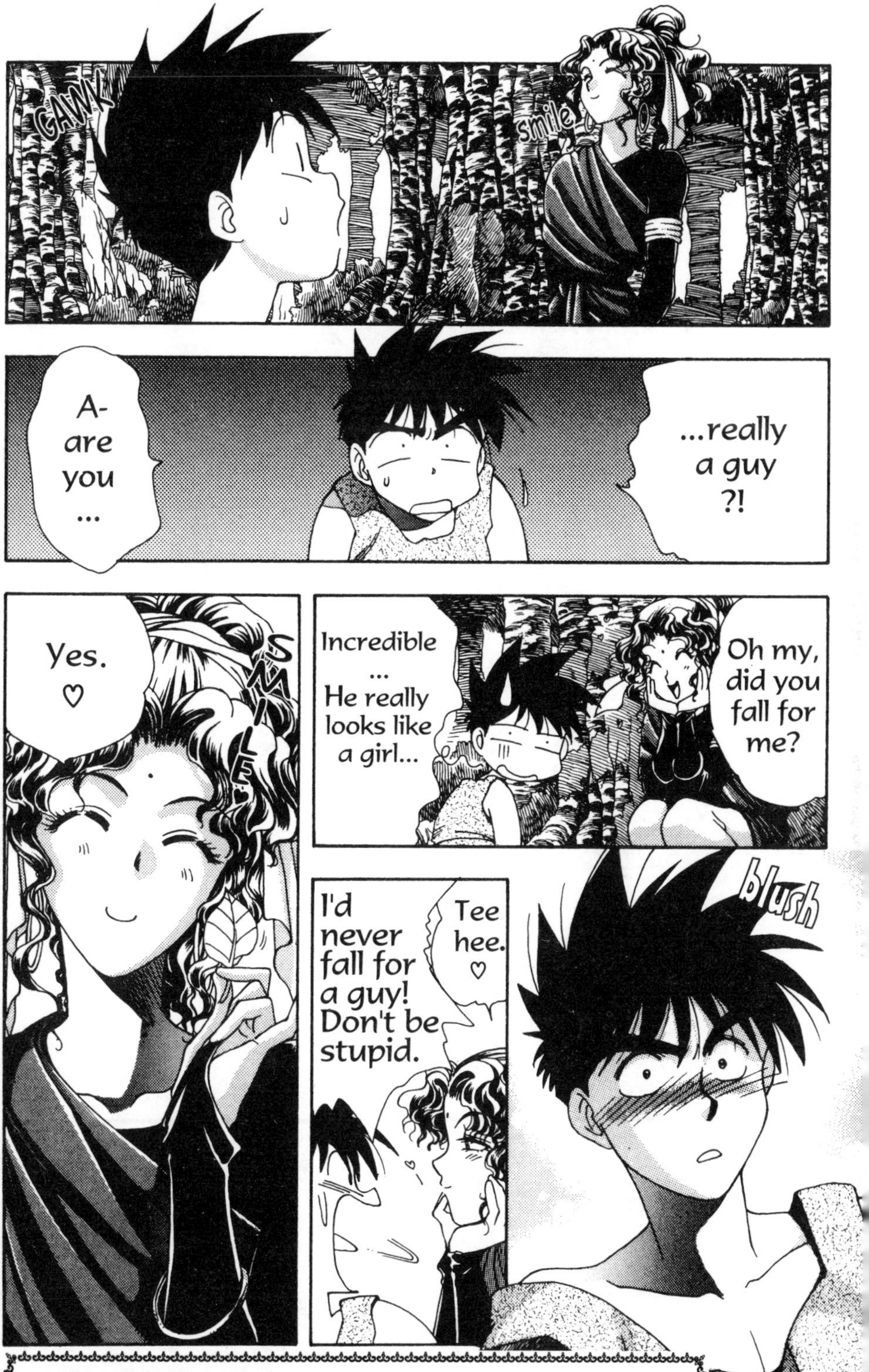
GAWK
smile
A- are you ...
...really a guy ?!
Yes. ♡
SMILE♡
Incredible ... He really looks like a girl...
Oh my, did you fall for me?
I'd never fall for a guy! Don't be stupid.
Tee hee. ♡
blush

The Spellbook of the Necromancer - Part 2

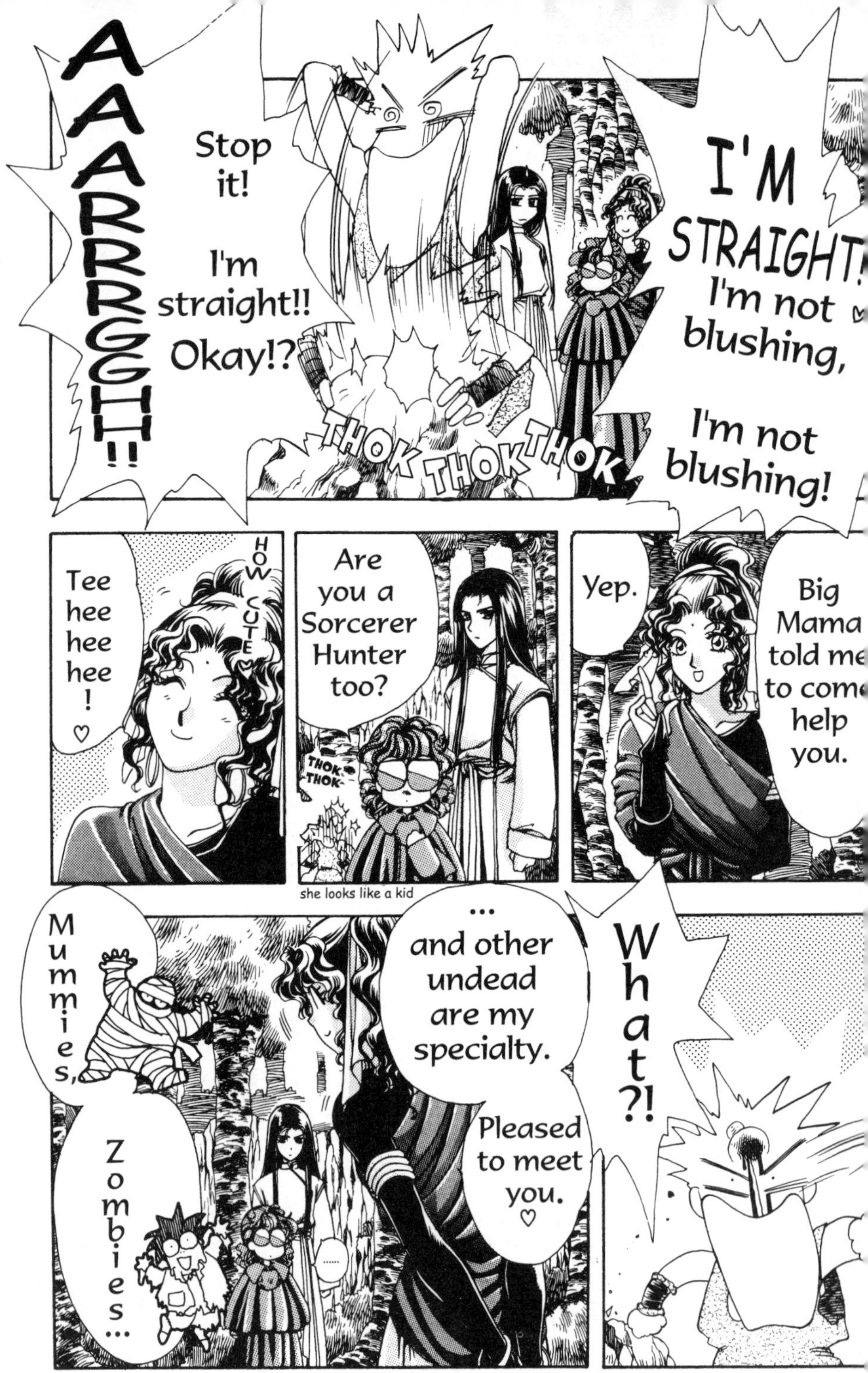
AAARRRGGHH!!
Stop it! I'm straight!! Okay!?
THOK THOK THOK
I'M STRAIGHT!
I'm not blushing, I'm not blushing!
Tee hee hee hee! ♡
HOW CUTE ♡
Are you a Sorcerer Hunter too?
THOK THOK
she looks like a kid
Yep.
Big Mama told me to come help you.
Mummies,
... and other undead are my specialty.
Zombies...
Pleased to meet you. ♡
......
What?!

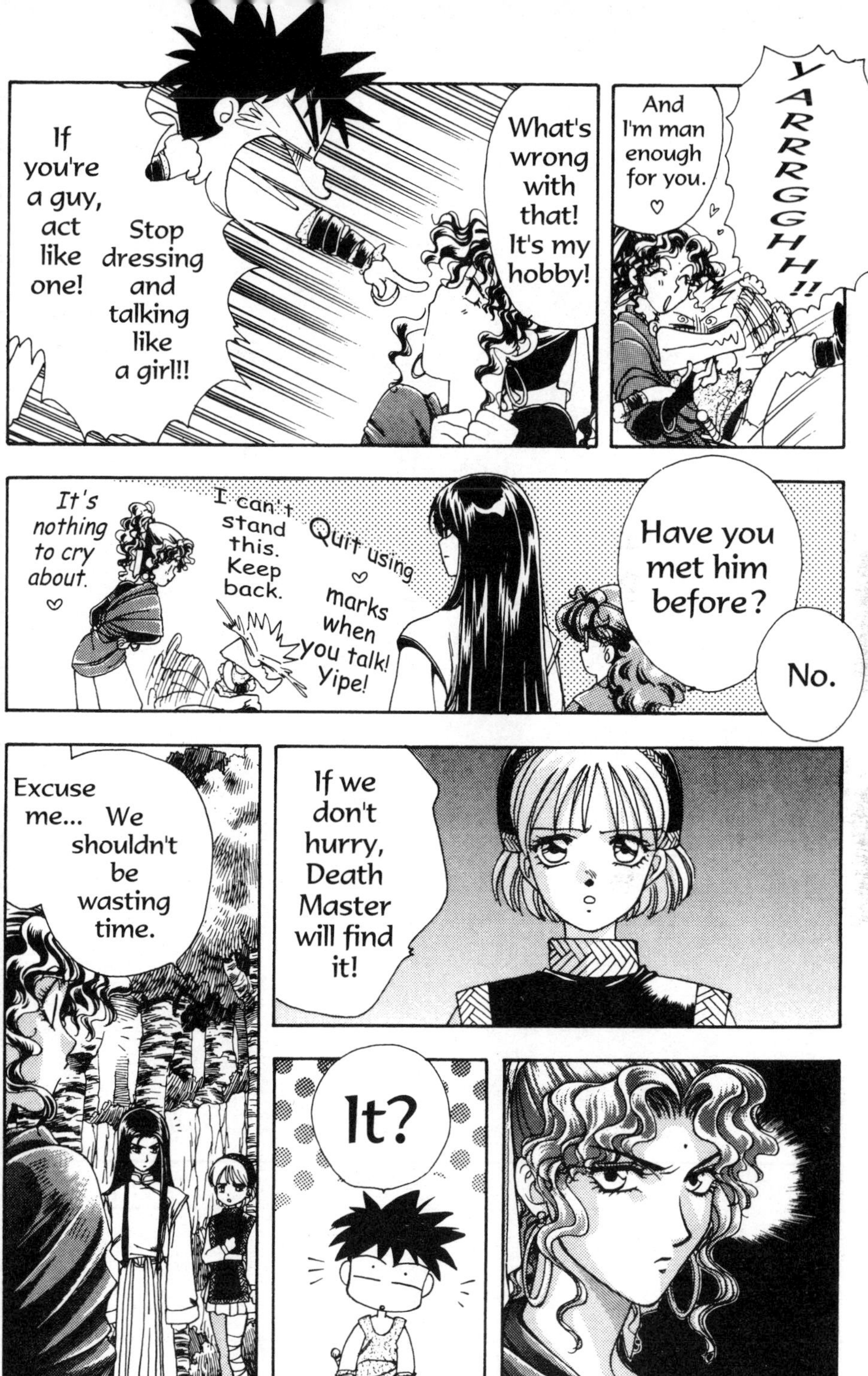
If you're a guy, act like one!
Stop dressing and talking like a girl!!
What's wrong with that! It's my hobby!
And I'm man enough for you. ♡
YARRRGGHH!!
It's nothing to cry about. ♡
I can't stand this. Keep back.
Quit using ♡ marks when you talk!
Yipe!
Have you met him before?
No.
Excuse me... We shouldn't be wasting time.
If we don't hurry, Death Master will find it!
It?

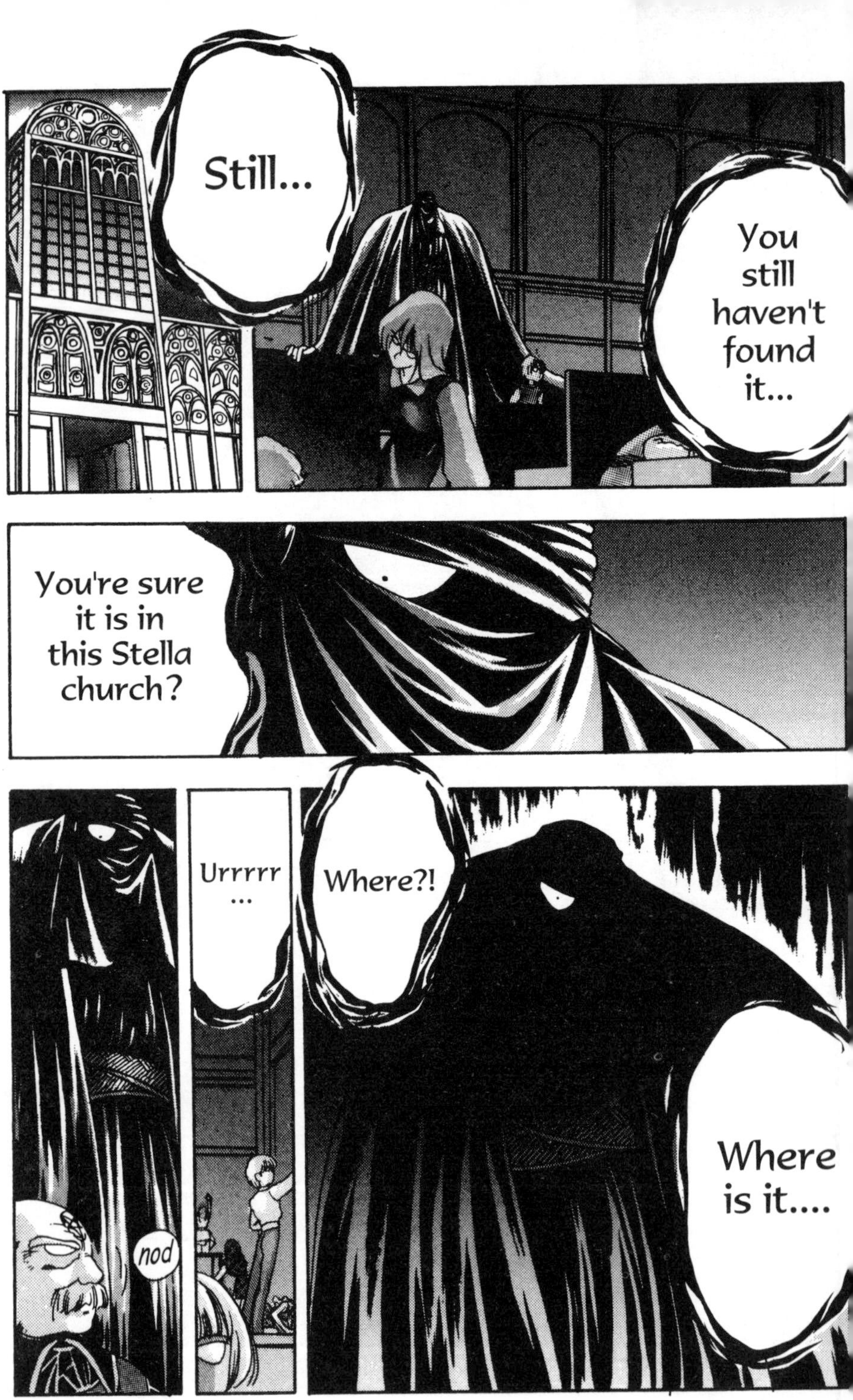
Still...
You still haven't found it...
You're sure it is in this Stella church?
nod
Urrrrr ...
Where?!
Where is it....

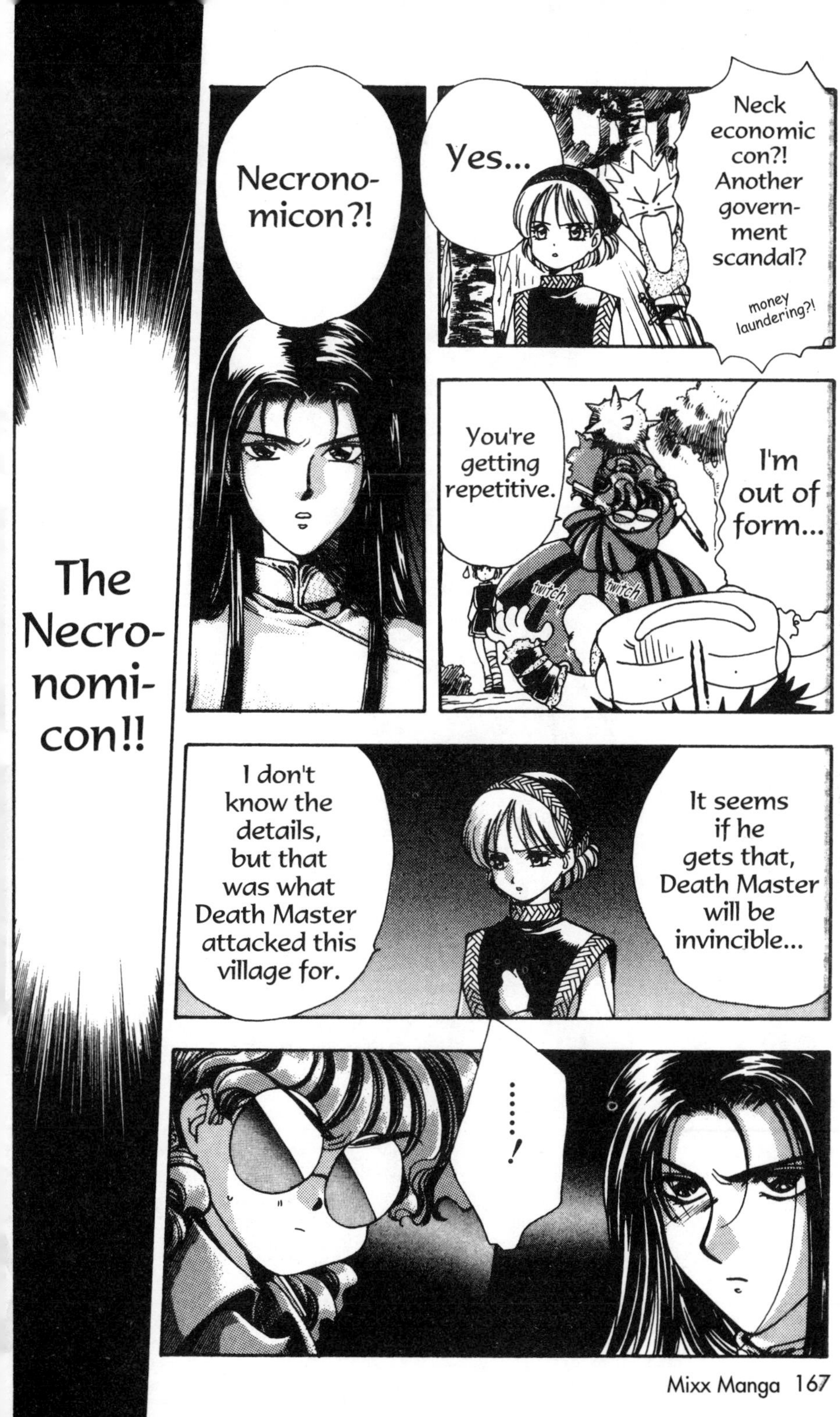
The Necronomicon!!
Necronomicon?!
Yes...
Neck economic con?! Another government scandal?
money laundering?!
You're getting repetitive.
I'm out of form...
twitch
twitch
I don't know the details, but that was what Death Master attacked this village for.
It seems if he gets that, Death Master will be invincible...
......!

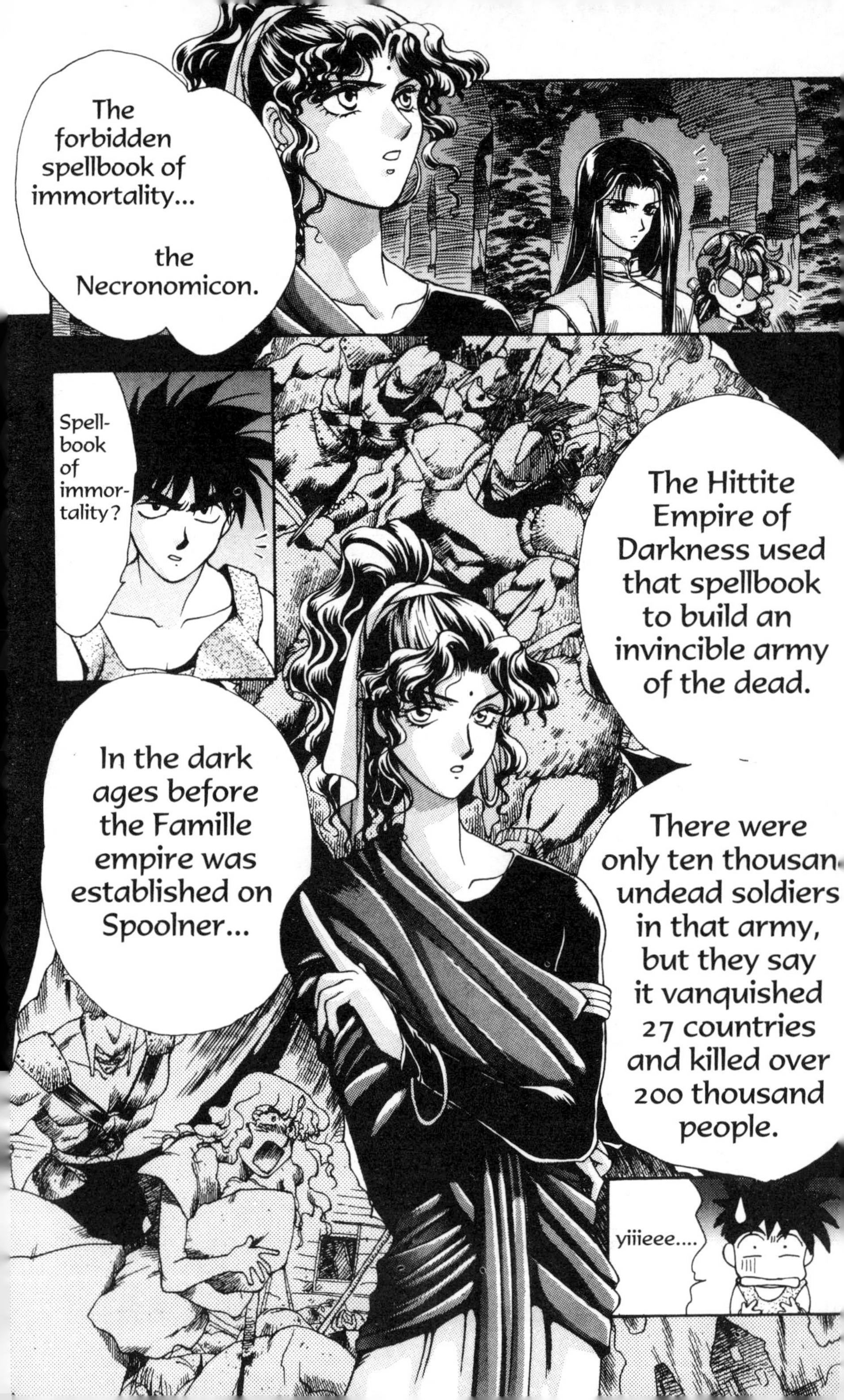
The forbidden spellbook of immortality...
the Necronomicon.
Spell-book of immor-tality?
The Hittite Empire of Darkness used that spellbook to build an invincible army of the dead.
In the dark ages before the Famille empire was established on Spoolner...
There were only ten thousan undead soldiers in that army, but they say it vanquished 27 countries and killed over 200 thousand people.
yiiieee....

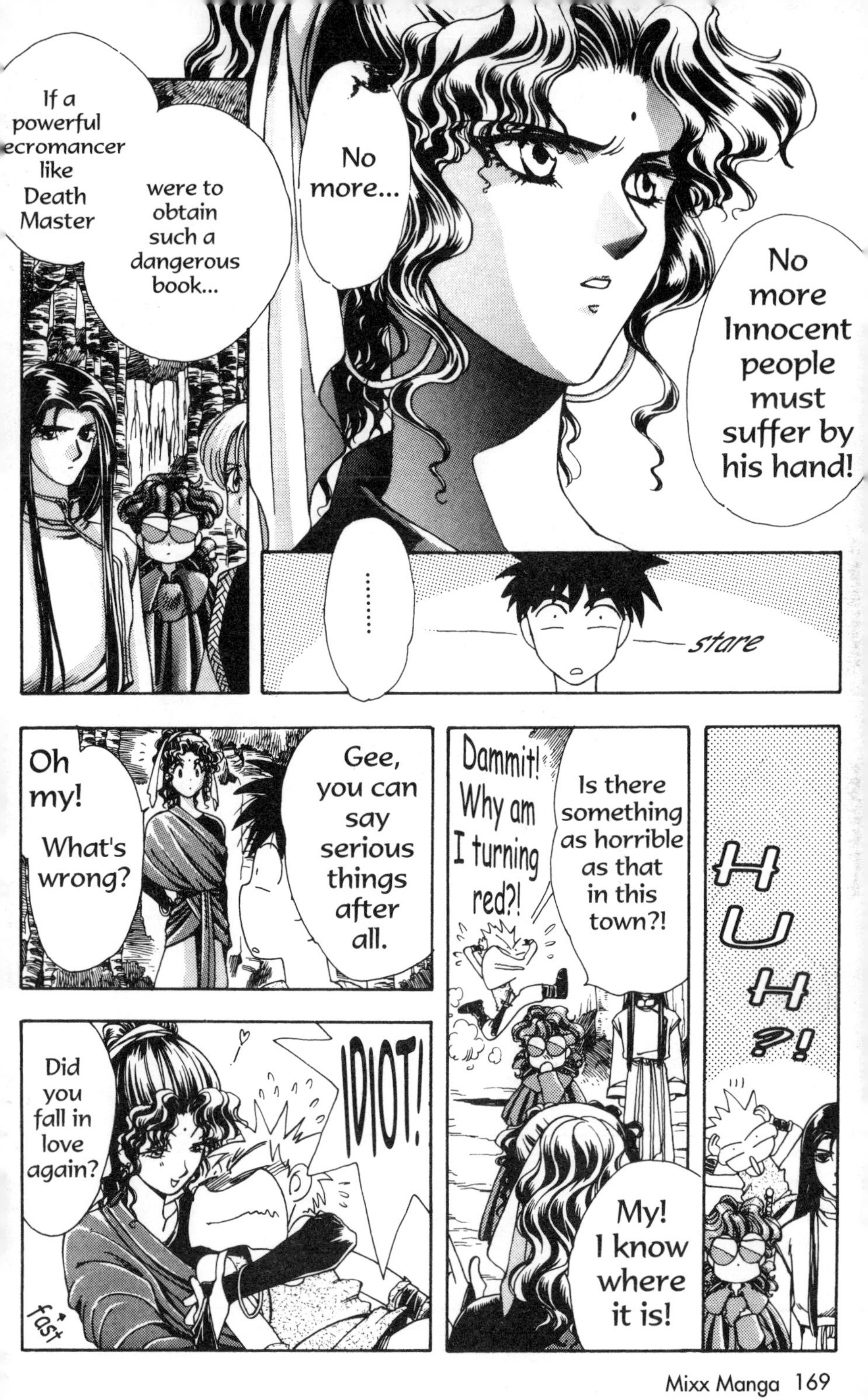

If a powerful ecromancer like Death Master
were to obtain such a dangerous book...
No more...
No more Innocent people must suffer by his hand!
....
stare
Oh my!
What's wrong?
Gee, you can say serious things after all.
Did you fall in love again?
IDIOT!
fast
Dammit! Why am I turning red?!
Is there something as horrible as that in this town?!
My! I know where it is!
HUH?!

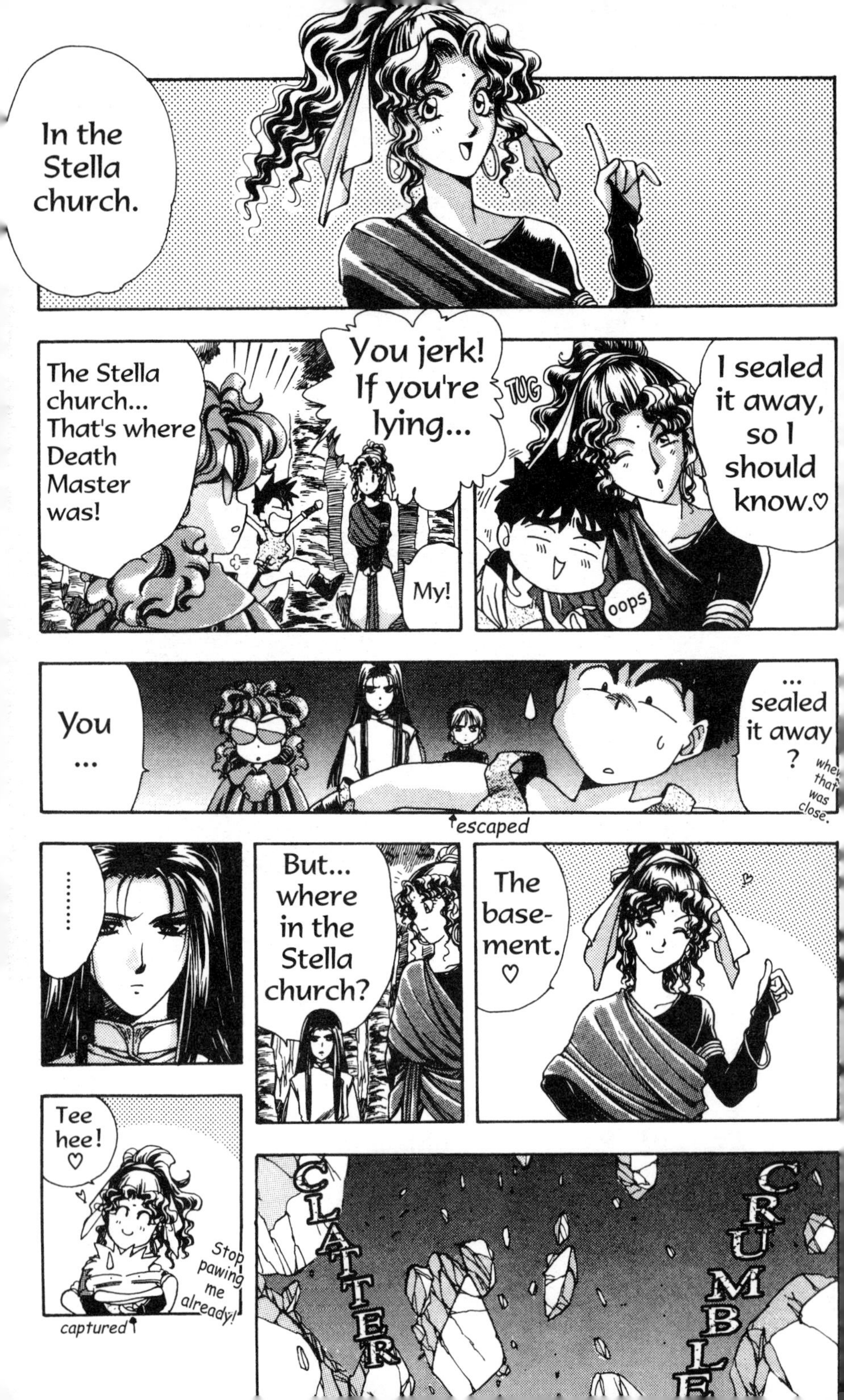
In the Stella church.
The Stella church... That's where Death Master was!
You jerk! If you're lying...
My!
TUG
I sealed it away, so I should know.♡
oops
You ...
... sealed it away ?
whe that was close.
escaped
....
But... where in the Stella church?
The basement. ♡
Tee hee! ♡
Stop pawing me already!
captured
CLATTER
CRUMBLE

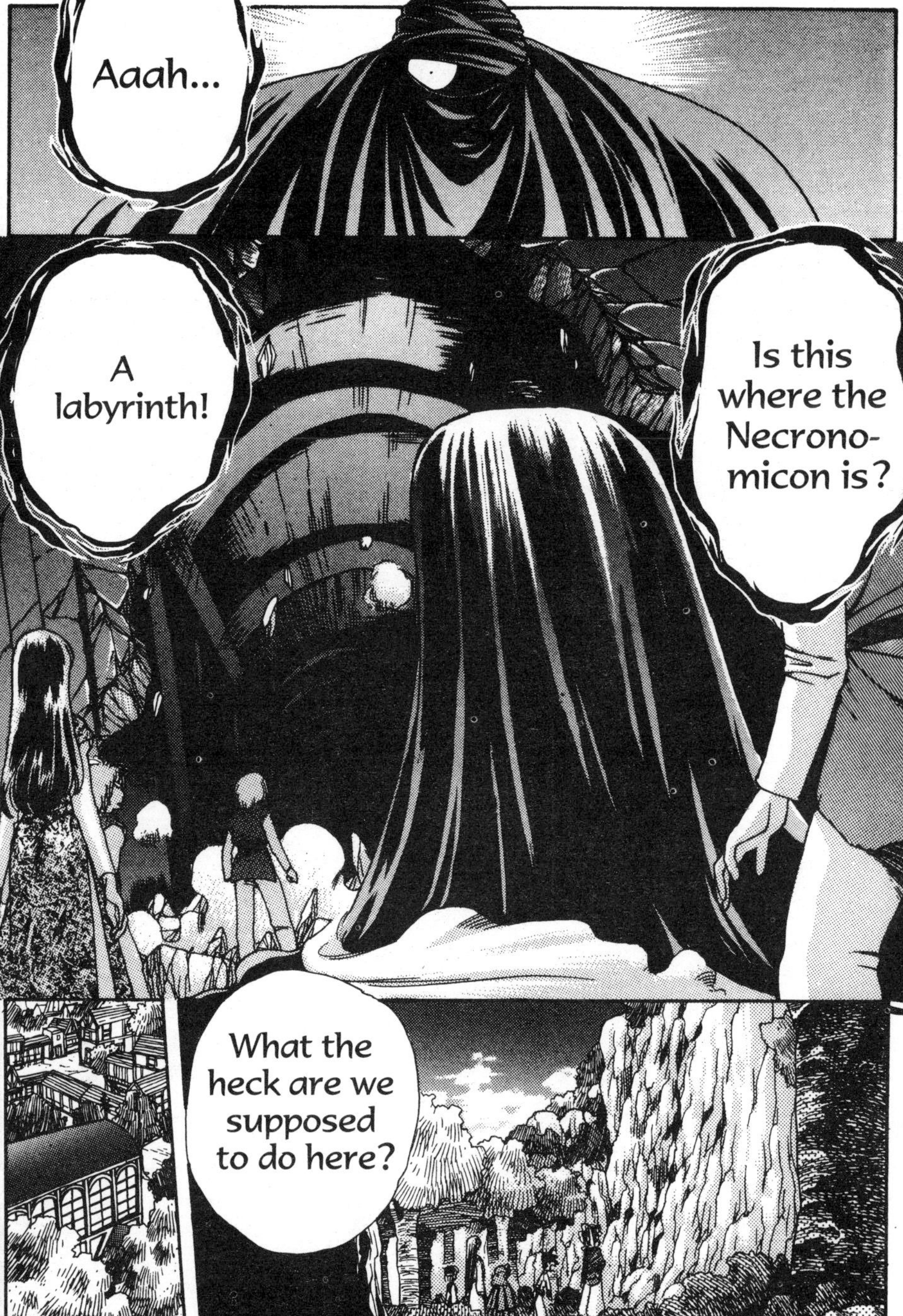
Aaah...
A labyrinth!
Is this where the Necronomicon is?
What the heck are we supposed to do here?

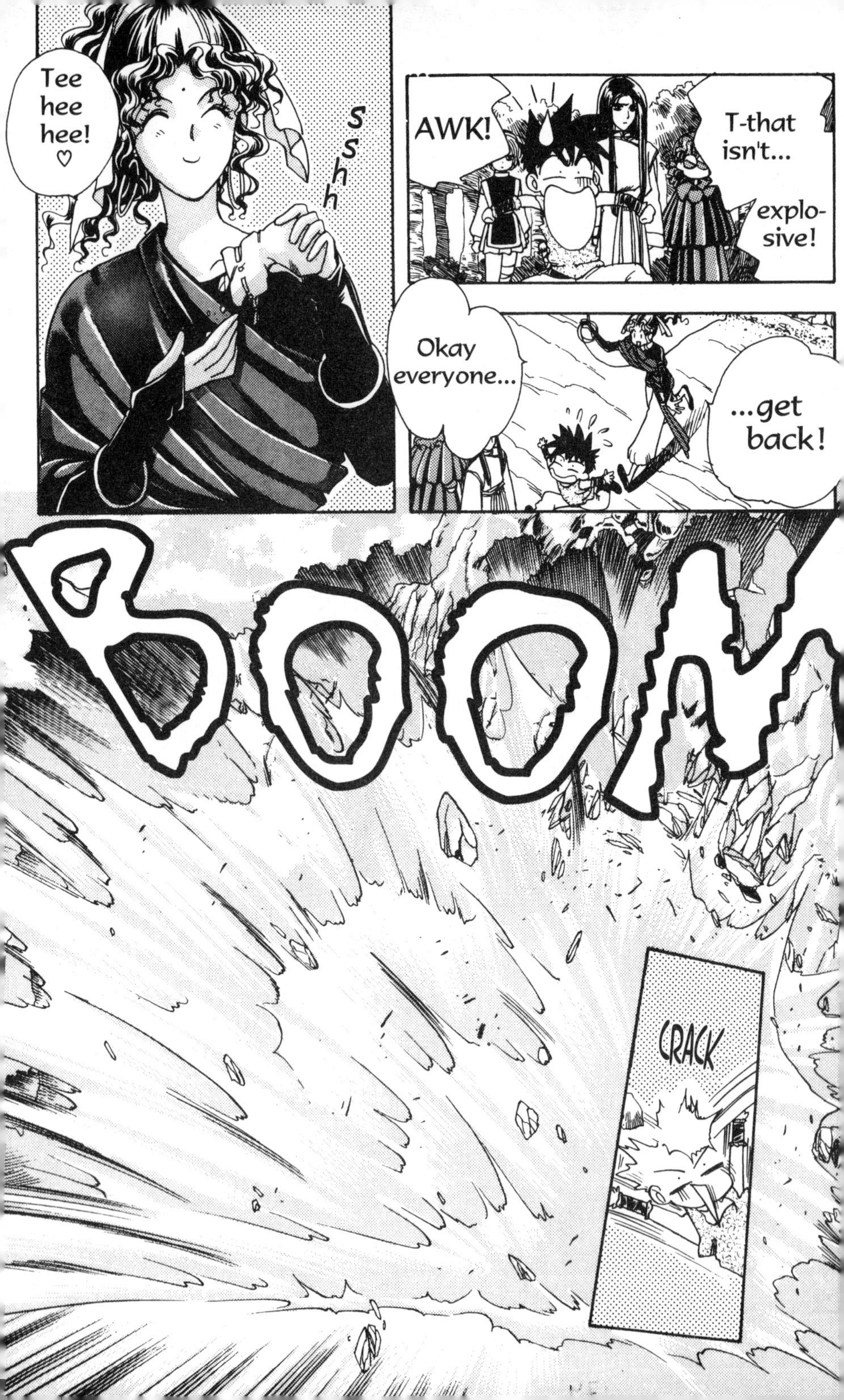
Tee hee hee! ♡
sshh
AWK!
T-that isn't...
explo-sive!
Okay everyone...
...get back!
BOOM
CRACK

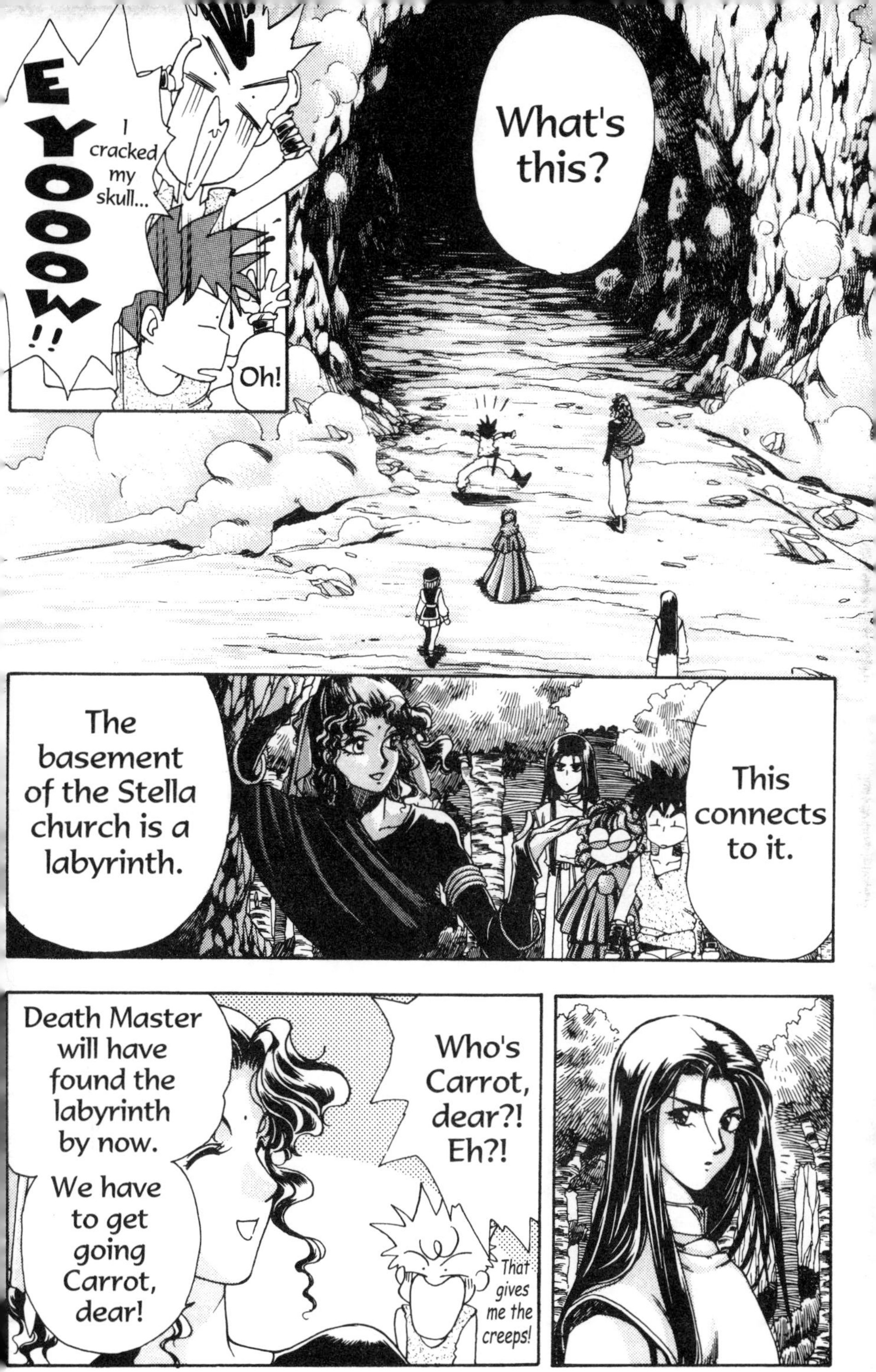
EYOOOOW!!
I cracked my skull...
Oh!
What's this?
The basement of the Stella church is a labyrinth.
This connects to it.
Death Master will have found the labyrinth by now.
We have to get going Carrot, dear!
Who's Carrot, dear?! Eh?!
That gives me the creeps!

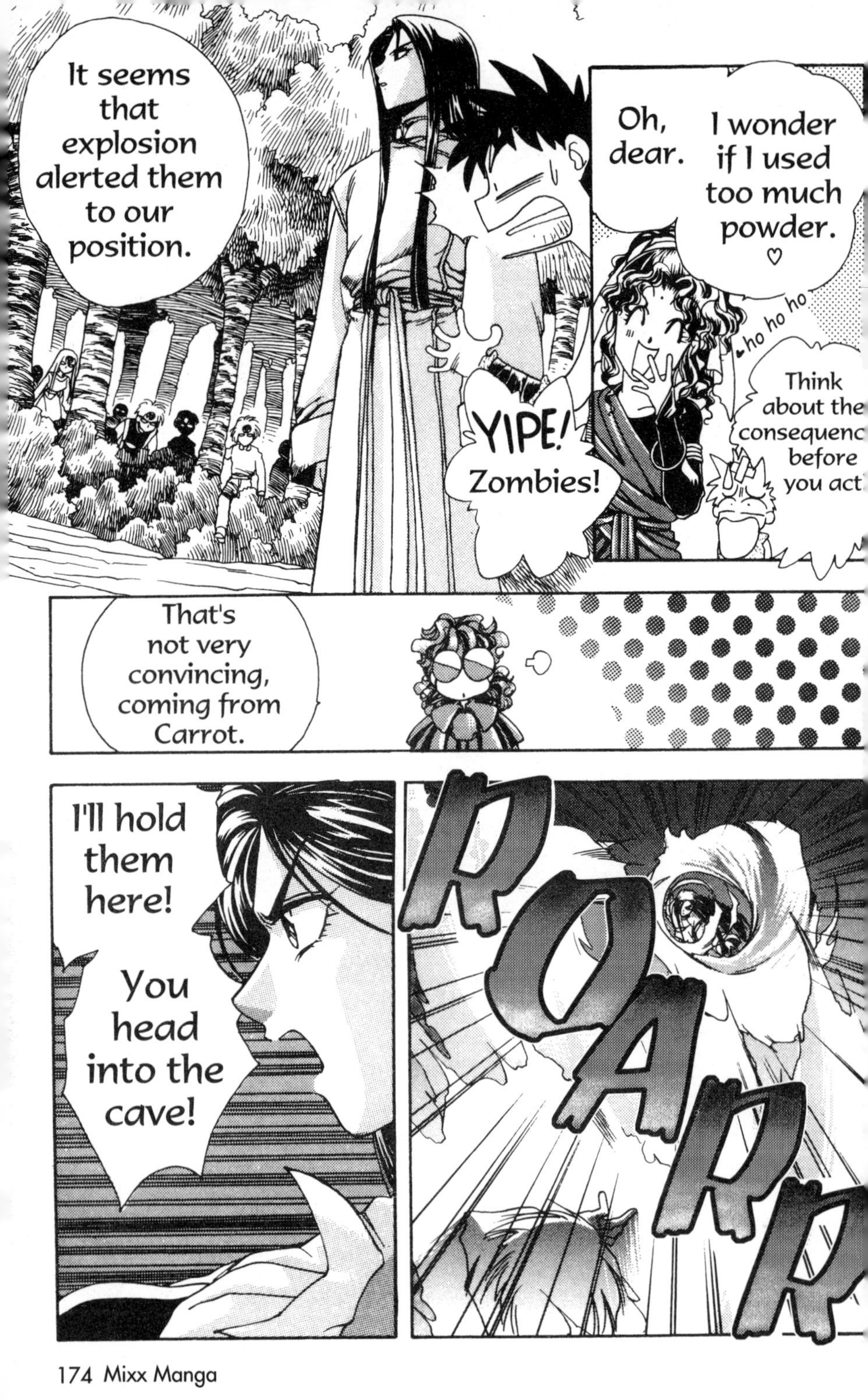
It seems that explosion alerted them to our position.
YIPE! Zombies!
Oh, dear.
I wonder if I used too much powder. ♡
ho ho ho
Think about the consequenc before you act
That's not very convincing, coming from Carrot.
I'll hold them here!
You head into the cave!
ROARRR

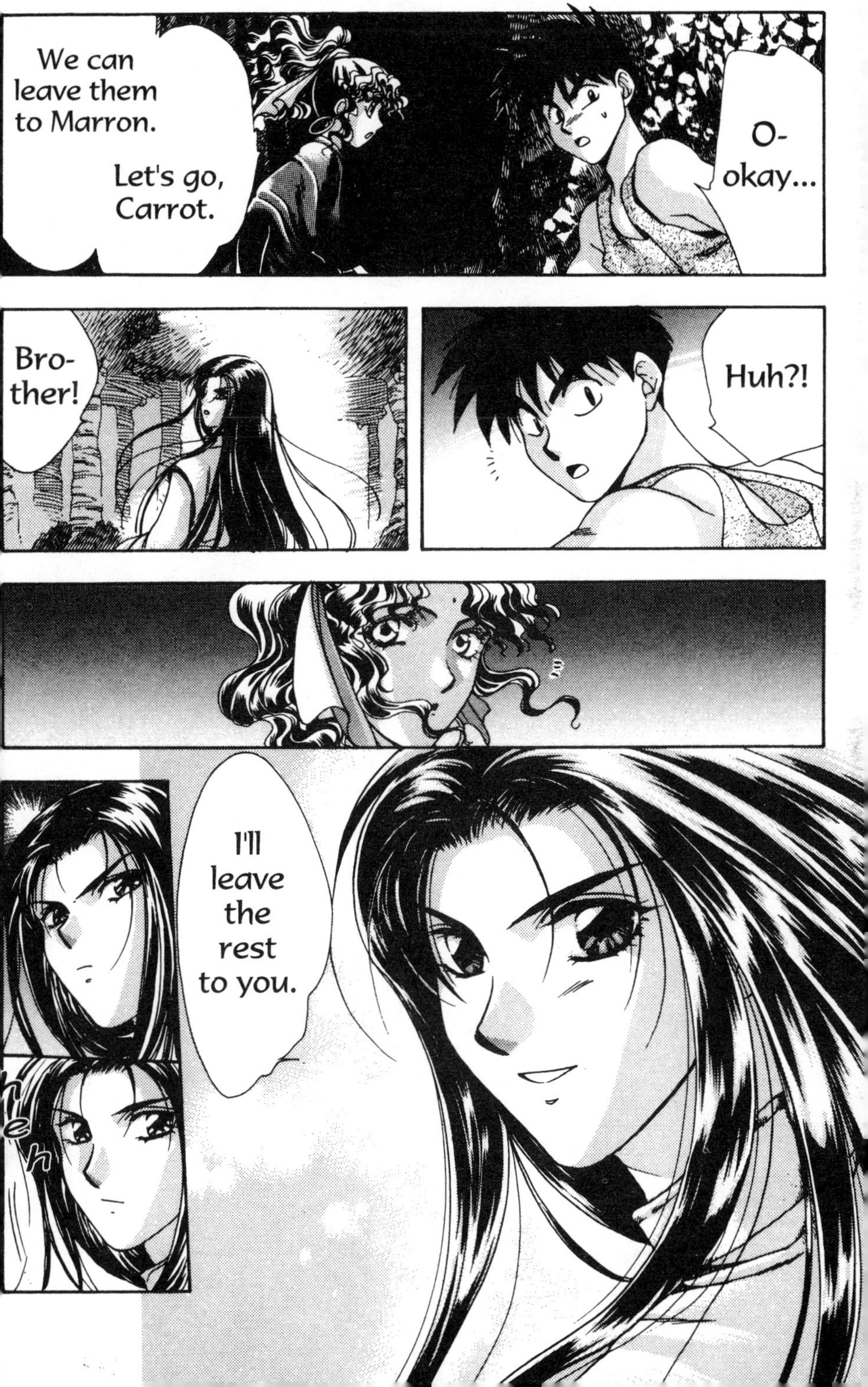
We can leave them to Marron.
Let's go, Carrot.
O- okay...
Bro- ther!
Huh?!
I'll leave the rest to you.

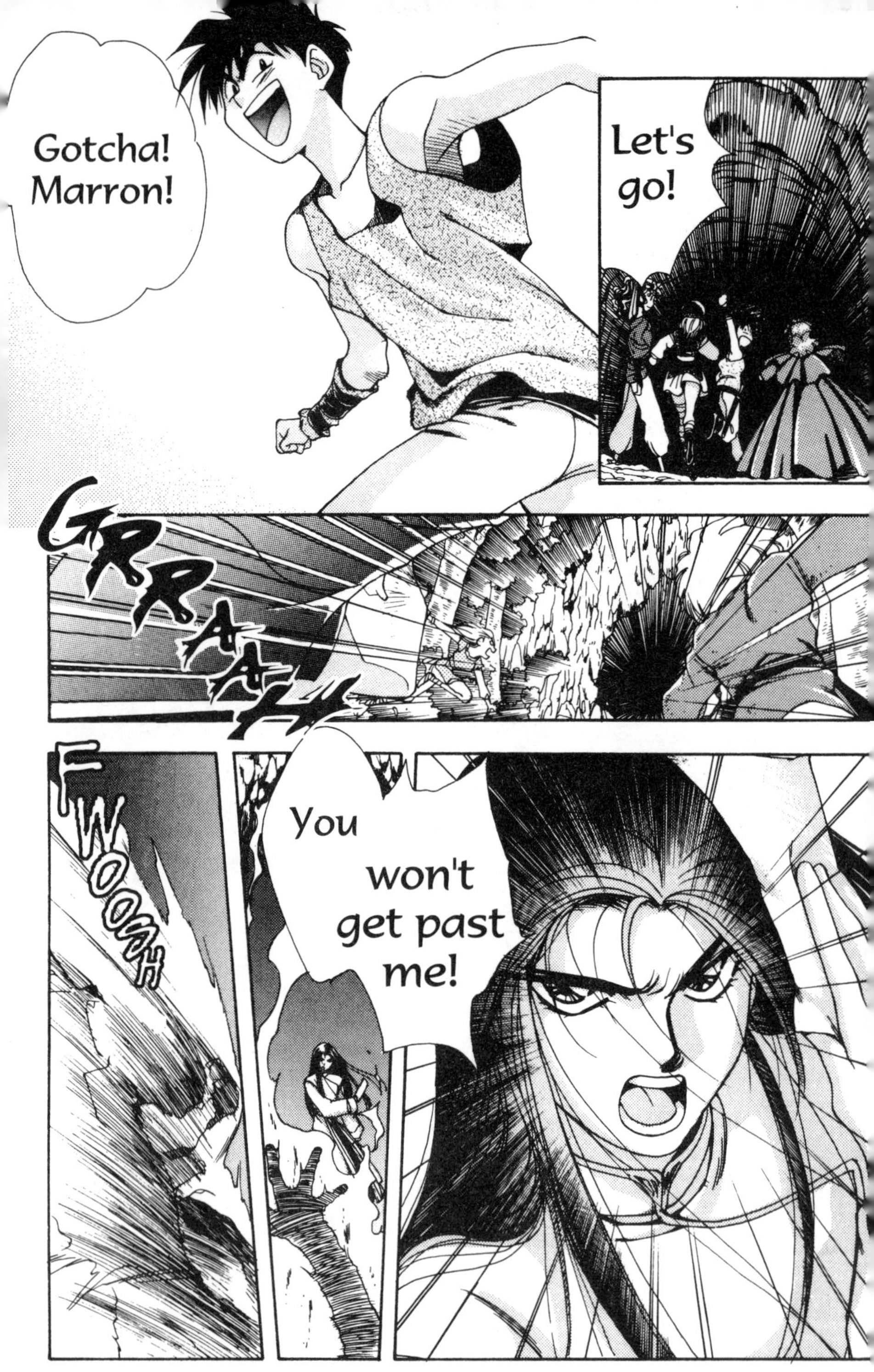
Gotcha! Marron!
Let's go!
GRRAAHH
FWOOMH
You won't get past me!

I hope Marron is alright...

You don't need to worry about Marron!

You should worry about your-selves. What will you do when you face Death Master again?

That's right... Marron's Eastern Magic didn't even budge him...

uh-huh

My! But we have Carrot.

eep ...?

Me?!

Your powers are Aranju, the power to absorb magic; and Zoanthropy, right? You should be able to absorb Death Master's poison and transform.

Are you sure?!

I wouldn't turn into a zombie ?!

Probably not.

Pro-bably ?!

Now look, you!

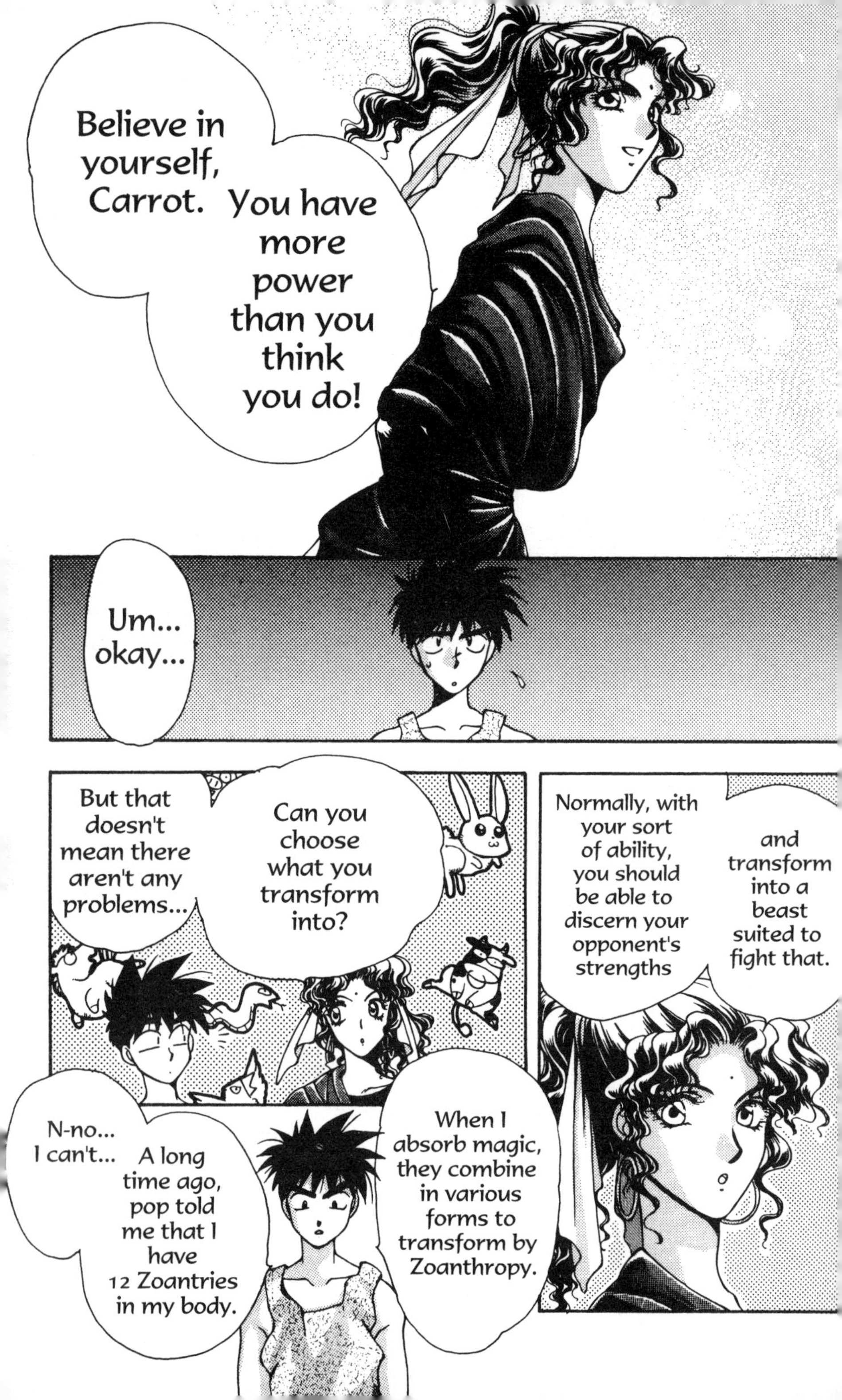
Believe in yourself, Carrot.
You have more power than you think you do!
Um... okay...
But that doesn't mean there aren't any problems...
Can you choose what you transform into?
N-no... I can't...
A long time ago, pop told me that I have 12 Zoantries in my body.
When I absorb magic, they combine in various forms to transform by Zoanthropy.
Normally, with your sort of ability, you should be able to discern your opponent's strengths
and transform into a beast suited to fight that.

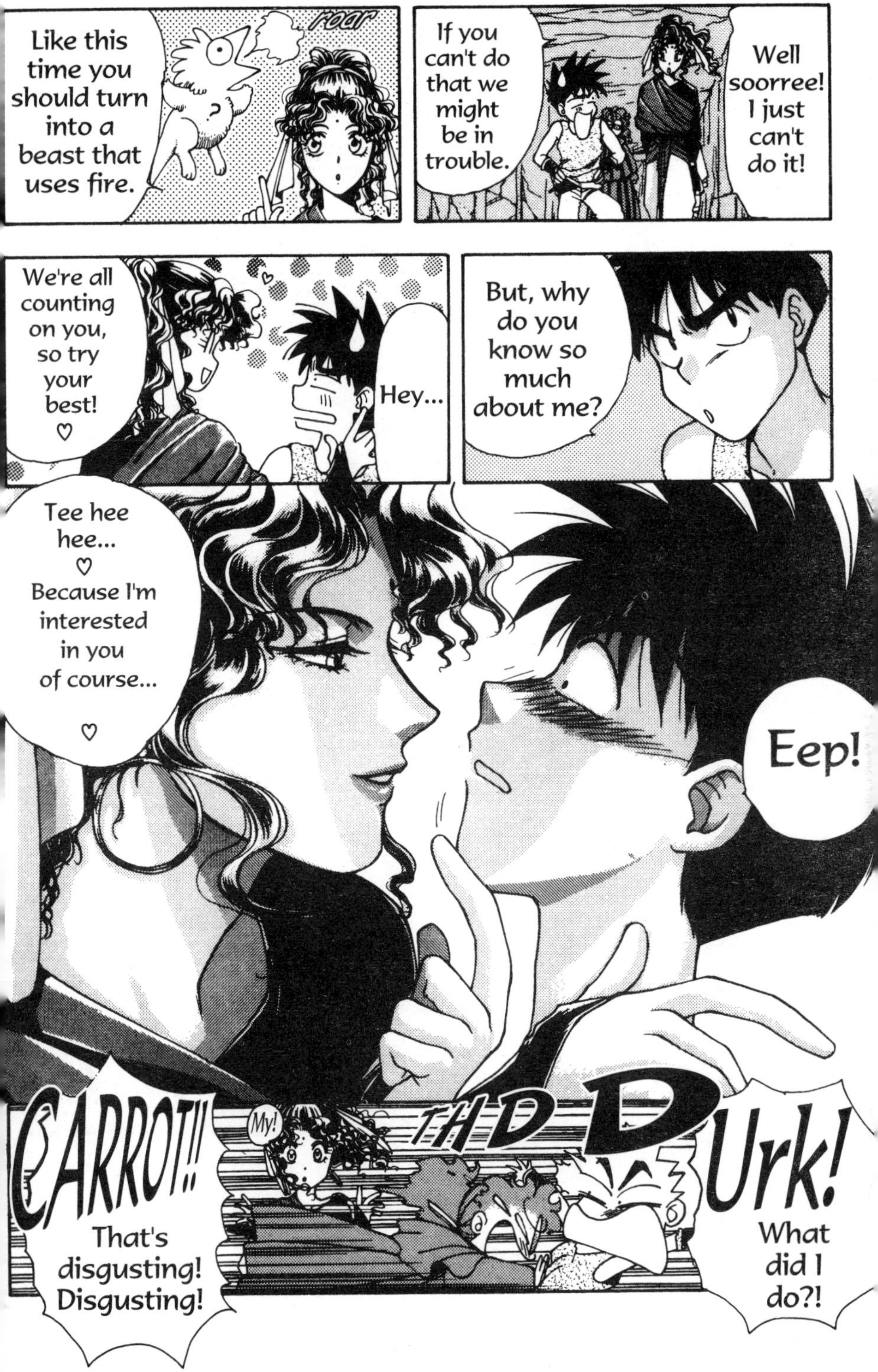
roar
Like this time you should turn into a beast that uses fire.
If you can't do that we might be in trouble.
Well soorree! I just can't do it!
We're all counting on you, so try your best! ♡
Hey...
But, why do you know so much about me?
Tee hee hee... ♡ Because I'm interested in you of course... ♡
Eep!
CARROT!! That's disgusting! Disgusting!
My!
THDD
Urk! What did I do?!

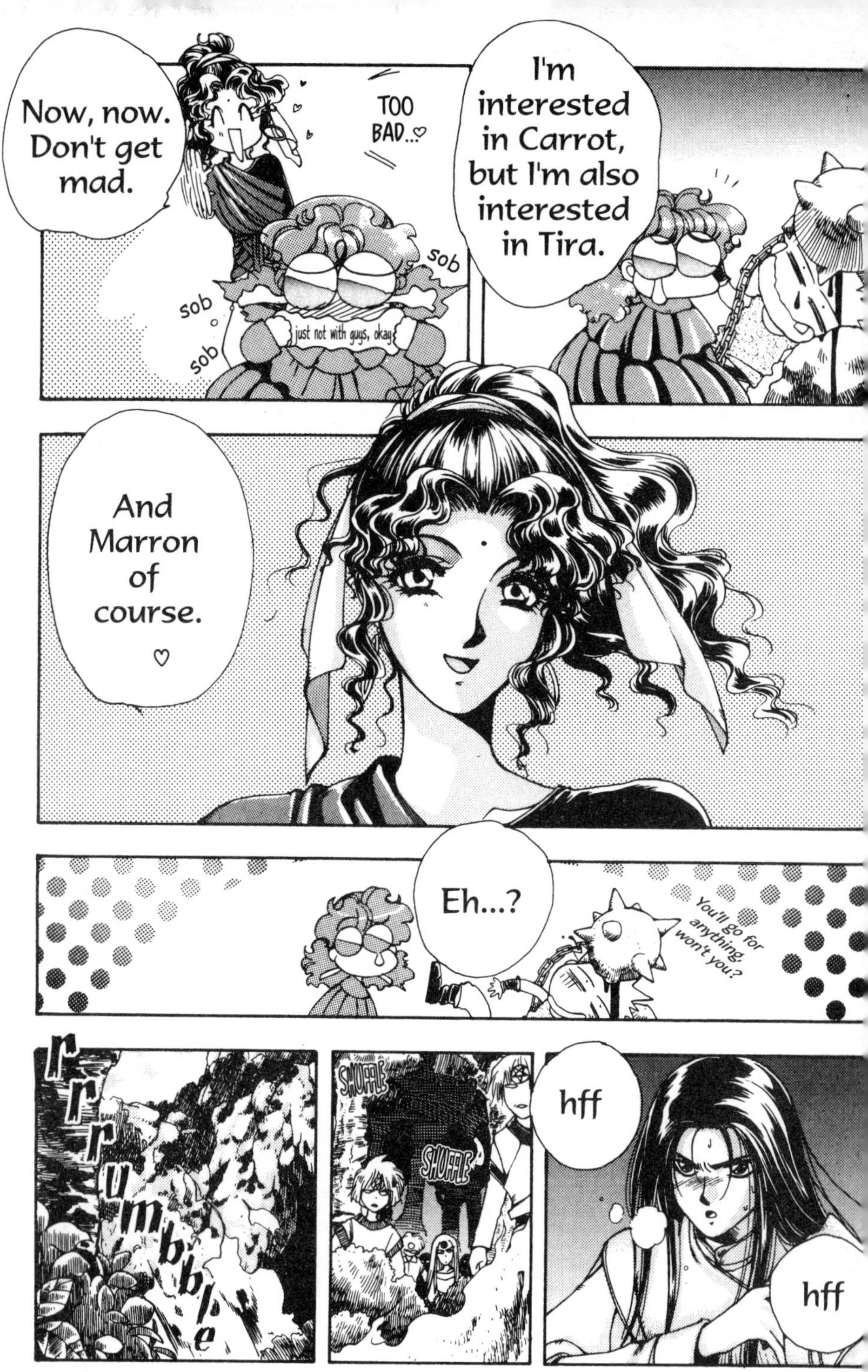

Now, now. Don't get mad.
TOO BAD...♡
sob
sob
sob
just not with guys, okay
I'm interested in Carrot, but I'm also interested in Tira.
And Marron of course. ♡
Eh...?
You'll go for anything, won't you?
rrrumbble
SHUFFLE
SHUFFLE
hff
hff

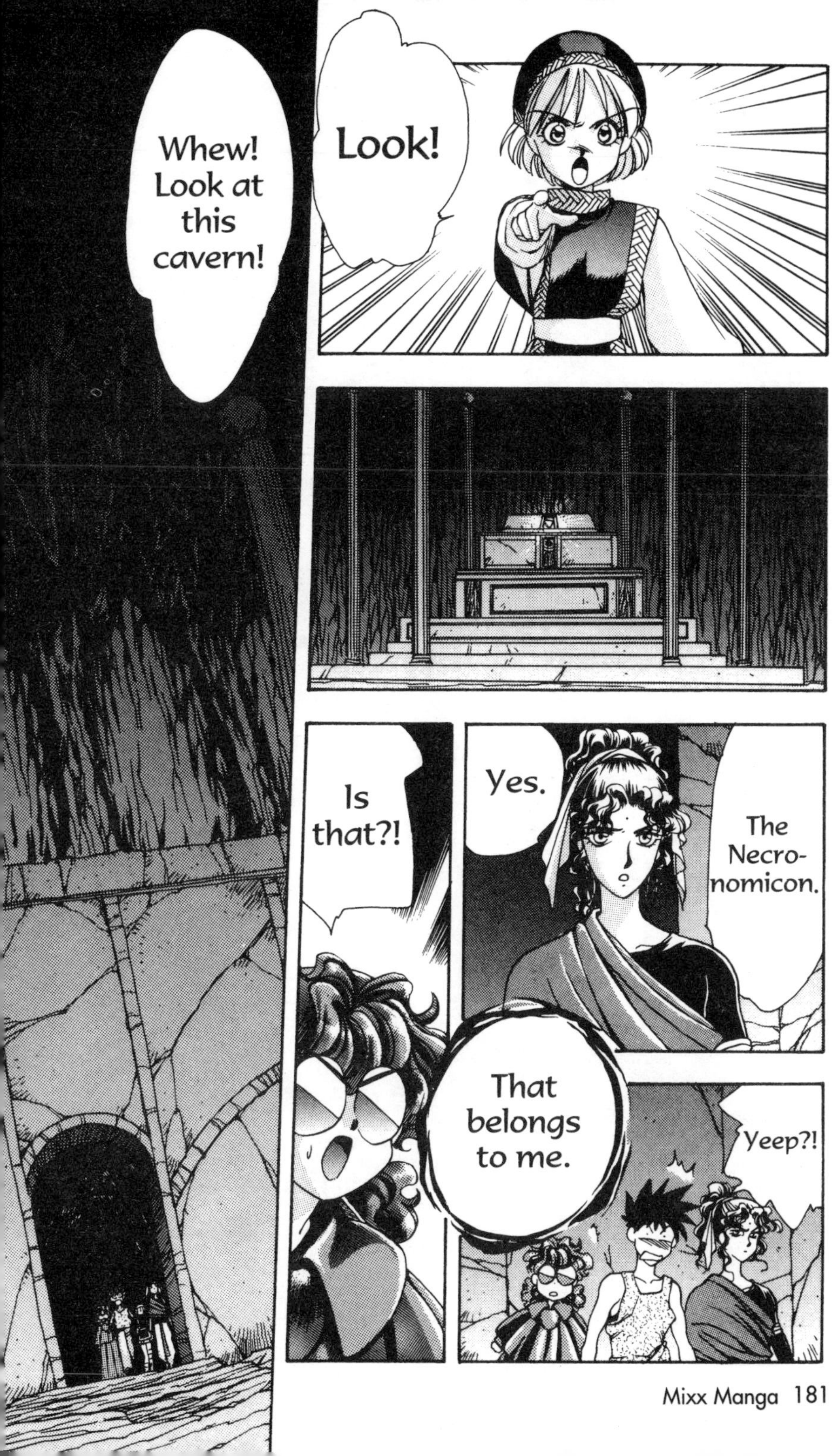
Whew! Look at this cavern!
Look!
Is that?!
Yes.
The Necronomicon.
That belongs to me.
Yeep?!

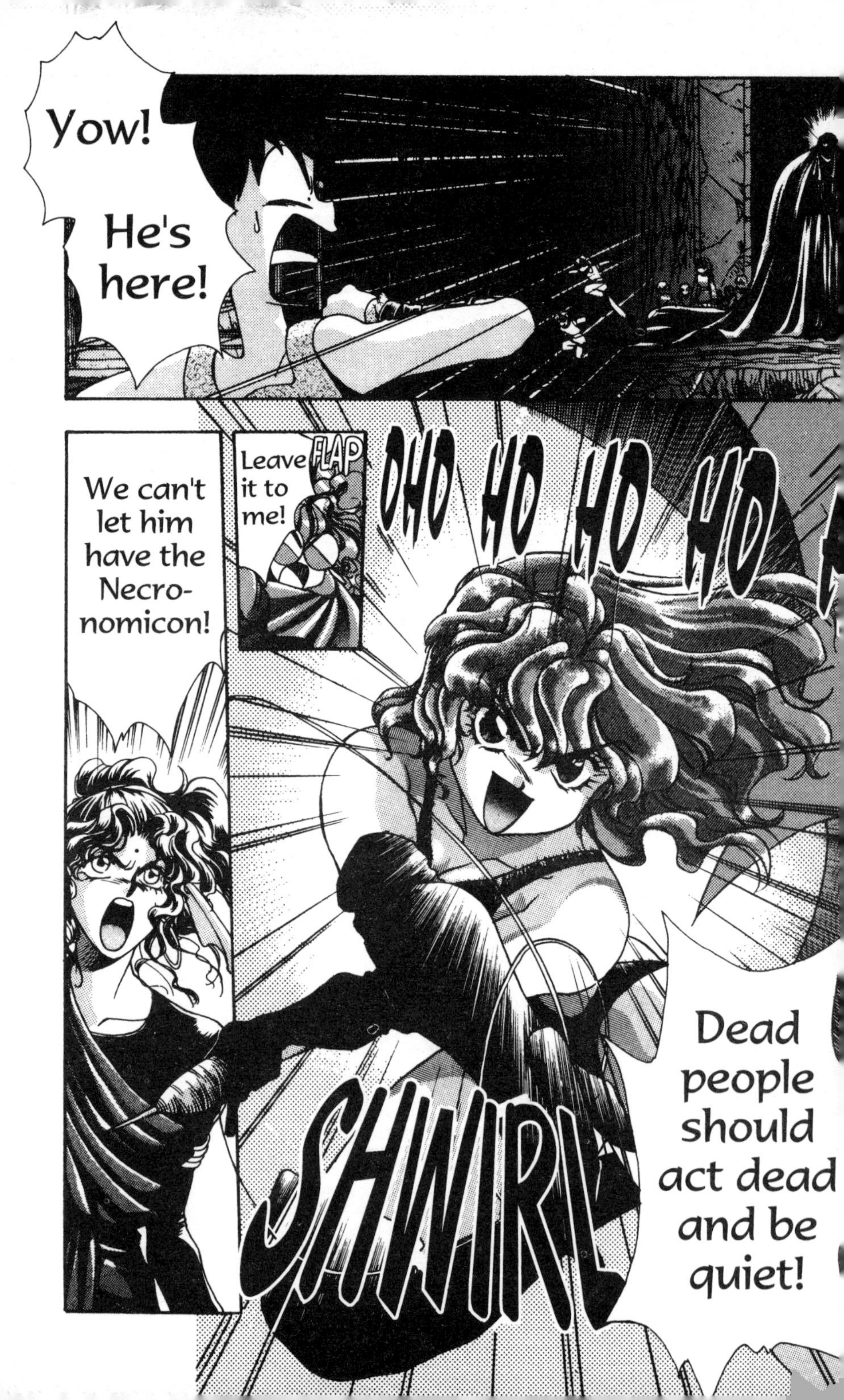

Yow!
He's here!
We can't let him have the Necronomicon!
Leave it to me!
FLAP
OHO HO HO HO
SHWIRL
Dead people should act dead and be quiet!

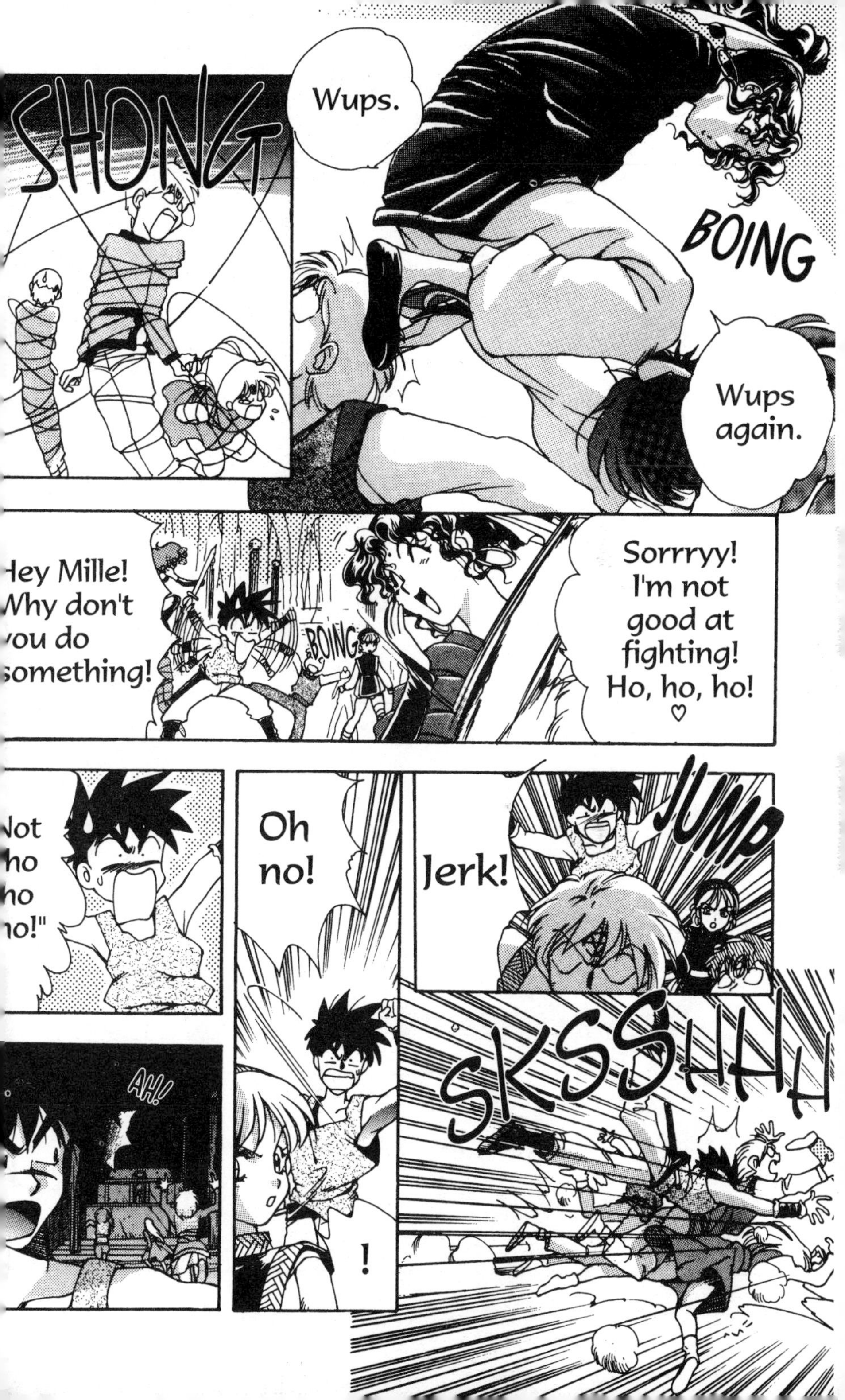
SHONG
Wups.
BOING
Wups again.
ley Mille! Vhy don't ou do omething!
BOING
Sorrryy! I'm not good at fighting! Ho, ho, ho! ♡
Vot ho ho o!"
Oh no!
Jerk!
JUMP
AH!
!
SKSSHHH

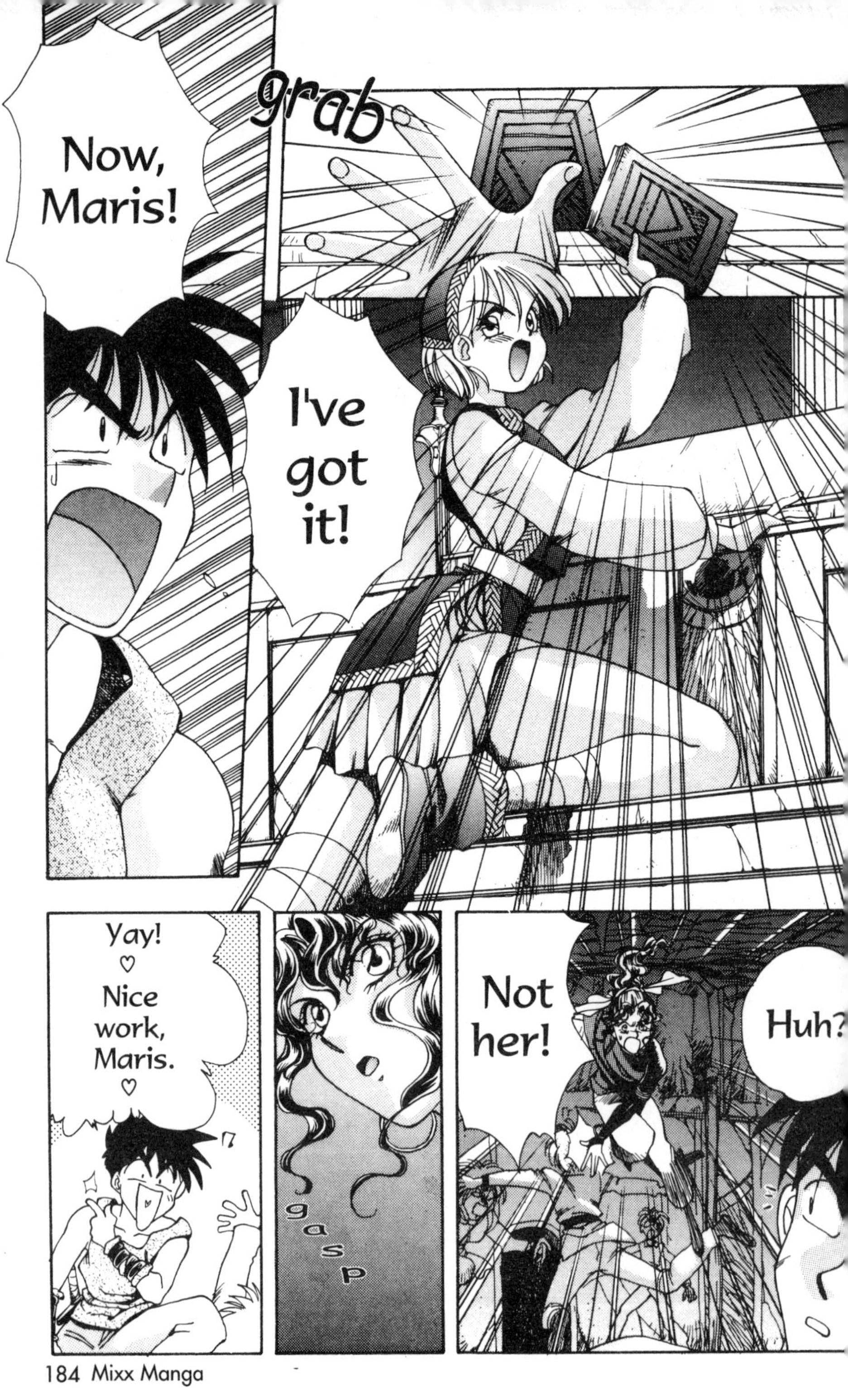
Now, Maris!
grab
I've got it!
Yay! ♡ Nice work, Maris. ♡
gasp
Not her!
Huh?

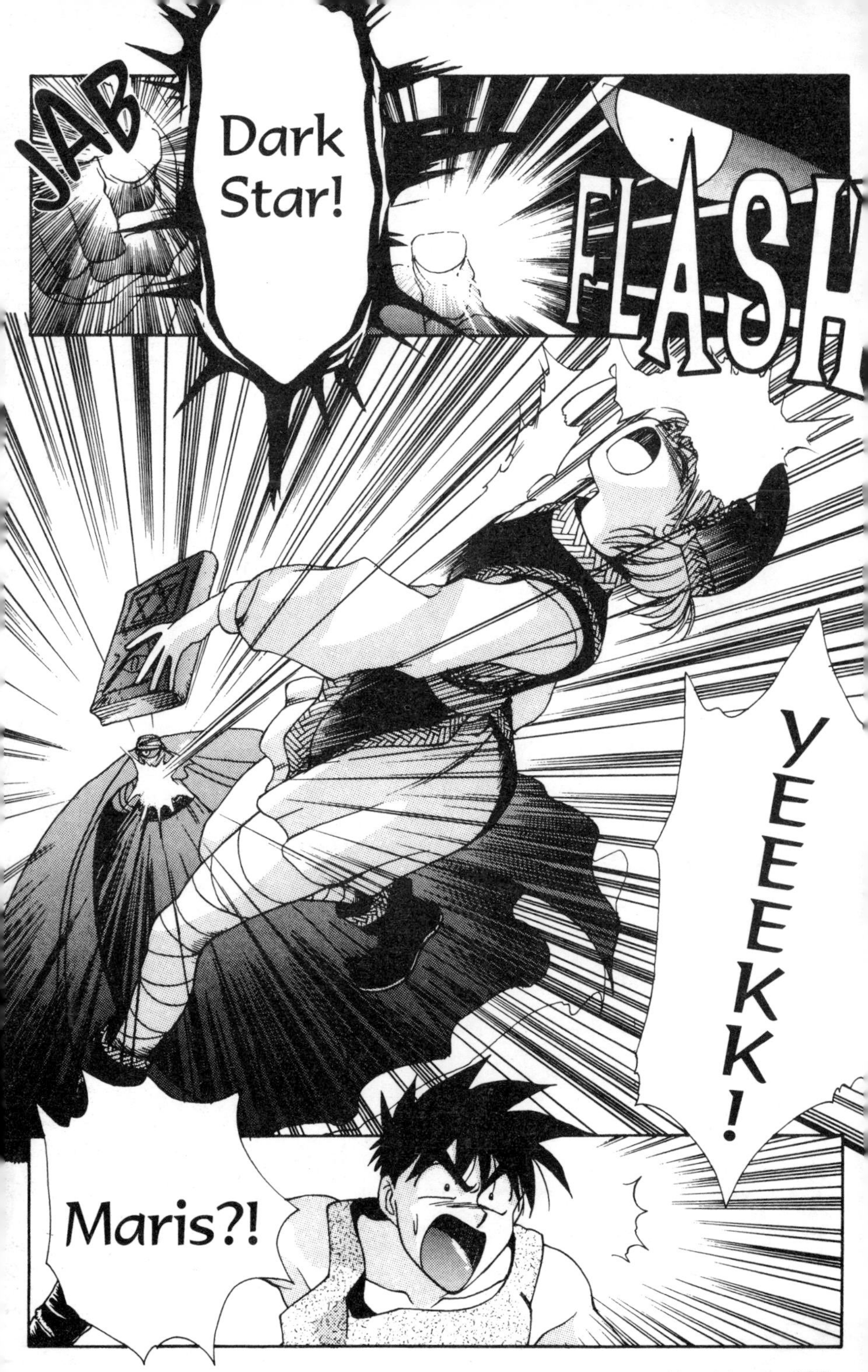
JAB
Dark Star!
FLASH
YEEEKK!
Maris?!

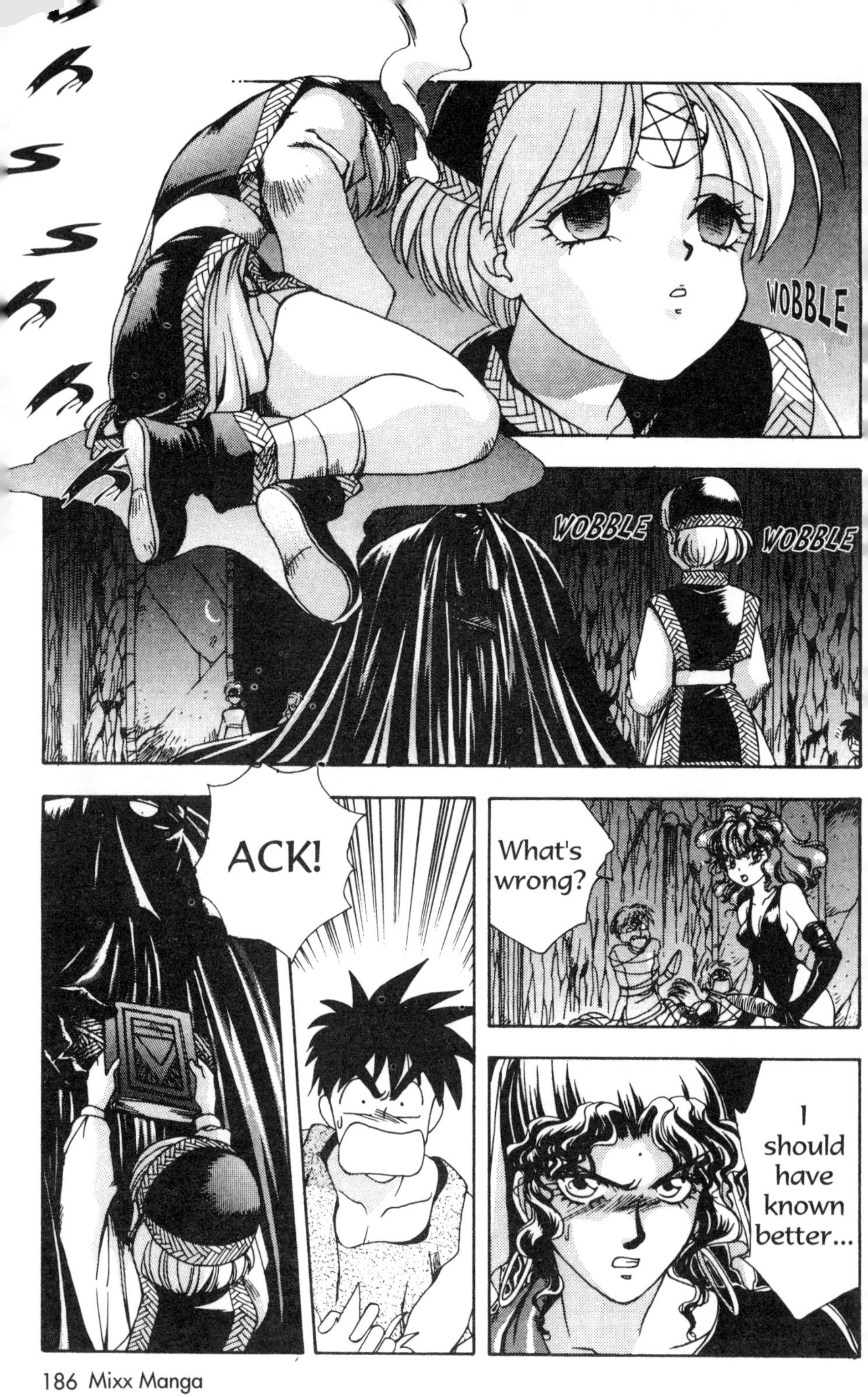
WOBBLE
WOBBLE
WOBBLE
ACK!
What's wrong?
I should have known better...

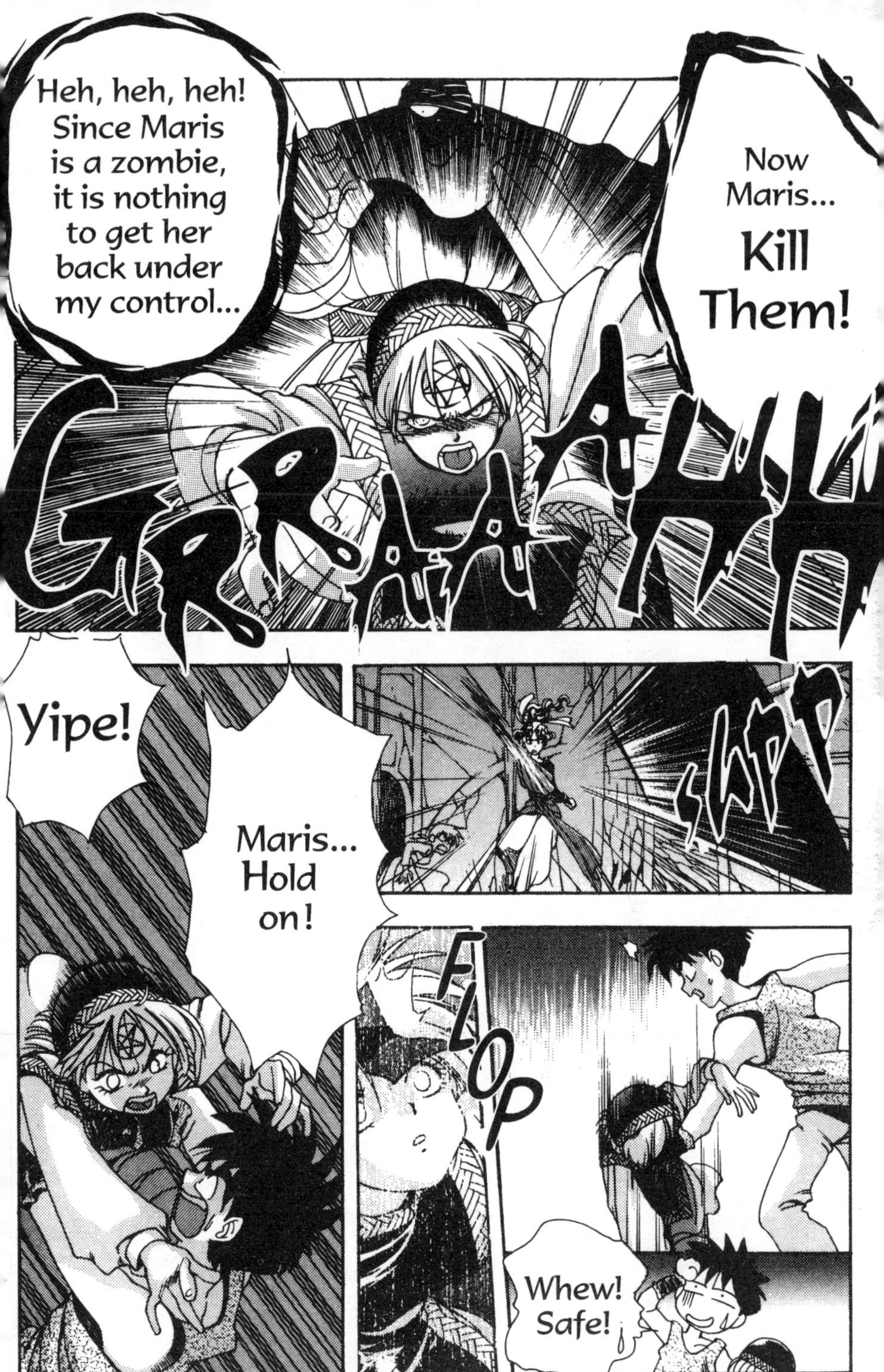
Heh, heh, heh! Since Maris is a zombie, it is nothing to get her back under my control...
Now Maris... Kill Them!
GRRAAAHH
Yipe!
SLPP
Maris... Hold on!
FLOP
Whew! Safe!

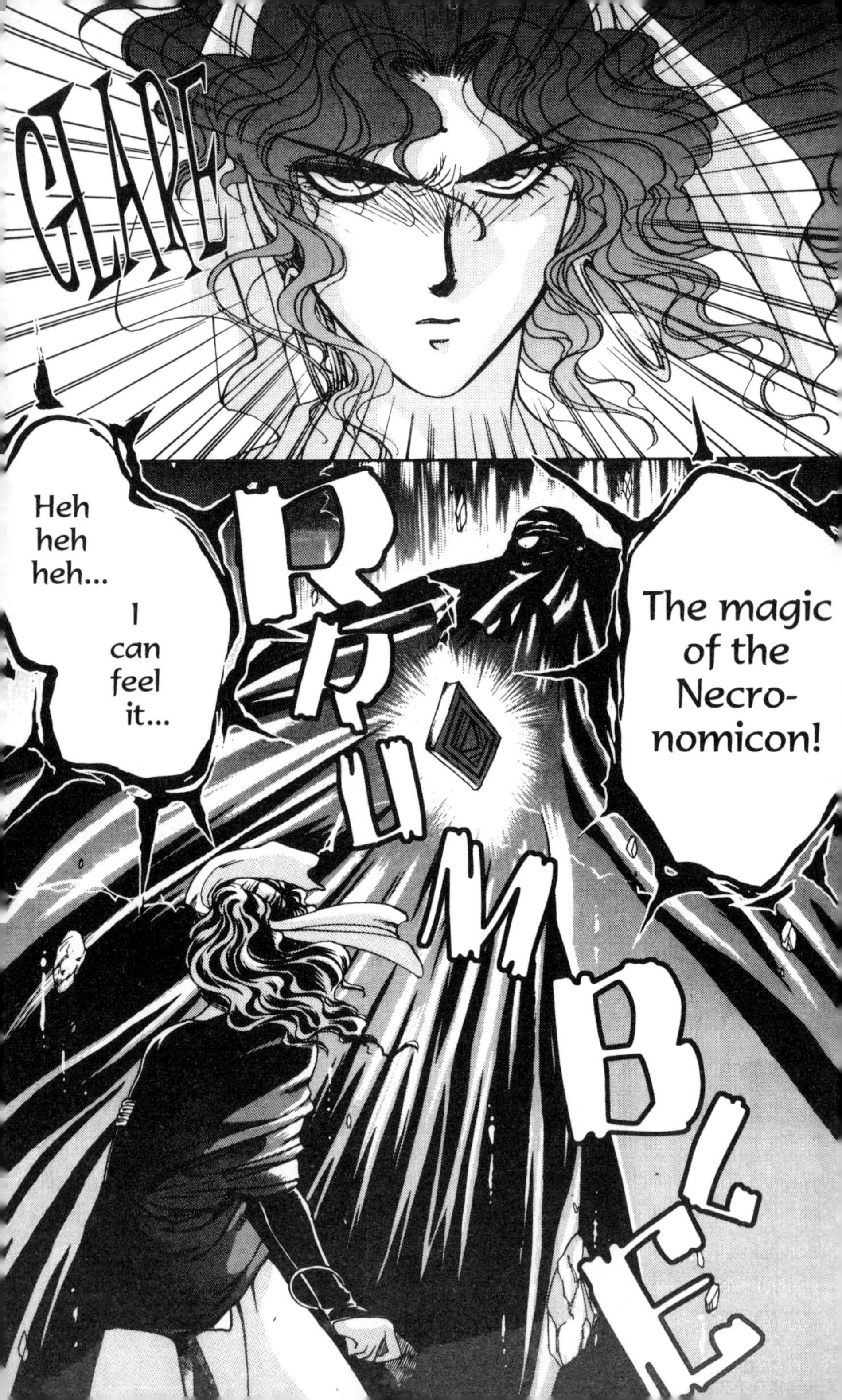
GLARE
Heh heh heh... I can feel it...
RUMBLE
The magic of the Necro-nomicon!

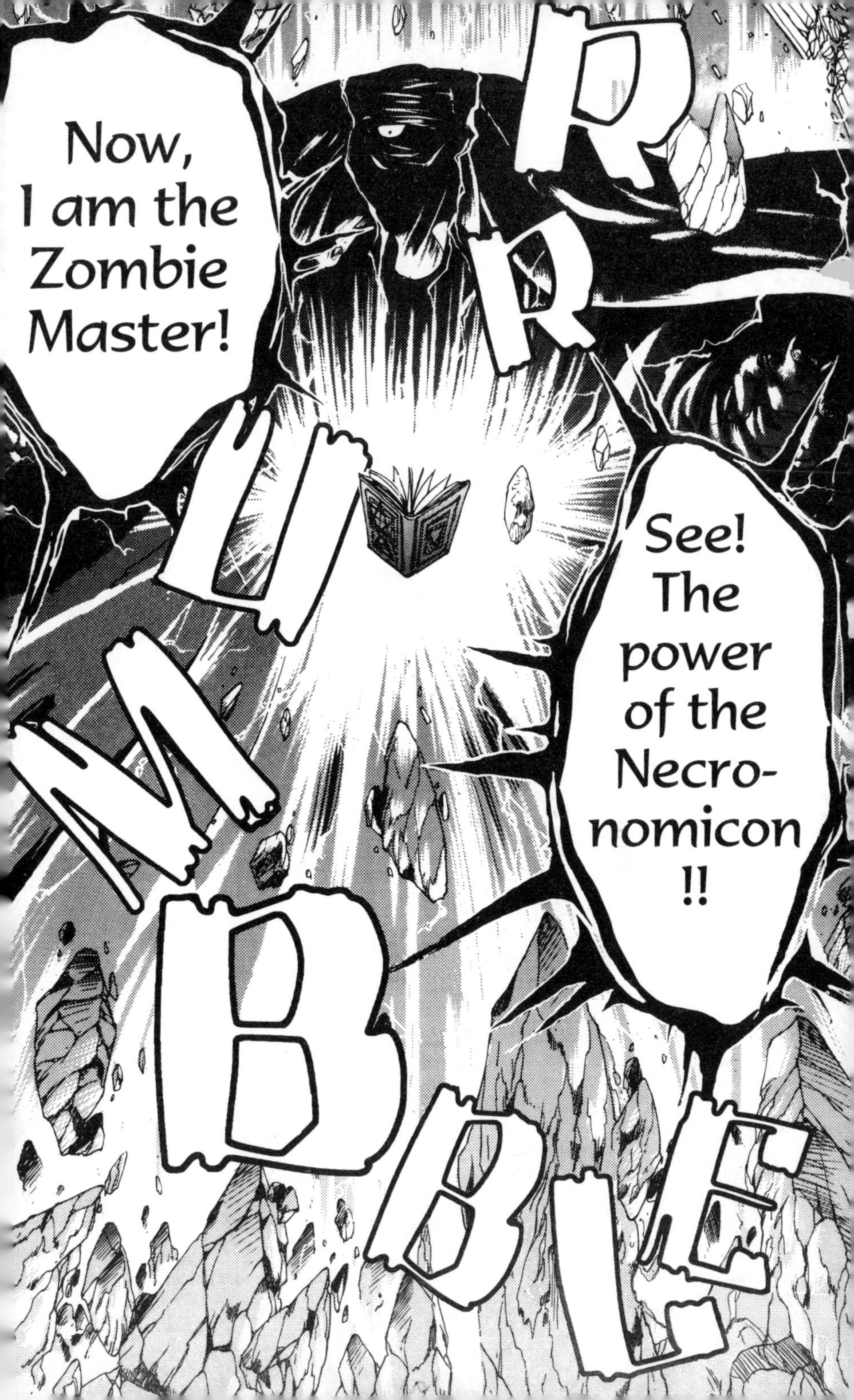
Now, I am the Zombie Master!
See! The power of the Necro-nomicon !!
RRUMBBLE

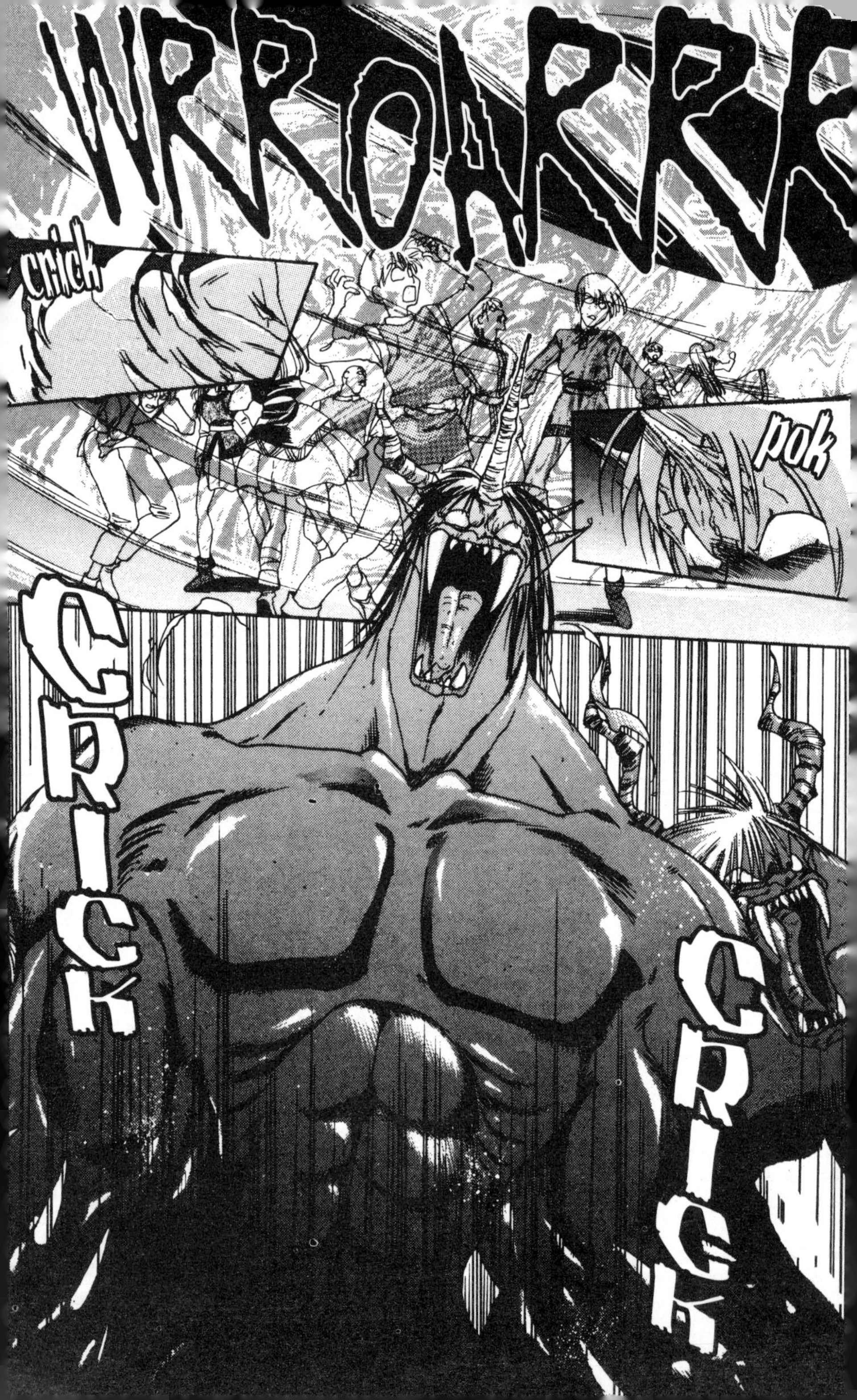
WRROARRR
crick
pok
CRICK
CRICK

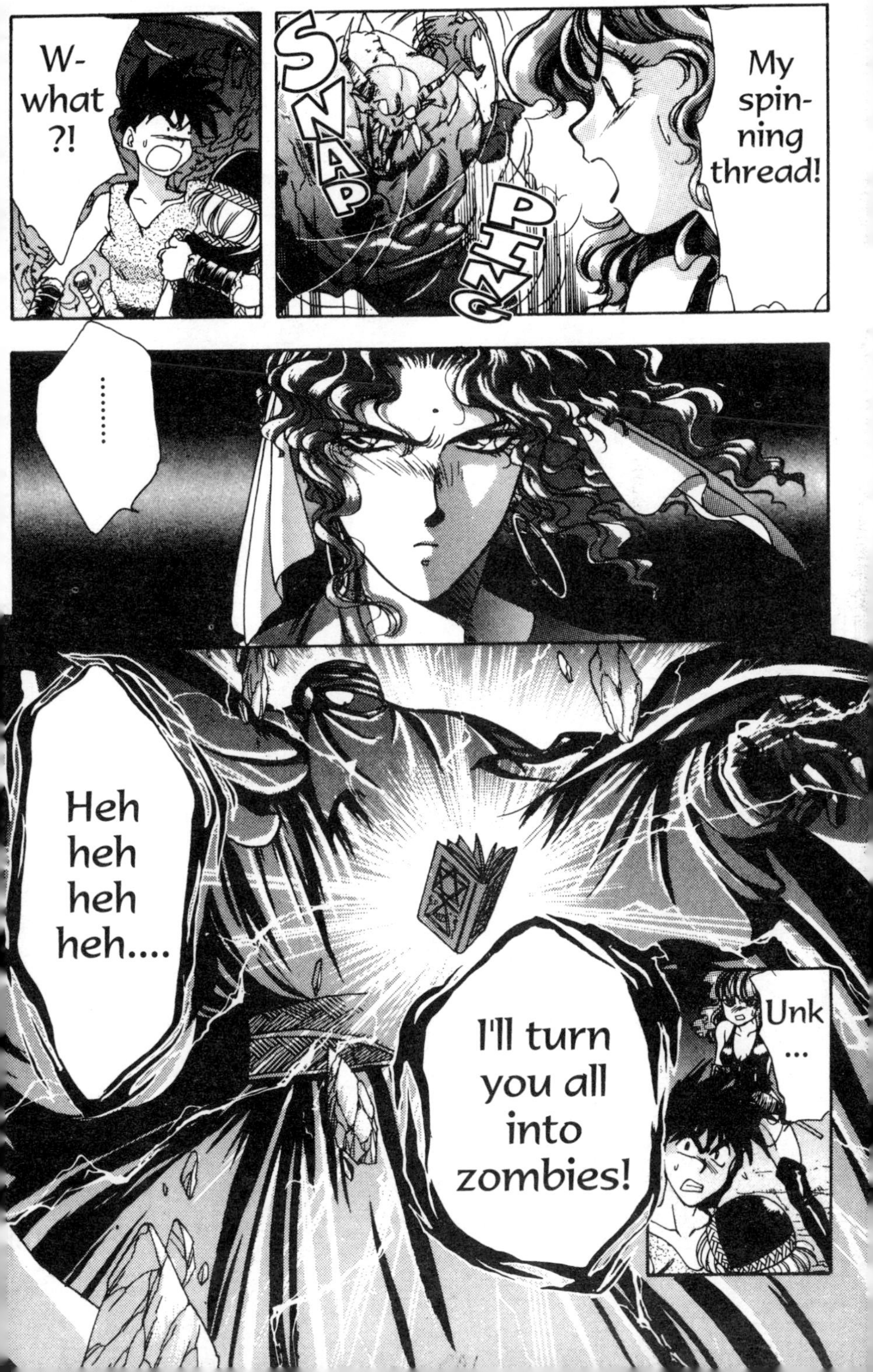
W-what?!
SNAP
PING
My spinning thread!
......
Heh heh heh heh....
I'll turn you all into zombies!
Unk...

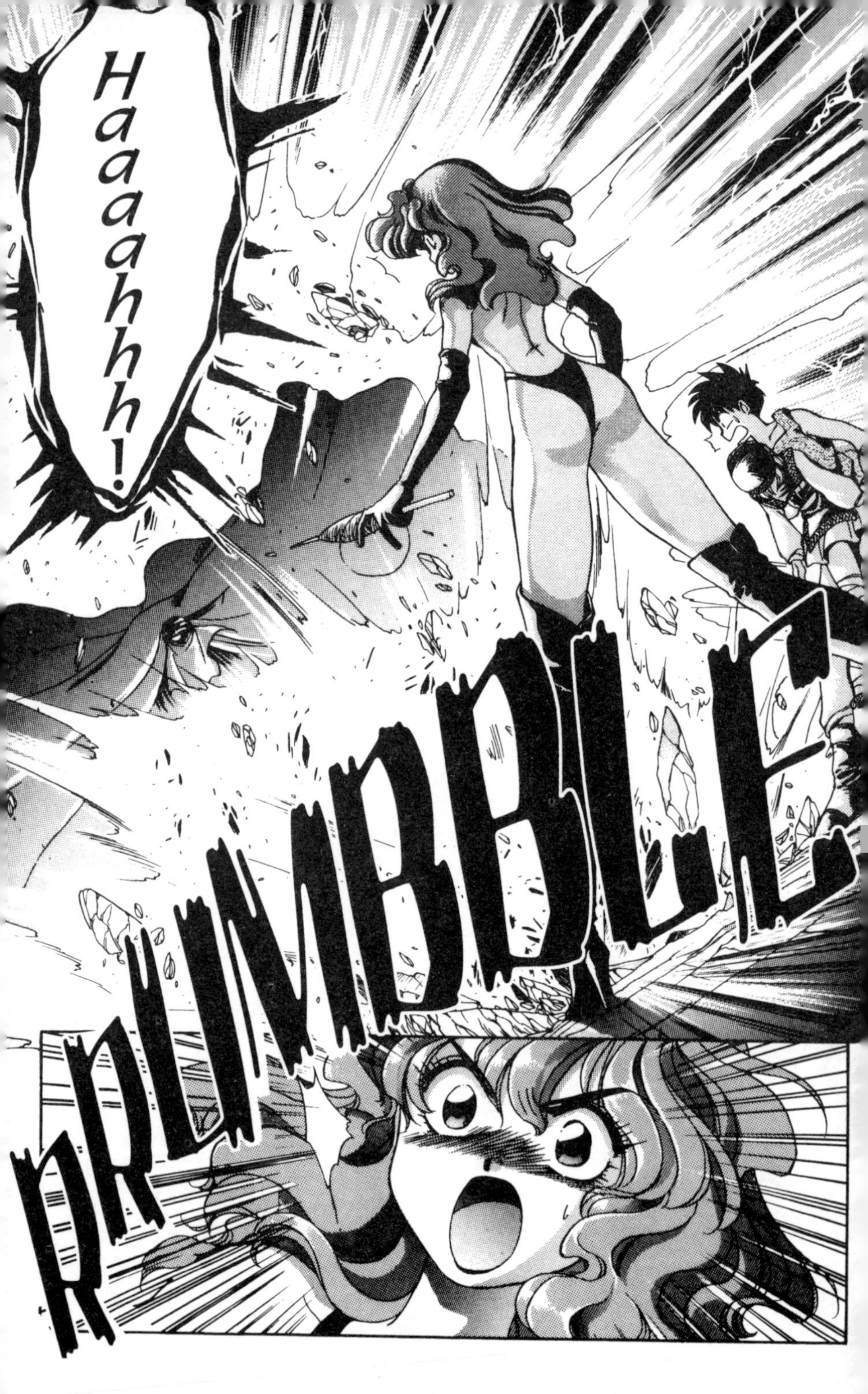
Haaaahhhh!
RRUMBBLLE

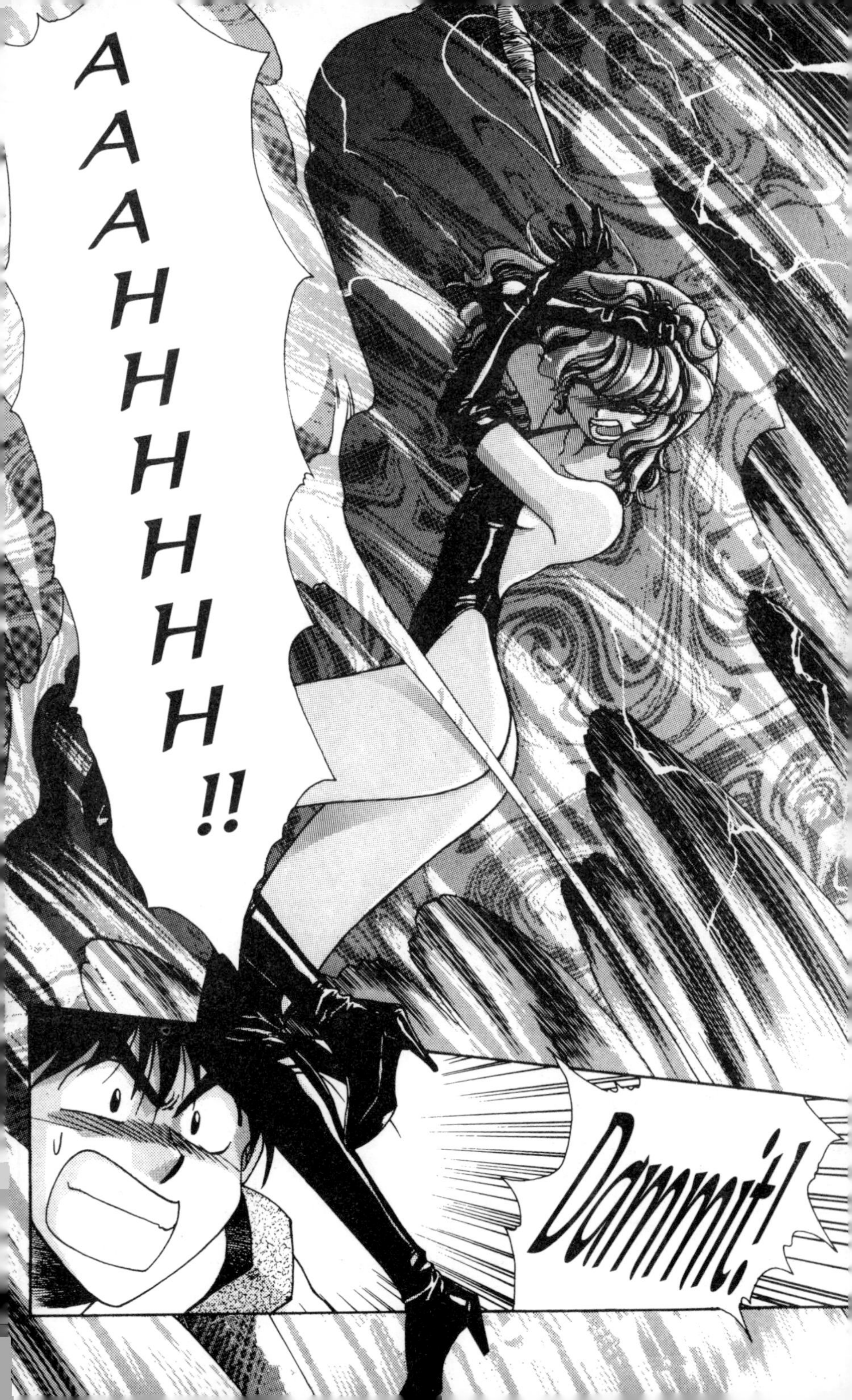
AAAHHHHHHH!!
Dammit!

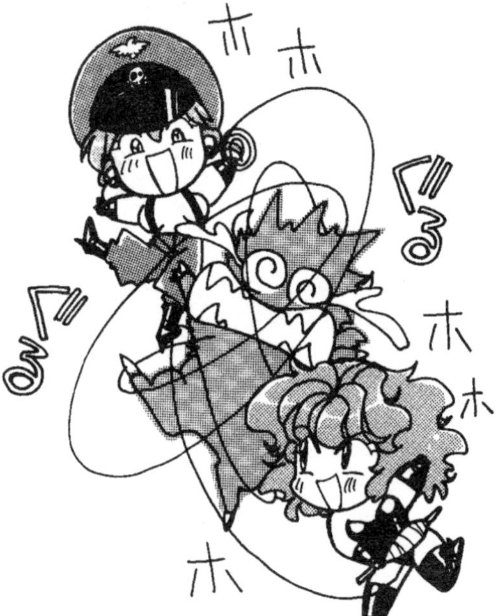
ホホ
ぐる
ホホ
ぐる
ホ

AFTERTHOUGHT

I'm so happy to be doing this a second time. It's Ray Omishi. For those reading this for the first time, hello. Please keep reading with us♡ Well, Mille Feuille make his appearance didn't he? Ray is so happy to draw one of my favorite transvestite characters. On a tangent, she also has a young-boy and older girl fixation. Looks like there are going to be a lot of new characters appearing in SH. Part of me is excited ♥ and happy, but part of me is scared... I'm have trouble drawing beautiful people, so I want to get better at them. But I'm hopeless. If I could pour some of the energy I spend on drawing girls, into drawing guys I like twins too, I wonder if we're going to have any of them... Ah-ah... This passage has no theme... What kind of an afterthought is this... I'm sorry Well then, I'll see you next time Ray Omishi

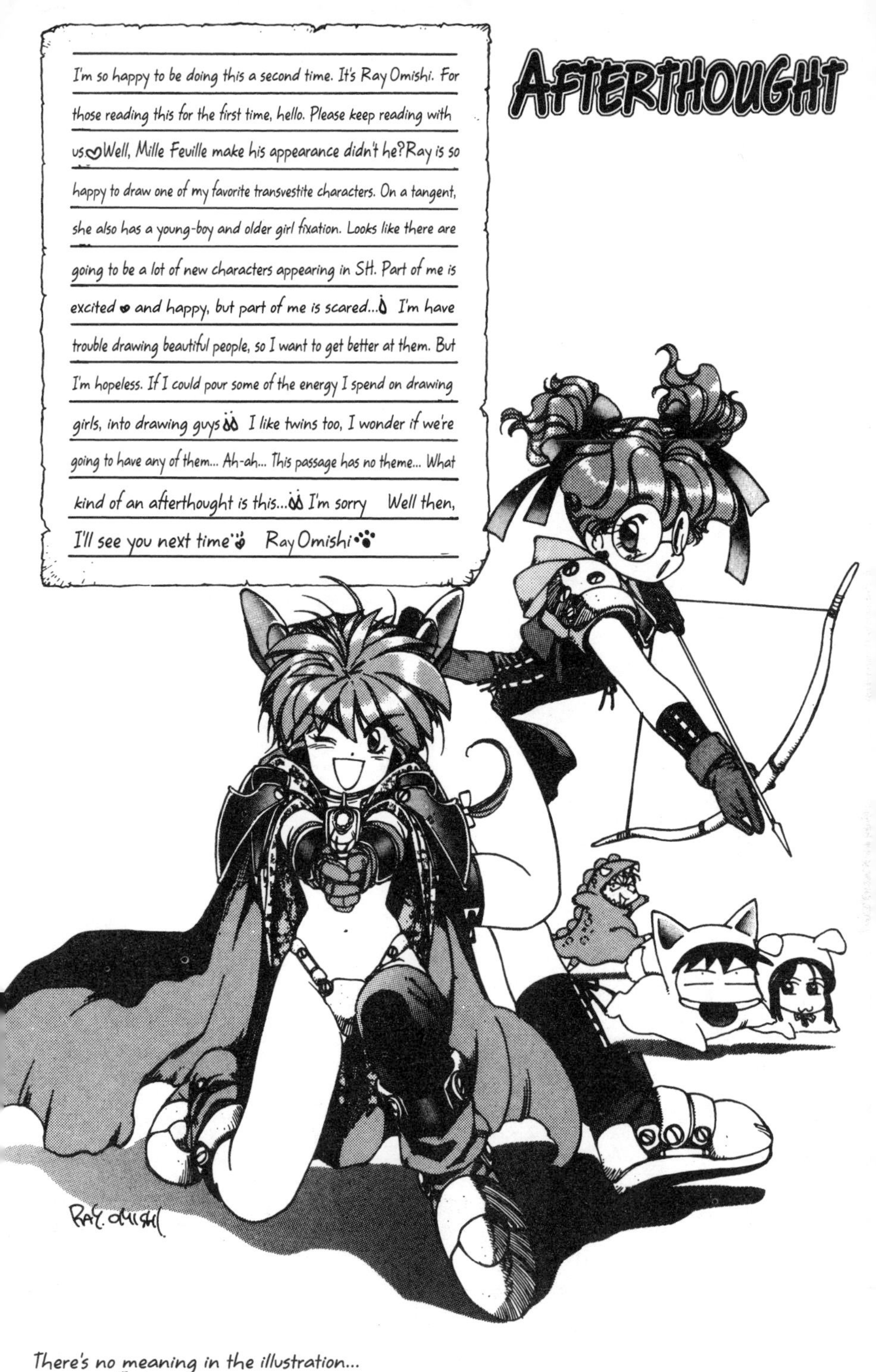
RAY. OMISHI

There's no meaning in the illustration...
Just wasting space.

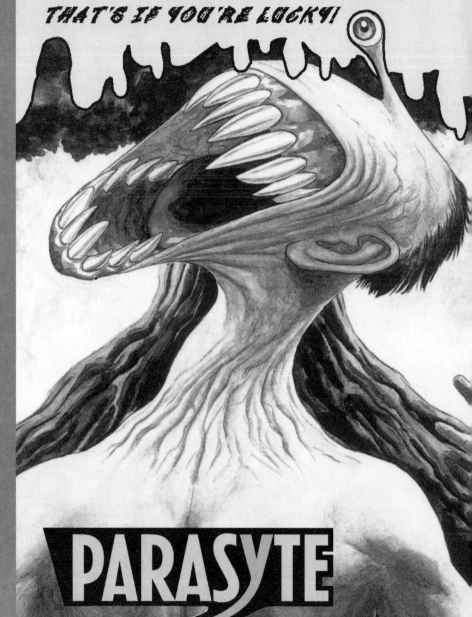

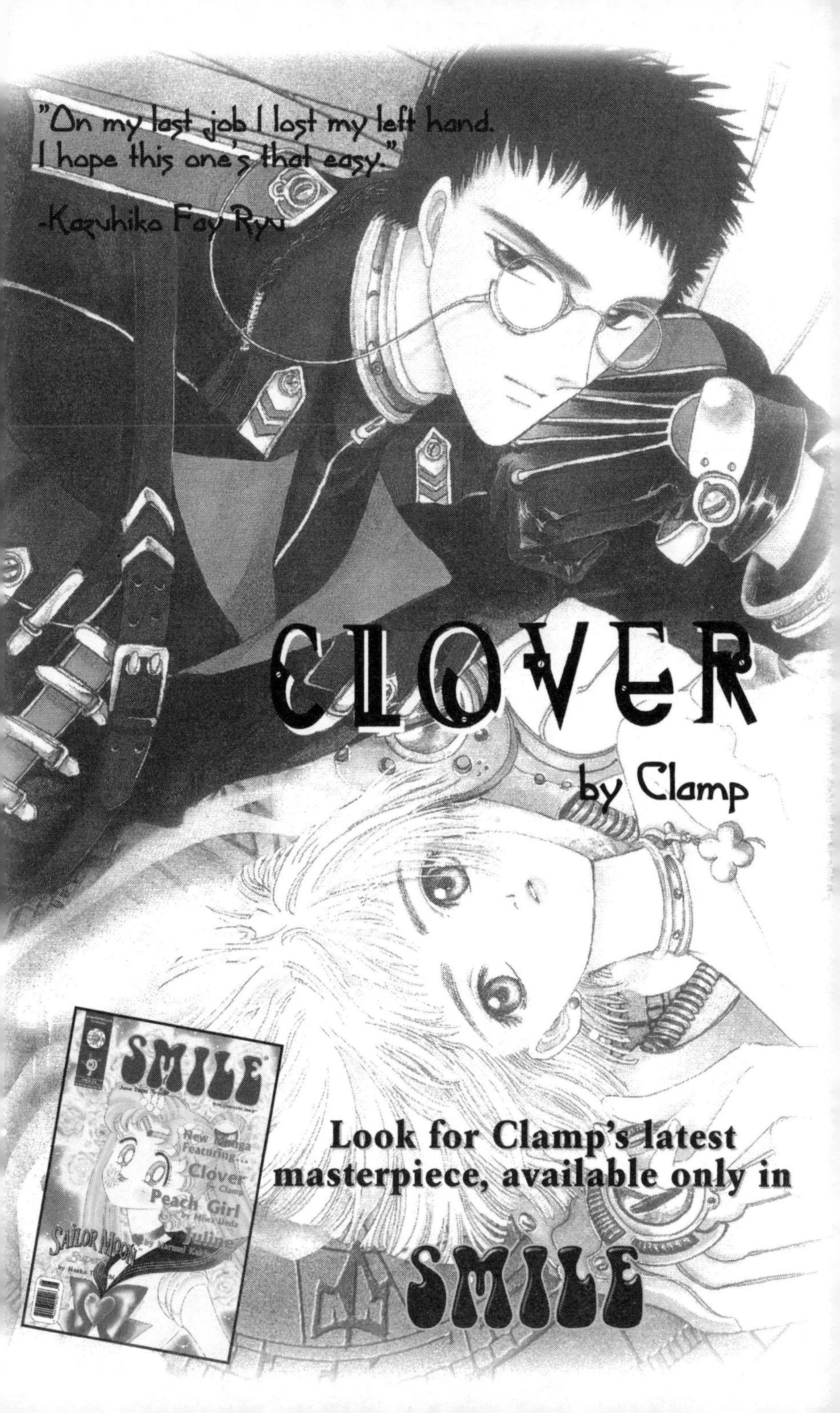
"On my last job I lost my left hand.
I hope this one's that easy."
-Kazuhiko Fay Ryu
CLOVER
by Clamp
Look for Clamp's latest
masterpiece, available only in
SMILE

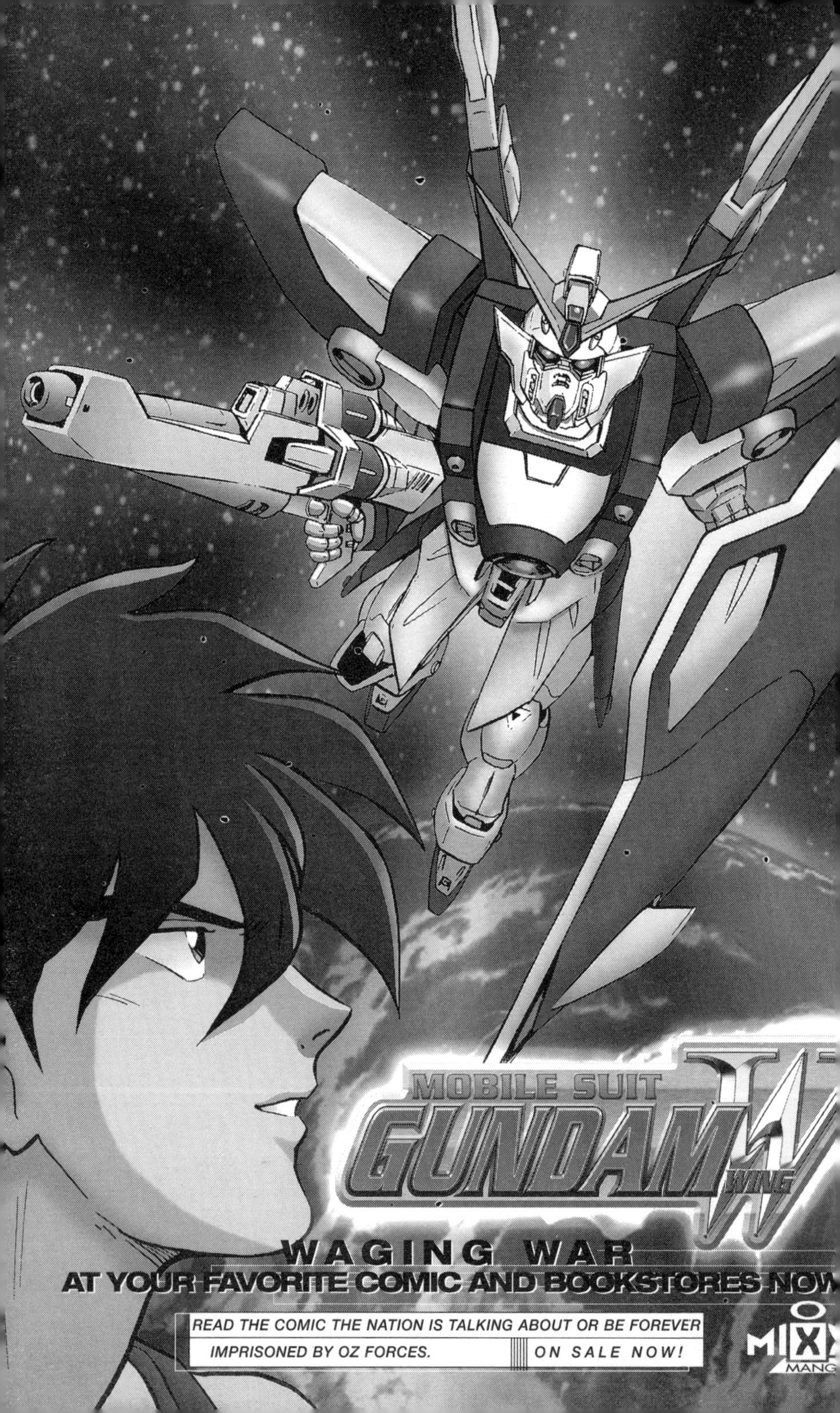
MOBILE SUIT
GUNDAM WING
WAGING WAR
AT YOUR FAVORITE COMIC AND BOOKSTORES NOW
READ THE COMIC THE NATION IS TALKING ABOUT OR BE FOREVER
IMPRISONED BY OZ FORCES.
ON SALE NOW!